11-8-65

REPORTING THE NEWS

REPO

THE

SELECTIONS FROM

EDITED, WITH AN INTRODUCTION, BY

LOUIS M. LYONS

RTING NEWS

NIEMAN REPORTS

THE BELKNAP PRESS OF HARVARD UNIVERSITY PRESS

CAMBRIDGE, MASSACHUSETTS 1965

Distributed in Great Britain by Oxford University Press, London

Library of Congress Catalog Card Number: 65–19825

Printed in the United States of America

Book design by David Ford

ABOUT THIS BOOK

Louis M. Lyons, newspaper reporter, television news commentator, and for twenty-five years Curator of the Nieman Fellowships for newspapermen at Harvard University, retired from his Nieman position in the summer of 1964. He also retired as editor of *Nieman Reports,* the quarterly publication of the Nieman Fellows, which he had guided since its founding in 1947. For distinguished service in his three overlapping careers he has won many awards and a national reputation. In the words of Dwight E. Sargent, his successor as both Curator and editor, Mr. Lyons has built an institution of recognized significance and lasting value to the world of journalism.

During the seventeen years of Mr. Lyons' editorship, the quarterly published many thoughtful and lively articles on newspapering—its responsibilities, its changing problems, and how its professionals go about their jobs—by Nieman Fellows and other persons well qualified to speak on those subjects. Harvard University Press accepted with enthusiasm the opportunity of publishing Mr. Lyons' own selection of those articles, asking him to write a long introduction of a personal nature and expecting him to include a number of the many excellent pieces he himself wrote for the magazine. He did both.

The task of selection turned out bigger than Mr. Lyons had imagined. After much toil he exhibited a preliminary stack of one hundred and twenty-eight articles, all of which he thought deserved to be in the volume, though he knew they could not all be. More weeks of struggle finally reduced the number to fifty-one, a small enough pile to put in a grocery basket, which he did (we still have the basket). He has made a few minor editorial changes in the pieces (for example, to reduce topicality) and has condensed some of the longest ones. These fifty-one articles, with Mr. Lyons' general introduction and his brief introductions to the seven parts of the book, we are proud to publish.

CONTENTS

VI. GOVERNMENT AND THE PRESS

VII. BOOKS AND MEN

APPENDIX

REPORTING THE NEWS

INTRODUCTION

Nieman Reports and the Nieman Fellowships

One thing a newspaperman should learn early is that memory is a very unreliable reference for any matter of fact. I thought I had learned this. But a letter from Dean Norval Neil Luxon of the University of North Carolina Journalism School jolted me. For years I had been replying to questions about the origin of *Nieman Reports* by saying that it was started in response to one of the recommendations of the Hutchins Commission on Freedom of the Press. That commission in its report in 1947 urged, among other things, a continuing appraisal of the performance of the press. My memory was that the Nieman Fellows picked up this suggestion and undertook to try to meet it in a modest way by launching a quarterly in journalism. And I would certainly have gone on thinking so if Dean Luxon had not written me to suggest that, after seventeen years, the best, or most durable, articles of *Nieman Reports* be collected in a book.

This, he said frankly, he was proposing for the convenience of instructors in journalism who found the quarterly a continuing source of material for use in their classes. I had of course known that journalism school staffs were among the most appreciative subscribers to *Nieman Reports* and that many of them, notably Neil Luxon himself, had become valued contributors.

His suggestion led me first to the files. For the earliest issues had long been out of print. I wasn't even sure that in all cases file copies remained. There was just one of the first issue, February 1947. To my amazement, there was nothing at all in it about the Hutchins Commission report. It was the second issue that was devoted to this epochal document.

The April 1947 issue led off with a long review of the report and followed with a comprehensive summary and abstract of the report itself. The next issue was full of reactions from the newspaper press, almost all negative, some scoffing at this Ivy Tower notion of a bunch of professors who set themselves up to criticize the press. Actually they didn't set themselves up. Henry Luce, publisher of *Time, Life,* and *Fortune,* set them up with $200,000 to make a study of the state of freedom of the press. It was the commission that expanded its report, as the title indicated, to *A Free and Responsible Press.* "Responsible" was the key word, and freedom and responsibility were linked: only a responsible press could remain free. Responsibility of the press is a concept introduced by the Hutchins Commission, or at least given currency by its report. The publishers who scoffed at it as an academic notion in 1947 have long since adopted it into their vocabulary. I am sure many of them think they invented it. It became at once the basic theme of *Nieman Reports* and has threaded through the reviews, critiques, and articles occupying seventy-two issues. My memory was off only by two months. For once started, *Nieman Reports* took its tone, found its philosophy, and built its course on the responsibility of the press.

This coincided of course with the purpose of the Nieman Fellowship program at Harvard, eight years old in 1946 when the former Nieman Fellows gathered in Cambridge to organize, in the inevitable ways of alumni, into the Society of Nieman Fellows. The Society was merely a visible symbol of the strong sense of solidarity of the newspapermen who had held the fellowships since Agnes Wahl Nieman had left to Harvard her share in the *Milwaukee Journal,* which her husband had founded. This bequest, she said, was "to promote and elevate standards of journalism and educate persons deemed especially qualified . . ." James Bryant Conant, as president of Harvard, gave much thought to the use of this very special gift. Finally he established the Nieman Fellowships, which, starting in the fall of 1938, have brought each year to Harvard an average of a dozen newspapermen to spend a year on leave from their papers, pursuing studies of their own choice, to strengthen their background for journalism.

It was a unique enterprise and remains such after twenty-five years. Harvard had no journalism school. Many newer universities had. Conant decided that a special bequest should be turned to a special use. What a university could best do for journalism was to open its doors to a certain number of selected newsmen each year, to let them take the university on their own terms and carry on individual studies, both to fill gaps in their education and to explore fields of specialization. To ensure that the program would serve their own felt needs, Conant's plan stipulated there should be no degrees and no credits for courses taken. Indeed they need not take courses if they could find shorter cuts to what they wanted. (Conant had no reverence for college lectures, but the Fellows down the years have found the quality of Harvard lectures exciting.) The program was to be individual, informal, tailored to their own particular needs. The one rule the Harvard Corporation laid down was that applicants must have had at least three years of newspaper experience, this to keep the program to those who had already found their careers in journalism.

It may have been an afterthought of Conant's, but if so, one that was to prove of strategic vitality to the Nieman program, that he added one element to this otherwise wholly individualist scheme. Either Conant or Archibald MacLeish, whom he persuaded to leave the staff of *Fortune* to devote half his time to guiding the first group of Nieman Fellows in their initial explorations of Harvard, felt that somehow there should be a thread of journalism running through their Nieman year. This thought developed into the Nieman dinners, weekly events of the first year. To each, a leading journalist was invited to lead an evening's discussion. Half a dozen or so Harvard faculty guests were invited to join each dinner discussion.

This held a lively interest and inevitably focused the Fellows' thinking on some of the basic questions, problems, issues, and concerns of journalism. Without the stimulus of these discussions, *Nieman Reports* would never have been born, nor would the remarkable esprit de corps of the Nieman Fellows have developed as it did, so that within a few seasons what began as an educational opportunity had become one of the prized distinctions in American journalism.

Under the brilliant direction of Archibald MacLeish, the Nieman dinners in that first year established a tone and tradition that endured. Felix Frankfurter, then in his last year at Harvard, seldom missed one. Edwin A. Lahey, pungent, able, irreverent, at that time a labor reporter for the *Chicago Daily News,* was a member of that first group, and his insistent prodding questions soon developed a let's-get-right-down-to-cases style for the dinner discussions. Lahey's thrust and sally method quickly created a respected status for Nieman Fellows with the Harvard faculty and "Laheyisms" became legendary. "Your Fellows are the only people who'll talk back to me," a professor told me in the early days. One session, after a long and fairly complex discussion by an economist, Lahey asked, "Now, professor, if you could just sum that up in about two thousand well-chosen words?" Heywood Broun was a dinner guest that year. He chose to stay over a day to visit with Lahey. His next column was on the Nieman Fellowships: Broun suggested they should go only to newspapermen who had never been to college. Ed Lahey was the one in that group who fitted Broun's prescription. Our faculty guests reacted to the candor of the dinner meetings. When Henry Luce came, he described the editorial principles of *Time,* as committed to democracy and private capitalism. It was one of our political scientist colleagues who persisted in asking which Mr. Luce put first.

A parallel program, started the second year, added a dimension to the Nieman discussions. That was a weekly seminar, Tuesday afternoon, four to six, over beer and cheese, each session led by an invited member of the Harvard faculty to discuss some topic in his field. These topical discussions often applied directly to the background of current issues, and very often led naturally into discussion of the performance of the press on these issues. The questions raised and answers offered at the Nieman dinners and seminars carried on into the luncheon conversations and other gatherings of the Fellows through the year. Often the Fellows followed up a seminar by inviting a provocative faculty guest to luncheon to continue the argument. Soon they were initiating their own meetings and listing guests they wanted to hear.

Such discussions were facilitated by the hospitable arrangements of Harvard. From the first the Nieman Fellows were associated with the Harvard Houses, which brought them into the main stream of the academic community. They were all members of the Faculty Club. The Signet Society, an old literary club, became the gathering place for Nieman dinners, and its talented steward, Archie Gibbons, under Nieman tutelage, was soon to earn a Nieman Oscar for the improvement in his Martinis. The *Harvard Crimson* started an annual dinner with the Nieman Fellows, as later did Harvard University Press. The young scholars of the Society of Fellows invited them to one of their Monday dinners. Student groups, political clubs, law clubs often wanted Nieman Fellows as speakers.

After a time, Dean Erwin Griswold of the Law School appointed a liaison committee of three distinguished law professors, Arthur Sutherland, Mark DeWolfe Howe, and Archibald Cox, to set up three or four meetings a year with the Fellows. These sessions were seeded with law professors who dropped in, Zechariah Chafee, Paul Freund, Milton Katz, Ernest Brown, Benjamin Kaplan, Henry Hart, Phillip Areeda, Charles Haar, and others, to join in the discussions. These began with the law of the press, libel and privilege. But soon the Fellows proposed going beyond their parochial concerns, and the sessions dealt with the Supreme Court in its controversies, with segregation, with crime and the police, and inevitably with the frequent conflict between a free press and a fair trial.

As new issues arose—the war, atomic energy, science reporting, education reporting, urban renewal—the Nieman Foundation on occasion sponsored special programs for newspapermen beyond the membership of the Fellows. Thus the resources of the Harvard faculty were again brought to bear on lively concerns of the press, and the sessions of course were also open to the current Nieman Fellows. Extracurricular life at Harvard was a continuing dialogue, much of it focused on the press.

No age limit for the fellowships had been set when the program was announced. The first group in 1938–39 ranged from twenty-six to forty. Two who were to be among the most distinguished of journalists, Irving Dilliard, later editorial page editor of the *St. Louis Post-Dispatch,* and Ed Lahey, later Washington bureau chief of the Knight Papers, were thirty-four and thirty-six. I was the patriarch at forty. But John Clark, who at his untimely death in a New Hampshire flood twelve years later was successfully publishing his own newspaper, the Claremont, New Hampshire, *Daily Eagle,* was only twenty-eight. This has been a typical Nieman age range, averaging about thirty-two, after eight, ten, or twelve years of newspaper work.

It was in the second year that I first had to wrestle with applications, for the third group. I was puzzled by the large number of senior journalists applying, men in their upper forties or fifties, managing editors or chief editorial writers. They clearly sought a sabbatical. I had, myself. But on any competitive basis, their numbers would eliminate the younger men. Education is a bet on the future. I mulled and worried over this for some time until one day I was passing President Conant on a cross-walk. He stopped me to ask, "How is the Nieman business going? It's going all right, isn't it? That's all I hear." This was his invariable and almost only comment in the early years, and the extent of his intervention in an enterprise he had created. I said yes, it seemed to be going all right. But then I mentioned the problem with the applications.

"Why don't you put on an age limit?" Conant asked instantly. "Say forty. You may later want to start a program for the older men that could be a sabbatical. But right now I should think you'd have to put on an age limit."

It seemed the only answer. We did. It has remained the most often protested element in the program. The selecting committee has always allowed itself the privilege of making an exception, but only in the exceptional case. Such a case, for example, was Tillman Durdin of the *New York Times,* who had been in East Asia for some fifteen years. It seemed good sense to respond to his desire for a year of reorientation in America, though I don't suppose he put it that way; and especially because the special East Asian program that was one of the regional programs developed at Harvard out of the war provided a unique opportunity for the background studies in his field.

It seemed natural to waive the age limit when America was deep in the war and many of the younger men were in the military service. But with the war over, there was no question about putting it back. The war's end brought a sharp rise in applications, many of them, naturally enough, from newspapermen who had been in war service and saw their best chance for such a year of study before they returned to their jobs. Also their war experience had opened new fields of interest. Some wanted to prepare for foreign correspondents' work, others to study the convulsions in Europe, the changed map of international relations, the psychology of such political extremism as led to Hitlerism. Out of the veterans' group in the years following the war, the Nieman program, like all parts of the university, found some of its most mature and earnest students.

But the age-limit question led me to examine the experience of the first ten years of the fellowships and it left no doubt that the most visible results of the Nieman Fellowships could be measured in the progress of the younger men. Of course there were variations. What is the "right" age for one man may be different for another. But, over and over, the growth that was remarked on by their Harvard associates and later by their professional colleagues was among the younger men. I mean age twenty-five to thirty. In this age group were Harry Ashmore and Nat Caldwell, later Clark Mollenhoff and Anthony Lewis, all to win Pulitzer prizes; John Clark and Edwin Paxton, to become publishers of their own newspapers; Robert Manning, later an Assistant Secretary of State and then an editor of the *Atlantic;* Thomas Griffith, to become Senior Staff Editor of all Time, Inc., publications; Carroll Kilpatrick and Selig Harrison, later of the *Washington Post;* George Chaplin, later editor of the *Honolulu Advertiser;* Millard Browne, later chief editorial writer of the *Buffalo Evening News;* Neil Davis, editor of the *Lee County Bulletin,* Auburn, Alabama; Vance Johnson, later assistant to the publisher of *Collier's* and then promotion manager of the Field Enterprises; William J. Miller, Cleveland reporter who became a *Life* editorial writer; James Daniel, associate editor of the *Reader's Digest;* John Day, later a managing editor and still later CBS News Director, now owner of his own paper in England; Boyd Simmons of the *Detroit News;* and Tom Sancton, political reporter, author, and teacher.

One factor in the youth of some of the earlier Fellows was that they had gone into newspapering without going to college or without finishing college. In the 1940–41 group eleven of the fourteen had no college degree. This of course changed with the later groups as college became a more common experience. Still, for the first ten years one in six was having at Harvard his initial contact with a university. This very seldom appeared a handicap, a fact that tells something about newspaper work and the men in it. The newspaperman has to learn to look things up. He doesn't call it research, but he must be able to read rapidly through reports and studies in varied fields and get the gist of them. Most college studies of primary interest to journalists are relatively nontechnical. Even economics and law require only getting onto a fairly short vocabulary of special terms. Learning the ropes in the library stacks and catalogue was always a project of the opening week. For the rest they found their own way, with plenty of counsel accessible when needed. Of course these were selected men, and journalism is a self-educating process. But the Nieman experience suggests that anyone of intelligence can tackle education to meet his needs if he wants it enough.

For the right man at the right time, such a fallow year for intellectual exploration can be immensely rewarding. Indeed the reports the Fellows submitted at the year's end often read like testimonials. The final passage of William J. Miller's, since I have it before me, will illustrate:

> Circumstances having dictated that I write this report some weeks and several hundred miles removed from Harvard, I am in a position to assess the year from a greater distance and perspective than if I had written it while there. It has already begun to take on a glow, a patina, like a fondly remembered dream. I know even now that I shall always cherish it as a golden year, a *Wander Jahr.* I know that I am certainly a great deal broader, both mentally and spiritually. Blind spots in my mind have contracted, tolerance and understanding have expanded. I am no longer as certain as I was about anything, other than my own ignorance. Most important of all, I have shed considerable of the inferiority complex endemic to the non-college man.
>
> For me, the year has been a priceless experience. If I were forced to enumerate any particular things I had learned, I might be unable to give a satisfactory answer. The gain is a difficult one to express, but nonetheless real. Chief of all I would count the opportunity it has given me to regard men and their affairs from a greater distance than a working newspaperman obtains. Gertrude Stein, in a rare burst of lucidity, once told me: "A newspaperman is too immediate to be immediate." I think I know precisely what she means. We are too involved in the deeds of the moment to appraise them validly. I suspect every newspaperman has, at one time or another, felt a desire to go off to Samoa and twiddle his toes in the sand while, like Miniver Cheevy, he "thought and thought and thought about it." Well, here we have a chance to "think about it." My thinking has produced no conclusions, but it has enabled me, I believe, to reach a much broader perspective. I always knew, intellectually, that is, that nothing is ever black, or white, but gray; emotionally, however, I always judged them as one or the other. I believe I have at last achieved an open mind.

A corollary to the experience with the younger men was that the largest leakage from journalism came in the upper age group. This was a surprise. The Harvard Corporation, in setting a minimum of three years of news work, had been concerned only that the Fellows should have got securely on the journalistic track. But, as it turned out, after fifteen or eighteen years in the news room some had had it. The applicants who seemed most securely anchored in their newspaper careers were most apt to leave for government information service, public relations, advertising, authorship, teaching. Often this meant growth and an economic gain for the individual. It was only within our peculiarly circumscribed program, focused singly on journalism, that we had to count such departures against our record. Or anyway others did. The program was under continual and often unsympathetic criticism from many of the managers of the press, and they scored any movement of Nieman Fellows out of the news room as a failure of the Nieman program. Of course there is constant movement out of news rooms, always has been. A few years of newspaper work has always been rated as valuable basic training for the many allied fields which have immensely expanded with the enlargement of "communication," and which invariably offer more money than the newspapers have had to pay for work that, at least till recently, has had a glamorous attraction that made it unnecessary to do the recruiting or institute the in-training programs or offer the money that has been necessary in other employments.

The difference between Nieman Fellows and other newspapermen in this was simply that the Nieman Fellows were marked men. Their lapses were noted and publicized.

The war years, of course, shook up newspaper staffs along with others. Nieman Fellows and others enlisted or were drafted or drawn into special services, some of which offered unique opportunities after the war. Moreover there had been active recruitment of the early groups of Nieman Fellows, by *Time,* by the then new newspaper *PM,* by Marshall Field's new *Chicago Sun,* and by others. This, altogether, accounted for considerable movement in jobs. A decade or so later it was sometimes the newspaper, not the Nieman Fellow, that disappeared during his Nieman year. Mergers and the disappearance of newspapers left a number of Fellows on the job market. Of course the rapidly expanding broadcasting industry and the ever-widening need of government at all levels, particularly the U.S. Information Agency, absorbed them.

The Nieman Foundation has long since ceased to worry about some carping when a former Fellow yields to the seductions of a Washington bureau or a job with the *New York Times.* But in the first years an institution that was dependent on cooperation of newspaper managements to give their staffers leaves of absence had to be sensitive to newspaper critics. Often I bit my tongue when, on being introduced to a Southern publisher who had lost a Nieman Fellow, I was greeted with, "Oh, yes, you run that employment agency at Harvard."

It was a struggle not to retort: "Yes. We had to raise Jim's stipend over what you were paying him so that he could live in Cambridge."

Early in World War II the Foundation passed through its most critical period. Harvard, like other universities, sought ways to help the war effort. Its president was soon preoccupied with developing the atom bomb. Its most distinguished professors were commuting to Washington or taken over wholly by the government for the duration. Harvard historians made up the core of the Office of Strategic Services. The Air Force sent its procurement and ordnance men to the Harvard Business School. Special area and regional programs were set up in Cambridge for the officers and civilians who would administer occupied territory in Germany and Japan, and for others who needed the languages and customs of new lands.

With all this conversion to war the suggestion naturally arose of suspending the Nieman Fellowships for the duration. President Conant decided to do this. A proposal was made to convert the Nieman program to a wartime center for propaganda research. The war urgency certainly made a sufficient case for suspending the fellowships. On the other hand, there was no one with any status in the university to present the case for not doing it. MacLeish had been drawn into Washington after his one year of directing the Nieman program. It was then operated on an ad hoc basis through the war years. My newspaper job was right next door, on the *Boston Globe,* and President Conant had asked me to take charge of the program the year after MacLeish left. The *Globe* was cooperative in letting me have time for this. Twice in the first few years I had turned in my Harvard resignation when the term seemed up, only to have Conant come on the long-distance telephone from Washington weeks after, to ask if I'd stay on till he could give it more attention. "It's going all right, isn't it? That's what I hear." Once he had said: "I suppose eventually we'll want to appoint some wise old professor. But I don't know who it would be."

So the program was on this stopgap arrangement when it was proposed to suspend the fellowships for the war. Actually, while I am at it, I should go on to say that the Fellows on their own during the war years did some very effective organized study of propaganda, serving as a committee of the Harvard branch of the William Allen White Committee to Defend America by Aiding the Allies. The Harvard chairman was Ralph Barton Perry, philosopher, whose own published contributions to America's problems in the war and toward the peace came to fill a useful book shelf. But it was another professor and friend who saved the Nieman program from suspension.

Arthur M. Schlesinger, more even than others of a hospitable faculty, had taken a personal interest in the Fellows from the start. They studied American history with him; they consulted him on their programs; they enjoyed his good talk and wise counsel. He enjoyed their companionship, attended their dinners, entered into their discussions of public issues and the press. He was later to serve for many years on the Nieman Committee which interviews and selects the annual groups of Fellows, and to become for all of them the very symbol of their friendly and stimulating relation with the Harvard faculty.

Professor Schlesinger was disturbed to hear that the fellowships were to be suspended. He felt that the question hadn't been fully considered, indeed that now more than ever Harvard should be preparing newspapermen—for what lay ahead after the war. He persuaded me that even my limited and temporary status at Harvard gave me a responsibility to put my oar in. We went to see Mr. Conant. It turned out that a factor in his thinking about it had been the manpower shortage. He'd assumed newspapers couldn't or wouldn't spare men from their war-reduced staffs to go on leave to study. The upshot of the conversation was that he asked me to query about fifty newspaper editors and publishers for their views. It came out fifty-fifty. This result impressed Conant.

We'd had no reason to think that more than half the newspaper managers would be for us anyway. Many of them had given Conant a very cold shoulder when he consulted them about starting the Nieman Fellowships. Most had brushed it off as a most unlikely proposition. Conant himself was to say, long after, that it began as a very dubious experiment.

But if half of a group of leading newspaper executives advised going ahead in the face of war and manpower shortage, that was good enough. The fellowships were never interrupted; so we never faced the question whether, had they been, the proposed propaganda research institute would ever have been reconverted to newspaper fellowships after the war.

Once again while I was still only a temporary part-time employee of Harvard, Professor Schlesinger was to lead me to the president's office. This was to reverse a decision against women as Nieman Fellows. Harvard had been a stag university when the program started. Radcliffe had not yet been merged into Harvard in what Conant was to describe to protesting alumni as coeducation only in practice, not in principle. But some dauntless women had applied for fellowships from the start. Then after years of struggle the Medical School admitted women. Finally a woman became one of the Littauer Fellows in Public Administration. That gave Schlesinger his cue. He knew we'd had to reject applications from women every year. We had chuckled together over Conant's response when I had brought the question up to him the year before: "Why, you serve whiskey at these Nieman dinners, don't you? Let's not complicate it. It's going all right, isn't it?"

The one thing I'd learned about Conant was that if I left him alone, he'd leave me alone. That was as much as one could ask of any boss. Having no notion of making a career at Harvard, I had let the Nieman Fellowship program move on its own momentum, which actually was what Conant wanted. As an administrator he was a good "No" man. He had on his desk a crystal ball the alumni had given him. It was his habit, when anyone came in with a project that sounded dubious to him, to say, "Let's look at the crystal ball." The crystal ball had a big "No" painted black on the bottom of it. His answer to any proposal about the Nieman program was, "Let's not complicate it."

But college presidents held no terror for old Arthur Schlesinger. He had disagreed with all he had served under. He argued with Conant that women were newspapermen and women were at Harvard. I filled in the details of women in journalism. Conant had heard of Anne O'Hare McCormick and Dorothy Thompson anyway. Finally he yielded the point. "The blood be on your own head," were his parting words to me. So we had two women in the

1945–46 Nieman group and several after that and the program survived.

In his mission to admit women to the Nieman Fellowships, two of Professor Schlesinger's keenest interests coincided. If there was a more ardent feminist in Cambridge than he, it was Mrs. Schlesinger. In his autobiography he says that, next to his own professional work, the two activities in which he took greatest satisfaction at Harvard were as a trustee of Radcliffe College and a member of the Nieman Committee. He also dedicated a book on the press to "the Nieman Fellows, past and present." This was his *Prelude to Independence: The Newspaper War on Britain, 1764–1776.*

Reviews of Professor Schlesinger's books in *Nieman Reports* sometimes alternated with reviews of books of his son, Arthur Junior. The inescapable confusion between the two Schlesingers, both historians in the same field and both winners of Pulitzer prizes, always entertained Professor Schlesinger. Even the official *Harvard Gazette,* on announcing appointment of the younger Schlesinger to a full professorship, published the biography of his father. When Harvard gave Professor Schlesinger an honorary degree, his son, who was a marshal of his twenty-fifth-anniversary class that year, was his commencement escort.

Professor Schlesinger's long service on the Nieman Committee was memorable to a generation of applicants because of a habit he had of opening an interview with "What have you been reading lately?" This always threw the applicant into a tiz. Under the exigencies of the situation, the candidate usually couldn't think of a thing he'd been reading. Assuming this was a test question, many a successful applicant left the interview in a state of nervous anxiety; often an applicant would go home and send in a list of books he really had been reading. Professor Schlesinger was much amused when finally one of the former Fellows told him of the upsetting effect of his innocent question.

Next time I had occasion to go to the president's office was after the war and Conant was asking me to give up a plan to go abroad, and instead to take a full-time appointment at Harvard.

I reminded him he'd been going to appoint a wise old professor as curator.

"Did I ever say that?" he replied.

The title of "curator" has proved a conversation piece all these years. It has a curious bit of history. Announcement of Mrs. Nieman's bequest in 1937 brought a plea from the Harvard Library for $5,000 a year of the Nieman fund to put foreign newspapers on microfilm. This was granted before the Nieman Fellowship program came into being.

When President Conant persuaded Archibald MacLeish to leave *Fortune* and devote half his time to guiding the first group of Fellows, a title for this unorthodox academic appointment was suggested by the new library project. MacLeish became "Curator of the Nieman Collection of Contemporary Journalism." The start of the Second World War cut off the library project before it was developed. Several years later we bought off the library's lien on the Nieman funds. But when President Roosevelt, at the end of that first year, appointed MacLeish as Librarian of Congress, it must have helped MacLeish's cause with the Senate committee to have what looked like a librarian's title appended to his name.

When President Conant asked me to fill the gap till he could think of his next move, he started me with the title "assistant curator" and it amused him that I was to be "assistant to a nonexistent curator of a nonexistent collection." After one year "assistant" was dropped from the title, which was also shorn of the nonexistent collection. In its abbreviated form it has provided innumerable people the pleasure of quipping that they thought a curator had charge of old bones in a museum. But my charges proved a very lively lot and have done quite a lot of rattling of old bones.

In 1946 it was Conant's idea to launch the new chapter of more organized administration of the program with a Nieman Reunion, and out of that *Nieman Reports* was born. As the one permanent Fellow, I became inescapably the editor and the Nieman office its publishing place.

Nieman Reports was not the first publication to grow out of so much talk at Harvard about newspapers. The Fellows of 1941–42 conceived a project of their own that became a book of essays on newspapering, published by Harvard University Press under the title, *Newsmen's Holiday*.

The first group after the war, in 1946, asked that the Nieman dinner guests for the second half of the year be chosen to relate to a project they had assigned themselves, to develop a blueprint for the kind of newspaper they would like to see. Among the Nieman dinner guests that season were Joseph Pulitzer of the *St. Louis Post-Dispatch;* Helen Reid of the *New York Herald Tribune;* Barry Bingham, editor of the *Louisville Courier-Journal;* Ralph Ingersoll, editor of *PM;* Thomas L. Stokes, Washington columnist; John Tunis, writer on sports; Fred Stein, editor of the *Binghamton Press;* Theodore White, China correspondent; and I. I. Rabi, atomic scientist. The Fellows went into these sessions with their own lists of questions and challenges to their professional guests. They followed up with their own post mortems and out of their endless discussions came the book, *Your Newspaper: Blueprint for a Better Press,* by Nine Nieman Fellows. There were eleven Fellows that year. It was characteristic of their individualism that two chose not to enlist in a project that had so Utopian an aspect.

By then Nieman groups had had considerable experience judging newspapers. Various newspaper organizations had begun to make it their practice to ask the Nieman Fellows to judge entries in their contests—for example, the New England Weekly Publishers Association, the regional Associated Press managing editors, the labor press editors, and special award committees for the Tom Stokes Award, the Amasa Howe Award, and others. So the Fellows had been dragged into the role of critics and appraisers of press performance.

It was several years after the "blueprint" book, and after *Nieman Reports* had been well established, that the Nieman Fellows of 1949–50 fell into the most successful publishing venture of any. This was a special issue of *Nieman Reports* entitled "Reading, Writing and Newspapers." I say fell in, but they were pushed, and by one of their most valued faculty colleagues. Theodore Morrison, teacher of English, had for some years been critic and coach of the writing of Nieman Fellows and had helped in shaping a fast-growing shelf of books by former Fellows, many of them begun in chapters submitted to his writing course. His part in "Reading, Writing and Newspapers" really begins long before 1950.

Curiously, or maybe not, almost none of the first few groups of Nieman Fellows had taken any studies in English. They were already professional writers, and their interests were in the studies that make the background of the journalists' issues in public affairs —chiefly history, government, and economics, with variations into specialties in science, the Soviet Union, sociology, labor relations, law, what have you. For happily the range of a great university spans the universal dimensions of journalism.

It was not until A. B. (Bud) Guthrie became a Nieman Fellow in 1944 that the Fellows' interests were sharply directed to their own writing, the tool of their trade. This was under Guthrie's enthusiastic and characteristically aggressive concern for journalistic writing. He was then executive editor and had long been city editor of the Lexington, Kentucky, *Leader*. The city editor is the key man in the newspaper. His is the strategic desk. Assignments flow from it; copy returns to it. Here if anywhere in the newspaper is the best chance for useful criticism and development of talent. Guthrie must have been a stimulating and influential city editor. He'd been working at writing himself, and he was an American history buff, his best friends the history professors at the state university in Lexington.

Guthrie was forty-four and he never would have been a Nieman Fellow at all had we not taken off the age limit of forty in the last two years of the war. Another of equal age in that same group was Houstoun Waring, editor of the most famous weekly paper in America, the Littleton, Colorado, *Independent*, a one-man Nieman Foundation himself, starting all manner of enterprises to "elevate standards of journalism" in Colorado, where they now have what they call the "Little Nieman Program" at their state university.

The most distinguished issue of *Nieman Reports* grew out of Bud Guthrie's discovery of Theodore Morrison's writing course. Guthrie had earlier discovered, as almost all Nieman Fellows did, Professor Frederick Merk's course in American history, "The History of the Westward Movement." This was a rich slice of the story of the nation's development that took up all the movements and issues and changes wrought by America's "course vaguely realizing westward." This was Guthrie's bread and wine. He made Merk's course the basis of his own researches into America's westward movement and found the source material for his books, *The Big Sky*, *The Way West*, and *These Thousand Hills*. As he began to write, he looked for ways to improve his writing. Morrison gave a course in the short story. But he dealt sympathetically with any form of writing and welcomed Guthrie. The relationship was to last through the production of Guthrie's books, the mails carrying chapters to Harvard for the criticism which the author gratefully acknowledged in one of his first dedications.

Guthrie urged his colleagues that Morrison's course was a practical road to improvement of their writing which they couldn't afford to miss. When he'd converted them, he recommended a special seminar on writing for the Fellows. As a result, during the next two decades Morrison worked with a good many Nieman Fellows, either in seminar discussions, private consultations, or in his regular course. The shelves of books by Fellows in the Nieman rooms testify to part of his influence; the other and vastly larger part, of course, goes into their daily newspaper pieces.

Morrison always felt that newspapermen had a certain hump to get over, to shift from journalistic writing to a more literary form. He used to argue about this with the Fellows, whether there wasn't something artificially restrictive about the traditional form of the newspaper story. Was this necessary? Couldn't you have better writing, a more natural style, without losing anything necessary to the condensed form and active movement of the newspaper story?

Finally in 1949–50 the Fellows responded to his urging and went to work on it. They organized themselves to produce the symposium called "Reading, Writing and Newspapers." Morrison wrote the introductory essay, a challenging one. The others dealt with the form of the newspaper story, with the conditions of newspaper writing, with the copy editing, the editorial page, the interpretive story, the specialist's report.

By this time *Nieman Reports* was well established, and its April 1950 number was given over to the symposium. It quickly went through three editions, for 7,000 copies, to meet demands from newspapers and journalism schools. Some newspapers ordered enough copies for all their staff members. It has long been out of print. Two of the essays, including Morrison's provocative challenge to newspaper writing, are included in this collection. Space alone prevents reprinting them all.

Guthrie's other enthusiasm at Harvard, Mr. Merk's course, was shared by generations of Nieman Fellows. Harvard undergraduates used to comment on eleven Nieman Fellows in the front row of old Harvard Three, where the wooden benches were carved with initials of students dating back into time. When Professor Merk retired and the announcement went out from Harvard, editorials sprouted in newspapers across the land. We collected some twenty of them along with a large batch of appreciative letters to present to him at commencement time in a big scrapbook.

The flabbergasted professor blinked at the offering.

"You Fellows have made me famous," he said in affectionate accusation.

The first issue of *Nieman Reports* announced its intention. The announcement simply stated that:

> The ninety-six newspapermen who have held Nieman Fellowships in the past eight years organized the Society of Nieman Fellows in 1946 and their Council voted to start a publication in journalism.
>
> It is intended to publish a quarterly about newspapering by newspapermen, to include reports and articles and stories about the newspaper business, newspaper people and newspaper stories.
>
> The Nieman Council hopes to make it of enough interest to the newspaper profession so that newspapermen generally will want to subscribe to it and write contributions for it. It has no pattern, formula or policy, except to seek to serve the purpose of the Nieman Foundation "to promote standards of journalism in America . . ."

The magazine got out of bounds with its first issue. Some Fellows had suggested that a mimeographed job would do; others proposed sending out printers' galleys. The serious postwar paper shortage was part of the problem. But the Crimson Printing Company, which prints the Harvard newspaper and other publications, agreed to print in magazine format if we would accept a heavy white butcher paper they had in stock. This was better than we'd expected.

The first issue attracted some newspaper attention, which, curiously, we hadn't expected. The *New York Herald Tribune* reported it in detail, describing its articles, with the result that about 300 applications for subscriptions came in immediately. This was more than three times the number of the Nieman Fellows up to that time. The Fellows and former Fellows have ever since been a minority among subscribers and they soon became a minority among contributors. For no similar periodical existed. *Editor & Publisher,* the trade paper, and the *Journalism Quarterly,* a publication of academic research in journalism, just about made up the field.

Nieman Reports offered a forum for articles, reviews, critiques, proposals on any aspect of journalism. It was the one place a speech or lecture could be published, and, if important enough, published in full. To provide full texts, if significant, was accepted as one of its functions. Soon most of the articles came from outside the Nieman circle, though the current group of Fellows at Harvard always supplied most of the book reviews and could be counted on for one or two articles in each issue, often the liveliest and most provocative. Contribution was always voluntary and in the nature of things uneven. But there were always some who could turn out acceptable reviews and sometimes a distinguished one. Sometimes a member of the group would take over in effect the role of book-review editor. If one turned in an interesting article, this often stimulated others to try their hands. A literary style is not a universal characteristic of newspapermen. To discover one writer with some distinction of style in a group was always a delight. But literary style was not demanded if a Fellow had something important or interesting to say. Copy editing is a more common talent and that helped, and there were always willing hands to share the tedious chore of proofreading.

The first issue narrowly missed disaster over the proofreading. In our innocence, we thought the printer read proofs. He assumed that it was our responsibility. The result was lugubrious. Of the two pages of letters to the editor in the following issue, most had references to the incredible number of typos in the previous number. Our first letters department was headed "Complaints and Otherwise." One of these letters will do as a sample of the rest. Brooks Atkinson wrote, "I'd like to subscribe, providing the proofreading improves." Some years later when Brooks was in Cambridge to talk at a Nieman dinner, he dropped in at his old haunt, the Crimson printer, and told them he was glad they were printing *Nieman Reports,* which he found a valuable publication. This immensely enhanced our standing with our printer, for the *Times* drama critic was a former *Harvard Crimson* editor, revered by his old printers.

In the war Brooks insisted on closing down his critic's desk and switching to war correspondence (he came back from Russia and China with new distinctions and a Pulitzer prize). The Nieman Foundation had arranged a two-week program of background on the war and invited fifty editors and correspondents to it. Brooks joined the group at the last minute, having just then completed his conversion at the *Times*. With all our planned-for facilities filled, I had to put him up in one of the ancient buildings outside the Yard. I apologized as we climbed the stairway into its vast archaic interior.

"You couldn't have pleased me more," Brooks said. "This was part of the famous Harvard Gold Coast and I was never inside it in my student days." (The Gold Coast had been a series of apartments, luxurious in their day, occupied by well-heeled undergraduates. When the Harvard Houses were built, about 1930, these buildings became part of the university system.)

That first issue led off with one of the most provocative articles the magazine ever printed. As I now read it again years later, what interests me is that we had no qualms at all about leading our first issue with it. It was lively, interesting, and valid. Its title was "What's the Matter with the Newspaper Reader?" Its author was William J. Miller, and its point was that the reader must be an undiscriminating fellow to put up with the fare most newspapers served him. Bill Miller was a vital, tough-minded reporter on the *Cleveland Press* when he came to Harvard. Everything about his article was utterly out of tune with almost everything that followed, both in that same issue and in those to come. It seems paradoxical, to go back and read it, that this was our introductory tone. Whether Miller sought a shock treatment, or wrote with tongue in cheek, or felt in the cynical mood he then ascribed to newspapermen generally, would, at this distance, be only a guess.

His opening is sufficiently descriptive:

> Whenever two or more newspapermen get together the talk sooner or later turns to the sad state of the nation's press, and what should be done about it. That was true of every one of the nine groups of Nieman Fellows so far. A majority in nearly every group felt that the press generally was doing an inadequate, and too often a biased and venal, job. Like the weather, everybody talked about it endlessly but found no solution for it.
>
> Many reasons have been advanced for the publishers' cussed persistence in continuing to publish newspapers that are far from being as honest, as fearless or as outspoken as most of their writers would wish them to be. One possible reason is perhaps too simple to have merited much discussion, and that is that the general public may not want a better press. I have come to the conclusion that the people get about as good a press as they deserve.

The rest is more of the same, with suggestive detail. What saves it from mere carping is its humor.

> If you will make a careful study of newspaper readers on street cars, subways, busses or elsewhere, you will quickly note the moods which conflict with the tepid desire to be informed . . . At the time when most people read newspapers, either going to work or going home, they tend to be absorbed in day dreams . . . One man is torn between a desire to read and a desire to look at girls' legs. Usually he settles on a particular girl and thereafter maneuvers his paper in such a way that he can pretend to read it and at the same time watch her . . .

As Miller settles to his theme, it is that "the majority of American newspaper readers do not like to read anything that forces them to think. That is why *PM* has made such a miserable showing. *PM* has been plugging along for seven years with the notion that so long as your heart is on the side of the angels, your news does not have to be either fresh or interesting." (*PM,* the adless newspaper, was then rapidly running out of readers, soon to fold.)

Miller did a fast turnabout at the end of his piece. "Any time a sufficient number of readers become really dissatisfied with the daily newspaper they are getting, they can pool their money and roll their own."

If any thesis has been utterly routed, it is that one. Miller mentions particularly labor unions as a likely group to set up their own newspaper. The subsequent experience of the big Typographical Union in operating a number of newspapers proved a fiasco. A later Nieman Fellow, and a very able one, was persuaded away from a good job on a good newspaper to become managing editor of one of these big union papers. He was very soon telling his friends what a mistake he had made. If he had thought to escape the dictates of the Chamber of Commerce, he found the dictates of the union ownership just as arbitrary and even more parochial. He soon grasped at a chance to escape back to conventional journalism, which had at least learned to come to some kind of terms with the minimum necessity to print the news.

Newspapermen could get together and run their own newspaper, Miller suggests. When this was tried in Cincinnati it was one of the fastest flops in the history of failures. It ended with the mortgagee owning the paper and selling it to the same outfit that now owns all the papers in town, a situation that has become familiar through the economic forces that Miller brushed off. His advice to the potential newspaperman ownership was to let their paper be "short, simple, sexy and full of pictures. I predict it will sell like hell. If on top of that it is honest, unprejudiced and unslanted, the public won't mind. The press the American people get is pretty bad, and it is just what they deserve."

The nine Nieman Fellows who were at that moment completing their "blueprint" for a different newspaper chose the opposite tack. They took the reader seriously and proposed to provide him the kind of newspaper an informed citizen needs to keep up with the score in his public affairs. A couple of their chapters first appeared in *Nieman Reports*. As I have already recorded, the theme of press responsibility became the touchstone of *Nieman Reports* starting with its second issue.

In that first one, the other principal articles are "Crusading in a Small Town," by another Nieman Fellow, Ernest Linford, then editor of the *Laramie Republican-Boomerang,* now chief editorial writer of the *Salt Lake Tribune;* and "I Always Wanted My Own Newspaper," by William Townes, a Nieman Fellow from the same news room in Cleveland as Bill Miller. The piece by Townes tells of his excitement and satisfaction in developing the Spartanburg, South Carolina, *Herald* by providing leadership in its community problems. "News enterprise, quality and editorial integrity were the first requirements in my formula." They spelled business success besides building a strong community newspaper. Townes was to repeat this success on the same formula as general manager in Santa Rosa, California. But he was disappointed in a long search for financing to buy the kind of newspaper he wanted and finally went back to working for other publishers, to become managing editor of the *Los Angeles Examiner* until it succumbed to the thinning out process in newspapers, when he went to Baltimore as assistant managing editor of the *Evening Sun.*

In one important aspect, that first issue set a role for *Nieman Reports* which was to continue. It published four and a half pages of text of a Senate committee study of the forces tending to monopoly in the newspaper industry. Called the Murray Report because its chairman was Senator James E. Murray, it was titled "Survival of a Free Competitive Press." It was in two parts: "The Small Newspaper" and "The Newsprint Industry."

The subheads on our summary of the Murray Report tell its story:

I. Giants Control Newsprint
II. Crisis for Small Papers
III. Press Monopoly Cannot Stay Free

As it turned out, that was as effective a background setting for the Hutchins Report, which would occupy our second issue, as could have been contrived had we been conscious of the sequence to come. It also set the pattern for our comprehensive report on the British Royal Commission study of the monopoly trend in British journalism which came out the same year.

Nieman Reports gave full treatment to these three examinations of the forces affecting the press in America and Britain. The Murray, Hutchins, and British reports, with summaries, reviews, and comment, occupied fifty-five pages, some 16,000 words, of the first three issues of our new magazine. Nowhere else was such comprehensive treatment given to these illuminating studies of the forces at work in the newspaper business. If nothing else, this, we felt then, and still feel, justified our venture. It filled a gap.

From the start we accepted it as a responsibility to publish texts of studies and reports which because of their length and special nature would not find publication elsewhere. Thus we ran the full report of the inquiry by a committee of the American Society of Newspaper Editors into Senator McCarthy's investigation of James Wechsler, editor of the *New York Post.* The incisive part of that was a separate report of four members who were the only ones ready to speak out forthrightly against this instance of McCarthyism threatening freedom of editorial expression.

Similarly we ran the full survey of the California newspapers' performance in the 1950 Senatorial election, a joint enterprise of the Newspaper Guild and the Stanford journalism school. We were later to run a number of studies and criticisms of press bias in elections, and some account of such positive measures to guard against it as the staff memorandum of the *Washington Post* editor, J. Russell Wiggins, before the 1956 election.

In 1950 we aspired to publish the texts of Pulitzer prize stories, since nobody else did. We started (July 1950) with Meyer Berger's extraordinary reconstruction of a series of killings by a maniac in Passaic, New Jersey.

But we were soon stopped in this project when we found Pulitzer awards given for a long series of articles or sometimes for the work of an entire year. So in July 1950 we were able only to describe, not reproduce, Edwin Guthman's investigation for the *Seattle Times* that reversed the dismissal and loyalty-board charges against a University of Washington teacher, Professor Melvin Rader.

We did run (July 1957) the text of the fearless speech of Buford Boone to a segregationist group in Tuscaloosa, Alabama, which he had printed in full as an editorial in his *Tuscaloosa News*.

One little investigation of our own exposed a journalistic abuse that needs continual exposure; indeed it had it several times over the years in *Nieman Reports*. In gathering press reaction to the Hutchins Commission report (we printed editorial reaction from dozens of papers), I was struck by the number of identical editorials in numerous small newspapers. I assumed they came from a syndicated editorial service. But, soon after, William Pinkerton, old AP man and former Nieman Fellow, director of the Harvard News Office, called me up one day to say he had something interesting to show me. Bill had a batch of clippings, fifty-nine of them almost alike. They were the same editorial in fifty-nine papers, referring to the annual report of James B. Conant, then president of Harvard.

The editorial had twisted a statement of Conant's to set up a straw man for an attack on college teachers as "warped or leaning to the party line": this under the heading "House Cleaning Due in Colleges." This was the absolute opposite of the position Conant had expressed. It didn't take elaborate detective work to discover the source, a public relations firm, E. Hofer & Son, in Portland, Oregon, serving the private power interests. I pieced together an article (July 1948) called "Editorial Writing Made Easy."

We named the fifty-nine papers that used the propaganda. The reactions, which brought letters to fill five columns in the next issue, further documented the Hofer enterprise as subsidized by the private power interests, and as claiming to reach 14,000 papers. "Reproductions of our articles appear almost invariably as original editorials, as we ask no credit," they had boasted to their backers.

A year later, when Richard Neuberger was in the Oregon legislature, he discovered the same source of editorial attacks on his conservation bills and his espousal of a Columbia Valley Administration, like TVA. Neuberger sent us an article which we ran under the title, "Prefabricated Editorials—The Hofer Factory Revisited."

Some years later a graduate student in journalism discovered this Hofer factory and was referred to *Nieman Reports* as a source. We ran his more detailed report on it. So far as I can make out, this repeated exposure had no effect whatever. The papers unabashedly using this canned bias are below the level reached by any journalistic standard, run by businessmen with axes to grind or willing to grind axes for others. They are of course small and undistinguished, but their total readership, which is regularly subjected to such stuff, must be considerable. I was reminded of this long after by a statement of Governor William Scranton in his desperate belated effort to head off the 1964 nomination of Senator Barry Goldwater by the Republicans. Scranton said two hundred Goldwater delegates were from Southern states where no Republican was ever elected; they had no responsible constituency; they were consequently "immune to public opinion."

Neuberger, before he entered politics, was the most energetic journalist of the Northwest, ranging from Alaska to California for his material. He had almost a monopoly on the magazine market for articles from the territory he covered so assiduously. Neuberger early became an enthusiastic supporter of *Nieman Reports* and sent us a number of articles. These continued after he got into politics. A notable instance was his article on the press neglect of the state legislature. The same press that complained of centralization of power in Washington was focusing all its own attention on Washington and covering its own legislature in slapdash fashion, he wrote. This was, and still is, largely true. In New England north of Boston, it's been a struggle for the smaller papers, which can't afford their own correspondents, to get anything like adequate statehouse coverage out of the wire services.

Dick Neuberger stopped writing for us when he became a United States Senator, but he came up to Cambridge for a breakfast session each season and his off-the-record talk about the adventures of a new member of the Senate were some of the most entertaining and illuminating sessions of the year. After his untimely death, his wife, Maurine, succeeding to his Senate seat, continued these visits for several seasons.

Texts for court decisions about the press were always grist for our mill, and these included vigorous assertions of the right of the press to access to court records, and equally vigorous denunciation of irresponsible pretrial publicity which led to reversals of sentences.

The issue of free press versus fair trial runs through our pages as it does through the endless controversy between lawyers and newspapermen. It was the theme of numerous sessions of the Nieman Fellows with the Harvard Law School. We have run articles by judges indignantly excoriating the press and retorts by such militant editors as J. Russell Wiggins, challenging the judges' premises. This issue is not going to be resolved to satisfy everyone. The British system that keeps the press on a tight rein just won't go in America. Indeed it often seems to lapse in Britain. The more irresponsible elements of the press fall into Governor Scranton's category of those immune to public opinion. The press, unlike law and medicine, has never achieved an effective discipline to hold all its members to a minimum standard.

Newspapermen often question how effective are the vaunted disciplines of law and medicine. I have always maintained that the law can exercise much more control than it does over pretrial publicity. The sources of the "confessions," on which prosecution so often stubs its toe in a trial, are invariably either police or prosecuting attorneys. These are officers of the law and certainly subject to court discipline, which is rarely attempted. If these sources were disciplined, there'd be mighty little pretrial publicity of the sort that can invalidate a conviction. But prosecuting attorneys are in politics. Judges too are elected in many areas. The temptation is to claim that a crime is solved when an arrest is made.

The Baltimore Supreme Court ruled in 1939 that it would be cause for contempt to issue to the press or to publish any admission by an accused in a pending criminal case. In 1948 the police made an arrest and claimed a confession in an atrocious murder of a little girl. The Baltimore newspapers adhered to the rule, but three radio stations in the area broadcast the confession. They were convicted of contempt. But the Maryland Court of Appeals quashed both the conviction and the Baltimore court rule as in violation of freedom of the press. The U.S. Supreme Court refused review, and there the issue has rested. No action was taken against the police commissioner, who testified he had issued no formal press release, only answered reporters' questions, an interesting distinction.

This, like all other issues of public concern in press performance, comes down to responsibility of the press. Endless articles in *Nieman Reports* have taken up this theme. Responsibility is increasingly accepted by most newspapers. Indeed we have come to describe "a responsible newspaper" as one that accepts standards of an institution very strategically affected by a public interest.

This leads into another endless and unanswerable question that has occupied considerable space in *Nieman Reports:* is journalism a profession? I have always cut through this to say that the responsible journalist acts as though it was, that his attitude must be that the reader is his client and his only client. This, too, I think, is increasingly accepted, certainly by newspapermen of the quality of Nieman Fellows. But the newspaperman is not a member of a profession in the same sense as doctor or lawyer. He is not a licensed practitioner. Nobody examines his qualifications to admit him to practice. He does not serve an *identifiable* client. He is employed by a businessman, a publisher. In the cynical view, journalism, if a profession, is a captive profession. The ultimate responsibility is the publisher's, whose most immediate concern is to sell enough papers to get enough advertising to make the operation pay. Standards in journalism are consequently very individual. Each man has his own. Those of the boss cannot always be guaranteed, let alone those of the yellow rag across the street with which both the journalist and his boss must compete.

One of the most provocative arguments for the advantage of "monopoly" newspapers, developed by John Cowles in *Nieman Reports,* is that, freed of competition, the newspaper can be more responsible. Nothing then prevents its putting the news in the perspective of its own professional judgment. Irving Dilliard carried that a point further: the newspaper without competition has lost all excuse for sensationalism.

The question, however, is whether it has also lost incentive to keep a sharp eye on city hall and the utility rates, to disclose unsavory facts about politicians it may have supported, to uncover conditions that need correction but that influential interests would prefer to sweep under the rug.

The newspaper without competition may have less zest for crusading or reform. As it undertakes to cover the whole market in its role as merchandiser of advertised products, its tendency is inevitably toward blandness, to be all things to all men. It is apt to adopt a posture of "independence" in politics, and this may drift to sterile neutrality on issues that matter.

In an era of mergers and reductions of the number of newspapers, from roughly the same causes that bring the same results in other industry, the newspaper stands out as a strategic institution, its relation to its community unlike any other. The community is terribly dependent on luck in the kind of publisher it has. It may build its own stadium, museum, auditorium, parks, hospitals, orchestras, but for its baseball team and its newspaper it depends on pot luck. So far as I can find, chance more than anything else determines that one city has a distinguished newspaper giving vital community service and another a humdrum paper or one that is unreliable, uninformed, narrow, or even hysterical. The theory that the public deserves the kind of newspaper it gets is hard to demonstrate. Are Louisville and St. Louis populations so much more deserving than the people of Indianapolis and Columbus? Was the generation that had great newspapers in San Francisco and Portland more deserving than the next generation? Have the people of Los Angeles suddenly become more deserving? Are the people of Providence so superior to those of Manchester, New Hampshire, that they deserve one of the most responsible of newspapers while the community a hundred miles away must put up with one of the most irresponsible? True, I think one can see that in Vermont the character of the population would discourage sensationalism, while in Nevada, considering its chief industries, this might not be so. But these are small and atypical territories.

Newspaper mergers and the reduction in the number of newspapers focused attention through all this period. *Nieman Reports* was fortunate in having this discussed, not only by persons who viewed the trend with alarm, but also by a number of publishers of "monopoly" papers, Barry Bingham, Paul Block, John Cowles among them. It was noted as early as the Hutchins report in 1947 that some of our most informed and adequate newspapers were monopolies. Des Moines, Kansas City, Atlanta, Providence, Toledo, Minneapolis have long had single newspaper ownership. It remained for John Cowles to spell out the advantages to the reader of having a newspaper unaffected by competition. Nothing pushed it off its own standards. Its own professional perspective on the news was not thwarted or frustrated by the threat of competition from a different standard, or none.

The disappearance of many newspapers with the consequent constriction of the channels of information and public opinion that Morris Ernst worried about in his *The First Freedom* went on apace through the 1950's. In 1964 when the *Houston Post* bought the *Houston Press,* the *New York Times* reported that only three cities were left with as many as three newspaper ownerships, fewer than twenty with as many as two. This left the rest as "local monopolies," typically one ownership printing morning and evening editions on the same presses. The obvious economy was in the overhead—one set of presses, one advertising department, one circulation department, one purchasing office. Only the news and editorial departments were separate to "compete" in such degree as their managements might find compatible with their complete control of the market. In some places the news competition was real and keen, in others nominal.

It always sounded a little silly for a publisher to say his two editorial pages operated independently; it only "happened" that both supported Dewey, Eisenhower, or Nixon. But this blind grew harder to sustain in the increasingly open climate of news production. By 1956 the Associated Press thought it news that the central offices of the Hearst and Scripps-Howard chains had directed their papers to support the Republican candidate and had transmitted a supporting editorial. This increasing candor in reporting protected the reader from the more blatant pretenses. It seemed to me to have become an inevitable concomitant of our open society and universal instantaneous communications, and it had established my own theory of the news in America: that murder will out. If the Republicans don't tell it, the Democrats will; if not the press, then television or the news magazines, or a paperback on a lively issue, coming off the presses almost as fast as the Sunday papers. There may be a time lag, and sometimes time is crucial, but little that is important is going to be bottled up very long. I think there is evidence that our latter-day news managers recognize this and adjust to it. If a publisher often has a rude shock at seeing his own front page, he realizes there is little he can do about it. The momentum of the news has taken charge.

This, of course, was in the direction all critics of the press sought.

It left little to the position of those who urged government regulation of the press or a government press. Indeed few ever had. The Hutchins Commission had specifically ruled this out, seeking only more responsibility and self-discipline within the press. This was the direction also of the British press inquiry and the resulting British Press Council.

Further, the experience with broadcasting, under nominal government regulation, has been disillusioning. Even when the Federal Communications Commission has occasionally sought some minimum reform in the public interest—like restraining the length and loudness of commercials—Congress, under pressure of the broadcast-advertising forces, has overruled it. This obviously suggests what government regulation or operation would come to. Congress controls the government. But the academic critics, as in the Hutchins Commission, that set off the yowls of publishers in 1947, were thinking in a conservative groove. They were all for private enterprise. Their criticism was in the main stream of American political thought, seeking reform, not revolution.

The press learned, of course, not from its critics, but from its own bitter experience. McCarthyism was the test it failed, and it soon confessed the failure. McCarthy exploited the news convention that what a public man says is news, and that the reporter doesn't go back of the quotation to test its truth. But McCarthy forced the press out of this. It had to come to "interpretive" reporting to look beneath the surface of the demagogue's claims as to the facts. It moved into an era of reporting in more depth, in order to explore and explain the meaning of the event. Competition with the swift pace of broadcasting may have forced this anyway. The slower newspaper needed to offer something beyond the first flush of the television bulletin. But it was McCarthy's exploiting of "objective" reporting that first forced the change.

Interpretive reporting brought a whole chapter of self-conscious debate over whether objectivity was sacrificed, whether reporting was taking over editorializing. When abused it did. But the basic journalistic discipline of objectivity can govern reporting in depth as well as on the surface. The effect was that the public was more informed. More competent reporters were required to deal with the background of the story. If this led to inclusion at times of a reporter's judgment as to the facts, I for one welcomed this aid. If the reader disagreed with the judgment, he could discount it and still welcome the fuller report.

Newspapering was, throughout this period, opening up, loosening up, the reporter given his head more. In and out of *Nieman Reports,* I had been pushing for this, cheering for it.

This seems to me at the very heart both of freedom and effectiveness. Too long and too tightly, the reporting staff had been held on short strings to assignment from the city desk. But the city desk knows only what it learns from its reporters. It must make out a schedule of coming events, of predictable developments to cover. But the reporters must be out where things are happening. Nobody gets a story sitting at a desk, that is, nobody but the reporter who has been so active in building acquaintance and earning confidence that people will telephone to make sure he doesn't miss something, or will talk frankly when he telephones *them.* The reporter needs to be associating with the people who make the news in his field; and that way he knows when a situation has developed to the point of being news. He knows it in depth and can write a piece that informs the reader. He never reaches this point if he is put down at a desk to be sent hither and yon at the bidding of a city editor. Of course the city editor has to have a mobile staff available for shipwreck and fire, accident and flood, for press conference and interview. But it is equally important that the seasoned staffers, responsible for areas of news, be free to explore, and to tell the office when they have a story worth writing. The tyranny of the old city editor was legendary; it lasted too long, and it inhibited reporting and limited the range and depth of the newspaper's coverage. One of the reasons why sports reporting has been livelier and, relatively, more informed than general city staff reporting is that it has been free of the city desk. Of course another reason is that you can't libel an umpire. Also the sports fans are informed and highly sophisticated about their sport. The reporter has to keep up with them.

One of the curious lapses of *Nieman Reports* is that it never marked the transition in the city room. Neither did anyone else. One day in 1963 the *New York Times* announced in an inconspicuous item that city editor Frank Adams was appointed to the editorial page staff and that foreign correspondent Abe Rosenthal, back from India, was appointed *metropolitan news editor.* In an explanatory paragraph, the *Times* stated that the development of the metropolitan area required replacement of city editor with metropolitan editor. Of course this explained only a part of it. Abe Rosenthal was soon developing stories that had no locality except to use the manpower of the city staff. At the same time the *Times* installed a national affairs editor, Harrison Salisbury, to try to close the gaps in national coverage. Interesting that they brought in foreign correspondents to direct these more explorative editorships. Joseph Herzberg, an acquisition from the *Herald Tribune,* where he had followed Stanley Walker in the tradition of the city editor who "knows his city like the back of his hand," was appointed cultural news editor, with a similar function to see that the arts obtained adequate coverage over all. Specialization was moving up from reporter to editor.

Of course in one degree or another something of this sort was happening all over, as the newspaper sought to adjust to changing conditions which required both more fluidity and more attention to what was going on outside the conventional news "beats" which had been conventional too long.

One can detect a gradual change in the tone of *Nieman Reports* down the years. The earlier issues show a sharper critical note. One time and another it has been suggested to me that the earlier Fellows were more radical. That, I think, is too easy an answer. Some of the same writers reappear through the years and their tone has moderated too. I note it in my own contributions. Of course the whole tone of American society has grown more conservative. The bulk of these articles ran from just after the end of the New Deal through the Kennedy administration. But the change in the press itself, I think, has been pronounced. Erwin Canham was writing of a "crisis in confidence" in the newspapers in the early period of *Nieman Reports,* and nobody would call the editor of the *Christian Science Monitor* either radical or carping. A frequent note in the early issues is about the extreme conservatism of publishers. It was true. There was also then perhaps a sharper cleavage between the attitudes of news room and business office. The Newspaper Guild was still new and publisher resentment of it strong. Reporters very generally felt an inhibiting hand at the news controls. Reporters thought of copy editors as hired to sit on the lid. News executives reflected the rigidities of publishers. "Little brothers of the rich," Edwin Lahey called them.

The difference in newspapers came in the change in generations across the board. You can put a finger on it in enough places to illustrate: most recently in the *Los Angeles Times,* but earlier in the *Washington Post, Atlanta Constitution, Charlotte Observer, Denver Post, Boston Globe, Minneapolis Star* and *Tribune, Houston Chronicle,* to a degree the Gannett papers. Even the *New York Times,* never reactionary, became liberal. One can claim that this has been offset by the papers that have fallen into bad hands or just fallen from their earlier standards. This has happened in a number of cases because of an interruption in the continuity of family ownership. William Pinkerton, in his interesting series on the sociology of the newspaper that ran in *Nieman Reports* through 1947, describes the newspaper control as typically a family ownership. But things happen to families to break them up and let in other controls. Those communities are in general fortunate where family continuity of control has kept up. But they are fewer than in 1947.

Another factor can also be demonstrated. As the business of the newspaper has preoccupied the publisher more, he has had to leave news and editorial direction more in professional hands, and news executives are more professional than a generation ago. It is more generally accepted that the news shapes the paper than the other way around. Our instantaneous communication has something to do with this. It has brought with it vast development of the news wire services, which now largely determine the flow of the news. They serve broadcasting equally.

It is much harder to intercept or divert the torrential news flow; also, through the competition of broadcasting, the reader has become more aware of what he should expect in the paper. This has made for greater uniformity and, along with increased syndication, has squeezed many of the distinctive differences out of regional papers. But, if newspaper work is leveling, it is at a higher level, a more professional handling of the news.

Criticism, consequently, tends to be more of technique and lapses, also more self-examination by staffers of their own role. It used to be too easy to put all the blame on the publisher. Another factor is a great increase in job security. People don't have to stay on a bad newspaper. Chances to move into television, public relations, government, or other allied fields continue to expand. The newspaper has to work harder to keep its good men—and to get them.

Newspapers have been very late to realize this and have lost much talent as a result, as the deans of journalism schools have been lamenting for years in articles in *Nieman Reports*. Only recently, and still very scantily, have newspapers done any active recruiting for staff or introduced any in-training programs. Mostly, channels to newspaper employment vary from chaotic to nonexistent. The *Wall Street Journal* has made a positive contribution through its Newspaper Foundation, with scholarships for college students who will take summer jobs on newspapers and prepare for journalism.

Of course, too, the education and competence of editors and reporters have risen. Specialization has increased. The first group of Nieman Fellows was divided between general reporters and editorial writers. Now as many are specializing—in science, labor, the Soviets, economics, Latin America, municipal finance, international relations, urban problems. This reflects the change in staff makeup and in the organization of the newspaper to cover the more complex areas of news in a world whose interests have been expanding in all dimensions. The content of *Nieman Reports* reflects this. The later issues deal with covering the schools, church news, strike news, the problems of science writing, of presidential press conferences, of foreign reporting.

The war and the bomb and the cold war brought new problems of security, secrecy, censorship, and complaints of "news management." These intensified as correspondents struggled with officialdom to tell the story of Korea, Cuba, Vietnam.

When Robert Miller of the United Press did us an article on the Korean War correspondents' problems with MacArthur's censorship, the *Reader's Digest* bought it, after our publication, paying both the author and us, and our share paid the printer's bill for a whole issue. In Vietnam the correspondents' difficulties became even more complicated. One of our most timely and illuminating articles was "The Correspondents' War in Vietnam," by Stanley Karnow, who was in the Far East for *Time-Life* and then for the *Saturday Evening Post*. Karnow is one of a notable group of foreign correspondents among the Fellows. Others include George Weller and Keyes Beech of the *Chicago Daily News;* Watson Sims of AP; Selig Harrison, first for the AP, then for the *Washington Post;* Dana Adams Schmidt, Henry Tanner, Richard Mooney, Henry Raymont, and Tillman Durdin of the *New York Times;* Alexander Kendrick of CBS; Dean Brelis of NBC; Piers Anderton of ABC; John Hughes of the *Christian Science Monitor;* Christopher Rand and Robert Shaplen, with the *New Yorker;* Robert Manning and Jerrold Schecter with *Time;* Robert P. (Pepper) Martin of *U.S. News & World Report;* Henry Shapiro and Robert Miller of United Press International; Robert Korengold and Walter Rundle, two UPI correspondents who joined *Newsweek.* Typically thorough in his preparations, Karnow wrote us that he was planning an article on the opium trade in China—would we please hire someone to get him a list of all the books on opium in the Harvard Library? Christopher Rand's system has been to walk over as much of a country as he could and talk to as many people as he could encounter.

The international dimensions of *Nieman Reports* expanded with the contributions of our Associate Fellows from other countries. Their articles about the newspapers of Japan, Taiwan, New Zealand, and South Africa, were detailed and informing. They also proved live bait to bring us many other articles from outside our own ranks, about the press of Chile, Sweden, Italy, Canada, France, and Germany.

These Associate Fellows came to us on the initiative of others. First the Carnegie Corporation arranged, in 1951, to finance three fellowships from Canada, New Zealand, and Australia. A few years later the Asia Foundation suggested a parallel program by which they would send us annually three Asian journalists. Later the U.S.–South Africa Leader Exchange Program began appointing one newspaperman each year from South Africa. The Commonwealth Fund a number of times had a journalist from Britain or Western Europe among its grantees who wanted to take up resident study at Harvard. After some years the period of the Carnegie grants ran out. Later the Canadian Associate Fellowship was taken up by the *Reader's Digest* of Canada. These various agencies added five to seven Fellows a year to our numbers and extended the dimensions of our discussions.

The first article by an Associate resulted from the Fellows' asking our first Japanese member to take over a seminar to discuss the Japanese press. He had full notes and we got him to develop them into a piece for the *Reports*. Sometimes we got a reverse twist on this, a discussion of the American press by one of our Indian members.

The leading topics in the *Reports* reflect the historical changes and the shifts in public attention.

The press of the NATO countries is the subject of an article in the early postwar period. Africa becomes an issue in 1959 that runs through several years, finally the subject of an entire special number of the magazine. We had by that time Associate Nieman Fellows from South Africa, both white and African.

Latin America rises as a subject first in the early 1950's and continues with variations until our publication in March 1964 of a long article on the wire services in Latin America, by Peter Barnes, from a book in process. Barnes had gone to South America to study American news sources and processes there on appointment as a research Nieman Fellow, supported by the Center for Latin American Studies at Harvard. Several Nieman Fellows by then were concentrating on Latin American studies. Cuba and its coverage, its press and what was happening to it were explored in the *Reports* through the early Castro years.

With the expansion of American interests around the globe, the fast rise of new nations in Africa, and revolutionary upheavals in the Middle East and Far East and Latin America, the wire services became increasingly important, their world-wide news a growing element in every newspaper. Studies of the flow of news and of the adequacy of our foreign news report began to present a new type of *Nieman Reports* article. The increased importance of the wire services focused attention on them. Criticism turned on the directions wire-service competition took, with its emphasis on getting in first, even by seconds, and on producing a more exciting report than the rival.

Sensationalism has ever been the bane of the press. The intensity of wire-service competition did nothing to abate this, nor did the practice of the services to mix sales and promotion with news coverage. The practice of making the bureau chief also the area salesman is of course utterly incompatible with single-minded concern for the news. This opens the door to abuse which at times seemed inescapable, especially in Latin America where rich influential newspaper clients had obvious axes to grind in the "image" of their governments or parties abroad.

A more subtle, perhaps inescapable, element in wire-service reporting in the postwar period has been its note of nationalism, often strident, often far from objective, in reporting on the Soviet Union, China, or Cuba. The sensitive telegraph editor who collected the most flagrant examples of this nationalist slant in wire-service reports could document a critical article, as occasionally one did. On a few occasions, when such a piece was offered, it seemed to me unanswerable, though it invariably inflamed the wire services. That such articles were submitted so seldom to *Nieman Reports* suggests that a nationalist point of view was an unconscious bias we nearly all shared, or else became so accustomed to it that we ceased to be sensitive to it.

I had a sharp illustration of how this looks from outside when I was invited to speak at a conference on public issues in Toronto. The theme was "communications," and Canadian editors were the chief performers. The crisis in American relations with Cuba was reaching its height. The Canadian editors were asked why Canada had to see the world through Washington eyes. Couldn't they have their own world-wide news service? The editors explained that it would cost too much for Canada to support. An editor from Quebec was the one contented participant. He had both the AP and Agence France-Presse. "I wouldn't think of using Agence France-Presse on Algeria or AP on Cuba," he said. The others sounded envious of this detachment that the French-language press could enjoy.

That the controlled press of authoritarian lands was more biased was beside the point. Zechariah Chafee first brought this out in a very temperate, persuasive piece, in *Nieman Reports,* April 1948, that reflected his own experience in the United Nations, where he had to defend the "capitalist" press from Soviet onslaught. He found he was often defending what his own sensitive nature found indefensible. And it was not only the Russians, but more significantly our Allies, who worried about the too frequent onesidedness of American reporting on foreign affairs. Out of similar UN experience, Erwin Canham, Carroll Binder, and Charles Sprague reported in like vein.

A recurring theme, noticeable in my frequent contributions, has been the relation of the publisher to his paper. Twice, on anniversaries, we ran C. P. Scott's statement about the *Manchester Guard-*

ian. Perhaps, said Scott, almost the chief virtue of a newspaper is its independence . . . it should have a soul of its own . . . At the peril of its soul it must see that the (news) supply is not tainted . . . Comment is free but facts are sacred.

We ran the eloquent statement in which Josephus Daniels bequeathed his paper, the *Raleigh News and Observer,* and the responsibility for it, to his sons. We ran the report of the trust set up to protect the integrity of the *Washington Post* in case of change of ownership; and we printed accounts of such trusts set up to protect certain noted British newspapers, one of them the *Times.* We noted the continuity of character that a newspaper has attained through several generations of family ownership, especially the *New York Times,* the Daniels paper in Raleigh, the two fine Washington papers, *Post* and *Star,* and for a century the *New York Herald Tribune* in the Reid family. The passing of the *Springfield Republican* after four generations was the occasion of discussion.

When biographies of the great editors and histories of individual newspapers were published, we liked to give them extensive reviews. One such book was *History of the Times* [of London], *1884–1912.* This is a most distinguished journalistic history, and anonymous, like everything in the *Times.* It is a great story and in a distinguished style. Some of it I can almost quote, over the years, with my eyes shut. After several generations "the editors of the *Times* had come to consider not so much their own views as 'what would be in character for the *Times.*' Taking the *Times* had not only become a habit" [with the most respectable elements in Britain] "but a habit that was handed down."

My own view had long since jelled that the most hopeful prospect for the control of American newspapers would be for their publishers to accept the same relation to their papers that they do as trustees of their universities: to provide the resources and protect the independence of the institution. This is not chimerical. It describes the attitude of the Sulzbergers on the *New York Times,* of the Pulitzers in St. Louis, of Barry Bingham in Louisville, of the Daniels family in Raleigh. It describes the attitude that Philip Graham had on the *Washington Post,* I believe, and it would hold for John Cowles in Minneapolis and now Otis Chandler in Los Angeles, and some more, not enough, but enough to be suggestive. Arthur Sulzberger came close to spelling out his publisher's creed in responses he had to make when awards were given to the *Times,* and we seized on such occasions for publishing him.

Professor Theodore Morrison included me on his staff at the Bread Loaf Writers Conference for two summers, and the lectures for that produced a short series on "Writing" for the *Reports.* Lectures of other people provided us some thoughtful critical essays on journalism. Nieman Fellows like Harry Ashmore, Clark Mollenhoff, Irving Dilliard, Anthony Lewis, and John Hulteng were among the recipients of awards for distinction in journalism, and occasions like the Elijah Lovejoy Award at Colby College always called for an address. The texts of what was said at such times were often sent to us by the journalist or by the host institution. Thus we had chances to publish articles by Mark Ethridge, Mark Childs, Barry Bingham, Joseph Pulitzer, Arthur Sulzberger, John Oakes, Gordon Gray, Clifton Daniel, Herbert Brucker, Russell Wiggins, Robert Estabrook, Alfred Friendly, James Pope, Thomas Storke, Charles Sprague, Palmer Hoyt, Ralph McGill, John Cowles, Robert Farquharson, James Reston, and others whose names were household words in the journalist's lexicon. Some of these men were in frequent demand on editorial occasions, and after an initial experience in the *Reports* often sent us later speeches. Others, especially the publishers, were men who seldom spoke, and, when they did, were likely to distill in the speech a lifetime's experience and convictions about their work.

Still other contributions arose from our associations with the journalists who came up to talk to the Nieman Fellows. All such sessions were off the record. This meant that many stimulating and informing discussions were retained only in our minds. The rule, of course, was essential to a full, free, candid discussion. You didn't want a man to be on guard against committing himself to something that might trip him up in print. But such speakers often came prepared with notes and occasionally with a full manuscript. In some instances, as in Paul Block's discussion of monopoly newspapers and Edward Behr's brilliant analysis of the French army at the time of its Algerian revolt, they were persuaded to write out their notes and let us publish. In Behr's case this led on to a book.

The visit of Harry Grant, the redoubtable publisher of the *Milwaukee Journal,* led to publication of a biographical profile of Lucius Nieman, founder of that paper, for whom the Nieman Fellowships were named. Mr. Grant did it for us and his paper published it in a brochure. His Nieman dinner talk was one I recall for another incident too. In recounting the development of that strong independent paper, he mentioned its current value. Out of the corner of my eye I witnessed the treasurer of Harvard, one of our guests that night, evidently having a nervous paroxysm. I realized that the figure the publisher had named in his exuberance was far beyond the figure arrived at in the negotiations the Harvard treasurer had carried on with the *Journal* lawyers to arrive at the value of Mrs. Nieman's bequest to Harvard from her $27\frac{1}{2}$ per cent share in the paper. But Mr. Grant's figure was not challenged on that occasion.

Mark Ethridge, one of the great newspapermen of his generation, always had a warm Dutch-uncle feeling for the Nieman Fellows and came up a number of times to talk to our meetings. The *Louisville Courier-Journal* with its sister paper, the *Louisville Times,* at one time had more former Fellows than any other paper. The paper was hospitable to their applications for leaves of absence. Mark had had a Rosenwald Fellowship himself when he was young and counted it a valuable experience. Also it was the kind of paper people didn't leave. Mark Ethridge and the owner, Barry Bingham, made a great team for newspapering. They became interchangeable parts of the management. Indeed they eventually changed jobs. Barry made Mark publisher so that he could be editor. But this meant the paper had two top editors and two top publishing minds. It needed both, for both were in demand for public service. Barry would run the paper while Mark was reporting to President Truman on crises in Greece and the Balkans. Mark would take over while Barry was off to war or serving as ambassador to Europe under the Marshall Plan. These big-league editors were always at home with reporters and vice versa.

During one session with Mark, the question arose why the *Louisville Times,* under the same Bingham ownership as the *Courier-Journal,* would continue to publish the columns of Westbrook Pegler, even when he wrote scurrilous pieces about people of the quality of Eleanor Roosevelt. Mark's defense was that their papers (morning and evening) were the only ones in town. They never sought a monopoly but had it thrust upon them. They wanted to state their views full strength but the political opposition was entitled to its spokesmen too. "But it doesn't have to be as bad as Pegler," Mark was challenged. "Yes, they're entitled to the worst there is," he retorted. When he got back, the *Louisville Times* published a piece, "Why We Run Pegler," which we reprinted.

Pegler himself was a guest on an occasion that rates as disastrous. I should explain that he resisted coming, said he was no speech maker, etc., etc. But I was persistent because the Fellows kept after me. This was the period when Pegler was crusading against the Newspaper Guild, calling it communist. A large part of the Fellows were, in the nature of their work, members of the Guild. Inevitably when Pegler appeared he was challenged about his charges against the Guild. One Fellow, who later became a top executive of one of the great news services, was especially persistent in his questions, trying to pin Pegler down. As moderator of such sessions I have often had moments of anxiety over whether a hot controversial discussion would stay within acceptable bounds. It almost always did, sometimes with a little pressure from the chairman. This time I was quite relaxed, feeling that the questioner would soon find there was nothing to be gained by further probing. But as I knocked out my pipe, Pegler suddenly swung around to me to say, "I didn't come up here to be cross-examined by collective bargainists." This collapsed that session. He wouldn't say any more. A few others ventured half-hearted attempts at conversation. But it was no good. We offered Pegler a ride back to his hotel but he said he liked to walk.

This was almost the only real disaster in twenty-five years of Nieman dinners. We had a few, but very few, other embarrassments. One of the most surprising to us, and devastating, came when a Fellow quoted a poem of Robert Frost's against a political position the poet was taking. The offender was quite innocent, an admirer of Frost. He just didn't know the rules Frost played by. That was off limits. It was intolerable to Frost and he said so vehemently, and wouldn't take on the Nieman Fellows for several seasons. Later when I had come to know him as a Cambridge neighbor, Frost relented and returned and was again affectionately revered and enjoyed as a dinner guest by successive annual Nieman groups. But the evening he blew up was a vivid experience. I recalled a line of Carl Sandburg's in a Harvard commencement address in 1940: There's a time coming that will blow your hair off.

There was at least one time when the embarrassment ran the other way. This was the miserable night when an aging editor from the American Southwest sat and read a prepared text about his visit to South Africa, extolling the virtues of a system where the Blacks tended the beautiful flower gardens of the Whites and the the Whites fed the Blacks. The brilliant and sensitive South African Black in the Nieman group just laughed, but everyone else was upset.

The Fellows for the most part learned that you can ask almost any question, if you ask courteously; that you can argue a point, treating a guest's views respectfully; but that there are civilized bounds of discussion and obligations of hospitality. They learned, too, to hold back the stickier questions until they had become reasonably well acquainted with the guest and he had got well warmed to his talk. The couple of highballs after dinner helped some. There were just two, for after the second round Archie locked his liquor closet and went home, leaving us to close up the club.

Professor Zechariah Chafee, great and lifelong champion of freedom of speech, became intensely interested in the press through his service on the Hutchins Commission. Out of that experience he wrote two volumes on the government and mass communications. Chafee, Professor Schlesinger, and Professor Ernest Hocking of Harvard all served on that commission, as did Archibald MacLeish, who had been and later was again at Harvard. Schlesinger brought Chafee over from the Law School for several sessions with the Nieman Fellows, both while the commission was working on its report and after it was published. It may well have been from some of the Nieman Fellows that Chafee got an expression that appears in the report and that he used in a press conference in New York when the report was issued. He said he found good newspapermen "frustrated" at their inability to inform the public more adequately through their newspapers. This roiled Arthur Sulzberger, publisher of the *New York Times.* He demanded to know if Chafee had found any *New York Times* men frustrated.

This was fresh in Chafee's mind when he joined us at a dinner with Joseph Herzberg, then city editor of the *Herald Tribune.* Just before the evening was over, Chafee put it up to Herzberg: did he find that reporters had a feeling of frustration in their work? Herzberg grimaced and wriggled and scratched his head over that one. "Well," he said, "I'm not so very stable myself."

This became a byword with the Fellows for a long time, whenever anyone was stumped by a question. Joe Herzberg was a terrific city editor, besides a man of rich humanity and droll humor. There seemed nothing about New York City he didn't know. It seemed one of the most incredible evidences of malfunctioning of the *Trib* under its final generation of Reids that they moved Herzberg off the city desk onto the Sunday paper. He soon escaped to the *Times* with other top *Trib* men of that period.

Herzberg did a book, *Late City Edition,* one of the best things on journalism. He got his colleagues to contribute a chapter each on the various departments. He was kind enough to let us choose a chapter to run in *Nieman Reports.* We chose the piece about the editorial page by Geoffrey Parsons, who must have been a very tolerant and wise chief. He believed in giving writers their heads. A man would write best on a subject of his choice. And if he had any style of his own, it was sabotage to try to edit him into your own style. That system produced a lively and vigorous page, with a flavor of its own.

Our luck with Nieman dinner speakers was uneven, like newspaper conversation. It was almost always informing, interesting, and candid. But some of our journalistic heroes proved disappointing speakers.

Tom Stokes was a blunt honest columnist for Scripps-Howard. He never got over being a reporter who chose to dig into situations in Washington that weren't getting much exposure. But Tom's talk proved to be about the length of one of his short columns. Then he'd said it. To get more out of him was like pulling teeth, though he enjoyed the general conversation into which the evening drifted.

Joe Liebling was unpredictable. He came a number of times, seemed to like to come. But sometimes he lapsed into a Buddha-like silence after he'd stated his brief thesis that publishers were no damn good. Then he'd just beam benevolently on anyone else who wanted to talk until it reminded him of a story, when he'd come to bat for another brief inning. Having got used to this, not only in Cambridge but in joint appearances with Liebling on panels here and there, I used to tell the Fellows, when they asked for Liebling, that they'd better be prepared to provide the conversation. My calculations went way off the last time he came. He had just finished writing that marvelous story, *The Earl of Louisiana.* The book wasn't out and, in the course of a luncheon session that stretched out to four o'clock, he told most of the stories in it. It was fascinating talk that filled the room with laughter all afternoon.

James Thurber's reminiscence of Harold Ross of the *New Yorker* was then running in the *Atlantic Monthly*. Naturally we asked Liebling about Ross. As the session broke up, Liebling said to me that he'd written a piece about Ross, and if I wanted it for *Nieman Reports* I could have it. This was a wonderful bonus from his visit. The next issue of *Nieman Reports* published Liebling on Ross.

For a period the *Christian Science Monitor* had the Fellows around annually to a session with their editors. Later the *Boston Globe,* when it got into a new building, took this up. The Fellows were at dinner at the *Monitor* when the news came that President Roosevelt was dead. I remember Erwin Canham giving the announcement. That changed the conversation drastically, but made it a memorable occasion.

Over a long period the *New York Times* extended hospitality to the Nieman Fellows when we made an annual trip at mid-year to the United Nations where, from Eleanor Roosevelt through to Ambassador Lodge, the American delegation as well as the Secretary-General's staff gave us illuminating briefings. The *Times* would have us around that evening for cocktails, dinner, and a long evening with publisher and editors. The *Times* would even bring up their Nieman Fellows from Washington to join the evening. The talk was all about the *Times,* which fascinated our members from the hinterland. Our hosts answered the most searching questions with amiability: why didn't they publish a national newspaper? How did they decide whom to support for President? What went on at their editorial conferences?

In later years *Time* and *Newsweek* arranged dinners in Boston for the Nieman Fellows and brought up top members of their staffs.

The dinners with the *Globe* would come early in the fall. These always got rapidly around to criticism of the Boston newspapers, a gambit of the Fellows from other places, who were used to newspapers that didn't have front-page ads or such black headlines or so many jumps from the front page. The *Globe* editors must have braced themselves for these affairs, but they were most tolerant hosts and great fellows. They knew by then what to expect, for their executive editor, political editor, Washington correspondent, and science editor had all been Nieman Fellows, and I was a *Globe* alumnus.

My *Globe* days were my preparation, if there could be said to be any, for the role of moderating Nieman dinners and seminars. The best talk I ever knew was in luncheons with newspaper colleagues and the richest was the talk of our old editor, James Morgan, whose wisdom and limitless knowledge of political history, his kindness and personal interest in all of us, overcame any shortcomings in our jobs and led some of us, at least, to share the feeling he expressed at ninety, after more than three score years on the paper: "I wouldn't swap my luck for any other."

I had always felt that way about newspapering through my twenty-five years on the *Globe,* eight of them overlapping my twenty-five years with the Nieman Fellows. If anything could have utterly unfitted me ever to become a critic of the press it would have been the consuming interest of newspaper work, the intellectual excitement of starting on each fresh quest in the infinite variety of journalism, which has of course all the dimensions of human activity and human interest. But later I realized how exceptional my experience had been.

The *Globe* was still operated on an older system (or lack of system) than prevailed on many papers. There was no distinction between reporters and rewrite men. One would do both jobs and not be aware of the difference. The same staff wrote for daily and Sunday papers, or some of us did. There was a minimum of specialization. One might be covering politics today and a shipwreck tomorrow, a murder trial or a series on unemployment or social security, writing a column or filling in on editorials. The variety was stimulating without necessarily making us superficial. For while a man was covering a public-utility rate case or exploring war production or the finances of the city, he needed to get his mind around the problem and, for the days or weeks involved, know as much about it as anyone in town. When it was over, he tackled a new assignment. The paper had its limitations and inhibitions, but these were not mean or venal and seldom commercial.

When the publisher squashed a proposal of mine for an article on mushrooms, his reason was succinct. "Good God, you'd poison half the population." When I had wrapped up the story of a threatened withholding of milk by the New England dairymen in a price dispute with the distributors, the city editor greeted me with "The publisher says no milk strike story." To my protest that the *Globe* couldn't suppress a situation its farm readers knew all about, he said, "All right, you go downstairs and get your head beaten in. Not me." There was nothing to be afraid of but a little picturesque profanity. So I went down. "Of course we'll run the story," said the publisher. "All I told them was not to use the term 'milk strike.' People would think it is the milk wagon drivers." When I was covering legislative hearings on regulating the cosmetics industry, which had a strong lobby of big advertisers, I got a characteristic note from the publisher, who had certainly been besieged by his advertisers. He said, "Give both sides."

On assignment, I explored a fantastic Wall Street effort to get control of the cranberry industry, which was concentrated among small growers on Cape Cod. When my first piece had run, the publisher sent for me to say he'd been told I'd been "had." This made me indignant, but the managing editor quickly went down to straighten him out. That night a real estate operator called on me to plead that I stop the series. It was costing him a $250,000 commission, he said. It sounded more and more like Alice in Wonderland. I told him there was nothing I could do; he'd have to see the publisher to stop a series in the *Globe*. "I have seen him," he groaned. "He was insulting. He practically threw me out of the office." I felt pretty good about our publisher after that. Of course the absurd scheme fell through. It couldn't stand publicity. But they had rounded up options on hundreds of the small cranberry bogs on the Cape. This was in the booming twenties when the sky seemed to be the limit on speculative schemes.

With this background I used to prickle all over at first encounters with the academic skepticism and cynicism about the press. Even when I found that many of my newspaper colleagues shared the same views, I was a long time growing callouses over my sensibilities. It seemed a wry joke to learn that some publishers were saying "Lyons infects the Nieman Fellows with this attitude of looking down their noses at the Boston newspapers." Of course it wasn't just the Boston newspapers that the Fellows criticized, but they had to get used to front-page ads and black streamer heads, which were such old hat to me that I never noticed them.

All who venture any criticism of the press become acutely aware of the hypersensitive reaction of many newspaper managers. Professor Charles Higbie wrote an article for *Nieman Reports* on "Our Nervous Press and Its Nervous Critics" (January 1959). Some publishers' reaction to criticism is at times practically paranoiac. It has restrained all but the hardiest souls from criticism. It has intimidated most journalism-school faculties from exercising any critical function at all, so that journalism has been all but denied the wholesome effect of the continuing professional criticism to which law is exposed in our law-school reviews.

This occupational allergy of publishers is often noted but seldom explained, if it can be explained. One partial explanation may be that the newspaper is so much more personal an institution than law or medicine. The controlling individual is identifiable. His product is highly visible to his community. He naturally takes it more personally than the lawyer, doctor, educator, or civil servant do when their institutions are criticized, as of course they are constantly. Yet the newspaper is critic of everything else. It is a paradox that it should be least capable of taking what it daily dishes out. It is the least criticized institution in our society and so strategic in its relation to all others as to require the most attention.

Almost at once *Nieman Reports* got the whole Nieman Fellowship program into hot water which developed into a serious crisis and came close to severing my connection with the program altogether. The editor of a publication without staff is bound to have to undertake himself those reviews and subjects he feels most essential; so I began for the first time writing critical pieces about the press. It was undoubtedly impolitic to name newspapers and compare their performance with that of others. I am sure it was my production more than anything else that soon roused the wrath of certain publishers. Some of them were influential Harvard alumni, and President Conant could hardly brush them off. Their attitude led Mr. Conant to remember that he had been going to have an appraisal of the program after five years, but because of the war had let this lapse. It was now the tenth year and he announced that it was appropriate to appoint a review committee of newspapermen.

I was shown a list of those it was proposed to appoint and was asked for suggestions or changes. I had none to make. It was a representative group. But it seemed to me that if the program was in trouble the short way out of it was for the curator to resign. Colleagues closer to the president's office insisted this was not the answer. But what really dissuaded me from resigning was the hubbub the word of an "investigation" of the program stirred among Nieman Fellows. A reunion was due shortly and I shrank from the prospect of a public commotion. The Fellows on one paper, who suspected their publisher of being a chief critic, wrote me they intended to leave the paper. My mail was disturbing. So, determining not to be made a martyr by the intensity of Nieman loyalty, I wrote assuaging answers to letters, taking my line from the president's office that such a review after ten years had been foreordained.

President Conant had the committee up for two days at Harvard to hear from deans and professors and from the curator and current Nieman Fellows. Such members of the committee as James Reston, Mark Ethridge, Mark Childs, and Erwin Canham must have had some weight with the conservative publisher members. The final report endorsed the Nieman program. It made some criticism of the selection process (and I have no doubt some managements had played the old army game and supported applicants they would miss less than others). The committee made only two recommendations, both easy to accept.

One recommendation was to have some newspapermen on the selecting committee each year. I had proposed that to Mr. Conant myself at the end of the first year. The other was that every Fellow should be required to take at least one full course complete, with examinations. Professor Schlesinger had often urged this, but I had held out for the complete freedom I had so much enjoyed the first year. Actually most Fellows were taking more than one course complete. It was no hardship for a Fellow to select one course, most central to his purpose, and do all the work in it. This never proved a problem. The Fellows almost invariably got the high marks one would expect of such mature students choosing their own subjects. No record was kept of their marks except in the Nieman office. But it unquestionably promoted our public relations within the faculty. Often a professor wrote me a note of his pleasure over a distinguished paper by one of the Fellows. Some of these papers made us good copy for *Nieman Reports*. If there was any grousing by a professor about the visiting firemen who just listened in on his lectures, one of his colleagues could testify to the performance of the same Fellows in his course. By the time of the reunion that June (1948) the crisis had passed. The only reference to it I can recall was in a sally of Mark Ethridge, opening a talk with, "I hear that some of you write books," which drew an appreciative response. *Nieman Reports* continued on its way.

One problem with many manuscripts we could not use was the tendency to criticize "the press" as all of a piece. So doughty a critic as A. J. Liebling seldom made any allowance for the vast range of difference in the quality and performance of individual newspapers, responsible and irresponsible. Even in the irresponsible group there is a distinction to be made between the narrow, reactionary, or slanted paper, which nevertheless reports in some relation to the world of reality, and the absolutely zany press, such as Max Hall describes in his adventures with two now-defunct Hearst papers, "Can a Yellow Rag Change Its Color?" (March 1964).

Our first couple of issues included even short stories and other literary forms which we soon decided were out of our line. Had we kept on with this, the quarterly might have attained a more literary flavor. For, besides Bud Guthrie, a number of Fellows, Robert Shaplen, George Weller, Hoke Norris, Henry Hornsby, Clark Porteous, Tom Wicker, William McIlwain, Hodding Carter, Frank K. Kelly, Tom Sancton, Herbert Lyons, and Ian Cross, among others, proved to be novelists as well as journalists, and Charles A. Wagner a poet. But it was unquestionably sound to stick to our last, and for a long time the quarterly filled a vacuum in its field. Without staff or resources, we could not take on more than we did.

No one is more conscious of the limitations of the quarterly than its first editor. The Fellows' dues and our subscriptions barely paid the printer's bills, though we did not hesitate to subsidize one issue out of four when necessary, on the ground that publishing was part of the job. We never could present detailed commentary on press performance with the immediacy of "CBS Views the News" in the brief intervals when, first Don Hollenbeck on radio, and later Charles Collingwood and Ned Calmer on TV, were assigned this useful chore. Nor had we the professional staff with which the *Columbia Journalism Review,* endowed and handsomely published, began in 1962 its graphic surveys of newspaper performance on the most important issues. We were unable to pay contributors, and consequently unable to assign articles, save for a brief period after I received the Lauterbach Award in 1958. The Lauterbach committee turned over the residue of their funds with the award, for support of *Nieman Reports*. It was amazing how fast the $4,000 melted away in publishing even a modest quarterly. We maintained the award, at a reduced rate and finally only a scroll, to complete the decade from its establishment. The purpose of the award was to honor the memory of Richard Lauterbach, a Nieman Fellow and brilliant journalist, by the recognition of distinguished service in the field of civil liberties. Herblock was our first year's selection, then Ralph McGill and Thomas Storke. In the case of Mr. Storke, we had the added satisfaction of seeing the Pulitzer prize for public service follow our lead.

Had the editor been enterprising enough to raise funds and promote the quarterly, presumably we could have entered more actively into appraisal of current journalistic performance. But our own members in the Society of Nieman Fellows were too busy in their own pursuit of journalism for us to ask them to undertake elaborate research on a problem. Thus we never could have such an extraordinary analysis of a newspaper strike as Abe Raskin's in the *New York Times* after the New York strike of 1963. Equally extraordinary was the objectivity of the *Times* in publishing this uninhibited account of a strike to which the paper was a party. But even had we felt free to impose assignments on our members, they were always involved themselves.

But it was not wholly a liability that we had to depend upon the product of reflection and detachment. Such an article as James McCartney's on the "Vested Interests of the Reporter" (March 1964) would hardly have been produced under other conditions than the fallow year of his Nieman Fellowship. The yield of such experience is almost unique and, I hope, justifies a modest venture in publishing. From former Fellows, active in their own work, anything they sent us was a byproduct; but it too was apt to be thinking out loud about a situation on which they had been able to get some perspective. It was the occasional insight of such a piece that provided the chief satisfaction of editing.

I am sure we published too many pieces about What is the matter with editorials? or weeklies? or the wire services?—though the best of these were effectively provocative. As I think back over it, I realize that we labored also under a certain inhibition, not to be dogmatic, not to claim to have all the answers. Although our effort had been stimulated by the Hutchins Commission, we shied away from their proposal for a Commission on the Press. This proposal was kept alive and actively promoted down the years by William Benton and Harry Ashmore, both closely associated with Robert Hutchins. The practicality of this was under recurring discussion. I was never convinced. But beyond that, we resisted involvement in the implication of a board of review that would pass continuing judgment. We wanted a forum of open criticism and appraisal, but drew back from the establishment of a commission to render judgments. We were accused, of course, of doing just that; but so long as we had not presumed to do it, we could stand the accusation.

But we kept the *Reports* open for descriptions of such commissions in Britain and Australia, which to be sure were quite different, and, it seemed to me, of little effect. We published with interest a proposal of Arthur Sulzberger's for a "newspaper court" to deal with abuses of pretrial publicity and the like. Barry Bingham was to suggest a local committee in Louisville for appraisal of the press. As owner of both papers there, he would unquestionably have desired such organized informed criticism from outside. In Littleton, Colorado, Houstoun Waring had organized a group of citizens to present periodic criticism and suggestions on the performance of his *Littleton Independent*. This was the effort of a publisher to be sure he was meeting his community's needs. But these were very limited applications of the Hutchins idea, as of course was *Nieman Reports* itself.

I. A RESPONSIBLE PRESS

We start with a review of the Hutchins Commission's analysis of the state of the press and its challenge that "only a responsible press can remain free." This 1947 review describes better than anything else the purpose and tone of *Nieman Reports*. The selections that follow it develop naturally as the discussion unfolds in some of the infinite variations encountered in the universal dimensions of the press. The press is provocatively challenged by Zechariah Chafee in "The Press under Pressure." Some of the other titles are eloquent of the fervor and dedication of the authors—"The Full Dimensions of the News," "Take a Forthright Stand," "Responsibility of the Reporter and Editor." The issue of responsibility leads to the thorny problem of pretrial publicity, illustrated here by Judge Sobeloff's article, and to such abuses as the use of prefabricated editorials provided to newspapers by a publicity firm for the electric power industry. Some of the most illuminating and candid discussions of the press as an institution have been the articles facing up to the monopoly issue by three publishers of "monopoly" papers, John Cowles, Paul Block, and Barry Bingham, of which the one by Mr. Cowles must suffice here.

A Free and Responsible Press

LOUIS M. LYONS [APRIL 1947

In December, 1942, Henry R. Luce of Time, Inc. suggested to President Robert M. Hutchins of the University of Chicago an inquiry into the freedom of the press: both its present state and future prospects. President Hutchins selected a dozen scholars to serve with himself on a Commission on Freedom of the Press. Their conclusions now published mark an important event in the history of American journalism.*

For the first time an examination of the performance of the press has been undertaken by a highly competent, independent body with adequate resources. They spent three years and $200,000 of Mr. Luce's money, then $15,000 more that President Hutchins dug out of the Encyclopaedia Britannica.

The variety of experience of the Commission membership lends weight to its findings. Besides President Hutchins, they were: John Dickinson, general counsel of the Pennsylvania Railroad; Beardsley Ruml, then president of the Federal Reserve Bank of New York; Archibald MacLeish, formerly assistant Secretary of State; Reinhold Niebuhr of Union Theological Seminary; George N. Shuster, President of Hunter College; Harold D. Lasswell of the Yale Law School; John M. Clark, economist of Columbia University; Charles E. Merriam, political economist of the University of Chicago; Robert Redfield, Dean of Social Sciences at that institution; and three scholars of Harvard University, Zechariah Chafee of the Law School, Arthur M. Schlesinger, historian, and William E. Hocking, philosopher. As director of their staff they had Robert D. Leigh, former president of Bennington College, assisted by Llewellyn White.

Their extensive inquiry included all agencies of mass communication—books, magazines, movies, radio, newspapers. But with books they found little problem, and with magazines less than the other media. They are bringing out separate studies on the movies and radio. Their central report is largely concerned with the newspaper.

They considered freedom of the press in terms of a responsible press and they came out with the warning that only a responsible press can remain free. Failure of the press to meet the needs of a society dependent on it for information and ideas is the greatest danger to its freedom, the Commission finds.

Its answer to the question "Is the freedom of the press in danger?" is a flat "Yes." But the reasons do not echo the familiar assumption

* *A Free and Responsible Press,* ed. Robert D. Leigh, the report of the Commission on Freedom of the Press (University of Chicago Press, 1947).

of the publishers that freedom of the press is their proprietary right to act as irresponsibly as they please.

The Commission's reasons are:

1. As the importance of communication has increased, its control has come into fewer hands.

2. The few in control have failed to meet the needs of the people.

3. Press practices at times have been so irresponsible that if continued, society is bound to take control for its own protection.

The citizen also has a right to truthful information on public affairs, the Commission asserts. "No democracy will indefinitely tolerate concentration of private power, irresponsible and strong enough to thwart the democratic aspirations of the people. If these giant agencies of communication are irresponsible, not even the First Amendment will protect their freedom from government control. The Amendment will be amended."

This is an urgent warning to the interests in control of the press. It is going to be a hard one to brush off or forget as so many criticisms of less weight have been brushed off and ignored.

The Commission recites the communications revolution that has made the press big business and shows it acting increasingly like big business and increasingly in alliance with the interests of other big business. The vital necessity of the citizen to have access to clear channels of adequate information on public affairs has never been more painstakingly presented. His right and obligation to secure such information is insistently put.

Then the Commission comes to a sticking point. How to protect the public right to access to truthful information is a complex problem. The Commission's remedy is less convincing than its diagnosis. That has been true of course of all earlier criticism of the press. The Commission shies away from public regulation to make the press accountable, lest other freedoms be endangered. This is the dilemma of a modern society enormously dependent upon a press in private hands, inevitably controlled by large capitalists whose interests are not always the public interest.

It is easy to show that accountable service in communication is as essential as pure food, public health, and fair trade practices. But these other needs are protected by law. If we accept the view that government regulation of the press is a danger to freedom, then the public is cut off from the traditional means of a democracy to protect its interests by public regulation.

That the Commission has not taken us out of that dilemma is both the weakness of the report and the riddle of the problem. If you refuse the public the sole public recourse to protect its rights, you haven't much left but hope and prayer. The Commission prays that the press may make itself more responsible. It urges that the press restore the professional status of journalism, long a captive to the publisher's business. It wants professional standards applied to the performance of the press. It insists that the press cease shielding its own miscreants by the device of refusing publicity to the malpractices and libel suits of its fellow members. It asks a sense of trusteeship by publishers. These are indispensable reforms.

But the only means to these ends that it finds to recommend are public concern, public appraisal, public criticism of press performance. It proposes an endowed agency to supply continuing appraisal of press performance. This is a very mild poultice to apply to the organic and spreading disorder of irresponsible giantism which it finds in the institution of the press.

But the report is not to be judged by failure to find the cure. Its value is in alerting the public and warning the publishers of the failure of the press to meet the public need. The definition of "common carrier of public discussion" as the function that a responsible press must accept is one for all journalism to paste in its hat.

The great strength of the report is its penetrating examination of the performance of the press. It has the courage to challenge the whole rigamarole of press clichés as to what is news and the silly game of scoops and headline hunting. "The news is twisted by emphasis on the novel and the sensational . . . Too much of the regular output consists of a succession of stories and images that has no relation to the typical lives of real people anywhere. The result is meaninglessness, flatness, distortion and perpetuation of misunderstanding." It finds the press preoccupied with the sensational and trivial "to such an extent that the citizen is not supplied with the information and discussion he needs to discharge his responsibilities to the community."

Every newspaperman knows how generally this is so. With a few notable exceptions which the Commission might well have emphasized more than it did, newspapering in the United States is pretty sloppy business, casual, trite, almost ritualistic in its clichés, and so stereotyped that the individual differences among newspapers in widely differing communities are hardly more distinctive than among the different brands of canned corn. The easy flow of such stuff as comes from the police blotter gets so much of the attention of the press as to squeeze out most of the information on public affairs that makes any sense. The giant modern press has exploited our high literacy and the rapid technology of communication. But its own contribution in serving the one with the other remains for the most part as primitive as the hand press and post rider. It is directly because newspaper publishers as a class are among the most conservative groups in America that newspaper performance is as uninspired, as unoriginal, and uninformed as it is. It makes its own definition of news which is often so peculiar and parochial as to exclude most information that has any use or any meaning. The value of this report lies in its jolt to the mentality of those who control most of the press to their own profit.

The honorable exceptions are easily identified. The public stake in the issue runs parallel to its stake in self government and peace, for both, as the Commission shows, are threatened by the frequently irresponsible and often false presentation of government activity and international relations. They are threatened even more by the usual absence of useful information on these vital areas.

The Commission might have made note of, but did not, those exceptional newspapers that operate on a very high level of responsibility to serve the reader with information essential to the citizen. But they are highly exceptional as every one knows who has tried counting them up and found fingers left over.

The Commission's recital of the increasing concentration of newspaper control and consequent contraction in the number and diversity of outlets for information and ideas is a twice-told tale. Morris Ernst explored it in his *The First Freedom*. But it will bear emphasis. Even as this report was in the press, the sale was announced of the *Philadelphia Record* to the *Philadelphia Bulletin*. That leaves the third city of America at this writing with one morning and two evening newspaper ownerships.

It underscores the Commission's point that: Through concentration the variety of sources of news and opinion is limited. The insistence of the citizen's need has increased.

True, but some instances would have been in order. With $215,000 and a research staff and three years to work, the facts about the press handling of such stories as the destruction of the OPA and the wrecking of the housing program would have illuminated the report. It was possible to measure how much the public was told of the lobbies and pressures and industry sit-down strikes to end price control and to muscle out Wilson Wyatt's program. It would have been possible to show how little attention was paid to the profits made out of the removal of price limits when the headlines were crying over strikes for more wages. Facts are the most telling evidence. Had the Commission been more journalistic in its own report, its conclusions would have more effect.

The report is a philosopher's summation of the state of the press. It would be more informative if it contained more research into instances. The Commission cites "charges" of distortion and says "bias is claimed" against consumer cooperatives, food and drug regulations, and Federal Trade Commission orders on fraudulent advertising. "Many people believe," it says, "that the press is biased on national fiscal policy." The Commission had the means to run down these charges.

It is hard to believe that it did not. It heard fifty-eight witnesses from the press and its staff recorded interviews with 225 others. The report is derived from 176 separate documents developed in the study. Some of the cautious language of the report is quite evidently a device to appease the more conservative members in the interest of the unanimous agreement which they present.

Very usefully, the Commission shows that radio rates far below the newspaper as a responsible channel of information. Public affairs take from zero to 10 per cent of radio time. The Commission says bluntly that before it can be respectable radio must take control of its programs away from the advertisers: "Radio cannot become a responsible agency of communication as long as its programming is controlled by the advertisers. No newspaper would call itself respectable if its editorial columns were dominated by its advertisers and if it published advertising, information, and discussion so mixed together that the reader could not tell them apart."

It sums up radio programs with this: "The great consumer industries which in 1945 gave the networks three-quarters of their income determine what the American people shall hear on the air. A dozen and a half advertising agencies place contracts and prepare programs. The result is such a mixture of advertising with the rest of the program that one cannot be listened to without the other."

The devastating report on radio recalls the curious results of certain polls that have found more public confidence in news heard on the radio than read in the newspapers. There is no accounting for this except by the magic many people still feel in hearing a voice. Any newspaperman who at times performs on the radio has had the experience of receiving a charmed response from neighbors and acquaintances who never mention his familiar daily reports in his newspaper. Yet he knows, and so do they if they ever think about it, that he contributes far more to their information in the less restricted channels of the paper.

After reading its report on radio one can better understand the Commission's lack of enthusiasm for government regulation, though it doesn't offer that as a reason. Radio has been under regulation from the start, and obviously regulation has failed to result in adequate radio service. To say that the FCC has been prevented by the power with Congress of advertiser-backed radio pressures from ever trying real regulation does not add much comfort or increase anticipation of benefits from press regulation.

This is not the reason the Commission seeks to avoid governmental action to require press responsibility, but it is a consideration not to be overlooked by those who disagree with them about it.

The Commission finds the quality of the press affected by the fact that "wages and prestige of the working newspapermen are low and their tenure precarious." This is an understatement. The newspaper is a prep school for the fields of radio, magazines, movies, and public relations. The most talented of its staff are grabbed off by these competing enterprises often for an extra $20 or $30 a week and all the years of their development lost to press and public. This is one of the sorest points about American newspapering and one of its grievous ills.

Everybody else appreciates the value of a trained newspaperman except the newspaper publisher. So journalism is drained constantly of the men capable of operating at a level of public service.

It would have been easy to show this. Take the number of men in government agencies who left newspapers for a little more money. Take the whole personnel of radio and see how many were trained in newspapers. Take the salary levels of radio and compare with newspapers. Take the staff of a few representative papers of fifteen years ago and show where the featured reporters of that time are working now. This forfeiture of the press' own human resources has reached a point where even *Editor & Publisher,* the trade organ of the press, has been plaintively editorializing on it.

But a deeper disturbing note is the Commission's discovery of the "frustration" of reporters and editorial writers. "The Commission was disturbed by finding that many able reporters and editorial writers displayed frustration—the feeling that they were not allowed to do the kind of work which their professional ideals demanded. A continuation of this disturbing situation will prevent the press from assuming effective responsibility toward society."

As remedies, the Commission urges that the press "use any means that can be devised to increase the competence and independence of the staff."

That is all very well. And very true. Better reporters and better paid reporters are needed. But to say this and stop there misses the central issue.

Can the Commission imagine a journalist being "independent" and working for Hearst, McCormick, or the paper controlled by the First National Bank?

What is it that turns idealistic newspapermen into frustrated cynics? It is the context of the job itself. It is the very irresponsibility the report complains of. The Commission is going around in circles to say that the press is irresponsible, that it should be responsible, that it requires professional standards, and that the press should develop professional standards in its staff. The newest tyros in the city room have the standards desired until they are conditioned on the job to something else that defeats and frustrates the best of them.

It is a very insidious thing. The Commission has sensed it, explored it, been revolted by it, but never quite come to grips with it. The Commission realizes that a profession has been taken over and exploited. There is no parallel for that in other professions. It clearly baffles a Commission made up of members of the professions of law, education, religion, science, and philosophy. Any of their "frustrated" newspapermen could have told them more than they understand about the catch in the game. But their contribution is in describing the problem. That is a large contribution. They leave it as they must in the lap of the public:

"We have the impression that the American people do not realize what has happened to them. They are not aware that the communications revolution has taken place. They do not appreciate the tremendous power which the new instruments and new organization of the press place in the hands of a few men. They have not yet understood how far the performance of the press falls short of the requirements of a free society in the world today. The principal object of our report is to make these points clear."

The Press under Pressure

ZECHARIAH CHAFEE, JR. [APRIL 1948

Mr. Chafee, professor at the Harvard Law School until his death in 1957, was serving as U.S. member of the U.N. Sub-Commission on Freedom of Information in 1948. He had also been a member of the Hutchins Commission on Freedom of the Press.

The newspaper press is so familiar to us that we easily forget what an incongruous phenomenon it is in a highly controlled society like ours. Think of the tightly organized societies of the past. Rameses II, Tiberius, Diocletian, Henry VIII, and Louis XIV could govern without being bothered by newspapers. Within only two centuries little news sheets issued by obscure printers have turned into enormous enterprises in each of which a handful of men can inform and influence millions of citizens. How they will go about it is often unpredictable. In 1919, for example, Hearst's love for the underdog led him to give opponents of sedition legislation space which most journals refused, whereas today he urges that every Communist be harried out of the land. The owner of the *Chicago Daily News* dies and the whole character of the paper changes. Comic strips, colored cartoons, boiler-plate editorials—we don't know what will happen next. Yet if the press is to be alive and vigorous, it must be unpredictable. The press is a sort of wild animal in our midst—restless, gigantic, always seeking new ways to use its strength.

Of course the press does not represent the only enterprises which since 1700 have grown from small beginnings to great power. The Standard Oil Company, General Motors, the Bank of America, the New York Stock Exchange, the CIO, to name only a few, developed as fast as the *Chicago Tribune* and the *New York Times*. Yet there is a striking contrast. Sooner or later the enormous power of these private bodies arouses public alarm, and they are put under some measure of governmental control to restrain possible abuses. They can no longer run loose. It is the first principle of our Bill of Rights that the government must let the press run loose. All of us, I fervently hope, believe this to be a wise taking of risks. The First Amendment presupposes, as Learned Hand says, "that right conclusions are more likely to be gathered out of a multitude of tongues, than through any kind of authoritative selection. To many this is, and always will be, folly; but we have staked upon it our all."

Nevertheless, we must face frankly the risks we have agreed to run. The press has become an "imperium in imperio." No other powerful business organization in the United States now enjoys such almost complete independence from the federal government. Even among nonprofit organizations there is nothing to compare with the immunity of the press for abuses of power except the churches. A church's behavior can at least be predicted from its settled doctrines, and by its very nature its members are accountable to God. The sovereign press for the most part acknowledges accountability to no one except its owners and publishers.

Of course, there are notable exceptions to this attitude of self-sufficiency. We can all name some of them. The American Press Institute at Columbia and the Nieman Foundation at Harvard are in their different ways inculcating a different conception. Sevellon Brown said in opening the Press Institute: "We are here because we recognize the tremendous social responsibilities which are ours, responsibilities of a scope and complexity scarcely dreamed of by newspapermen a short generation ago." The question remains, however, whether the leaders of newspapers and radio and motion pictures will of their own accord move fast enough toward giving the kind of service which American citizens need in order to govern themselves intelligently and encourage the President and Congress to make our country do what is necessary to maintain a durable peace. There is less time at our disposal than we used to think before Hiroshima.

In 1947 two wholly different efforts were made to create a greater responsibility in the American press.

The first was the publication in March of the general report of the Commission on Freedom of the Press. It was unfortunate, though quite natural, that most attention of reviewers was concentrated on the final chapter of recommendations. We had felt unable to urge any sensational remedies, and hence the book was often brushed aside. Much more important, I believe, are the opening chapters which analyze the problem of what sort of press the public needs in a free society. The following passage strikes the keynote:

"Today our society needs, first, a truthful, comprehensive, and intelligent account of the day's events in a context which gives them meaning; second, a forum for the exchange of comment and criticism; third, a means of projecting the opinions and attitudes of the groups in the society to one another; fourth, a method of presenting and clarifying the goals and values of the society; and, fifth, a way of reaching every member of the society by the currents of information, thought, and feeling which the press supplies."

The book went on to examine the present performance of the press. It then stated that, despite some examples of "extraordinarily high quality of performance" in newspapers, radio, and motion pictures, "when we look at the press as a whole . . . we must conclude that it is not meeting the needs of our society. The Commission believes that this failure of the press is the greatest danger to its freedom." And so we appealed to the leaders of the press itself to recognize the gravity of the situation and "assume the responsibility of providing the variety, quantity and quality of information and discussion which the country needs . . . They must . . . themselves be hospitable to ideas and attitudes different from their own, and they must present them to the public as meriting its attention."

Some leaders of the industries reacted gratifyingly to this appeal, but most remained apathetic. A typical reaction was shown by the writer in *Editor & Publisher* who cited the total number of newspaper buyers in the United States as conclusive evidence that the public is satisfied with the press as it is. In 1910 there were millions of passengers who rode on steam and electric railroads, and some apologists for the railroads might as well have cited that astronomical figure as proof of the complete public satisfaction with trains and trolleys. Yet that was on the eve of terrific legislative attacks on the railroads and the financial ruin of trolleys. Of course millions of citizens read the newspapers they can now get, because they can't get anything better.

An incident at the last annual meeting of the Associated Press illustrates the newspaper leaders' lack of interest in their task—as the Commission described it—of providing information to enable the American people to make for themselves "fundamental decisions necessary to the direction of their government and their lives." After the election of officers for the ensuing year and other routine business, the publishers present from all our leading papers were asked whether they had any suggestions for a wider coverage of news by the Associated Press. There was a long silence, which was broken at last by one man. Did he ask whether the public could be told more of what goes on inside China beyond the birth of eight children at once? Did he regret the drastic reduction of Associated Press correspondents in Europe, or express the wish that we might learn more about the way American soldiers were governing our own zone in Germany? No—he complained because the Associated Press did not carry news of the Irish sweepstakes.

The second group of criticisms of our press in 1947 came from foreign representatives in the United Nations. The attack began mildly in the Sub-Commission on Freedom of Information in May, warmed up during the summer in the Economic and Social Council, and reached fever heat in the General Assembly. Newspapers at last awoke from the apathy with which they had received the report of the Hutchins Commission. Mr. Vishinsky in effect adopted the methods of King Rehoboam: "My predecessor hath chastened you with whips, but I will chasten you with scorpions."

Needless to say, I do not agree with Mr. Vishinsky. But this is not just a question of Mr. Vishinsky. As soon as I reached Lake Success, I became aware of a strong current of feeling in other nations that the sort of irresponsibility the press here and elsewhere has often displayed is a threat to peace which ought to be restrained, by moral suasion if not by law. Varying resolutions imposing responsibility have been constantly proposed in the U.N., not only by more moderate representatives of the U.S.S.R., but also by delegates from countries whose good will to us is unquestioned, like France, Norway, Chile, India, and Australia. At least three points in these proposals deserve examination in order to ascertain what lessons for us they convey.

First, the Soviets regard the press as an instrument of government policy and not as a neutral vehicle of information. My Soviet colleague, Mr. Lomakin, urged our Sub-Commission to list as one of the main tasks of the press: "To organize the struggle for democratic principles, for the unmasking of the remnants of Fascism and for the extirpation of Fascist ideology in all its forms." The fact that this particular formula was decisively rejected should not blind us to the fact that there are plenty of adherents in America to the philosophy behind the formula. They want the communications industries to make specific political decisions and inculcate specific political ideals in citizens instead of providing citizens with the material for making their own decisions and ideals. The recent movie investigation in the Un-American Committee stands for just the same philosophy as my Soviet colleague—only the Committee's enforced aim is "free enterprise" or "Americanism." There is a much greater need for extirpating this philosophy in our country than for extirpating the remnants of Fascism—whatever that is now. By contrast we should insist, as my Norwegian colleague Mr. Christensen said, "That the basic task of the press and of other media of information is to tell the truth."

The first lesson, then, from the U.N. discussions is that no narrow political ideals of any sort should fetter the obligation of the American communications industries to ascertain the truth and furnish it to our citizens.

My next point is that Soviet writers and speakers use the phrase "freedom of the press" in a sense quite different from ours. To us it means that the law does not prevent anyone from saying what he wishes, within our sort of legal rights. Their constitution provides that "printing presses, stocks of paper . . . and other material requisites" shall be put at the disposal of working people and their organizations. Hence we feel that Soviet censorship by officials negates free presses in Russia, and they feel that our press is not free because owners and publishers can interfere with presentation of views unacceptable to them.

If, as I believe, the Commission on Freedom of the Press is right in asserting on the first page of its report that "the development of the press as an instrument of mass communication has greatly decreased the proportion of the people who can express their opinions and ideas through the press," then it is time something was done about it. I do not underrate the practical difficulties—newspapers cost money to produce and space cannot be "free" like free air. And I do not think the remedy lies in more laws. It is a matter for the conscience and professional skill of owners and publishers and everybody else engaged in the communications industries.

Although a newspaper cannot practicably open its pages to dissentient writers except in the column of Letters to the Editor, the journal is under a moral obligation to present fairly in its news and special articles the significant views of the various substantial groups in the community, and not merely the views of the particular group to which the owner and publisher belong. Both sides of a public controversy should have a reasonable chance to reach the readers of newspapers of general circulation.

That is my second lesson from foreign criticisms of our press.

My last point relates to my first. It is a specific application of one of the broad ideals of the press already stated—"To help maintain international peace and security through understanding and cooperation between peoples." It is very significant that when this aim of the press went from our U.N. Sub-Commission to the Economic and Social Council, the Council added, "and to combat forces which incite war, by removing bellicose influences from the media of information."

Of course, American papers are not alone to blame, but the fact that others do wrong should not prevent us from doing right. This, again, is not a matter for law. Not law but the consciences of editors and other writers should lead them to weigh with unusual care proposed publications which will aggravate international ill-feeling. Especial attention should be given to the phrasing of headlines.

Is our press responsible? Yes, to some extent, but it should be more so. Is our press free? Yes, in our sense of freedom, but the different sense of "accessible to all significant views on public questions" is also important, and there we might do more. Finally, freedom *from* something is not enough. It should also be freedom *for* something. The wide immunity from governmental control which the press claims will be empty if it be a mere negation. Freedom is not safety but opportunity. Freedom ought to be a means to enable the press to serve the proper functions of communication in a free society.

The Full Dimensions of the News

JAMES S. POPE [JANUARY 1949

Mr. Pope gave the talk from which this article was taken to a group of German editors attending seminars at the American Press Institute. He was then managing editor of the *Louisville Courier-Journal,* since retired.

When an editor has decided to print as much news as his readers can digest, he has only begun the complex job of designing his newspaper. How much is enough? How much space can be used for current news? How far must he go in printing non-news material in order to attract and hold circulation?

A few years ago a survey was made of the *Louisville Courier-Journal.* It showed the preferences of men and the preferences of women.

Out of every 100 men, 94 looked at the pictures on the picture-page (we no longer have enough newsprint to carry an entire page of pictures, but many American newspapers still do this) ; 69 of each 100 men read "Blondie," our most popular comic; 71 read the weather forecast; 60 looked at the editorial-page cartoon; 44 at the radio schedules; 72 read a cartoon called "Private Lives," showing how easy it is to stimulate curiosity with a title; 36 read a sports column. Most of the other comics ranked close to "Blondie"—over half of our subscribers read them.

The front-page banner headline of that day (April 12, 1940) reported that 18 German ships had been sunk. Mr. Churchill was quoted as saying "We're on the Road to Victory." He did not say how long that road was to be. With such news, the front page was well read. Seventy-eight of the same 100 men read the leading story. But after the front page was passed, readership of news dropped off sharply.

If you were designing a newspaper from that survey, and knew nothing else about your job, you would carry a front page of news and fill the remainder of your paper with comic strips, cartoons, and sporting features.

Such a product ought to be perfect. But it would not be. It would be like a huge market which displayed meat and bread in the windows, but offered for sale over the counters inside nothing but chocolate candy. Your customers would soon get the stomach-ache. They would look elsewhere for meat and bread.

We have never made news one half as appealing as it should be. News is the most interesting item we could offer. It is life. It has no other limitations. Its limits are merely those of human activity—mental, physical, spiritual. News is our very selves, multiplied and magnified to a world-wide stature.

News is the basic stuff from which is copied the little ersatz images, the comic drawing and the photographs. We have let the image-makers surpass us, though we have the blood-and-bone original to offer. For this I think every American newspaperman should feel shame.

News is endless in variety, but the comics and pictures are monotony itself. Comic characters go through familiar adventures day by day. They meet the same obstacles, triumph in the same old way. There is little novelty or surprise in them, and almost no real imagination.

And what of the pictures? Americans have looked at so many of them so many times, it now takes a touch of magic from the photographer to get a photograph worth printing. For every dramatic news picture there are dozens that are simply tiresome.

Of course people look at pictures. It is a basic human instinct. But how many of them hold a fresh interest? The reader polls have not found a practical way to measure quality. That is our job, as editors.

Are we to admit that a cartoonist's stale bag of tricks and an album of shopworn pictures can interest more readers than living news of living people, freshly gathered and told with humor, with drama, and with penetration?

We must always remember that these surveys have been made of newspapers as they are, not of newspapers as they should be. We have not begun to exploit the rich store of material that is ours. We have not trained reporters who can make a diplomatic conference —which may settle our fate for 100 years—as vital as the capture of a comic-strip crook by a witless detective.

What we need is a survey of our minds, of our imaginations, of our timidities and failures as editors. We need a survey to tell us why we have to push our priceless product with so many free confections.

When we begin to learn to reflect the true color that is a part of the news, we must be very careful not to pour false color into it.

I am sorry to say there is disagreement in this country about what we call objectivity in news reporting. That simply means that the reporter tries to keep himself out of his report. He gives the reader full information, avoiding words that throw a favorable or an unfavorable light on the event. The reader thus can form his own opinion; the reporter's opinion is not pressed upon him.

Many newspaper and magazine editors openly question whether it is possible to be objective, and even whether it is desirable to be. There is a belief that what is objective is dull. But this is a part of the foolish myth that news is so pale it must have rouge smeared on its face with blatant adjectives and adverbs. This is not true. It is seldom the news which is dull, but the manner in which it is told. Truth is not only stranger than fiction, it is much more exciting.

There is a great danger in writing "color," which usually means bias, into straight news. Every good newspaper has an editorial page. On this page the editor may express his opinion of the news. If he introduces those opinions into the columns where his readers expect to find only factual information, he is being dishonest, and in time his readers will find him out.

It is my argument, then, that news can be more interesting than any other material we choose to print, little news as well as big news; that it must not be accepted and printed in the form given to it by those with a selfish interest; that it must be offered to the reader in its rich, natural color.

There is still another thing to consider in the proper handling of news. It must reflect vision and understanding on the part of the editor if it is to bring vision and understanding to the reader. No intelligent citizen of this world believes any longer that what happens in his own town, or his own county, or in his own nation is all that matters to him, and all that he needs or wants to know.

What has happened in Germany in the last fifty years has had more influence in our lives in many ways than what happened here at home; and what happens in America and in Russia in the next ten years may easily determine the future of your children and grandchildren. Therefore, the editor who does not attempt to give his readers a clear account of foreign affairs is putting a blindfold over their eyes. They will be helpless pawns in the international game of chess.

On the *Courier-Journal* and the *Louisville Times* we have the world-wide news reports of the United Press and the Associated Press, and also the superb accounts of the foreign staff of the *New York Times*. In addition to this we buy the articles of the North American Newspaper Alliance, the *Chicago Daily News* Service, the Overseas News Agency, and the work of many independent writers. In recent months we have printed on some days as much as 15 or 20 columns of foreign news, out of the 45 or 50 columns of spot news in the paper. But we have not been content with that. We want the people who handle and comment upon the news to know something of the lands and the people whence it comes.

Within the past few years our editor, Barry Bingham, has been to Germany twice, studying the problems of reconstruction there and throughout Central Europe. Mark Ethridge, our publisher, has twice been to the Balkans. We have been repaid for his total absence of some eight months on government missions by his grasp of the problems we face along the borders of the Soviet Union.

When it became clear to us in 1945 that India would not live in colonial bonds after the war ended, I flew to New Delhi and traveled over the country. I tried to learn something of the political and religious and economic background of India's struggle for independence.

These are merely examples. Other editors on other American newspapers have done likewise, and the frontiers of our understanding are steadily being pushed outward.

The world has a basic hunger for news. It is as deep, I believe, as the hunger for food in many regions. This craving for information is being felt among millions who never had it before. And if we will satisfy it, we can remake our world into a vastly better place, a community in which peace can live without fighting daily for its life.

Take a Forthright Stand

THOMAS M. STORKE [DECEMBER 1962

Thomas M. Storke, at age 85, was awarded a Pulitzer prize in 1962 "for his forceful editorials calling public attention to the activities of a semi-secret organization known as the John Birch Society." At that time he was editor and publisher of the *Santa Barbara News-Press*. In 1964 he sold the paper but agreed to stay on as editor and publisher emeritus. This article is from an address which was read for him at the Elijah Lovejoy Convocation at Colby College, November 8, 1962 (Colby gave him its Lovejoy award that year for defense of civil liberties). A year earlier the Nieman Foundation at Harvard had given him its Lauterbach award. Appended to Mr. Storke's article is one of the editorials in which he challenged the Birch Society.

I believe with deep sincerity that the responsibility for maintaining all of the freedoms—freedom of speech, freedom of religion, freedom of assemblage, and freedom of the press—rests on the shoulders of the men and women who ARE the press. I believe that the greatest threat to those freedoms lies in our failure to be true to our convictions—our failure to speak out when we see freedom jeopardized, even in what may seem to be a small way.

I have frequently read that newspapers have had to resist pressures, or have been threatened by some governmental action to curb their stand for freedoms. To me this is all sheer nonsense.

Let me make one point perfectly clear: During my 62 years as an editor, no one has ever questioned my right to stand up for justice or freedom whenever they were under attack, either directly or indirectly. No one has ever attempted to bring pressure against me, commercial or otherwise, in an effort to silence me on any issue. No governmental or legislative action has ever been a threat to the press so far as I could discern.

I believe that the greatest sin of the American press is the sin of omission rather than the sin of commission—the sin of refusing to take a stand on issues that might become too "hot" to handle.

There would be little reason for apprehension if all of our newspapers were as forthright and conscious of their responsibilities as the *New York Times, Christian Science Monitor, Washington Post, St. Louis Post-Dispatch, Louisville Courier-Journal, Milwaukee*

Journal, Los Angeles Times, San Francisco Chronicle, San Francisco Examiner, McClatchy's *Bees,* and some others. But too many newspapers, large and small, do not meet the standards of those newspapers, I regret to say. Too many newspapers do not speak out on the vital issues with clarity and conviction.

There is nothing that should have seemed remarkable about my own clash with the leader of the John Birch Society, Robert Welch. I did only what any other newspaperman would or should do in the same circumstances. I took a close look at what the Birch Society was doing to my own community and I told my readers what I thought about it.

I saw a steady pattern of undercover attack against school officials, against churchmen, against governmental leaders, against university professors and administrators. With rising anger I read Robert Welch's charges of Communist conspiracy, directed against a former President and one whom I consider to be a great Chief Justice of the United States. I read such undiluted Welch poison as this, and I quote: "While I too think that Milton Eisenhower is a Communist, and has been for 30 years, this opinion is based largely on general circumstances of his conduct. But my firm belief that Dwight Eisenhower is a dedicated, conscious agent of the Communist conspiracy is based on an accumulation of detailed evidence so extensive and so palpable that it seems to me to put this conviction beyond any reasonable doubt . . . There is only one word to describe his purposes and actions. That word is 'treason.' "

After my newspaper—a relatively small newspaper of 35,000 circulation—disclosed in a dispassionate series of articles what was going on in our community, I spoke my editorial mind. My opening statement may have been more forceful and less eloquent than was called for, but it did give me a platform from which to direct my fire in the weeks to come. This is what I said:

"The editor and publisher of the *News-Press* is in his 85th year. His entire life has been spent in this community. His memory takes him back many years and his reading even further. He lived when conditions were rugged. When West was West and men were men. He lived during periods when if a man or a group of men openly by word of mouth, or the printed word, called our president, our vice-president, our secretary of state, the president's brother, members of the Supreme Court, and others at the head of our government, traitors, they were made to answer. Such slanders often called for a visit from a courageous and irate group which brought with them a barrel of tar and a few feathers . . . It is in the light of this background that the *News-Press* tells where it stands on the John Birch Society."

The results were amazing. An outpouring of support for my position came from the moderates in the community, both liberal and conservative—the people in the middle who are heard from too rarely. Community leaders who had been attacked stood up and fought back, realizing that the newspaper was behind them.

But most amazing—and in many instances distressing—was the reaction around the country as word of my editorials spread. It was amazing to me that within a few weeks requests came for almost 20,000 reprints of my editorials.

It was distressing that among the hundreds of letters I received were many that read like this:

"The Birchers are moving into our community. Already they are making life miserable for our teachers and preachers. They are dividing our town. What can we do to combat their activities? We have appealed to our local newspaper, but it won't take a stand. It is helping the Birchers for its silence."

It is distressing that even now I can count on the fingers of both hands the number of major newspapers that have come to my attention that have taken a position on the Birch issue. I am not saying what position other newspapers should have taken. I am only saying that they should not have ducked the issue, sensitive though it may have been or may be today.

Whatever position newspapers choose to take on an issue, they MUST speak out if they are to continue to deserve the protection of the First Amendment to the Constitution. The greatest threat to freedom of the press lies within ourselves—the press. We are truly the custodians. Freedom can survive only if we newspapermen fulfill well the responsibilities the Founding Fathers had in mind when they singled us out for the protection of the First Amendment. Freedom can survive only if newspapers, first, inform their readers fully and fairly about the issues that affect their lives, and, second, take vigorous, honest stands on those issues. Both information and comment contribute to informed, lively discussion of issues—discussion which is an essential ingredient of the democratic decision-making process.

It matters, of course, which side of an issue a newspaper takes. But what matters more is that it take a stand—a firm editorial position which it proclaims clearly. From the clash of ideas and opinions on an issue, we can expect that human decency and democratic principles will prevail in the end. From silence and evasion we can expect only public confusion and apathy.

I do not mean, in all this, to exalt the editor's position unduly. I do not mean to suggest that even the best of editors cannot go wrong or do not go wrong on occasion.

But I do say this: The editor worth his salt will have conviction and a regard for human decency and he will be articulate about it.

The following editorial by Mr. Storke was in the *Santa Barbara News-Press* on February 26, 1961, and was reprinted in *Nieman Reports,* April 1961.

During recent weeks, the *News-Press* has sought to enlighten its readers about a semi-secret organization called the John Birch Society.

We believe that the *News-Press* has performed a public service by bringing the activities of the society to the attention of the community. Hundreds of our readers have agreed. But a newspaper would be derelict in its duty if it did not express its opinion of the way the society is organized and the tactics it employs.

First, let there be no mistake about this: Communism must be opposed vigorously. Its gains throughout vast areas of the world are shocking. Every American must be alert for Red infiltration. But that does not lead logically to the conclusion that to fight Communism at home we must throw democratic principles and methods into the ashcan and adopt the techniques of the Communists themselves, as the John Birch leaders would have us do.

The *News-Press* condemns the destructive campaign of hate and vilification that the John Birch Society is waging against national leaders who deserve our respect and confidence.

How can anyone follow a leader absurd enough to call former President Eisenhower "a dedicated, conscious agent of the Communist conspiracy"? Those are the words of the national leader of the John Birch Society, Robert Welch, in a manuscript entitled "The Politician," of which photostatic copies are available.

The *News-Press* condemns the dictatorial, undemocratic structure of the society.

The *News-Press* condemns the tactics that have brought anonymous telephone calls of denunciation to Santa Barbarans in recent weeks from members of the John Birch Society or their sympathizers. Among victims of such cowardly diatribes have been educational leaders, including faculty members of the University of California at Santa Barbara, and even ministers of the Gospel.

The *News-Press* condemns the pressures on wealthy residents, who fear and abhor Communism, to contribute money to an organization whose leader said that "for reasons you will understand, there can be no accounting of funds."

In the Blue Book, the society's "Bible," leader Welch said that the organization needed one million members. He also said that the dues are "whatever the member wants to make them, with a minimum of $24 per year for men and $12 for women."

One million members, divided equally between men and women, would bring him 18 million dollars a year. Quite a sum to play with without accountability!

The *News-Press* challenges members of the society to come into the open and admit membership. A local enrollment "in the hundreds" is claimed, but so far only a few of those who have joined the organization have been unashamed enough to admit it.

The John Birch Society already has done a grave disservice to Santa Barbara by arousing suspicions and mutual distrust among men of good will. The organization's adherents, sincere in their opposition to Communism, do not seem to understand the dangers of the totalitarian dynamite with which they were tampering.

The *News-Press* challenges them: Come up from underground.

And if they believe that in being challenged they have grounds for suit—let them sue. The *News-Press* would welcome a suit as a means of shedding more light on the John Birch Society.

Free Press and Fair Trial

SIMON E. SOBELOFF [JANUARY 1956

This author was then Solicitor General of the United States. He was later appointed a federal judge. The article is from a talk he gave at Temple Ohabai Shalom Brotherhood, Brookline, Massachusetts, at the Brotherhood's fifteenth annual dinner for the Nieman Fellows, November 29, 1955.

I suppose that all editors would agree as an abstract proposition that the right of a man to a fair trial should be respected and all judges would assent to the proposition that the press should be free. Let us look away from the necessarily imprecise legal boundaries that have been sketched out in various decisions of the courts, and consider more generally the interests of society that are at stake.

The courts and the press both have their responsibilities. The courts have a duty to assure fair trials; the press has a duty, no less vital, to inform the public. Each of these functions is essential in a civilized society. But while the direct burden of ensuring fair trials is on the courts, the press, too, carries a responsibility for the fairness of court trials. It should be equally clear to the judges that while journalists naturally have a primary role in maintaining the freedom of the press, the courts are also concerned to preserve this freedom. Freedom is indivisible.

Fair trials could not be held if newspapers were free without limit to intrude in pending judicial proceedings, and conversely, it is equally certain that trials would not long remain fair if newspapermen were not free to observe and report proceedings in court, and then comment freely upon the court's performance.

In our society both the judge and the editor enjoy special status. Our system has no special consideration for judges and editors either as individuals or as a class, beyond assuring to them independence in the performance of their respective public duties. If special powers and freedom are granted them, it is not in tribute to their individual merits or to exalt them, but to protect the functions they perform. It is the simple but august task which the Declaration of Independence calls "securing the blessings of liberty." The editor and the judge are set apart from other citizens only that they may act as guardians of other men's liberties.

Both judges and editors sometimes forget this and think only in terms of their privileges and immunities. Both need to be reminded that it is neither the judges' rights nor the editors' rights that are of primary importance; the area is completely filled by the citizens' rights. When editors or judges forget their responsibilities they sink, not to the common level, but below it, for they are recreant to their trust.

I hasten to add that I realize that not all newspapers are alike. With 1700 papers, performance is bound to be unequal. So also, not all judges are alike. The profession has a quaint saying that equity varies according to the length of the chancellor's foot. Generalizations are misleading. Most courts operate with dignity and effectiveness while a few cover up under the protective label of "judicial discretion" the most extreme indiscretion and arrogance. It is not flattery but simple truth to say that, by and large, newspapers are mindful of their public responsibility, as are courts. And if there are abuses, we can take comfort from Chief Justice Marshall, who said that we must bear with the inaccuracy of the press as "the calamity incidental to freedom." But newspaper publishers, as businessmen, are not immune from the laws regulating business.

Courts are not exempt from scrutiny and criticism by the press. My illustrious fellow-townsman, Henry L. Mencken, once gave an irreverent definition of a judge. "A judge," he said, "is only a law student who marks his own examination paper." If that were really so, what a happy existence it would be—for him; but it is not so. No judge marks his own examination papers. The examination papers of judges are marked by other judges, at all levels of the judicial hierarchy, even in the rarefied heights of the tribunal from which there is no appeal to any other human tribunal. And their examination papers are constantly being marked by the public. To make this possible is one of the reasons for newspaper reporting and commenting on court cases.

It is a great illusion shared by too many that only the courts are the guardians of our freedom. The courts have on numerous important occasions made historic contributions to freedom's cause; but while I hold the judicial function in reverence, I submit that it is a limited one. It is not the only branch of government that is charged with the preservation of freedom. Nor is the government as a whole the sole custodian of the people's freedom. In a free society each individual has a responsibility, but the press has a unique responsibility.

Mr. Justice Black has said that free speech and fair trials are two of the most cherished policies of our civilization, and that it would be a trying task to choose between them. His associate, Mr. Justice Frankfurter, has pointed out that the core of difficulty in judging is that there is hardly a question that comes before the Court that does not involve more than one so-called principle. He remarks—"Anybody can decide a question if only a single principle is in controversy." In support he quotes Mr. Justice Holmes' wise words: "All rights tend to declare themselves absolute to their logical extreme. Yet all in fact are limited to the neighborhood of principles, of policies which are other than those on which the particular right is founded." The truth is that both principles—the independent judiciary and the free press—have to be made effective. The advocates of one side or another make a mistake when they insist on arrogating to either principle an importance which would ignore or unfairly subordinate the other.

Recently the Court of Appeals of New York invalidated the conviction of a socially prominent young man charged with profiting from the immoral activities of young women. The ground of the reversal was that the presiding judge had barred the press from the trial. The law that insists that trials be kept public is not for the benefit of the press; public trial is deemed essential to a fair trial.

The horrors of the Star Chamber were fresh in the minds of those who wrote the First Amendment. The press is given a status here only as it serves a larger public purpose. I think that your profession and mine both welcome the doctrine laid down by the Court of Appeals of New York in the case I mentioned. Courts may not take unto themselves the power to enforce their notions of public decency and morality and suppress the sensational and the vulgar, if in doing so they sacrifice basic rights.

We will all agree that it is better not to have a court sit in judgment over what is good and what is bad for the public to know. Granted, judges are no more competent than other men to act as censors of public information, even information emanating from the courts. But is this an end to the question? Does it, therefore, mean that the press has no further obligation, but should avail itself to the full of its legal right and publish with impunity every sordid detail of a vice trial, or divorce proceeding? One of our greatest newspapers has coined the phrase: "All the news that's fit to print." Lesser journals, I am told, have changed it to "All the news that fits." Does not the press owe an obligation to consider the question of fitness, and ask itself earnestly whether the public's "right to know" really requires the indiscriminate spreading of such matter before them?

In some places interrogation of discharged jurors is not allowed. In others it is legally permissible, but it is a serious question for the press to ask itself how far such inquiries may be pressed without embarrassing former jurors or inhibiting future jurors.

I would like to suggest, in all good spirit, that in the frontier cases, in areas where the law is still in the making, if the press abuses its freedom, restrictive decisions may emerge. In England, as you know, far less latitude is permitted the press than in this country. There proposals were pressed for still further restrictions, and apparently this led to the creation of voluntary committees of journalists to police the profession from within.

There have been, as we know from observation, useful by-products of great public advantage from the full and free reporting of public proceedings, judicial and other. Fraud, corruption and dishonesty, in and out of government, would in many instances go undiscovered but for the vigilance of the press. Many social evils would go uncorrected, because unnoticed, if it were not for the activity of the newspapers.

The turbulence which surrounds this question of the freedom of the press in relation to judicial proceedings and elsewhere is not something to be deplored. It proves the vitality of the idea of freedom. Much more to be feared would be a condition in which the question did not arise, for quiescence on the part of the press would be the surest sign that freedom was on the wane.

In all walks of life there is an unfortunate disposition to treat legality as synonymous with propriety. Not everything which is lawful is wise: not everything which is permissible is decent and just. The thesis which I respectfully submit is that even if a publication is within legal limits, a newspaper has an obligation to weigh the propriety and fairness of what it publishes. Indeed, in this area, where it is so largely free from control, it is the newspaper rather than the judge that bears the greater responsibility. It is interesting to point out that judges operate within a framework of law which cabins them; we are fond of speaking of a government of laws rather than men. But what of the editor? If he is to a large degree exempt from judicial or other government control, what is to guide him? Has he not a heavy responsibility?

Three times in recent years (since 1941) the Supreme Court has considered the validity under the First Amendment of convictions of newspapers and editorial writers for contempt for editorial comment on pending cases. In each case, a majority of the Court concluded that on the facts before them they could not find a sufficiently serious threat to the administration of justice to warrant abridgment of the freedom of the press to comment on the trials in question. But it would be a disservice to journalism to suggest that the scope of the freedom to report and to comment on pending trials that the Supreme Court has recognized is a license to abandon self-restraint. Such reserve is frequently desirable, if not absolutely essential, to the attainment of impartial justice.

So, may I, in this spirit, and without presumption, suggest that even where there is no legally enforceable obligation there is a high moral duty to act with as great a measure of discriminating judgment as is possible under admittedly difficult circumstances. It is your high ethical obligation to avoid injuring the good name of an innocent person or to prejudice one accused of crime or a litigant in an ordinary civil case.

Headliners have a facile formula—action verbs and few qualifiers. Is it an answer to plead the limitations of space in the headline? Many do not read beyond the headline, and sometimes people are injured by this kind of hit-and-run treatment.

I am not even remotely intimating that there should be legislation to restrict reporting any time in any way. I raise no question as to whether you are within your rights to publish. What is more, in most cases you may not even be answerable in a libel suit. But is the indiscriminate megaphoning of abuse consistent with sound and wholesome journalism? It seems to me that though you are free, you are not discharged of responsibility. Rather, because you are free, you are the more responsible. What I have been saying is so general that it may offer little help in specific instances. I have purposely avoided here all pretense of particularity. You will know better than I the precise application of what I am saying. What is important is the spirit in which these matters are approached in the day to day decisions you make.

And let us never forget that one of the reasons for press freedom is to enable it better to pursue the task, so indispensable in a democracy, of educating the people to enable them to perform their civic duties intelligently. May I raise the question whether newspapers, in selecting what to report of court proceedings, and how, are acting with due regard for their educative function. If a Sadie Zilch is haled before the police court for entertaining strangers in her home, there is likely to be adequate press coverage of every detail. If the Supreme Court hears a case involving the constitutional powers of the president to make agreements with foreign nations, not much is likely to be said about it, even in good papers. I can assure you that there is good, interesting news, and real drama in the higher courts. It isn't all technical by long odds, but these sources are often neglected on the assumption that the public is not interested. Are readers really on such a low level of taste and intelligence? Are you sure that what you give them is really what they want? And how far is it legitimate to pander to prurience even when there is a market for it? I have nothing against Sadie Zilch. I speak merely for better coverage of more important court proceedings in the sharp competition for limited space, and I am thinking of the newspaper's role to educate, as well as titillate, its readers.

Editorial Writing Made Easy

E. Hofer & Son Do the Work for 59 Papers with 390,008 Circulation

LOUIS M. LYONS [JULY 1948

The tradition of the newspaper editorial is that it presents the view of the newspaper editor. In the editorial his readers expect to find the editor's considered judgment on the news. That is what they have been led to expect.

What would be the readers' judgment of an editor who farmed

out his editorials to someone else without letting them know? Suppose this someone else was an anonymous person not resident in their community or within a thousand miles of it—someone not working for the interests of their community or even the interests of their newspaper—but working for some special interest with an axe to grind of which the readers are not told.

Well, there are at least 59 newspapers in the United States with a total circulation of 390,008, which do just that. Within a few days of April 1, 1948, 53 of these 59 papers all printed as their own an identical editorial under the same identical heading in the 53 different communities in 25 states, and none of them wrote it. Not one. It wasn't even written by one and copied by the others. But all 53 presented it to their readers as their own editorial. The other six of the 59 changed the title on it or added or subtracted a sentence or two before running it. It was still the same editorial.

The editorial was actually prepared and distributed by the Industrial News Review, owned and operated by E. Hofer & Son of 1405 Southwest Harbor Drive, Portland, Oregon. This concern distributes prefabricated editorials to newspapers on behalf of power interests, especially in opposition to federal power. This outfit has discovered that there are editors either too lazy to write their own editorials or venal enough to present the paid-for propaganda of special interests as their own views.

E. Hofer & Son evidently consider that the interest of their clients is served by opposing and discrediting any or all federal government programs and in smearing such independent minds and free institutions as do not supinely fall in line with the views of their special-interest clients. Such free and independent minds are to be found in colleges where their function in teaching economics and government parallels the function of the honest, independent editor.

So E. Hofer & Son put out editorials attacking bills for federal support of education, and look for opportunities to attack the teaching in free universities. They saw such a chance in March and exploited it. They plucked a sentence out of context in the annual report of President James B. Conant of Harvard, applauded him for it, then twisted their interpretation until they had concocted an "editorial" saying precisely the opposite of what President Conant was saying—and sent it out to complaisant editors to use as their own material. The 59 did so use it. Its heading in 53 of them was:

"House Cleaning Due in Colleges," a smear on college teaching as biased. That was not the considered view of any of these editors. It was not President Conant's view. It was a view that E. Hofer & Son evidently thought would please their clients to have disseminated through the anonymous editorial columns of a wide distribution of newspapers.

Not all of these newspapers are insignificant. They include Maine's *Biddeford Journal* and *Bath Times,* both dailies. They include the *Port Huron* (Mich.) *Times-Herald,* a daily of 26,000 circulation; the *Nashua* (N.H.) *Telegraph,* a daily of 10,000 circulation; the *Lockport* (N.Y.) *Union-Sun* and *Journal,* with 10,000 circulation; the *Wheeling* (W. Va.) *News-Register,* a daily of 25,000 circulation; and the *Beckley* (W. Va.) *Post-Herald,* a daily of 16,869 circulation.

These 59 newspapers are not the whole score. For the *Oskaloosa* (Iowa) *Herald* credited the editorial to the *Newton Daily News.* It may have been misled into believing it was reprinting an actual editorial by a contemporary. The *Newton* (Iowa) *News,* a daily with 6,016 circulation, is not among the papers clipped by the press clipping bureau (Burrelle's) from which these 59 papers were tallied on this one editorial. So we know the score is incomplete. Indeed, 20 or 30 other papers have been revealed by the same clipping service to have used identical editorials on other issues.

Now there's no question here of whether a paper has a right to print the camouflaged views of special interests. The question is one of dealing honestly with the readers of a paper's editorials. There is no problem about handling such stuff as E. Hofer & Son put out by a paper that wants to use it. The *Mesabi News* of Virginia, Minnesota, published it under a boldface head: "Editorial Opinion of Others," and with a credit line to "Industrial News Review, Portland, Oregon." The editor of the *Mesabi News* may be as lazy as the other 59, but every reader and writer of editorials will agree he is more honest. (More is redundant. Scratch it out.)

Of these 59 papers, 53 used the canned editorial without changing a word. Six others changed the head on it or changed the opening or closing sentence to give it a slight touch of their own. Thus the *Terre Haute* (Ind.) *Tribune* changed the head and wrote its own sentence in place of the closing one of E. Hofer & Son. It's still the same editorial. The *Hibbing* (Minn.) *Tribune,* with 7,913 circulation, wrote its own lead and added a punch line, but left the body of the editorial as it came in. The *Concord* (N. C.) *Tribune*, the *Columbia* (Tenn.) *Herald*, the *Cadillac* (Mich.) *News* and *Port Huron* (Mich.) *Times-Herald* changed the heading to "Academic Freedom" and did some penciling of their own in the editorial before palming off the views of E. Hofer & Son as their own editorial.

The accompanying table gives the papers that ran the editorial. Of course these 59 papers and their 390,000 readers are only a fraction of those exploited by the prefab editorializing of E. Hofer & Son on behalf of their clients. These 59 were picked up by one clipping bureau in one month quite by accident because their editorial happened to mention the annual report of the president of Harvard. But it is something to think about that these 59 "editorials" which were all one "editorial" and this not an editorial but a propaganda sheet item, add up to more than all the news clippings on President Conant's report, which was nationally distributed by the press associations. More papers carried the twisted commentary of E. Hofer & Son than carried any news on the president's report. No news account of the president's report was found in any of these 59 papers. So all that these 59 communities got a chance to read of the annual report of Harvard's president was this perversion of it by E. Hofer & Son.

E. Hofer & Son found the president's report applicable to their purposes. How many other people among the 390,000 readers of these 59 papers might have found it applicable to their interests, we don't know, but we know that none of them had a chance because all they had served to them was the capsule that E. Hofer & Son chose to twist to their purposes. The clippings on President Conant's report just happen to make the subject of our exhibit. On how many other subjects of public concern does the same state of affairs obtain?

The medical profession has a procedure for malpractice. So do the lawyers. There is an American Newspaper Publishers Association and an American Society of Newspaper Editors, and there are ethical codes for journalism sponsored by these and by state press associations. This exhibit is offered to any who accept any responsibility in these matters.

NEWSPAPERS PRINTING EDITORIAL,

"HOUSE CLEANING DUE IN COLLEGES"

	Circulation
Alabama	
Mobile Post (w)	3,012
Connecticut	
Bridgeport Life (s)	15,695
Delaware	
Middletown Transcript (w)	2,492
Florida	
Dade City Banner (w)	—
Illinois	
Blue Island Sun Standard (w)	8,400
Indiana	
Terre Haute Tribune * (d)	26,662
Iowa	
Newton Daily News (d)	6,016
Oskaloosa Herald ** (d)	6,660
Louisiana	
Minden Herald (w)	1,800
Maine	
Bath Times (d)	3,929
Biddeford Journal (d)	8,624
Massachusetts	
Cambridge Recorder (w)	(not given)
Dorchester Beacon (w)	10,123
Orange Enterprise & Journal (w)	2,400
South Boston Gazette (w)	7,409
Michigan	
Cadillac News * (d)	4,234
Ishpeming Iron Ore (w)	983
Port Huron Times-Herald * (d)	26,881
Minnesota	
Austin Herald (d)	9,549
Hibbing Tribune * (d)	7,913
Virginia *Mesabi News* † (d)	—
Missouri	
Moberly Message (w)	2,685
Trenton Republican-Times (d)	2,775
New Hampshire	
Dover *Foster's Democrat* (d)	3,085
Hampton Union & Gazette (w)	1,200
Keene Sentinel (d)	5,069
Nashua Telegraph (d)	10,616
New Jersey	
Carteret News (w)	2,800
Gloucester City News (w)	3,100
Hillsdale Herald (w)	921
Hillside Times (w)	2,312
Park Ridge Local (w)	1,390
Pemberton Times-Advertiser (w)	2,619
West Orange Chronicle (w)	2,502
Westwood Chronicle (w)	1,120
New Mexico	
Hobbs News and Sun (d)	6,500
New York	
Lockport Union-Sun & Journal (d)	10,093
Tottenville *Staten Island Transcript* (w)	1,500
Yonkers Times (d)	2,020
Yonkers Record (d)	8,210
North Carolina	
Concord Tribune * (d)	6,961
Ohio	
Piqua Call (d)	6,974
Bucyrus Telegraph-Forum (d)	6,181
Pennsylvania	
Blairsville Dispatch (w)	2,750
Kittanning *Simpsons' Leader-Times* (d)	9,810
Masontown *Klondike Bulletin* (w)	4,730
Oxford Press (w)	1,500
Philadelphia *Frankford Bulletin* (w)	32,500
Phoenixville Republican (d)	5,320
South Carolina	
Gaffney Ledger (w)	3,650
Tennessee	
Columbia Herald * (d)	2,918
Virginia	
Narrows News (w)	1,987
Radford News Journal (d)	3,015
West Virginia	
Beckley Post-Herald (d)	16,869
Wheeling News-Register (d)	25,153
Williamson News (d)	6,280
Wisconsin	
Janesville Gazette (d)	17,341
Shawano Leader (d)	4,605
Wisconsin Rapids Tribune (d)	8,165
Total	390,008

* Title changed to "Where to Draw the Line" or "Academic Freedom." Slight changes in text.

** Credited editorial to another paper.

† Credited editorial to Industrial News Review, Portland, Oregon.

The text of the Hofer editorial, which *Nieman Reports* printed alongside the above article, is as follows:

HOUSE CLEANING DUE IN COLLEGES

James B. Conant, president of Harvard, recently said: "The nation has a right to demand of its educational institutions that the teachers dealing with controversial subjects shall be fearless seekers of the truth and careful scholars rather than propagandists. But granted honesty, sincerity, and ability, there must be tolerance of a wide diversity of opinion."

No one can quarrel with that doctrine, and it could well serve as a model for any university in a free country. However, it is evident to anyone who has even a cursory knowledge of modern teaching that much of the instruction on controversial problems is warped and biased. This is done, in many cases, by individual teachers who are trying to sell some ism or other. And it is done in many other cases by text books which bend the truth in order to hew to what amounts to the party line.

It is one thing, for instance, to show the student what socialism and communism and the nationalization of industry involve, as contrasted with a capitalist or free economy. It is a very different thing to deliberately make it appear that the super state is the answer to the ills of mankind, and unfortunately that is an impression that emanates from many colleges today. It is all very well to discuss what may be wrong with the American system. But, at the same time, we must honestly teach what is right in the American system, as proved by the results it has achieved for the masses of people.

Academic freedom is as basic as any other freedom. It must be protected from fanatics on either the right or the left wings of political and economic thought. But it must justify itself, as Dr. Conant said, by fearlessly seeking the truth—not by tearing down the principles which make the freedom of some professors in American universities to promote political and economic philosophies which, if adopted, would destroy the liberties and opportunities on which our nation was built.

In the next issue, October 1948, *Nieman Reports* carried responses to the E. Hofer & Son exposure. Some of them, reprinted here, add data on the Hofer operation:

HOFER TO WASTEBASKET

I much enjoyed your blast at Hofer & Son, especially since for many years I regularly threw that pinkish-colored (such a strange tint for so conservative an outfit) envelope into the wastebasket. I hope the campaign agin 'em goes on. We will help out here.

Les Moeller
University of Iowa School of Journalism

UNSAVORY

This is a note of appreciation for your blast at that unsavory Hofer-newspaper relationship.

The Hofer organization has been exposed before, but apparently it still flourishes.

More reports like yours are needed, and they must be widely disseminated, before the enormity of this situation finally impresses itself upon the hundreds of editors who keep the thinkers of Southwest Harbor Drive in business.

Charles T. Duncan
Assistant Professor, University of Minnesota

CANNED OPINION

Thinking is already too stereotyped in America. Press and radio facilitate the process. But normally a person knows whose opinion he is picking up. Now, however, it appears that a surprising number of newspapers are offering to their readers, as their own, editorials that are actually produced in an "editorial factory."

This practice is exposed in the July issue of *Nieman Reports,* published by the Society of Nieman Fellows. It discovered almost by accident that a single editorial was carried by 59 newspapers, with a circulation of 390,000. *Nieman Reports* found that the material was prepared and sent out by a company in Portland, Oregon, which it says, "distributes prefabricated editorials to newspapers on behalf of power interests."

Of course, it has long been the habit of small newspapers to use "boiler-plate" features, especially pictures. Those who know the labors of the small-town editor will not condemn him if he doesn't get around to doing an editorial. Perhaps he is to be commended if he finds that others have said it better and so quotes them.

But in the case cited by *Nieman Reports* only one of the 59 papers acknowledged the source of its editorial, while only six even contributed a title of their own. Hiding the source—and the apparent propaganda purpose behind this material—is the real fault here. There may be a legitimate place for syndicated editorials—although something precious in the press must be lost where they come in. But at least there should be honest identification of the source. And certainly readers will do well to look behind the printed page.

—*Christian Science Monitor,* July 21, 1948.

CANNED EDITORIALS

While preparing a speech I am to give at the convention of the American Association of Teachers of Journalism at Boulder, Colo., September 1, I have just re-read your fine piece, "Editorial Writing Made Easy." Having been a country editor who was compelled in times of emergency to "borrow" from the "canned file," I was more than interested in your revelation and comments. I have seen the Industrial News Review and am aware of the many country papers which clip it, maybe without reading it, and use it in lieu of home-grown editorials. I suspect that the number of papers who use some of this stuff is many times 59.

I wonder if you are aware of the number of otherwise "high grade" papers who pass up the free Industrial News Review editorials but who pay for and use canned editorials of the NEA service. I understand this service goes to some 700 clients. Every day that I wade through the high stack of exchanges in the *Tribune* news office I see dozens of reputable daily papers of this region which use these identical canned pieces day after day. They differ from the Hofer & Son masterpieces in that they do not intentionally carry propaganda. Yet, it is obvious that Mr. James Thrasher, the editorial writer, aware of his 700 clients and the conservative ideas of the majority, tempers or even slants them in the direction of not disturbing very violently the status quo. I have followed Mr. Thrasher for years, even used some of his stuff in times of emergency. He is a good writer and I suspect that the quality of his editorials is far above what the home-grown staffs could turn out, at least in literary quality and accuracy. But the implications and dangers of having editorials turned out wholesale and used without careful examination and analysis—as I suspect most of them are—present quite a journalism problem.

Ernest H. Linford
Salt Lake Tribune

THE RECORD ON E. HOFER & SON

Chief purpose of this note is to say that I found your piece on E. Hofer & Son of considerable interest as a footnote on the subject of Public Relations for Industry. In case you are not familiar with it, I wanted to call your attention to a report of the Federal Trade Commission on the subject of Public Utilities Pressure Groups, in general, and E. Hofer & Son, in particular. This report was published in 1934 and, in a sense, your piece is a footnote to it that would seem to prove, among other things, that the market for propaganda in the press continues to be excellent.

In case you would like to look up the FTC report, here is the reference:

Federal Trade Commission, Utility Corporations: Summary Report, Resolution No. 83, 70th Congress, 1st Session: *Efforts by Associations and Agencies of Electric and Gas Utilities to Influence Public Opinion,* U.S. Government Printing Office, 1934, pp. 92–97.

A digest of this report can be found on page 529 of a book of journalism readings, published in 1942 (fourth printing, 1946) by Prentice-Hall, Inc., title: *The Newspaper and Society,* edited by George L. Bird and F. E. Merwin.

The digest quotes the 1925 edition of the annual gotten out by E. Hofer as follows:

"The work started by the Manufacturers and Industrial News Bureau in Oregon in 1912 has gradually grown until today, instead of reaching some 200 papers in 1 state with an editorial discussion of the subjects as outlined, we are reaching some 14,000 papers in the 48 states."

Later in the FTC report, Mr. Hofer makes the following claim, relative to his editorial achievements: *"Reproductions of our articles appear almost invariably as original editorials, as we ask no credit."* Here is a quotation from the FTC report which might interest you:

"A letter from G. W. Curren, secretary United Gas Improvement Co., to H. S. Whipple, vice-president Rockford Gas Light & Coke Co., June 10, 1927, also makes the claim that:

"'The articles are reproduced extensively as original editorial and news.'

"What their character was and what their appeal was that lured

$84,000 per annum from the private utility groups and companies are thus stated:

" 'We show the blighting effect government or public ownership has on private initiative and enterprise. We show that drastic and radical rate regulation which kills utility development hurts the community worse than the company; we show that exhorbitant taxation of business is simply indirect taxation of the consuming public.'

"In addition to the service, Mr. Hofer also carried on correspondence with editors giving at some length arguments against municipal ownership of utility plants . . .

"In corresponding at various times, Mr. Hofer stated the quantity of material reproduced in the rural press from 1924 to 1927, and showed that for 17 months ending October 1924, reproduction in all states was estimated to be 27,000,000 lines or about 25,000 pages; for 1926 the amount of publicity obtained was estimated to be 2,318,964 inches, or about 19,325 solid pages, and for 1927, the total estimated inches were 3,111,420."

Back in 1924, Ivy Lee made a talk to the American Association of Teachers of Journalism (published by Industries Publishing Co., New York, 1925, under the title of "Publicity") in which Lee stresses the point that "the essential evil of propaganda is failure to disclose the source of information," and this idea now seems to be so widely accepted as to be official government policy; that is, propagandists and lobbyists are required to register.

What E. Hofer discovered, of course, is that many a weekly and small daily will print editorials without revealing the source, and your piece is further evidence of what Hofer has been boasting about *for a few decades.* I suppose the explanation must be chiefly that these small papers are publisher-run without the buffer of newspaper men with a professional attitude. The publisher of a small weekly (usually a job printer) tends to keep his eye strictly on the balance sheet and considers an adequate staff a needless expense. In all the criticism of the press, the thousands of weeklies with their focus on hometown news and lack of professional standards are overlooked. Yet I would estimate that the weeklies and small dailies have a greater influence than the great daily newspapers. In Amherst, for example, more people read the two weeklies than regularly read daily newspapers. My point is that I would not call weekly newspapers "insignificant" as you did by implication in paragraph 7 of your piece, although, doubtless, you meant relatively insignificant.

Thinking the matter over, my opinion is that the editorial by Hofer is superior as a piece of writing to most of the editorials run in our weekly and small daily press and that the explanation for its use is that these newspaper editorial staffs operate on a shoestring; that is, these newspapers do not want to afford newspaper men, in the common meaning of this term, to put out the paper. This is the sort of situation that has contributed to the development of the booming modern vocation of public relations. I'd guess 80 per cent of a weekly is supplied free by someone.

Such educational institutions as the Institute of Propaganda Analysis and such publications as the *Journalism Quarterly* (and *Nieman Reports*) strike me as the only corrective to the use by shoestring newspapers of propaganda supplied by competent public relations men. Certainly, the A.N.P.A. or the A.S.N.E. are not going to undertake to educate the publishers of weekly newspapers. What the publishers need is some familiarity with the professional thinking that would prevent good newspapers from running an editorial, sent out by a special-interest group, without giving the source.

Arthur B. Musgrave
Professor of Journalism
University of Massachusetts

Attribution of News

Memo to All Hands

ALFRED FRIENDLY [JULY 1958

One of the most vexing of all problems of the news is the story that, for one or another reason, cannot be attributed to its source. After long wrestling with this puzzler, the managing editor of the *Washington Post* gathered himself together one day and got off this policy statement to all his staff.

Some questions have arisen recently about the various conventions about attribution of news and our policy on them. The following summary is in explanation.

Direct attribution is the best way of handling news and information about an event or conditions or situations of which we do not have direct, eyewitness knowledge ourselves. This is always the best way, inasmuch as it provides the reader with a knowledge of the source, enabling him to evaluate its credibility for himself. It involves no pretense of having direct knowledge which we do not have. It avoids the risk of having the newspapers used to disseminate material for which the author is unwilling to take public responsibility.

However, when sources will not allow attribution, or will not talk if there is attribution, we are driven, along with others, to move from the best way of presenting the news of which we are not the witness to second-best ways.

These methods, because they lack the virtue of complete candor and do not have the advantage of straightforward processes, get newspaper people into a great many misunderstandings. They are, in many cases, a means by which officials seek to evade responsibility for knowledge and information for which they should be willing to assume responsibility. In many cases, citizens have a right to know, not only the information, but the source of it.

Still, we do not make the circumstances under which some information is available. They exist. We have to live with them. It is the purpose of this memorandum to make it more convenient to live with them and to minimize the possibilities of misunderstanding between the newspapers and our colleagues and our sources.

1. OFF THE RECORD. In a small gathering, or an interview, if a news source asks to put the remarks he is about to make off the record, the reporter has the choice of agreeing or of asking the news source not to make the intended comments at all, in order to remain free to seek the story elsewhere. If the source persists in speaking off the record and the reporter does not accede, he must leave the gathering, for if he dissents and yet remains, he places himself in a challengeable position with respect to later independent discovery of the information.

If the reporter agrees to the off-the-record basis, he must then hold the disclosure in absolute confidence. He may not use it in anything he writes, even without attribution to the source, however guarded. A violation of a confidence of this kind is considered, and properly, a cardinal newspaper sin.

He may, unless forbidden by the original source, seek out the same information from another source, but without in any way indicating that he already has heard the news, or is in possession of it, from someone else.

If he accepts the off-the-record condition as to the information itself, he usually may use it upon its public disclosure somewhere else, but in all such cases where a question may arise about a breach of confidence, the reporter should act only after discussion of the matter with his editors and the appropriate desk.

An even more difficult problem arises with respect to disclosure of the source when that source has been publicly identified elsewhere. Again, the proper course is to bring the matter to the attention of the desk and the editors, who will determine what can be published and whether prior clearance with the source is called for.

The reporter will choose the other course (asking the source not to mention the subject if he can do so only off the record) when he believes that he has an opportunity to find out about the matter in some other way and does not, therefore, wish any conditions hanging over him or limiting his future inquiry.

In a public meeting or gathering, open to all without specific invitation, any attempt by a speaker to put all or part of his remarks off the record may be firmly and blandly ignored as an absurdity.

In a large gathering—say 20 persons or more—but sponsored by a private organization, club, committee or the like, where the reporter is present in his role as a reporter but also as an invited guest, he must protest vigorously any attempt by a speaker to go off the record. He should point out that the meeting was scheduled as open to the press, that any attempt at secrecy with a group that large is manifestly meaningless, ineffective, nonsensical, etc., and should declare he will not be bound by the limitation. If he is then requested to leave, he will do so and report the matter to the editors of the appropriate desk. They will decide what sort of a protest should be made.

1a. PHONY OFF–THE–RECORD. Many persons new to the Washington scene or to contacts with the press may say they are speaking off the record, having heard the phrase but misunderstanding it, and intending only to mean "for background only" (see #2 below). The reporter's objection may then serve to clarify the situation and put the story on a usable basis. In all cases, make sure you and the source are clear on the meaning of his injunction and its limitations.

2. FOR BACKGROUND ONLY. This convention, also known as "Without attribution," "The Lindley Rule," "The Rule of Compulsory Plagiarism," or simply as "Don't quote me," is a common one and is used—or should be—when a person of considerable importance or delicate position is discussing a matter in circumstances in which his name cannot be used for reasons of public policy or personal vulnerability. It is often abused by persons who want to sink a knife or do a job without risking their own position or facing the consequences to themselves.

Obviously, it is much better to obtain a story in circumstances which permit the identification of the source. In certain types of stories, particularly those arising on the police and court beats, it is often not possible to report the event at all without attribution. In some cases, attribution is needed as a matter of fair play to the other side of the controversy, or sometimes attribution may be needed to pin responsibility for potentially libelous statements where it belongs. In some cases, however, the "background only" procedure is legitimate and provides an honest, worthwhile story which could not be obtained in any other way.

In such cases the reporter may not, of course, identify the source and may not hint at, imply or suggest his identity. In some cases, the source may insist that no attribution be given even to the agency or organization of the source, forbidding the reporter even to indulge in such vague attribution as "State Department sources," or "Internal Revenue Service officials," and the like.

In all such circumstances, the reporter is on dangerous ground. He must take pains to establish clearly and without any ambiguity in his own or the source's mind exactly what the conditions are, and must tell the appropriate desk the circumstances of the story and the conditions applying to it. He will write the story, following instructions from the desk, as if on his own knowledge and discovery, or with whatever kind of attribution has been allowed.

In all, the reporter must remember that a violation of confidence is accomplished just as surely by disclosure of the news and/or the source to an unauthorized person as it is by printing it in the paper. He breaches the confidence he has undertaken by telling someone who was not included in the original session who the source was, and what transpired.

He has the right to, and should, inform his desk and editors of the event and the source, but making clear what the conditions were; if he writes a memorandum to his editors on the session he must precede it by a clear and obvious caveat about the circumstances under which the information was obtained.

For a reporter to give the story and/or source to another person who was not invited to the session is not merely a breach of his commitment; it is often a sure way to guarantee that he himself will be scooped. The other person, not bound by the original conditions or not understanding them, may blithely proceed to publish the account. The reporter who disclosed the matter to another cannot console himself with the thought that the second man may have acted unethically; the fact remains that he committed the initial breach of confidence himself.

If a story obtained on an Off-the-Record or Background-Only basis is published elsewhere with a disclosure of the source, the reporter who agreed to the terms in the first place must seek guidance from his conscience, his editors and, if possible, from the original source.

The ugliest and most lasting quarrels between the press and the news sources in Washington over the last thirty years have come from deliberate or, most usually, unwitting misunderstandings of the ground rules in situations of this kind.

3. NOT FOR DIRECT QUOTATION. This convention, fortunately now rare, is tailor-made for confusion. When someone speaks but asks, "Don't quote me directly," take infinite pains to make sure exactly what he means.

The custom came into being in press conferences of the President and the Secretary of State some years ago. It meant that the speaker's remarks could be fully and clearly attributed, but that his words must be paraphrased rather than used literally inside quotation marks. Thus a reporter could write, "The President said he felt fine and would go to New York next week," but not, "The President said, 'I feel fine and will go to New York next week.' "

The purpose, if any, was to spare the speaker the cold printing of the solecisms common in conversational remarks.

Now, with televised White House press conferences and a transcript made of the Secretary of State's conferences, the injunction is rarely used. Occasionally, a speaker whose native tongue is not English may ask to be spared the risible consequences of direct quotation. In such cases, common politeness requires compliance with the request.

But make abundantly clear whenever someone says "Don't quote me directly" that he means what he appears to say. Ninety-nine times out of 100 he means, in reality, "background only."

4. HOLD FOR RELEASE. Statements, speeches, handouts, reports, etc., are often embargoed for publication until a certain time, by a statement on the document. Ordinarily, there is no room for doubt; if there is, check with the appropriate desk, or the issuing agency.

Occasionally, in an interview in which several reporters participate, they may agree with the news source not to use the information until a certain time. Such bargains must be kept. Make sure that you understand the terms exactly and that all of those present do, too, lest you be double-crossed inadvertently or otherwise. The reporter who sees brewing a proposal to embargo the information after a news session, and ducks out deliberately in order to steal a march and contend that he knew nothing of the latter agreement, will not last long or do his paper and himself any credit. If he does not like the terms of the embargo, he can object and his sole objection prevents the deal, for this is a case where reporters are morally bound only by unanimous consent.

If a release is broken, accidentally or by design, it is customarily a sign for general release by all. But in all such cases, check first with the appropriate desk.

5. PRIVATE GATHERINGS. Reporters, if they are worth their salt, will pick up much information from conversations at parties, private visits and social gatherings. There is a real problem on what use may be made of the information so received. No flat and general rules about procedure can be made to take care of all cases of this kind.

Basically, however, the reporter's own sense of what is fit and morally proper will be the best guide. If the reporter is at a private gathering as an individual and not because of his position and profession, politeness and decent social relations require that he specifically ask the person who discloses the information whether it may be published, and under what conditions. He may choose to do it on the spot, or to call on the source at a later time, operating without ambiguity as a reporter and not as a social contact.

If the reporter has been invited to the gathering in his role of a reporter, and if he is told something by someone who knows he is a reporter and is working at it at the moment, he may ordinarily write what he learns.

In all circumstances, and whatever the conventions, stated or implied, remember that a cheap beat, won by cutting a corner, by a technicality, or by violating the spirit if not the letter of the understanding of the news source and of other newsmen, is empty, usually worthless, and is followed by penalties and regrets far heavier and longer enduring than any momentary gains that are obtained.

Conduct yourself so that you can look your source in the eye the next day.

Vested Interests of the Reporter

JAMES McCARTNEY [DECEMBER 1963

Mr. McCartney, of the Washington bureau of the *Chicago Daily News,* was a Nieman Fellow in 1963–64.

Some years ago in Chicago a dispute arose between the Federal Bureau of Investigation and the Chicago police department over who deserved the most credit for trapping a notorious peddler of narcotics. Each agency was convinced it had played the key role. City editors all over town were getting two distinctly different versions of what happened from their men in police headquarters and those on the federal beat.

The late Clem Lane, city editor of the *Daily News,* finally threw up his hands in exasperation. "Haven't we got anybody around here any more who hasn't got an ax to grind?" he cried.

Lane was wrestling with a phenomenon common in the newspaper business yet, for elusive reasons, often overlooked in serious discourse on problems of the press. He was dealing with reporters who had developed vested interests in their beats—interests so deep that both had difficulty in taking objective views.

To the police, FBI agents were overpaid "glory hunters." The federal men felt, as they often do, that the police were "dumb cops" who would have let the peddler escape. The reporters sided with their friends and Lane's injunctions budged neither.

The phenomenon would be of little interest if the kinds of problems it suggests were no more serious than whether the FBI or the Chicago police would get public credit for trapping a dope peddler. But the fact is that problems growing out of reporters' vested interests can be much more serious. They can be serious enough to have a bearing on great national decisions and the molding of public opinion on some of the most crucial problems of the times. Some of the most influential reporters in Washington, for example, have deep vested interests in their beats or in their specialties—so deep that they have as much difficulty in presenting objective views as the two Chicago reporters. The problem is undoubtedly universal in the news business. When national news is involved its import may be magnified.

A strong case can be made that many reporters covering such key spots as the White House, the Congress, the State Department, the Justice Department, or the Pentagon are plagued with problems of vested interests.

The symptoms of the vested interest are not always easy to detect, but the result in the extreme form is that reporters become spokesmen for their news sources rather than dispassionate observers. They become sloppy about recognizing that alternative views may exist and about digging out and including alternative views in their stories. Over a period of time some may as well be press agents for those they are covering and, indeed, sometimes perform that role, or something very close to it.

Obviously the mere writing of a story that is favorable, in effect, to the source is no sign that a reporter has sold his soul to his sources and lost his objectivity. But when reporting becomes consistently noncritical, when months or years go by without a critical story, it may be that the virus of vested interest has struck.

The difficulty in trying to understand the problem or in doing anything about it lies in the fact that the vested interest is frequently one of the most valuable of human possessions—personal friendship. No reporter can operate successfully without friends. But being objective about friends can be as difficult as being objective about one's wife.

Friendship is not all of it, however, by any means. A reporter may hesitate to take a critical view of regularly tapped sources for the very human reason that he prefers to be greeted pleasantly when he walks into an office, rather than to be treated as though he were poison. His vested interest is in maintaining a pleasant atmosphere. Another dimension to the problem involves the reporter who has come, through deep exposure, to understand and sympathize with the problems of his sources. He may become a sincere convert and advocate of their point of view. If he is reporting in a field where there are sharp differences of view he may be on the verge of losing his usefulness as a reporter. At the same time, however, his expertese may be valuable to his paper.

The price that the press, and perhaps the country, pays for reporters' vested interests can be high. When great national questions are involved a reporter's lack of objectivity may play a critical role in the public image of important government institutions. Consider some specific problems along this line in Washington.

In the Pentagon it is commonplace for reporters to make alliances with one or another of the armed services, presenting, by and large, that particular service's views on highly controversial problems of national defense. One particularly influential reporter has had a liaison with the Navy that goes back for years and has played an important role in influencing defense policy. Today he is working actively with the Navy in its battle against Defense Secretary Robert McNamara's attempts to reshape the nation's defense machine. Another influential reporter is, for all practical purposes, a spokesman for the Air Force. He may be counted upon to defend the Air Force's desire to maintain the manned bomber or to present, in great detail, Air Force views on strategic necessities for national survival. Both, in effect, have become creatures of the so-called military-industrial complex that President Eisenhower discussed, with grave foreboding, in his Farewell Address. Of course the Defense Department has its spokesmen in the press corps, too. It pressed many of them into service—without actually drafting them—to defend itself against the onslaught from Capitol Hill when Sen. John McClellan (D., Ark.) was investigating the TFX warplane contract.

The result of these practices and habits means that stories from the Pentagon frequently represent points of view of one or another of the Pentagon's warring camps. What is disturbing is that often the stories give no indication that the reporter has attempted to balance the story by obtaining views from other camps. The aforementioned friend of the Navy, for example, rarely mentions that he is writing a Navy point of view and that the Defense Department would disagree wholeheartedly. If the result were only public confusion the problem might not be too serious, for the public in a democracy is often confused. But often the public is misled—a somewhat more serious infraction.

Such specialized liaisons are relatively simple to detect in the sprawling Pentagon. They become more subtle in reporting from the White House. The White House press corps, by and large, is inclined to take the most sympathetic point of view possible toward the problems of whatever administration may be in power. In part, perhaps, because of the intimacy with which White House reporters live with the presidential press secretary, and depend on him, the White House press tends to be the most docile in town. Although there are exceptions, party ideology doesn't seem to be important. Some of the White House regulars who counted themselves as supporters in print of the Eisenhower administration managed to switch to Kennedy without outward sign of mental anguish.

Just plain fear may play a role in White House reporting. The awesome power of the presidency is, indeed, something to contemplate and few reporters relish the thought of arousing presidential anger. The tendency even in presidential press conferences is to throw the president home run balls rather than curve balls. It takes a man of some moral courage to brave the possibility of presidential ire or of presidential sarcasm before a national television audience. But the fact is that controversial questions often are simply not asked at presidential press conferences. If they are, one may be sure that White House staff members will not fail to make a mental note of the questioner. The next time the questioner makes an inquiry for his paper at the White House on a routine matter he may find staff members unavailable—for days. At least one reporter remembers months of difficulty in getting anyone at all to answer a phone call at the White House after writing a story about freeloaders on the President's private plane.

The White House beat presents special problems to a regular who might wish to exhibit a sign of independence. The beat produces so much front-page news without critical reporting that a sycophant can stay in business for years.

Some of the most intriguing problems of all arise on Capitol Hill, with perhaps the most intriguing results. The tendency of reporters who regularly cover the Senate, for example, is—naturally enough—to make friends with the Senate's ruling group, the primary source of important news. By itself this is certainly understandable. But over a period of time there seems to be a marked tendency to report the activities of the ruling group in a favorable light and to make challengers to that group appear as though they are social misfits.

The importance of this tendency to the reading public becomes apparent when one considers the political ideology of the ruling group in the Senate. For many years the power has been in the hands of Southern conservatives, often working in harmony with relatively conservative Republicans. Thus reporting from the Senate tends to have a bias in favor of these groups. Senate liberals—or in fact almost all who challenge the ruling group—are frequently pictured in terms that suggest that they are all but a lunatic fringe, when in fact those outside the ruling group in the Senate include some of the most dedicated and responsible legislators in the nation.

Possibly no story illustrates the limitations of Senate reporting as it has been done in recent years better than the Bobby Baker story in Washington. Baker, who resigned under fire as secretary to the Senate majority and became the object of a formal investigation, has been an important Senate fixture since 1955. Gossip about his power and influence as well as about the fortune he has amassed has been common in the Senate press gallery. Any reporter with eyes could see him wheeling and dealing on the Senate floor when important legislation was under consideration. The facts that he owned a restaurant franchise in North Carolina and has been the co-owner of a plush motel on the Atlantic Ocean have been common knowledge—expensive properties for a former page boy with a relatively modest Senate salary. Yet Senate press gallery regulars exhibited an astonishing lack of interest in writing about Bobby Baker. He was virtually unknown even in Washington outside the immediate Senate family when the story broke, because none of the Washington papers had ever made a serious effort to explain his role. Nor had the heavily staffed New York papers. This protectiveness reflected itself in at least some coverage of the Baker affair by major papers which staff the Senate even after the story broke. They tended to pooh-pooh the story in print and to suggest that Baker had no influence.

It is easy enough for an outsider to come along after a story has broken and say to reporters: "Look, see what you missed." Reporters can quickly come up with any number of reasons why a story couldn't be told. In the Baker case they could point to a lawsuit as a key first element making it possible to print material about Baker. Because such points are often at issue this argument is worth mention.

It may be that it would have been difficult if not impossible for any reporter in the Senate to have cracked the Baker story as it developed without the help of the private lawsuit, but that is not quite the point. The point is that reporters covering the Senate had consistently, over a long period of time, failed to report that a non-Senator had risen from page boy to achieve a position of astonishing power and influence—had become more influential in Senate affairs than many elected Senators. The press had, in effect, protected a key figure in national politics from the cleansing light of publicity.

It is not that reporters covering the Senate did not understand Baker's role. Most of them with political perception—a qualification that excludes some—did, in fact, understand Baker's role. They simply failed to write about him. It seems perfectly obvious that many Senate reporters were no more anxious to probe into Baker's affairs than the Senate itself. Perhaps some of them felt, with some justification, that the threat of losing friends and news sources in the Senate power structure was too overpowering—that writing about Baker wasn't worth the gamble. If this was the case the situation provides an incisive glimpse into the ramifications of reporters' vested interests.

The protective instinct also extends to reporters on the House side of the Capitol. Some of the most glaring excesses of House mismanagement have been reported with singular lack of enthusiasm by House regulars. An example is the new $100 million House office building, a monstrous monument to Congressional eagerness to spend money lavishly when accommodations for Congressmen are involved. The facts about the building have been reported, but largely by individual correspondents from isolated papers, not by most of the regulars in the House press gallery. Only a few of them bothered to attend the first formal tour of the building. A nonregular also wrote the first story about plans for an elaborate underground parking garage for Congressmen and Senators in which the cost per parking space was to be $24,700. The story killed the project, at least temporarily.

Actually, far more outrageous examples of reporters' vested interests in Washington could be furnished. Some reporters have been so closely allied to specific political figures that their copy, for all practical purposes, could be read as handouts. There are others whose identification with one or another political party is just as clear. They tend to represent newspapers with political views that are well known through their news columns, however, and thus can't be considered a general problem.

It would be unfair to suggest that the problems discussed here are unique to the newspaper business. It would probably be more accurate to say that perfectly natural human tendencies are at play.

State Department officials complain, for example, that United States ambassadors to foreign countries frequently fall into the same kind of trap. After serving in a country for a certain period of time and getting to know its officials and its problems they are inclined to become spokesmen for the country rather than spokesmen for the United States.

The U.S. bureau of the budget has the same problem with men it assigns to specialize in the budgetary problems of government agencies. Top budget bureau officials find that after a while the men begin to take on the thinking of the agency and pretty soon they are fighting to get it more money. "They try to sell the agency's case to us rather than to sell our case to the agency," said one budget official.

In the simplest sense, on virtually any beat in Washington, or possibly elsewhere, there are likely to be two kinds of reporters—the "ins" and the "outs." The "ins" are those who play along with the news sources, handle it their way, tend to overlook minor indiscretions and in general protect their sources. The "outs" fight their sources, or at least needle them. They get their news by insisting on their right to it or by sheer perseverance. They let the source know that they intend to play it straight. They get their news the hard way, running the risk of being ostracized not only by the sources but by the reporters who are "ins." A good reporter can probably do it either way, depending on the circumstances.

It is a sad commentary in general, however, that the news business in Washington has developed an exceedingly high percentage of "ins"—and far from enough "outs." It may be in part a mere symptom of the age of the organization man, the man who wants, above all, to be loved. But it's a bad thing for the business and it's probably worse for the country.

The trick for the "out," of course, is to retain the respect of his sources. To do that in some places may be no more complicated than simply playing it straight—which, as any experienced reporter knows, is not nearly as easy as it looks from the outside. But the problem in playing it straight can become somewhat more difficult in any situation where the number of sycophants becomes unduly large.

In Washington, where there are literally hundreds of reporters, the number of sycophants on virtually any beat is unduly large. This situation is in part because of circumstances. When a government press agent knows that he can count on a reporter to give him sympathetic treatment he is not inclined to want to take extraordinary measures to make sure that a man who plays it straight is counted in. Government press agents like to deal with their friends.

Unfortunately, the reporters who are under the most pressure in this kind of situation are frequently those representing the wire services, who supply most of the nation's news. The wire services staff more beats than anyone else and count on routine news for their bread and butter. If the wire-service reporter doesn't get the routine news he is, by the standards of his bosses, not doing his job. Thus he is under tremendous pressure to play along with the government press agent—the source of most routine news.

In defense of wire-service reporters it should be added that they normally try harder to play it straight than almost anyone else. You will rarely find their stories slanted. The primary method of slanting in the news business, however, is not in what is written—it is in what isn't written. And wire-service men are frequently trapped by circumstances. In a flash of independence they may write one good critical story. Then they may have trouble getting routine stories that their offices want for weeks to come.

The problems raised in this essay are not by any means simple, particularly in the light of the increasing trend toward specialization in the newspaper business. The increasing complexity of national news, and of news everywhere, has made specialization virtually inevitable. Frequently only an expert reporter is in a position to understand, let alone report, the news. Yet the problem of developing vested interests becomes more acute when reporters specialize. Thus unless reporters and editors are extremely careful in seeking to avoid the pitfalls of specialization the trend can easily lead to more noncritical reporting. Snooping general reporters in Washington continue to lead the pack in developing new stories, in delving into untouched fields, particularly in investigative stories. These reporters are often "outs" rather than "ins"—who aren't afraid to call a spade a spade in print. Nor are they afraid to ask critical questions that "ins" tend to shy away from.

Avoiding the trend to specialization cannot be the answer in the complex world of Washington news, although the business will be in a sad state if the general reporter is ever abolished. Some techniques can be employed, however, to avoid some of the pitfalls of specialization. For example, if a man is assigned to cover economics in Washington it would seem sensible to include both sides of the economics coin on his beat. He might be assigned to be responsible for the Labor Department as well as the Treasury. In that way he would be exposed to varying approaches to problems. Or if a man is assigned to the State Department, it might be wise to make him responsible, as well, for the Senate Foreign Relations Committee, from whence a critical view may come. Neither of these specific examples may be practical, but the basic strategy seems sound. The idea is simply to keep beats broad enough, when possible, so that a man is exposed to conflicting views in his daily routine.

Probably the most practical idea would involve the aggressive use of general assignment reporters, allowing them to probe freely on beats or in specializations as a regular procedure.

In the last analysis, however, the conclusion is inescapable that mere devices are not going to do the job. The basic problem must, inevitably, lie with editing and editors.

If a story from the Pentagon reports an Air Force or a Navy point of view it is certainly sound journalistic practice to require that the story make mention of the fact that the Defense Department violently disagrees. Unfortunately this seemingly simple practice—to check with the other side—is often abandoned on the so-called "higher" levels of journalism.

If a beginning reporter fails to check both sides, or all sides, of a story he is certain to incur the wrath of the city editor. But for reasons not always easy to understand, when a veteran political or labor writer, or a Washington correspondent, clearly fails to touch all bases—on much more significant material—it is often tolerated. By the same token, if a major scandal were to develop in most city halls under the noses of veteran reporters, heads would be likely to roll. But when a situation that might well be scandalous develops in the United States Senate, a situation that had been in existence for months or maybe for years, the attitude seems to be somewhat more tolerant.

The business and the world that we live in need the application of every sharp and suspicious mind available. They need more reporters who are willing to suffer the indignities of being "outs." They need more editors who read their newspapers with care and are able to pick up the telephone, place long-distance calls, and say: "What the hell!"

"No Other Allegiance"

The Impossible Role of the Press

ROBERT LASSETER [JULY 1947

Mr. Lasseter, a Nieman Fellow in 1943–44, was editor of the *Rutherford Courier* in Murfreesboro, Tennessee, when he wrote this, and for years after. He later went into business there.

No institution of our society is assigned a task more nearly impossible of complete attainment than the press. Essentially it is to furnish the people with information upon which they can base their decisions in governing themselves and conducting their daily relationships. The newspaper that perfectly performed this function would mirror the world aloft, for all to see, with no other regard than the fidelity of the image. With this as a criterion, the shortcomings of American newspapers today are apparent.

There is nothing innately wrong with the American system of newspaper publication—that is, nothing that cannot feasibly be corrected or in large part meliorated by public influence within the present limits of the constitution. The founders of our nation, who had a closer and more personal acquaintance with the evil of restraint on expression than is possible for us today, held a considered belief that, if the people were left free to print whatever they wished, the chemistry of popular democracy would provide a compensatory reaction to any abuse of the privilege. They saw newspapers operating by a rule of democratic principle: just as the government would be kept in line with the popular will by the votes of the citizens, so newspapers, legally unrestrained, would be persuaded to keep a position within the limits of public sanction by their need of the support and patronage of the people to survive. But the men who made our constitution, although they did detect an inherent danger in the growing commercialism of their young new land, did not foresee modern advertising, the connective by which newspapers would come to depend for their existence more upon the support of commercial interests than upon the people at large. Nevertheless, the logic upon which our forefathers reasoned, that newspapers can be expected generally to show an allegiance to that group upon which they are most dependent, was valid. It is reaffirmed in today's situation where newspapers tend to reflect the way of thinking of business, of property and privilege, rather than the viewpoint of the democratic community as a whole.

Briefly stated, the major defect of our American press system today is this: as a result of changes, economic, social, and technological, the base of support of our machinery of public information has shifted until today most of its burden bears upon one segment of our society instead of upon society as a whole. Business today pays three fourths of the cost of maintaining our newspapers; the public pays, directly, one fourth. It is inevitable, in this situation, that newspapers should tend to see from the business viewpoint. And the evil of this is that too often the public welfare, looked at from the privileged position of profit and property, does not have quite the same shape as when seen from the common level.

It is a serious error to assume that the peccancies of American newspapers are in any large sense the result of the deliberate intent of the men who control the press to misemploy their powers for their own personal interests. There are publishers, of course, who do not hesitate to deceive, conceal and otherwise manipulate the news, even to lie, for their own purposes. And there could be cited many instances of the prostitution of newspapers to mercenary ends. But, projected against the broad general background of the American press, these instances are exceptional. For every newspaper that deliberately abuses its moral responsibility to the public, scores can be named that have consistently shown their consciousness of a public trust.

The main valid general criticism that can be made of American newspaper publishers today is, not that they are morally irresponsible, but that they are primarily profit-seekers, and newspapermen only incidentally and secondarily. They think first of survival, and then of their public responsibilities, and too often the terms are not synonymous. Yet, it is pointless to sort out newspaper publishers by this criticism, which can just as correctly be laid against every other class of business or professional men in American life. What they do, most other men would do in their places. It is no mere accident that newspaper publishers tend to be liberal crusaders, exponents of democracy's need for dynamic forward change, while they are struggling for a start, and tend to acquire a conservative laissez-faire attitude when they become established and secure. It is no accident; it is human nature.

The second sound indictment that can be returned against the newspapers of America is their low intellectual level. The truth of this charge cannot be denied; yet, studied in the panorama of all its causes, this criticism, too, is largely a criticism of our whole American society. The rule that any publication seeking general distribution must adapt itself to general standards needs no exposition, and newspapers, by nature and practical definition, are publications seeking general distribution. People read things that they understand, that deal with what they are interested in; newspapers, needing readers to survive, attract them with whatever experience shows them the people respond to the most. The sad consequence of this, of course, is that readers above the average intellectual level must take the common fare.

Yet the more intelligent persons are not wholly ignored. An increasing number of American newspapers do publish editorials and features of fairly high content. And there are publications other than general newspapers edited especially for the more literate readers; they fill the demand, and the extent of their circulations may be taken as the measure of the demand.

But some critics see newspapers as the source-spring of all culture, and, assuming that it is a primary function of democracy's newspaper to lead the people into the paths of intellectual and social righteousness, proceed to the easy fallacy of blaming national imperfections on the newspapers. The premise is wrong, and the whole idea fallacious, for two reasons. One, we cannot charge the press with the responsibility of making public opinion without granting someone—and who but the newspaper publishers?—the right of deciding what public opinion should be, a right which the democratic idea inherently denies to any one. And two, the assumption credits the press with more power over public opinion than it, functioning legitimately and ethically, possesses.

There can be no doubt that broad thought patterns, what Philosopher Alfred North Whitehead has called the public's "tone of mind," are established largely on a basis of what the people read in the newspapers. But this influence is in the news itself, in the event, rather than the newspaper; the newspaper is merely the reporting agency, the mode of communication. Broadly, a newspaper's influence is like a law's influence; in a democracy like ours, as prohibition has shown, a law is effective in the degree that it is understood and its essential purpose approved by the mass of the people. A newspaper can crystallize, consolidate existing public opinion, can bring dormant opinion into life, but it cannot autocratically *make* or *mold* public opinion as desired, except as it interrupts the stream of news, distorts the image, by concealment, falsification, calculated selection or misinterpretation. It is only in the unanimity of newspaper publishers in their attitudes towards business—they are all necessarily businessmen, no matter how they disagree otherwise—that they have been able to impose their attitudes on the public mind.

Also contributing to the desultory texture of America's newspapers, their dullness, their shallowness, their incoherence, is the low state of journalism as a means of livelihood. News is a nebulous, tricky, elusive material; handling it with precision and probity is one of the most difficult of all modern jobs, requiring instant acute perceptions and immediate decisions, and also a great resource of general knowledge. Yet journalism, the reporting and editing of the news, has been one of the least rewarding endeavors of American life.

By the measure of the importance to the public welfare of competent and trustworthy news reporting and editing, the wage standard is low. It is low because it is not sufficient to justify the education and training necessary to proper execution of the job, not sufficient to attract the men who by talent and discipline are best fitted for the work. As a result, newspapermen have been too generally men striving beyond their capabilities. Every newspaper office knows the boy who practices typing in his spare time, learns the word formula and a few other tricks of the trade, and eventually becomes a fairly proficient reporter, able to do a slick job on any assignment. But despite the sympathetic appeal of this Horatio Alger picture, more than native intelligence and a slick way with words are required to do a proper job of reporting; it needs also a background of knowledge, of liberal enlightenment, to interpret events and analyze their significance in the broad lights of wisdom. There are too many miniature Westbrooks in the newspaper offices of the land: keen, eager youngsters and men, sincere and honest perhaps, but doing a job simply beyond the scope of their knowledge.

There is little criticism that can be cast at the social viewpoint of working newspapermen as a class. They probably tend more than any other occupational group in the country to be democrats at heart. News judgment requires constant thinking in terms of the many, and this is certainly an attribute of all good democrats. And the duties of reporting tend to expose them to all strata of our society, an experience which is usually conducive to the development of a sense of man's human dignity and of a realization, no matter how cynical, of the broad reaches into which our society has yet failed to carry the blessings of the community.

But perhaps the clearest and most present danger to the public welfare in the American press today is in the unmistakable trend towards newspaper monopoly. For the rule of democratic principle to apply to newspapers, it is necessary that there be competitive newspapers. The court of public opinion, rendering daily judgments on the press, can enforce its decrees only if there is a choice of newspapers.

It is astonishing to find these familiar names among the cities of the United States today where daily newspaper monopolies exist: Mobile, San Bernardino, Peoria, Evansville, South Bend, Des Moines, Topeka, Louisville, Springfield (Mass.), Worcester, Lansing, Duluth, Minneapolis, St. Paul, Jackson (Miss.), Kansas City, Butte, Omaha, Reno, Manchester (N.H.), Camden, Rochester, Utica, Asheville, Winston-Salem, Akron, Springfield (Ohio), Youngstown, Oklahoma City, Tulsa, Allentown, Reading, Wilkes-Barre, Charleston, Chattanooga, Nashville, Memphis, Wichita Falls, Norfolk, Richmond, Spokane, Huntington, Wheeling, Waterbury, Pensacola, El Paso, and Providence.

In 170-odd cities, one firm publishes both morning and evening papers, and in all but a handful of cases these papers appear under different names and in different makeup. And in 49 of these cities the morning and evening papers, although having the same owners, brazenly claim to espouse different political beliefs.

The newest device of newspaper monopoly is the "common law" merger, now in use in about half a dozen cities—Peoria, Topeka, Tulsa, Tucson, El Paso, Nashville, Chattanooga. By this method, competing newspapers combine their production, advertising and circulation departments, but attempt, at least outwardly, to maintain a competitive relationship editorially. The "common law" name was inspired by the comment of a Tennessee country editor following the announcement of such a merger in a nearby city. "The way we see it," said the country editor, "they admit they are living together but deny they are married."

Ownership of radio stations contributes to the monopoly hold on the news of daily newspapers in many cities. A recent report of the Federal Communications Commission showed that 285 newspapers owned interests in radio stations, over 200 of them holding majority and controlling interests.

The current tragedy of American journalism, however, is not the warped vision of a business-dominated press, nor the venality of a few newspaper publishers, nor the tightening news control, nor the low state of the Fourth Estate. Instead it is the sad example of New York's *PM*, which now has failed its design to build a mold for the adless newspaper.

Here, in *PM*, it appeared that the dream of all good newspapermen, for a paper free to practice the art of pure reporting, with no axes to grind, no cows to nurse, was to come true. Here, by a rich man's indulgence, newspapermen, who have always salved their professional frustrations with boasts of what they could do if unrestrained, were to get their chance. Here America, growing testy at a press that paid first deference to business, was to be shown that advertising is not essential to a newspaper, that a newspaper wholly dependent upon its readers could justify its existence. Here, in *PM*, was to be cut the pattern of a new American journalism.

But the art of pure reporting found no place of expression in *PM*. Instead of to calm, unbiased, dispassionate reporting, *PM* was dedicated to a type of dogmatic, bigoted, intolerant journalism. It was the colossal arrogance of opinionated journalism that was *PM*'s weakness. Every day *PM* undertook to answer the question that wise men have ever posed as unanswerable. What is truth? The adless *PM* failed for the simple reason that it performed the democratic function of a newspaper even less efficiently than its worst ad-carrying competitors. Readers could get at least a hint of both sides from the standard press; *PM* let not a drop leak through of the opposite view.

But although *PM* muffed its unique chance—unique in that Marshall Fields come only once—nevertheless adless newspapers still seem theoretically to offer an avenue towards the responsible and responsive journalism that democracy demands. And there are substantial reasons for hope that an ad-free press may yet develop in America.

Newspaper endowments may be one product of the growing national interest in the press and its functions as a democratic institution, as evidenced in the debates, polls, symposiums, and surveys of recent years. And an endowed press quite logically could be adless. The trend towards cooperative ownership and control of enterprises with public and semipublic functions has not yet reached the press, but possibly it will; it may be that the form of America's future journalism is an adless press owned cooperatively by its readers. Newspaper subscription prices have been rising steadily; the public now is becoming seasoned to a subscription price level that can support newspapers depending wholly upon circulation for their income. The government has a great potential weapon for encouraging ad-free newspapers in its control of the mailing privilege, a power already upheld by the Supreme Court; with public sanction, however tacit, this power might be put to use.

With even a small start, a trend towards adless newspapers could be expected to gather momentum. Special news and feature services would be likely to appear, once there was sufficient demand, and with their availability establishing adless papers would be still easier. A general access to the standard big news services, now that the government antimonopoly suits have been finally won, should be an encouragement. And ad-free newspapers have certain natural advantages, anyway, making them easier to establish than conventional advertising papers: they need only half the shop and press capacity to carry the same amount of news, use only half the paper and ink, require no advertising sales staff, and are a much less complex managerial problem all around.

What is needed now is a practical demonstration that a standard, serviceable, workaday ad-free newspaper can make its way in an average community; with that once shown, other ad-free papers will appear. And even though it is unlikely that the advertising press of America ever will disappear—advertising performs a valuable economic function—it is certain that an ad-free press, scattered over America, would be a valuable gauge and guardian of the responsibility of the advertising press.

And public pressure upon the government for legal reforms touching the press undoubtedly would have great effect. Laws respecting newspapers that now seem both feasible and advisable include one requiring newspapers to accept advertisements, within certain limits; this would at least guarantee minority groups their chance to be heard. A law requiring equal space and position to correct libels would seem only fair. While they would be difficult of enactment under present conditions, it is conceivable that laws establishing some professional licensing standards for newspapermen could be constitutionally upheld; if compulsory Guild membership is constitutional certainly professional licensing standards should be. Government competitive scholarships for newsmen, administered by educational authorities and with a free choice of institution, would elevate journalistic standards, as would the inauguration of a custom of sabbatical leaves for study for newsmen.

A proposal that the government could constitutionally place some limitations on newspaper ownership at least deserves consideration. A law prohibiting any individual from having an ownership interest in more than one newspaper could possibly be construed as not abridging freedom of the press, as long as no restrictions were put upon what a man could say in whatever newspaper he did own. There seem at least some grounds for a belief that newspaper ownership of radio stations is not in the public interest. Laws prohibiting newspaper ownership by individuals holding public office would certainly seem ethically advisable. And there could be legal restrictions tending to discourage absentee ownership, and to encourage local proprietorship and control.

The most immediately practical way of making American newspapers better is by improving the status of journalists, and thereby the standards of journalism. Ideally, newspapermen should be a group set apart, free from all influences except that of broad public opinion as expressed upon and through the newspaper. Short of this, however, there are quite definite things that can be done. Newspapering has made some strides as a means of livelihood in the past decade; newsmen are better paid today, more secure, and generally more capable, than they were before 1930. Much of this advance can be credited to the influence of the Newspaper Guild, and it is difficult to deny that the Guild has been, and is, in general, an influence tending to make better newspapers. But from the standpoint of broad democratic policy, there are questions as to the extent and type of union organization of newspapermen that would be most compatible with the best interests of the public.

Since newspapermen should be, ideally, a group set apart, it follows that a newspapermen's union should be an editorial craft union, and independent of any national union group other than its own. General laws and policies cannot always be applied, with full reason, to newspapers and newspapermen; what an ironworker thinks affects only himself, but what a newspaperman thinks is extended to all who read his newspaper. And it is the legitimate concern of the community to see that there is a minimum of unequable pressure upon a newspaperman's way of thinking, and also that newspapermen are not generally committed to any one viewpoint.

Schools of journalism are, increasingly, stocking newsrooms with men who have at least some degree of formal preparation for their calling. But there perhaps is a just complaint that too generally courses of journalism, by training men pointedly for practical ends, tend to perpetuate the existing pattern of journalism rather than to improve it. Journalism perhaps should be a graduate study, based on a liberal education; of the two, the liberal education is certainly more important, judged by the interests of democracy itself. Specialization in preparation for careers of journalism probably should be encouraged; master's degrees in journalism, after bachelor's degrees in concentrated liberal fields, should produce newspapermen well qualified to serve as the eyes and ears of the public, at least in respect to their subjects.

Whatever the practical possibilities of inaugurating changes in our newspaper system such as have been considered above, certain it is that widespread discussion of possible reforms, legal and otherwise, should have a salutary effect in itself. As newspaper publishers detect a possibility that the public is taking seriously suggestions for such reforms, the result probably will be critical self-examination by the press itself.

There must be a clear and stressed differentiation between Freedom of the Press, the individual's right, and State of the Press, the qualitative condition of our journalism. Blending of the two concepts dilutes the strength and clear significance of each. Unless the line between the two ideas is kept plain and unmistakable there is danger that we may, in our efforts to improve our newspapers, undermine a basic right. We would be stupid to deprive the people of the right to free expression, or to abridge this right, merely because of the failure of the press to be perfect, or the sins of a few publishers.

Our ideal must be a press that, while unrestrained in its expression, is both responsible and responsive to the people. In an important sense, America does not want a free press: it does not want a press free *from* the people, which is the sort of press that Germany had. America wants a press bound to the people, bound so tightly that the people cannot stir, however slightly, without that movement becoming visible in the newspapers. America wants a press that owes no other allegiance than to the whole community, and so established that any digression from the true course of that allegiance will bring its immediate corrective penalty. America wants a press so situated that the public interest is not only the moral course, but also the only profitable course. Such a press, it is true, would not be absolved of all the sins of today's press; indeed, such a press possibly would be more bound to the common level, more susceptible to public ailments. But America can better put up with a press that is limited by the common quality than it can risk a press independent of the people's touch.

And to obtain a truly responsive and responsible press, there are two requisites: one, its burden must be distributed generally, and not borne unequally by any class or group; and two, the people must have a choice of competitive papers.

Lastly, if we are to have better newspapers, we must have better newspapermen. The rewards of journalism must be such that the calling will attract to it the men best suited to perform its vital functions. And newspapermen must be, insofar as possible, free of any influences that may tend to distort the news image which they pass along to the public.

Responsibility of the Reporter and Editor

CLIFTON DANIEL [JANUARY 1961

Mr. Daniel is managing editor of the *New York Times*. This is from a talk he gave at Chapel Hill, North Carolina, October 21, 1960.

To be brief I could simply say that the responsibility of reporters is to get the facts straight and spell the names right. And the responsibility of editors is to fire them if they don't. That is really not a bad creed for newspapermen, but there is more to it than that.

I begin with the basic assumption that journalism in America is a calling—not a trade, not a profession, but a calling—that is not necessarily above politics, but should certainly be apart from politics. This may sound very austere and self-denying, but I mean it to sound that way. The man who embraces journalism as a career should be no less dedicated than the parson or the doctor. Like them, he should have his own standards—standards that are not subject to change by the shifting winds of public taste or political expediency.

My colleague Anthony Lewis of the *New York Times* said in a recent talk at Harvard: "There is no sure guide for all situations, but I think it is clear that the reporter must not become entirely committed—an obvious special pleader. His instinct should be all the other way. If he has a concern for the public good . . . he must reconcile himself to satisfying that urge by uncommitted reporting. Justice Frankfurter has put it that the reporter is an educator, not a reformer. I accept that definition, with the proviso that the educator must be allowed to harbor within him just a little of the spirit of reform."

The reporter, Mr. Lewis says, must satisfy his concern for the public good by uncommitted reporting. To translate that into practical terms, a reporter may belong to worthy organizations, he may contribute to good causes, he may campaign for civic virtue and public betterment, but he should never commit himself irretrievably to one cause, one organization, one course of action. In the words of the Code of Ethics of the American Society of Newspaper Editors, "Freedom from all obligations except that of fidelity to the public interest is vital." Actually, the reporter who understands his mission has a higher destiny than mere dedication to a single cause. His function is to create and preserve an atmosphere in which all noble causes may flourish.

These facts impose a peculiar responsibility on the journalist. It is a responsibility, not to his employer, not to a particular paper, not to a particular point of view, but to the public and to his own conception of the obligations of his profession. The publisher, the man who meets the payroll, is not alone responsible for the conscience of the profession. Each reporter and editor is the keeper of his own conscience.

"The modern journalist," as Louis M. Lyons has said, "is an employee. But his responsibility remains to serve the reader as his client. That describes the responsibility and the whole of it. He departs from it or compromises with it at the peril of his soul."

Mr. Lyons' conception of the responsibility of the journalist is based on the premise that information is essential to people who propose to govern themselves, and that those who supply the information must be above partisanship and self-interest. In other words, the duty of the reporter and editor, in Walter Lippmann's words, is to do "what every sovereign citizen is supposed to do, but has not the time or interest to do for himself"—that is, to gather information, pick out what is important, digest it thoroughly, and without partisanship or prejudice relate it to the problems of the day.

If the press is going to discharge this function fully, it must be among the bravest and boldest. It must say what no one else dares say, what no one else can afford to say. It must tell the people what they need to know, not what they would like to hear. If you ask me who decides what the people need to know, I can only say, "The editor." If he can't do that, he has no right to the title. If he allows someone else to do it for him—the government or some special interest—he forfeits his freedom.

There was a time when newspapermen seemed to be more outspoken than they are today, more contemptuous of authority, more defiant of restraints on their freedom. Nowadays, when we are engaged in a desperate competition with world communism, it is sometimes suggested that the newspapers should voluntarily restrict themselves.

This issue arose not long ago when it was proposed that the press limit its coverage of President Eisenhower's trip to the Soviet Union (the one that was canceled in May) and of similar visits by Soviet leaders to this country. A number of editors were questioned by the Associated Press Managing Editors Association. Nobody voted in favor of the press limiting its own freedom. One editor wrote: "If anybody proposes to limit the number of newsmen accredited to cover important international stories, let him do it if he dares. If such restrictions are imposed and found to be disadvantageous, let the enterprising newspaperman evade and defy them if he dares. If these opposite interests clash—and what is 'the American life' but a cacophony of colliding interests under the law?—then let the courts and the Congress draw the line, if they dare. But let's not circumscribe ourselves with our own pencils."

I like that fellow's spirit. It is the spirit with which I think we should meet the problem of official restrictions on news.

Somehow, I feel we newspapermen complain too much about the concealment of news by official quarters—"top secret" labels on inane documents, closed meetings of city councils, secret sessions of legislative committees, and so on. And we rely too much on the politicians to open these doors for us. The classic function of the aggressive reporter and editor—a part of the responsibility they owe to the public—is to open doors with the power of the press—pry them open, blow them open.

Of course, the issue of responsibility arises sometimes in matters more serious than a local political fight. It sometimes involves national security. Obviously, American newspapermen must not be irresponsible in the reporting of news that might affect the safety and security of our own country, our own homes. But the primary responsibility for safeguarding our national interests must rest always with our government.

When Nikita Khrushchev arrived in the United States, newspapers around the country received thousands of letters, telegrams and telephone calls urging them to boycott the visit, to ban Khrushchev from their news columns. So far as I know, there was not a single daily paper in the country that ignored Khrushchev entirely. However, there was one that gave him only six paragraphs on his arrival in New York. The *New York Times* printed 27 columns, and a very angry woman in New York called me up and demanded to know why we published a picture of that "Russian pig" on page 1. She said we should have printed pictures of President Eisenhower and the American flag instead.

While I appreciated her patriotism, I tried to explain—although she was too angry to listen—what I felt the responsibility of the press to be. Restricting news of Khrushchev's visit presupposes that it is more important for the press to show its disapproval of him than to inform the public of what he is and what he is doing. Perhaps the Russians would not have us so much on the defensive today if we had not, journalistically speaking, turned our backs on them for a whole generation and ignored what they were achieving in education, industry, and science.

There are still people who think it is unpatriotic to call attention to the Soviet challenge or to publish news that is in conflict with the opinions and policies of our government. What is the responsibility of the reporter and editor in *that* area? The answer is not simple, but it seems to me that, up until the time we are actually at war or on the verge of war, it is not only permissible but it is our duty as journalists and citizens to be constantly questioning our leaders and our policy.

Some people argue that newspapers should not print facts that might embarrass our government in its relations with other governments. But it may be that those very facts are the ones our people need to know in order to come to a clear decision about our policy. In our democracy, the purposes of the press and the government are not necessarily always identical.

Although our government does not recognize Communist China and prevents the Chinese government from being seated in the United Nations, there is no doubt in my mind that American newspapers should have correspondents on the Chinese mainland. We need to know what the Chinese Communists are doing because some day they may be doing it to us. It is nothing less than folly to let this great power grow up in the Pacific without our having any first-hand knowledge of its aims and accomplishments and its potential. Here is the most populous country on earth, and we have not a single diplomatic or journalistic representative there to tell us what is going on.

Looking back and second-guessing, I would say that we made a mistake in not sending our correspondents to China in 1956 when we had the chance. The Chinese government offered to admit a long list of newspapermen. But we declined. We did not want to embarrass our government. We did not wish to offend the sensibilities of those whose sons had died in Korea or were imprisoned in China. I think we were wrong. I think we overlooked our primary loyalty which is, as I have tried to suggest, to the American public—to give the public the information it needs to make intelligent decisions on our national policy with regard to China.

Our government has since changed its mind. A certain number of correspondents are now free to go to China. But Peiping has also changed. The Chinese are not prepared to admit our correspondents except on terms that Washington is unwilling to meet.

Without going into the diplomatic intricacies of this question, let me say only that any effort by journalism or government to break this impasse and see that the American people are informed about China would be a contribution to our national security.

In election years there are inevitably proposals, from inside the profession and outside, that the newspapers should guarantee equal space and equal billing to the two candidates for President. Of course, we should give them an even break. But the principle should not be carried to ridiculous extremes. Newspapers should be edited not with a tape measure, but on the basis of the best news judgment of competent, serious, responsible reporters and editors. A reporter knows pretty well when he is leaning toward one side or the other, and so does his editor. The only answer to that is: Don't do it.

Again and again these days we hear that factual reporting is not enough, that objectivity is out of date, that the news has become so complex that it must be explained, that interpretation is now necessary. A good deal of this talk is nonsense. Of course the news should be explained. There is nothing new about that. The news has always required interpretation, but interpreting the news does not exclude the possibility of objectivity in reporting it. As I have said, a reporter knows pretty well when he is being objective, and so does his editor. The important thing is that they should appreciate the need for objectivity, and its relationship to the role they play in our democracy.

Stripped to essentials, the responsibility of the reporter and editor is simply to serve the public—not the profession of journalism, not a particular newspaper, not a political party, not the government, but the public.

II. ROLE OF THE PRESS

Two problems of the newspaper press have attracted the attention both of its management and of observers of the journalistic scene in the postwar period, which is the period of *Nieman Reports.* The two problems are related. One is the competition from the newer, more dramatic medium of broadcasting, with its more immediate reports. The other is to obtain and hold the talent to sustain the newspaper's role against the excitement of careers in television, and also against the ever-widening area of communication in government, public relations, and allied fields—all of them seeking the same talents as the city news rooms and willing to pay a premium to get them.

The competition with broadcasting in news has forced the newspaper to seek new ways to hold its readers. The most definite result of this has been the increased emphasis on interpretive reporting, to put more depth in the story.

Interpretive reporting began with much headshaking over the dangers of departure from the tradition of objective reporting. For a long time the *New York Times* was meticulous in labeling as "news analysis" any story that ventured into more explanation and background exploration than the surface facts. The debate continues, though obviously the broader and deeper report has added a permanent dimension to the press.

The other problem, attracting and holding a necessary share of journalistic talent, has very slowly pushed newspapers into recruiting and in-training programs for which they felt no need before television had stolen so much of the glamour of the newspaper job.

The self-examination of the newspaper induced by these two

problems of the newer competition exposed also other factors that have lessened the appeal of journalism to many ably qualified young people. Questions have been raised as to the opportunity the newspaper affords to the idealistic reporter to uncover evils and campaign for reforms. How much has the business office restricted editorial freedom? How much has its merchandising role cramped the newspaper as crusader? Has it joined the ranks of big business as a bulwark of conservatism? Urgent discussion of all these aspects of the changing journalistic scene has occupied extensive space in *Nieman Reports,* some of it represented here.

As for television itself, the long-deferred hope to see television journalism free itself from its commercial blinders and realize its graphic potential has been reflected in the *Reports* from the first year. The complaint of the dominant control of the advertiser found classic utterance by television's great journalist, Edward R. Murrow, in his 1958 address to the news broadcasters. We ran this speech, and it is reprinted here. A companion problem of television reporting was dramatized by John Day, newspapersman who had turned news director for CBS. He asked whether a news broadcast is reporting or performing. His exploration of that question provides the final article in this part of the book.

There Is No Substitute for a Good Newspaper

NORMAN E. ISAACS [OCTOBER 1954

Mr. Isaacs now is vice-president and executive editor of the *Courier-Journal* and the *Louisville Times.* He was president of the Associated Press Managing Editors Association in 1953. This article is from an address to the National Newspaper Promotion Managers Association on May 10, 1954, when he was managing editor of the *Louisville Times.*

Three years ago I was called into the office of the publisher of the *St. Louis Star-Times* and told that the next day's editions would be the last. I do not intend to conduct here a public post-mortem. I raise the subject because I think you are entitled to a sort of backdrop for what I am about to say. The main point is that for five and a half months I was an unemployed managing editor. They may well have been the most important months in my whole life because for the first time—literally, the first—I had to think.

All of us use the word "think" very loosely. We "think" this and we "think" that. We do nothing of the kind. We operate by a kind of mental prearrangement. Rarely do we sit down and really think—to reason things out, to weigh, to balance and arrive at conclusions.

I grew up in newspaper offices. There was nothing else I had ever wanted to do. Like everyone else, I learned a thousand and one what *nots* to do. I also picked up bad habits. From assorted bosses, I picked up some good attitudes, discarded some bad. Mainly, I operated on instinct. My politics had been partly formulated by boyhood exposure to a voluble and partisan father; by debate around newspaper offices; by some personal experience. My newspaper attitudes—fortunately, I think—had been fashioned principally by a youthful exposure to some great crusading editors—men who had both ideas and ideals.

Like every other managing editor, I had had my battles with the business offices. Perhaps some of them had been more intense than others had experienced. But even these arguments were instinctive on my part. I cannot truthfully say that they were ever thought out and when I looked back I could see that many of my positions were arrogant and pig-headed.

At any rate, in the summer and fall of 1951—at the age of 43—I suddenly had to stop and think.

My friends were wonderful. They tried to rustle up many jobs for me. Some flattering nonjournalism business offers were made. But did I want to leave newspapering? If I did stay in it, did I insist on being a managing editor? Did it matter what kind of newspaper I went to work for—providing, of course, they would give me a job? What about newspapering anyway? Was it worth the effort? Wouldn't I be better off in some cushy spot in business or industry? What was it I really wanted to do?

Well, I preferred newspapering. But not at the expense of my convictions. That, it seemed to me, was an empty life. What good would money be if you had to walk down alleys to avoid the people you knew? I would like to go to work for a newspaper that rather reflected my own attitudes—an honest newspaper; a clean one; a decent one—a *responsible* one.

I must be candid and tell you that I had all but given up hope of such a connection when the unanticipated telephone call came from Louisville. And I am quite aware that I am probably the one in a thousand who got the lucky break at a decisive moment. If I never have good luck tap me again, I am still ahead.

This is the backdrop. If it were not such a painful and unsettling process, I wish all of you [the assembled promotion managers—ed.] could have the same opportunity to sit back and really think it through—not only to think backward, but forward as well.

If all of you had that opportunity, I am convinced that the field of newspaper promotion would move forward in seven-league boots.

For newspaper promotion, gentlemen, shares greatly in the indignities which are frequently heaped on good newspapermen and on potentially good newspapers. I have had my share of those indignities. In my time, I have had to promote old automobile contests, baby picture contests, bathing beauty contests, marathon dances, moving picture tie-in events, personal sketch artists, handwriting analysts, comic strip contests. You name it; I probably have had to promote it at some time or another.

Yet what did all these promote? The newspaper? No sir, not by a long shot. They degraded the newspaper. These events either made the advertising department think they were making some client delighted—which wasn't true—or the promotion manager had talked himself into believing that if he just promoted something, he was helping keep the newspaper's name before the public.

I shudder when I speculate on how many hundreds of thousands of dollars have gone down the drains in this type of inane, inept, unworthy, and useless promotion.

The conclusion is inescapable that there is no substitute for a good newspaper—honestly published, honestly sold, and honestly promoted. Check for yourself the list of America's top newspapers and you will find very little of the cheap and tawdry in either their production methods or their promotion activities.

Sure, you can buy circulation. And you can buy yourself broke, too. I do not have to defend that statement. The record also will bear that out.

Yet to this day there are publishers who will buy—on the recommendation of their circulation managers and promotion managers—contests, stunts, and assorted gimmicks designed to buy circulation. So the newspaper will add a few thousand papers. All the while, everyone knows that holding that circulation means paying a higher price on the next go-round. And still higher and higher. Nonetheless, this same type of publisher will have no hesitancy about sitting down to write a biting editorial about the insanity of a government permitting an ever-spiraling inflation.

I am one who has had my fill of newspapers which have to exist by peddling cheap insurance. Or by promoting newsboys' bands. Or by any other kind of expensive side-promotion to cover up the fact that what they are selling isn't really worth buying.

Some newspapers still believe that one way to get advertising clients and influence them is to give expensive parties and to buy expensive blocks of tickets for important events—charging the whole bill to promotion and then hammering down on all other expenses on the grounds that business conditions do not justify any leeway. These are the newspapers—the "Lucky Buck" promoters, the insurance peddlers, the sponsors of newsboys' bands, the party givers and the ticket buyers—which fail to understand Mark Ethridge's profound observation that the best newspaper dollar ever spent is the editorial dollar.

Men who choose not to understand can easily misinterpret that statement. It takes some thinking to understand it fully and I repeat again that too many have not had the opportunity to get sufficient time to sit down and think.

Looking back, I have become more deeply convinced than ever that the newspaper advertiser can never be bought by any phony promotional methods. He may listen because someone has been nice to him; but he will not buy space for that reason. There is only one justification for his advertising: To bring results.

My first experience with this came a long time ago. It made a tremendous impression on me and embittered me for some years because I didn't understand.

I was about 19 at the time, a kid sports writer. Boyd Gurley was editor of the *Indianapolis Times* and in the process of winning the Pulitzer prize for breaking up the Ku Klux Klan in Indiana. The Klan—in retaliation for the steady drumfire of exposure—called for a circulation boycott and later an advertising boycott. The Klan was strong and circulation did drop. You can understand my consternation when advertisers also dropped out with alacrity—even those advertisers whom one would judge to be so emotionally involved in the crusade that you would almost take it for granted that they would see it through to the bitter end.

No thanks to them, of course, the crusade persisted and was successful. The Klan was destroyed as an organization in Indiana. Circulation came back—then climbed. And the advertisers came back.

For years after that, I had only contempt for them. I looked upon them as moral cowards. Years later, I came to understand it more clearly and more tolerantly.

The advertiser has no morals. He is utterly and completely selfish —and undoubtedly has to be in order to survive. He may hate everything for which a newspaper stands—and yet be its greatest spacebuyer. He may read a newspaper avidly because he likes its editorial viewpoint; yet the moment he is solicited for advertising he becomes a cold, calculating businessman.

Nothing in the way of phony promotion can change this single overriding factor. And yet so many newspapers waste the talents and time of promotion men trying to build solicitations and campaigns that deal in fantastic extravagance and overstatement.

I am proud to work for a company that undersells itself ever so neatly. I consider this phrasing a masterpiece of sound judgment: "We publish two good newspapers. They are read by everybody in and around Louisville. We sell advertising space at reasonable rates. It produces sales."

Four sentences. An intelligent, proud statement. And it has stood up for years.

Don't you think, too, that the same approach goes for the reader? It does. Down to the last detail. Given a good newspaper and good service, you have a reader who is constant, dependable, and loyal.

Isn't it a dreadful admission of weakness to buy billboards shrieking about "the best" comic strips? Or to run full-page office ads promoting a contest of some type or another?

Wouldn't the dollars be better spent improving the newspaper as a product?

If newspapering is to move ahead, we have to quit kidding ourselves about the media we are working with. That is one of the big troubles with it. We haven't understood it well enough. For too many years, we've had too many charlatans running around, making fancy speeches—and almost all of them covering up, attacking anyone who dares to criticize us, wailing about the dangers to freedom of the press, and about the designs of a big, bad government against us—and almost all of them heavy with the dreadful economic perils that beset us on all sides.

Once radio was listed as one of the dragons in the list. Lately, television has taken its place. Such nonsense.

It is time we ourselves—we who work with newspapers—took stock. We need no St. Georges come to slay the dragons. We need an understanding approach to our work. We need a proper assessment of the role the newspaper plays in society.

The newspaper is a curious anomaly in a free-enterprise society. It is, on the one hand, a business enterprise—unregulated and uncontrolled by the state; yet given certain privileges of expression by the constitution; a business yet a public utility, serving the needs of the people. If it is to succeed in its multiple roles, it must have an appreciation of its position—a humility of its role as a public servant—it must have assurance of its power—and, most of all, it must have a deep integrity, going all the way from owner to apprentice. Every single one who works with the paper must have a pride in his calling and in his product. And everyone must *want* to keep the freedoms which are so precious to all of us.

I recall vividly the calumny heaped by so many newspaper owners and editors upon the Commission on Freedom of the Press—the Hutchins Commission—back in 1947 when the report was issued. Get a copy of the book, *A Free and Responsible Press,* read it and see for yourself the pathetic shortsightedness of so many newspaper executives. When you read it, you will readily see that the commission was serving nobly the best, long-range interests of the press.

It pointed out many of our weaknesses and it called for voluntary, internal reform in order to forestall any encroachment by government. The wiser and saner publishers and editors praised the report, but they were all but drowned out in the cacophony of those who to this day think almost every critic of the press is a violently dangerous enemy. These are the men themselves who are the most dangerous enemies to a free press. It is they who bring discredit on the whole profession by their money-grubbing, by their selfishness, and by their arrogance.

Let us look at the picture in its total form.

Newspapers have been, are, and probably will remain the most vital part of the nation's vast communications machinery. The total national circulation is tremendous. And it covers everything from the biggest cities to the smallest.

The news and picture magazines are popular, but they are a supplemental medium—no more than that. Where a newspaper in a city may have 100,000 circulation, a news magazine with more than 10,000 would be amazingly successful. I would estimate the figure to be half that.

Radio, I believe, has more news impact than the news and picture magazines. Television is still a lesser form of news competition. At this stage it is purely supplemental—but it has some great natural advantages and over a long period it may prove to have more adaptability than we presently believe.

Rather than being menaces, these competing media have had a salutary effect on newspapers. We have been forced to change emphasis; we have been compelled, by competition, to do many things better.

Let me hark back for the moment to the almost-forgotten day of the newspaper extra. Some of the older gentlemen here will recall with ease the day of the baseball extra. No week-day afternoon was complete without it—home delivery routes and all. I wonder how many extras are put out now in the United States. Not very many, I'd guess, in a year's time.

What killed the extra? Radio. That simple. We couldn't compete with instantaneous transmission. But while it may have killed the extra edition, it didn't damage newspapers in the slightest. Circulations dipped, recovered and climbed. We found that sports interest had increased. And where once we were able to get by with perhaps ten columns of sports news, we had to go up to twelve and fourteen and sixteen and beyond. We found that radio wasn't such a terrible villain after all.

I remember when I was told that the introduction of the weekly picture magazines, on slick paper, was the beginning of the end. This we could not possibly compete with. Today, our newspapers are equipped with wire transmission photo equipment and it is the rare big-city newspaper which cannot within an hour reproduce a photograph taken in Washington or San Francisco, or even on a battle front five thousand miles away. We publish more pictures in a week than even the flossiest picture magazines—and we not only give the top national and international pictures, but the one field the national magazines can't possibly touch—the local pictures, the meat and potatoes of our daily existence.

We do so many things better than we once did. We have newspapers today which if they are not great newspapers, at least are very, very good newspapers. To me, it is no accident that these good newspapers are also successful newspapers financially.

To me, it also seems no accident that these are the newspapers which are carefully promoted—and by carefully, I mean prudently, sensibly, cleanly. The whole import of their promotions is to emphasize the quality of their products, the quality of their editorial content.

Which brings me back, full-cycle, to some of our weaknesses. I suspect that our greatest weakness as a group is stubbornness.

Let me take it first from the news and editorial side. News and editorial men have fallen down in their jobs these past several years in quite a few respects. One of them has been in failing to keep pace with the changing quality of our readers. Another has been in clinging to outworn and outmoded techniques of writing, editing, and producing newspapers. And still another has been a sort of ivory-tower attitude toward all other departments on the newspaper—as if we in the news and editorial departments possessed all the brains available. Too many news and editorial men are contemptuous of the mechanical departments; supercilious toward the advertising and circulation departments; and blind as bats toward the usefulness of proper promotion.

I think almost the same things, in slightly different proportions, can be said of the failures of those in the promotion field. Promotion too, has failed to keep pace with the changing attitudes of the readers. It has clung to outworn stunts, presentations and assorted gimmicks. Promotion has seemed to be blind toward the possibilities of learning what the newspaper actually has to offer the customer.

Because some of us were trained in a certain way does not necessarily make that way the right one. I know of one publisher—now no longer a publisher—whose stubbornness was a thing of wonder. Once, many months ago, his newspaper had a big package deal with one of the major syndicates. He had all his comic strips in one basket. His major competitor made a backdoor deal, buying the whole package at double the price. You can imagine the publisher's consternation when the syndicate notified him that on the contract's expiration date there would be no renewal.

The publisher was in a panic. His plight was described to me in detail by the managing editor. The publisher tried desperately to talk the syndicate out of the cancellation. No soap. So—helter-skelter—he slapped together a whole new collection of comic strips and then waited fearfully for his day of doom.

What happened? Nothing. A few squawks here and there. A few stops and switches to the rival paper. But no catastrophe. You would think from this experience that the publisher would have learned that comic strips were not the answer; that good ones, bad ones, or indifferent ones, his newspaper's livelihood did not depend on them so urgently.

But, no. This gentleman proceeded then to enter into the most rigid deals for comic strips—long-term, ironclad contracts at fabulous prices—and some which never even appeared in his newspaper. And he called himself an astute business man. He was one of those who believed in billboards advertising comic strips as his paper's best offer and he continued these practices to the day he went out of business.

The cold truth of the matter is that all of our newspapers could dispose of comic strips today with no earth-shaking consequences. I have no particular desire to eliminate them. I think some of them are amusing. And I think the youngsters are particularly attached to them. My point is only that we are kidding ourselves if we insist they are essential. Any editor who has dropped a comic strip in recent years can testify that it makes practically no difference. I dropped one recently and as far as I know no one even knows it is gone.

Try dropping the vital statistics and see what happens.

The way to stay on top is to do the basic newspaper job—the printing of news—in clean and decent and complete fashion. Let's make our own advertising—the advertising of newspapers—a model for all other advertisers. Let us state the facts of the case honestly and with integrity.

The Story Behind Little Rock

HARRY S. ASHMORE [APRIL 1958

This is a slightly abridged version of the first Nieman Lecture to mark the twentieth year of the Nieman Fellowships, delivered by Mr. Ashmore at Harvard on February 21, 1958. He was then editor of the *Arkansas Gazette,* Little Rock. Later he joined the staff of the Fund for the Republic. He had been a Nieman Fellow in 1941–42. The lecture, besides being printed in *Nieman Reports* for April 1958, appeared in *Harper's,* June 1958.

They tell a story down my way—or used to—about a native son who, when he traveled in the great world, always replied to the inevitable query about where he came from by saying, "Arkansas—go ahead and laugh." That, however, was in a simpler time when those who live in the great cities, and are the most provincial of Americans, knew the state largely as a name which alternated in bad jokes with Oshkosh and Brooklyn.

Since September 1957 there has been nothing funny about Arkansas, or its capital, Little Rock. Outsize headlines have converted the name into a symbol which arouses strong emotions not only among Americans but among people everywhere. It has become a new battle cry for those on both sides of the great moral issue that has divided this nation through most of its history, and still divides it. "Remember Little Rock," proclaims the great seal that adorns propaganda-bearing envelopes going out from the headquarters of the Southern Citizens' Councils. The same words have been sounded by Negro hoodlums moving against whites with drawn knives in the slum streets of Northern cities.

The Little Rock story was, by universal judgment, the second biggest news story of the year—topped only by Sputnik. It attracted a concentration of correspondents, photographers, and radio and television technicians comparable to that which assembles for a national political convention. The newspapers, wire services, and networks sent their best men, too—seasoned hands to handle the fast-breaking spot news and think-piece experts to back them up. For many days the story had top priority on every news desk in this country and abroad—which meant the men on the ground could count on whatever space or time it took to report their findings in full. It is fair to say that journalism's best effort went into the Little Rock story.

Yet Harold C. Fleming, the perceptive executive director of the Southern Regional Council, whose business it is to chart the shifting pattern of race relations in the South, has written of the result:

"What do the millions of words and television images add up to? Have they given Americans—to say nothing of foreigners—a clearer understanding of the South's malaise? As a result of them, will the national shock be less or the insight greater if a similar eruption accompanies desegregation in Dallas or Charlottesville or Knoxville? We can hope so, but not with much optimism. Only a few major newspapers, like the *New York Times,* a few thoughtful television and radio commentators, and a few good magazines sought to give a meaningful perspective to their reports from Little Rock.

"Conspicuously lacking in most interpretations is any sense of continuity. The upheavals in Tuscaloosa, Clinton and Little Rock were not isolated events, but episodes in an unfolding drama of social change."

So speaks Mr. Fleming, and I can file no dissent from his verdict. All the traditional shortcomings of journalism were on display there on my doorstep. The cowboy reporters rode in to the scent of blood. They did not have to seek for drama; it was thrust upon them, with a complete cast of heroes and villains, and these readily interchangeable, depending upon point of view. I do not charge that the press sensationalized the Little Rock story; the facts themselves were sensational enough to answer any circulation manager's dream. Moreover, I believe that with only rare and negligible exceptions the men and women who wrote the Little Rock story were competent and conscientious. Similarly, I have no reason to believe that any but a tiny handful were bound by any home-office policy considerations or blinded by their personal prejudices. They performed their traditional function, within the traditional limits. They braved the mob that formed for some days around the high school, they interviewed the principals on both sides and many of the minor characters, they sketched in personalities and filled in color, and some at least tried hard to define the feeling of the community. Over a period of weeks they did a reasonably accurate job of reporting what happened at Little Rock—but as Fleming said, they have failed to tell why it happened.

The reason, I think, is that to American journalism the Little

Rock story had an arbitrary beginning and end. It began the day Governor Faubus surrounded Central High School with his state guard. It continued so long as there was a naked edge of violence. It ended when federal troops restored a surface order to the troubled city. It has had subsequent footnotes only when the edge of violence re-emerged in clashes between white and Negro children inside the school. It survives in the press today largely in the sort of occasional oblique reference that passes for the background of more immediate news.

Yet it is quite obvious that the Little Rock story did not begin in September. It is equally obvious that it has not ended yet. For Little Rock was simply the temporary focus of a great, continuing, and unresolved American dilemma which touches upon fundamental concepts of morality, of social change, and of law. Journalism has concentrated on only the exposed portion of the iceberg; the great, submerged mass remains uncharted.

It was, admittedly, an extraordinarily difficult story to handle. A journalist is trained to seek out spokesmen for both sides in any controversy. They were readily and anxiously available in Little Rock. The case for resistance to the federal court's integration order was made at length by Governor Faubus, and bolstered by the more flamboyant utterances of the unabashed racists in the Citizens' Councils. The case for compliance was made by the local school officials, the mayor of the city, and, belatedly, by the president of the United States, with somewhat more passionate arguments freely offered by spokesmen for the National Association for the Advancement of Colored People. But this was a controversy that had at least three sides. Caught between the committed and dedicated partisans was a substantial and silent mass of plain citizens—confused and deeply disturbed. They were people who deplored desegregation and also deplored violence. They felt, many of them, a deep compassion for the nine Negro children exposed to the anger and contempt of a white mob. But they also felt that the Negro children should not be attending the white school in the first place. They had been, most of them, willing to undertake what they considered the unpleasant duty required by the courts. But then, at the last moment, their governor had stepped forward and proclaimed that what they had accepted as the law was without substance—and that their failure to resist desegregation amounted to treason to their own traditions and to their own people. It may be true that most of those who accepted this thesis—and the majority have done so to some degree—did so with conscious rationalization. But it is also true that when emotion triumphed over reason they did not actively join the crusade of the governor and the Citizens' Councils; rather they simply subsided into troubled silence and by so doing withdrew their support from those few who attempted to stand against the tide. And because they were silent their attitude went largely unreported; the press took due note of the fact that in fairly short order Governor Faubus was obviously in command of the field; but here again it did not explain why—which is the heart of the story.

It can be argued that these matters are too subtle for the proper practice of journalism—that those who rode to Little Rock as though it were a four-alarm fire could not be expected to plumb the hidden attitudes of the populace, and indeed that the effort to do so would represent a dangerous departure from proper standards of objectivity. Perhaps so, but there were other aspects of the Little Rock story that were equally vital and by no means so elusive. There was, conspicuously, the failure of leadership in Washington which matched the default of Southern leadership and made the ultimate showdown between state and federal force inevitable.

Before pursuing this thesis I should, perhaps, note that I am, to borrow Sam Rayburn's description of himself, a Democrat without suffix, prefix, or apology. It should be noted too that I spent ten months in the wilderness with Adlai Stevenson in 1956, when the Democratic candidate's cries on this subject, along with all others, went largely unheeded. But, making all due allowance for my prejudice, I submit that the record shows that from May, 1954, when the United States Supreme Court reversed the old Plessy doctrine, until September, 1957, when the chickens finally fluttered in to roost in Little Rock, the Eisenhower administration took no affirmative action to pave the way for the sweeping social change the Court required or to temper the inevitable dislocations it would occasion. Indeed, the incredible fact is that the administration without preliminary moved directly to the ultimate resort of armed force, and then was confounded by its own belated audacity.

It required no delicate thumbing of the public pulse to chart the course of growing defiance in the South. It was evident in the violent utterances of some of the South's public men and in the silence of others. It was made a matter of record in the passage of a variety of restrictive laws in the Southern legislatures. A conspicuous public monument was erected in Washington when 100 Southern members of the Senate and House signed their breast-beating Manifesto in the spring of 1956. Yet Mr. Eisenhower's only reaction to all this was an occasional bemused press-conference statement about the difficulties of changing the minds and hearts of men. His administration, it is true, made token efforts to pass stringent civil rights legislation—which only served to lacerate the Southerners in Congress and certainly had an adverse effect upon their minds and hearts. And, of course, Vice-President Nixon, in the days before he sheathed his hatchet, along with other administration spokesmen, made the proper obeisance to their party's Abolitionist tradition when they were campaigning in those areas where the Negro vote is heavy. But at no time did Mr. Eisenhower attempt to use the great moral force of his office to persuade Southerners of the justice of the course the Supreme Court required of them, or his great personal prestige in the region to allay their fears that they were being forced into a revolutionary rather than an evolutionary course. Nor did he employ the vast political powers of his office to negotiate with the recalcitrant Southern political leaders from a position of strength.

I am not one who accepts without reservation the thesis that the Republican allegiance of most of the proprietors of the press has been translated into a conspiracy to wrap Mr. Eisenhower in bunting and protect him against criticism. I do not believe that this was a primary cause of the press' conspicuous failure to take due note of the troubles that were shaping up in the South, and of the administration's apparent unawareness. I suspect that it stems rather from the limiting journalistic axiom that what happens is news, and what doesn't isn't.

Thus the reporters rode into the region only when there was action—when a couple of red-necked hoodlums in back-woods Mississippi dropped Emmett Till into a river, or a mob ruled that Autherine Lucy couldn't attend the University of Alabama, or John Kasper incited the citizens of Clinton to wrath. In between, an occasional reporter, usually from one of the magazines, toured the region, but these too often caught only the sound and the fury on the surface.

If the reporting of the prelude to Little Rock was conspicuously inadequate, it seems to me that the postlude provides an even more distressing example. The stirring martial events of September were, it is true, somewhat confusing—particularly when President Eisenhower and Governor Faubus held their historic peace conference at Newport and there remained some doubt as to who came out with whose sword. Out of the communiques issued by the White House on this occasion, however, and the later meeting with the intermediaries from the Southern Governors' Conference, there emerged an assumption that the executive department of the federal government was prepared to back to the utmost the orders of the federal judiciary. This notion was reinforced by the arrival of the 101st Airborne Infantry, and by the presence in Little Rock of so many FBI agents they created a problem of hotel accommodations. Indeed, there was public and official talk of a vast document compiled by the FBI, at the direction of the United States Attorney General, presumably in preparation for court action against those who were clearly defying the injunctions of a federal judge. During those fall days the embattled Little Rock School Board, under fire from the state government for carrying out the judge's order and deserted by a city administration intimidated by a show of strength at the polls by a Citizens' Council slate of candidates, waited for the federals to ride to their aid. All they got, as it turned out, was a withdrawal of the regulars of the 101st and a perfunctory guard detail of federalized national guardsmen under orders to observe what went on in the school but not to arrest any malefactors within the school, who might come to their attention.

It soon became apparent that this was far from enough to preserve any semblance of order. The mob which once came close to forcing entry into the school did not re-form, it is true, but it didn't need to. A far safer course was to inspire a small group of whites against the isolated Negroes. And as it became apparent that Washington had done all it was going to do, the Citizens' Councils became bolder and bolder in their campaign of intimidation, coercion, and boycott directed against any who dared dissent from the defiant course they had charted. This week the campaign bore its first tangible fruit in the expulsion of one of the nine Negro children who had responded in kind to calculated mistreatment—an event greeted by the appearance of cards on the lapels of the student activists bearing the cogent notice: "One down—eight to go."

Here again, in spasmodic, uncoordinated fashion the surface of these events has been recorded by the press. But the other and more significant portion of the story has attracted little attention. In Washington, the decision to leave to the Little Rock School Board the entire burden of carrying out the court order against impossible odds has never been officially announced, in these terms, but has been clearly acknowledged by the Department of Justice. The new Attorney General, Mr. Rogers, said that there were no present plans for further legal action in Little Rock. He also noted that the administration had no plans for pressing for additional civil rights legislation at this session of Congress—a matter of some moment since the Justice Department had previously used as an excuse for inaction at Little Rock the failure of Congress to enact the enforcement provisions in the last civil rights bill. These pronouncements were followed by one of the most remarkable scenes enacted on Capitol Hill since adoption of the Missouri Compromise. Mr. Rogers appeared before the Senate Judiciary Committee to be interrogated as to his fitness as Attorney General, received cordial greetings, and was recommended for confirmation without a single question being addressed to him regarding his past or future course in the Little Rock case—and this before a committee that counts among its members Senators Eastland of Mississippi and Johnston of South Carolina. This singular occurrence was accorded no more than passing mention in the press and no one of consequence speculated in print or on a television tube as to the dimensions of what must have been one of the most remarkable political deals in recent years.

Just as the Little Rock story did not begin in Little Rock, it will not end there—whatever the ultimate fate of the eight children still remaining in the beleaguered high school. These events have already had tragic consequences in Arkansas and the South; those who were disposed to support an orderly adjustment to the new public policy have been discredited and disarmed—not so much by the extremists who are now in control, as by a national administration which deserted them in the first collision between federal and state force and declared in effect that the rule of law propounded by its own courts is not enforceable. And so, by default, what started out as a local issue has been built into a national constitutional crisis.

And it is no less than that—perhaps the most critical the nation has faced since 1860. I do not suggest that civil war is imminent, because of course it isn't. I do say that the drift in Washington has gravely compounded the dislocations that were made inevitable by the historical developments that were affirmed by the Supreme Court in 1954, and has left the country sharply divided on a complex moral and social issue at a time when national unity could be the price of national survival.

There are many who share the blame. There is reason to wonder if our system of education has served us adequately when in its ultimate flowering it has produced a generation, north and south, that appears not only unable to grasp the implications of the race problem but unwilling to face it squarely. I have said of the South that its besetting problem is not the accommodation of the rising aspirations of its Negro people, difficult as that may be, but its inability to reduce the issue to rational terms. In slightly different terms, the same thing is true of the non-South—called upon now to translate its pious principles into action and blinking painfully over the mote in its own eye.

But my concern here is with journalism. No one can say with certainty that the course of events in the South could have been altered had the president exercised firm leadership—or that Mr. Eisenhower would have been disposed to act even if those who are supposed to man the watchtowers of public affairs had sounded the alarm. And now, after the fact, this is perhaps not of consuming importance. But the watchtowers still remain largely silent, and I suggest that this is a matter of pressing concern. For it seems to me that the American people are still not aware of what Little Rock really demonstrated—that not only did the administration have no plan to meet the crisis when it came, but even now, with all the bitter lessons before it, still has charted no effective course of action nor displayed any disposition to do so.

I am the first to argue that time is of the essence in any resolution of the problem. In so delicate an area of human relations progress must be evolutionary. Yet time is of value only if it is put to some practical use; perhaps the most cogent single question yet raised was that put by Francis Pickens Miller of Virginia to a group of Southerners who at a national conference were pleading for a breathing spell. What, he asked, did they propose to do with it? It is clear that the Southern leadership has no program and no policy except the negative one of delay at any price—and part of that price will be a steady deterioration of race relations not only in the South but in the nation at large. And the administration has offered nothing except the politician's usual device for postponing unpleasant decisions—the creation of a study commission, which, if it does not founder on its partisan division, at some distant date presumably will come up with the facts the press should have been setting forth all along.

These then are some of the aspects of the Little Rock story which seem to me to be largely unrecognized or generally misunderstood despite the millions of words that have adorned the front pages and boomed out through the loudspeakers. I suppose that a patient man with endless time on his hands might have put together the lurid fragments that were hurled at him and divine their meaning—but readers and listeners are usually both impatient and busy. It remains, then, journalism's unfulfilled responsibility to somehow provide perspective and continuity—to add the why to the what.

Perhaps what we need most of all is simply the courage of our own convictions—to recognize that news is not merely a record of ascertainable facts and attributable opinions, but a chronicle of the world we live in cast in terms of moral values. We will err, certainly, and we will be abused—but we will at least be in position in the watchtowers, trying to tell the story in all its dimensions.

The Dynamics of Journalism

MARK ETHRIDGE [JULY 1958, SUPPLEMENT

The second Nieman Lecture to mark the twentieth year of the Nieman Fellowships was given by Mr. Ethridge at Harvard on March 20, 1958. He was then publisher of the *Courier-Journal* and the *Louisville Times*. After his retirement in Louisville in 1963, he became publisher of *Newsday*, on Long Island. This is a slightly abridged version of the lecture.

While what I have to say will deal largely with newspapers, it will be rather less about their narrower internal problems and more about their relationship to the changing structure of American life and their place in a society where we need to know more than we ever knew to survive. I hope it may have some interest also for those who have a concern that the field of communicating ideas is shifting from what comes through the eye to what comes through the ear, which I think much more tricky and much less reliable or enduring.

I claim the privilege of speaking as an authentic schizophrenic: a publisher talking about the newspaper *business,* an editor for many years and still one at heart talking about the newspaper *profession.* In either capacity I can pretend to some experience, if not authority, for it was 48 years ago that the Meridian, Mississippi, *Dispatch,* long since dead, demonstrated what I like to think was faith in me, but more likely its own poverty, by putting a callow high school boy on its payroll to cover sports at 50 cents a day.

My 48 years have not been continuous. Twenty-five years ago I became so angry at, and disillusioned with, newspapering that I quit. And I stayed out of it, too, for a full two months, until I was faced with doing something else that could not command, as Lincoln said, "that last full measure of my devotion." Or maybe it was true of me, as with so many other newspapermen, what one of Hamilton Basso's characters said in *The View from Pompey's Head,* that I was "still a little blinded by the dust of wonder that had got into (my) eyes."

And so I went back to writing as a staff member of the AP in Washington. For most of my life I have been in the news end and I would still be there if owners paid reporters, city editors, and editors as much as they do publishers. I became a publisher not, as Arthur Sulzberger jocularly said, by marrying the boss's daughter—I married the poorest girl but the best reporter on the paper—but by shooting off my brash young mouth: by shouting at the top of my lungs that the old-timers of personal journalism who preceded the corporate, business-office operation of newspapers, the old-timers who believed in the primacy of news and editorial pages, were indeed right.

What I believed in then I still hold to and repeat now to you who are concerned with gathering, handling and expounding the meaning of news: not only the best, but the cheapest box-office attraction a newspaper has is its editorial and news content. Let those who will, or feel they must, have gimmicks, their pogo sticks, their word games, their insurance schemes, their tangle towns and their charity tie-ups; give me a newspaper that prints the news fully, fairly, and fearlessly and comments upon it intelligently and vigorously and I will take my chances on circulation and advertising. Of course I would make sure that editorial excellence was coupled with hard selling and intelligent promotion.

Publishing a good and profitable newspaper becomes more difficult every day. Economic competition is stronger and the business operation more complex. Publishers who talk about costs rising out of proportion to revenues are telling the truth. It might be thought that the simple answer in such circumstances would be to do what the Lord did in *Green Pastures:* pass another miracle, which in the newspaper business generally means to raise circulation and advertising rates. But those who have tried that recently have found stiffer resistance than at any time within the past twenty-five years. We still have a hang-over from the penny-press days on the part of the subscriber and the vanity of numbers on the part of the publisher. Too many people who are willing to pay a thousand dollars for a color television set regard their five, or even ten cents a day, for a newspaper as the first point of attack in budget cutting. It seems to be particularly true in a recession such as we are having now that the installment payment on television or the washing machine is more important than news of the world.

But I am speaking of a longer range than a year or even the span of what we all hope is a temporary recession. If the economy dips much further, a good many newspapers will be pinched between the Scylla of rising costs and the Charybdis of the inability to raise rates to meet them. If we have a drastic reduction of national income it will be catastrophic for more newspapers than I care to think about. But in any case, with or without recession or depression, we are in a contracting business, or profession, if you will.

The day has long passed when a man with a shirt-tail full of type and a brain can start a newspaper. Only the very rich can embark upon what many consider the romantic venture of founding a daily newspaper and only the very few of the rich who own them can afford to die and leave them as part of their estates. Hence there has been a tendency in recent years toward trusteed newspapers, where ownership has been dissolved from the individual to employees, to charitable or pension trusts or public ownership.

The result is not always good. Widely held ownership tends to neutralize and vitiate editorial firmness. Employee ownership, though Utopian in sound, only creates more capitalists where one existed before. In an instance of which I am mindful, an employee-owned paper cut its news content drastically during the paper shortage of World War II because the employees wanted a continuation of the dividends to which they had become accustomed more than they wanted a good paper.

When I entered newspaper work, there were 2,600 dailies and 16,000 weeklies in the country. And there wasn't much else to do with leisure time but to go fishing and read. Automobiles were a scarce luxury; radio and its troublesome child, television, had not been born. The movies were pretty much the flickers and there were, of course, no drive-ins to compete for leisure time. But all these things and many others compete now for the hour we once had with the reader.

Today, there are 1,767 dailies and some 9,400 weeklies in the United States, a drop of 33 per cent in dailies, 49 per cent in weeklies. Thirty-five daily newspapers have disappeared since 1954. Since 1910, the trend toward fewer competitive newspapers has been progressing. Then only 42.9 per cent of the cities were noncompetitive; today the figure is 94 per cent. Only ten years ago, there were 76 chain operations, today there are 95, controlling almost half the newspaper circulation.

Absentee owners, who naturally care more about the balance sheet than about community problems, operate nearly 400 newspapers with about a third of the daily circulation. Twenty states contain only one city where competition exists. In 1910, 689 American cities had competing dailies; there are only 75 such cities now, not counting the 20 cities where business and production departments have combined for the sake of economy, and the publishers split the profits on some basis. Since 1924 we have lost a net 833 American dailies. New ones have been started during those years, but most of them have died, too.

Daily newspaper circulation in the United States gained 1.23 per cent in 1957 over the previous year. But the percentage of gain is by no means keeping up with the population growth. In the 43 largest cities, population grew 50 per cent in 27 years; newspaper circulation grew 27 per cent. We have been running hard to do less than stand still. The eleven largest Sunday papers lost almost 3,000,000 circulation between 1947 and 1957. From 1950 through 1957, New York dailies lost 639,344 subscribers and New York Sunday newspapers lost 1,572,913.

Nor can we gain much comfort from the advertising picture.

The three and a third billion dollars invested in newspaper advertising in 1957 was more than that spent in TV, radio, magazines, and outdoor put together. But that is not the whole or the long-range story. Total newspaper revenue gained 2 per cent in 1957. Media Records' 52-city study—covering the major cities—showed a loss in linage in those markets of 2.8 per cent.

Meanwhile, here's what our competitors were doing in revenue:

Television	Up 8.7 per cent
Radio	Up 14.3 " "
Magazines	Up 4.4 " "
Direct mail	Up 5.7 " "
Miscellaneous	Up 5.1 " "
Outdoor	Up 2.2 " "

Every medium did better than newspapers.

Since television came into the picture in 1949, there has been a small but steady decline in the percentage of advertising dollars to newspapers. In 1949 we got 36.5 per cent of the advertiser's dollar; in 1957 we got only 33 per cent.

I am sorry to have used so many figures, but they are pertinent because they add up to a picture of a contracting, rather than an expanding business, with more contraction coming over a long range: to a generally static if indeed not regressive circulation in the larger cities from which people are fleeing, and a host of other problems that confront publishers.

Here I can hardly do more than name the problems, certainly not try to give the answers, which lie in some measure with individual publishers rather than in a pattern. A great many of us are resorting to expedients such as leaving classified out of some editions, narrowing and shortening the page, cutting news content, splitting editions and trying to compete with suburban papers, which have made the only major gain—approximately 914,756 in circulation in the past seven years. (Suburbanites have generally cut out one metropolitan daily and substituted the local paper that gives them news of their friends and civic interests.)

But the ultimate answer does not lie in expedients. It may conceivably lie over the long range in the English pattern of small papers with high advertising and circulation rates. I suspect that whether we go that far or not, we are going to have to forego our linage and circulation vanity and charge what newspapers are worth. Certainly the monopoly and merger trend will continue; 52 cities are ripe for one of them now.

I do not argue the inherent virtue of monopoly, because there is no virtue in it. I leave its effects to the sociologists. The question is academic anyhow, since 95 per cent of the cities already have it. Besides, there is no such thing as a monopoly of news. Metropolitan radio and television stations in combination are broadcasting almost twice as many words a week as their opposite newspapers are carrying. I wouldn't concede for a moment that what they broadcast is nearly as full or as intelligent as what we give the reader—indeed a good deal of it is repetitious, superficial headline stuff, but with all the news programs on the air, only a moron could say that he was not aware of basic information or conflicting opinion, or that monopoly was depriving him of the right to know what was going on or what other people were thinking. My only defense of monopoly and merger is that in nine cases out of ten where they have occurred the newspapers are better and stronger and more independent.

Outside forces can't be wholly blamed for the economic squeeze in which too many newspapers find themselves. The bare, bald truth is that newspapers are even further behind in research than the United States government is on missiles or basic research—they are at least a generation behind in the sort of research that would make production more efficient. There has been no major improvement in the process of printing newspapers in the past 60 years. Publishers have done precious little to help themselves.

It has been only within the past few years that the American Newspaper Publishers Association has supported a research institute, now combined with the Institute of Newspaper Operations. The merged research bureau is operating on a budget of about $350,000 a year. Let me illustrate how piddling that is in comparison with other industries. In 1957 the aviation industry spent 7 per cent of its annual take on research. If the newspapers had spent that proportion of the $5,000,000,000 they get from the reader and the advertiser, the expenditure would have been $35,000,000 instead of $350,000. We are spending 70/100 of one per cent as an industry, in addition, of course, to what individual newspapers are spending.

That's almost criminal negligence of the field in which our greatest potential for efficiency lies. Even on so small a budget, researchers have pointed the way with teletypesetters, photon-typesetting, photon, plastic plates, to savings that may be realized. And nobody has yet touched the mail room, that greedy maw which yearns for automation—that room where the practices are about the same as they were 40 years ago.

If what I have said so far sounds like a Jeremiah, I assure you that it is only because I want to be extremely realistic. If I were a young editor again, as I intend to be for a few minutes, I would still argue that our salvation lies in better, not shorter or narrower newspapers. I could be much more optimistic as an editor than I have been as a publisher painting the economic picture. I could say in all truth that while a good many newspapers will die in the next few years, those newspapers which are alert to the changing patterns of life, which recognize their primary obligations to their country, their community and their readers and undertake to fulfill them, will survive.

I believe strongly that newspapers are indispensable to the full enlightenment of the American people and that in altered form they will survive through any period in which we may be interested.

There has been, in my time, a great lift in the intellectual level of newspapers. There has been, too, a change for the better in the concept of their responsibility to the public. There is less cheapness, less tawdriness, less pandering to the baser emotions and fewer newspapers that do it than when I came along. There is more sober and generally more independent discussion of issues; there is less blatant partisanship. There is better reporting; more background information, more reporting in depth, more graphic aids for the reader. There is better packaging, as Harry Ashmore called it.

There is more concern on the part of newspapermen for their professional status. The American Society of Newspaper Editors, the AP Managing Editors, Sigma Delta Chi, and the National Conference of Editorial Writers have all tended to emphasize the more serious approach to issues and to writing. The Nieman and Reid Foundations and the American Press Institute have been most useful factors in broadening the intellectual base of newspapermen. And newspapers themselves have become more strict in their educational and character requirements.

But there is still too much superficiality, too much over-writing, too much glamorizing of bums—male and female—too little digging for background. We have not substituted the decent, well-written human-interest story for the old sob stuff. As dreadful as a great many British papers are, there are still a good many things we can learn from them, such as tight writing and the sort of profiles and light essays which make the annual edition of *The Bedside Guardian* a pure delight and an exemplar of good writing. There is an open field on American newspapers for those of you who would become Max Freedmans or Alistair Cookes.

One of the best managing editors I know claims, "There is a tendency on the part of reporters to write in 'standard' style. The accident, the robbery, the theft, the obit—all fall victims to the process of journalistic automation, what, when, where. Unfortunately the how and the why are too frequently left out. Despite all the talk of interpretive writing, the average reporter tends to write much along the line of his predecessor of a generation ago. His sentence structure is shorter, but the basic news-story construction is strikingly similar. The story with the flair is still unusual enough to catch attention. Part of this is undoubtedly due to the quality of our manpower. As has been pointed out repeatedly, we are losing far too many men to the related fields of TV, radio, press agentry and industrial journalism. A large part of this is due to money; an equally large part to the failure of most newspapers to provide either emotional stimulus or to be the opportunity for journalistic service."

And, indeed, I might add on my own as a publisher that we could make the financial inducement stronger, particularly when journalism schools are turning out more and more announcers and television writers and relatively fewer newspapermen. I distressed some of my journalism friends two years ago when I said in a speech at Michigan that a good place to begin to emphasize content rather than the techniques, and thereby improve the content, was in the journalism schools.

I know that a great many schools are gallantly resisting the trend to become trade schools; that a great many journalism schools have vastly improved and have recognized that the best basis for writing is a well-rounded liberal arts education. I should like to see all of them recast so that the techniques of journalism become incidental and the emphasis is upon making the full man intellectually, upon learning more of what to write than how to write the five W's. My ideal school of journalism would be heavy in English and English literature (I might even require Latin); in history of every kind, including archeology; some natural science and political science and economics. I might be willing to consider psychology and sociology, but only if I could find somebody who had foresworn gobbledygook and talked in plain, unprofessional English, about human relations.

The time has come for schools of journalism to become professional schools in the fullest sense. Journalism teaching has been in existence in some form for more than 50 years. Today, 109 schools are listed in the *Editor & Publisher Yearbook.* According to Dean Norval Neil Luxon, of the University of North Carolina School of Journalism, there are 62 departments and 28 schools of journalism, with the remainder listed under fifteen different designations. I heartily subscribe to Dean Luxon's suggestion—unpopular as it was with his colleagues—that the time has come for a Flexner-type study of journalism teaching. As a result of the Flexner report of 1910 "the medical profession reduced the number of colleges of medicine from 148 in that year to 81 in 1957" by setting standards and eliminating the diploma mills. The American Bar Association has done the same thing.

We are willing to pour millions into medical schools to produce people who try to cure our bodily and mental ills—and that's important—or into producing lawyers who seem to be primarily interested in protecting property rights, or in turning out engineers and scientists on a mass-production basis, but we spend precious little in producing people who have the instrument, and sometimes the will, to protect the only thing that really means anything in this hydrogen world—our freedom at home and abroad.

My greatest apprehension on the news and editorial side has been whether newspapers, which are evanescent in nature, are accepting the awful responsibility devolved upon all of them by what Alistair Cooke called "America's vaulting into the saddle of power"; whether we as newspapermen are doing all we can to tell the public the truth about what that means: what it means in terms of the missile race, the relative strength of Russia and the United States, of NATO, the Baghdad pact, foreign aid of every sort, the United Nations, reciprocal trade, colonialism, and most importantly how our own governments, local, state, and national, are run. Our obligation is primarily to a free world in which there is no foreign story; all of them are local. We may have an uneasy seat as far as world power is concerned, but the simple fact is that we do not know how easy, or uneasy, it is.

Basic to any understanding of the truth is knowing the truth. As a nation we do not know it. I am not talking about freedom of the press; I am talking about its handmaiden, freedom of information, without which freedom of the press is a mockery anyway. I confess that I have indulged, or even nurtured, a sort of cynicism toward people who talked about freedom of the press, because they abused the term. Too often it meant the right to hire newsboys under age, or be exempt from the wage-and-hour law, or have special privileges as publishers. Even so recently as 1950 when Basil Walters, Russell Wiggins, and James Pope began to pull the bell rope of warning that there was a growing suppression of information, I had a supercilious attitude of amused tolerance. I did not realize that the bell was tolling for me, too. It tolls for all of us.

The brazen defense by Attorney General Rogers of the right and the use of secrecy by executive branches before a Congressional committee week before last was matched by the chief of the Foreign Service of the Department of Commerce, who, asked whether government business was not public business, told the Moss Committee, "It is *not* and you know it." Or by the Bureau of Internal Revenue, which told an ASNE committee that inquired about the secret settlement of an Albany, New York, case involving that most heinous of all domestic crimes, the watering of whiskey by bartenders, "The transaction is primarily of interest to the individual and the government." It turned out not to be; the public got interested also when a Congressional searchlight was turned on the revenue service. One hundred and sixty-six employes were purged, sixty for dishonesty, and the chief counsel, as the committee chairman said, "took flight under painful circumstances."

But there are secrets more vital that are being withheld. The military apparently wants only the successful missile tests reported, if the Cape Canaveral agreement reflects its attitude. The AEC has been revealed within the past ten days either to have indulged in sorry deception or to have been incompetent in connection with the subterranean atomic tests. Only under the spur of Harold Stassen and Senator Humphrey did the AEC amend its week-old report that the underground test could be detected only 250 miles away. It now admits that every seismograph within a thousand miles picked up the tremor and that the Geodetic Survey station in Alaska, 2300 miles away, reported it.

Truth was important to the people in this case, because the AEC has been opposing the suspension of atomic tests on the ground that the Russians can conceal them by carrying them on underground. A Senate subcommittee has absolved the AEC of deliberate deception. We must then consider it only incompetence which remarkably coincided with the political stand of the commission chairman with regard to the suspension of atomic tests.

The combination of a lot of things—the fact that the president wasn't told the truth about the Dixon-Yates power deal; the fact that he was not even told the last paragraph of his letter to Bulganin had been eliminated, plus a good many more serious evidences of the Papa Knows Best theory of government on the part of Washington bureaucrats—led me to subscribe most heartily to what Madison said: "Nothing could be more irrational than to give the people power, and to withhold from them information without which power is abused. A people who mean to be their own governors must arm themselves with power which knowledge gives. A popular government without popular information or the means of acquiring it is but a prologue to a farce or a tragedy, or, perhaps both."

We Americans may be playing the prologue to tragedy in our ignorance of where we stand in relative strength in the world. The White House has sat on the Gaither report since last October and is still sitting on it. Thanks to the enterprise of the *Washington*

Post, and to the privately financed Rockefeller report, the public does know a great deal about our strength or weakness, as opposed to the Russians. But no thanks to our elected leaders that we do know.

From whom are we keeping secrets? The Russians certainly know what their atomic submarines, for instance, can do and apparently so do we. The information is secret only from the American people. And we do have a right to know. We have a right to a better fate than those boys who lie in the hulk of the *Arizona* at Pearl Harbor. They never knew what hit them; we have a right to know what is likely to hit us. I stood up and cheered when Inez Robb, who flung one of her best flings, said: "I am sick and tired of being treated like a moral, intellectual and political idiot by the present Administration, which has decided that my fellow citizens and I lack the character and intestinal fortitude to face the grim warning that the United States is in the gravest danger in its history."

I don't agree with Inez that the attitude is all this administration's fault. The pattern has been there since the first World War. President Eisenhower did reduce the number of agencies authorized to classify material from 45 to 17. Some minor progress has been made. But it is the *attitude* that I am talking about: an attitude of Papa Knows Best, an attitude of fear of revealing some secret, a fear that was intensified during that awful, recent period of our national life when, as Holmes said, "that faith in the universe not marked by our fears" had temporarily left us, or, as the Quakers said, "we had a spiritual failure of nerve."

It was that period and that attitude which produced such a closure of scientific information that the scientists in one branch of the American government couldn't learn what others had found out. The Moss Committee developed the fact that seven different translations of the same book were made in different departments without any of the seven knowing that any of the others was making it.

Lloyd V. Berkner, a presidential science adviser, told the House subcommittee that 90 per cent of the nation's scientific secrets should be declassified to further scientific development. The administration is just getting around to asking that scientific secrets be shared with our allies, to prevent duplication of effort and speed our defense. We tend to forget that we would benefit most from a sharing of scientific secrets with friendly governments. We should not forget that it was Einstein, Lisa Meitner, Neils Bohr, Fermi and Teller, all refugees from tyranny, who contributed most to the development of the atom and hydrogen bombs. Or that it was Von Braun who finally rescued us from the humiliation of looking for only Russian sputniks in outer space.

If we are to have intelligent public reaction to requests for foreign aid, defense and scientific education money, we have more than a right to know what we are up against. Somebody should assure the frightened bureaucrat that he doesn't have to label "top secret" what was in yesterday's *New York Times* to keep his job. A good place for that to start would be the White House.

There is still too much a hang-over of the McCarthy era for any newspaperman, or for any citizen, for that matter, to relax the vigilance which Jefferson adjured, to force the truth out of the fog of secrecy. The genius of America, as a Russian woman exile said to me, is that it is a place where the people do not fear the government and the government does not fear the people. But only the greatest frankness between them can achieve that happy state. And in that relationship, newspapers can achieve their best service. There is plenty of vital truth to be mined, but not by reporters who regard the handout as gospel or a press club bar as an ideal base of operations.

"The gallery in which the reporters sit has become a fourth estate of the realm," Lord Macaulay said. "The publication of debates, a practice which seems to the most liberal statesmen of the old school full of danger to the great safeguards of liberty, is now regarded by many persons as a safeguard tantamount, and more than tantamount, to all the rest together."

The Built-in Bias of the Press

ROBERT FULFORD [APRIL 1962

Mr. Fulford, book and art critic of the *Toronto Daily Star,* gave this paper before the Winter Conference of the Canadian Institute on Public Affairs, in Toronto, February 17, 1962. The University of Toronto Press published the proceedings of the conference as *The Press and the Public* (1962).

My observation is that there is no Canadian community which is as dull as the newspapers which it reads. In general, I believe, English-Canadian newspapers follow rather than lead their readers, and I want to explore the possible reasons for this. Some of them are built-in tendencies of the press everywhere, tendencies which should be resisted; others are peculiar to Canadian communities. Now, my own feelings about newspapers are a mixture of pride and dissatisfaction, of love and hate. I have some intimate associations with newspapers. My great-grandfather edited copy in New York and in London, Ontario; my father was a newspaperman all his life; I started to work on a Toronto paper when I was seventeen; my wife and both her parents were reporters or editors. I read newspapers incessantly—newspapers from Canada, from England, from the United States. I sometimes pick up newspapers in languages I will never read, like Yiddish or Dutch, just to admire their typography or their illustrations. When I speak of daily newspapers I speak out of love; I can't imagine a world without them.

But I can imagine a Canada in which newspapers will play a more valuable role in the activities of the community.

In all the most obvious ways, newspapers serve their communities admirably. Charities couldn't exist without the pressure of daily newspapers; and building drives, like those for universities, regularly use the daily papers to create the proper climate for the extraction of money from the reluctant rich. The externals of politics and business are, I believe, fairly well covered and certainly our political system could not exist without the papers.

But in the less obvious ways, Canadian newspapers give less service than they could. One of the central reasons for this is the built-in bias of the press, a bias which has nothing to do with party political loyalty. Both the structure of the press and the character of the men who staff the newspapers force the press to lean in one direction, and only the most persistent and vigorous opposition can offset this.

The bias I refer to is in the direction of Authority, and in this case Authority means anything which is organized, which has a name, and which gives speeches. This bias is by now so natural and so much a characteristic of the press that it is rarely even mentioned. The bias may be towards industry, trade unions, department stores, governments, or cultural institutions.

In covering the news in all these fields the press tends—to what I believe is a harmful degree—to take its cues from established Authority. Because of the way newspapers are put out, both the news columns and the minds of the newspapermen are dominated by articulate opinion. On the most basic level it is much easier to cover a speech or rewrite a publicity release than to do a dozen interviews. It is much easier to accept conventional wisdom than to challenge it. And what is easier soon becomes what is natural; and this is the pattern of newspapers.

Murray Kempton, columnist for the *New York Post,* recently pointed out that one reason for this bias in American newspapers is the fact that journalists get their early training as police reporters. On the police beat you naturally look to Authority—the sergeant of detectives—for all the facts. You don't expect the criminal to have an opinion. This respect for Authority begins as an unfortunate necessity, develops into a habit, and ends by becoming a part of the reporter's personality. When he becomes an editor or a publisher, he becomes part of Authority himself, and this only increases his affection and respect for those people with titles, offices, and press agents.

In a country dominated by its middle class, where all our important institutions reflect a middle-class point of view, the newspaperman is now pre-eminently a middle-class citizen. His attitude is not far from that of the dead-center suburbanite—that is, again, an attitude which looks to organizations.

One of my favorite examples of the attitude I am talking about is the treatment of the automobile in Canadian newspapers in the last ten years. All around us, an important battle has been fought between the motor car and the pedestrian on one level and, on another level, between the superhighway and the public transportation system. It is my own opinion that in this case the middle class has fought the lower class and has won. But whether you agree with that or not, it would be hard to deny that this battle has been fought. It was one of the most spectacular social facts of the 1950's. Yet as I read the newspapers during that period I rarely saw this reported or commented on. The reason is that many people speak for the private automobile side of the question; and until recently very few people spoke for the other side; therefore, no contest. The newspapers were unable to report the anti-automobile view because that view was not organized and articulated.

In the same field, another development of the 1950's impressed me as significant. The North American newspapers I read during the last decade acquiesced in the development of the Detroit automobile. The auto makers were able to create a climate in which it was possible to produce, and sell in large numbers, monstrous machines which were frequently as dangerous as they were inefficient. It is true, of course, that the influence of newspapers in this regard was not nearly as great as that of automobile advertising itself. But to the extent that the newspapers refused for some years to criticize the Detroit cars, and frequently helped to publicize them, the newspapers were of assistance to the auto makers. Again, the auto makers were organized; consumers were not. It is too facile to say that this happened because automobile companies advertise. It would have happened, I think, whether advertised or not, simply as a result of the newspapers' tendency to adjust to organized opinion and to the status quo in whatever field they cover.

If it is natural for middle-class newspapermen to react in this way, then it is equally natural for them to become deeply and personally involved with the politicians and other officials they see regularly. This tendency has produced a special kind of newspaperman. An example is the sports writer who becomes so involved in friendship and professional association with the people he covers that he adopts their point of view entirely.

This is a tendency which is not limited to sports writers. Some years ago I worked with a reporter who had covered politics for a good many years. He knew more politicians than anyone else on our paper, and he was widely respected by both the politicians and his colleagues. But in the several years I knew him he did not write one story which would cause any discomfort to a politician. He simply covered the public meetings, and after a while he grew to be on such intimate terms with his subjects that he could no more attack them than he could criticize his children in public.

This friend of mine adopted without question the standards and opinions of those he was covering rather than investigating and challenging them. He was following a general tendency to its logical conclusion. Newspapers, which are rightly proud to be, as they say, "part of the community," sometimes grow so close to the community's dominant public values that they resemble house organs of official opinion. Because it is the easiest way, they adopt the standards of the community rather than try to shape them. This tendency is found in its most critical form in newspapers whose executives are deeply involved in public community activities, ranging from universities to football teams and from hospitals to television stations. It doesn't much matter whether the publisher has taken up these activities for pleasure, for money, or for the greater good of the humanity. In any case his presence on a board of directors inhibits or distorts the newspaper's coverage of the activities which those directors direct.

These are some of the reasons why newspapers tend to report and comment within the generally accepted public terms of reference. Politics, in the newspapers, means party politics. Culture means what the National Ballet Guild is doing. Social welfare means the annual report of the city welfare department. Labor means strikes and threatened strikes. This policy of concentrating on official action affects newspapers' judgment of what is news. For most papers and press services, the main news consists of shooting and voting, and secondary news consists of official statements. This leads to a kind of narrowness which chokes off news and comment on a large part of humanity. A newspaper, I think, should be a report and a comment on what the world is doing, not on what its elected officials are saying.

Consider the treatment of social welfare issues in our newspapers. Except in rare cases, this subject is handled either by political writers, who report on how it looks from parliament or city hall, or by feature writers, who manage to deal with the human beings involved but who are expected to glide easily from a story about starving children to a nice light piece about interior decoration. The country crawls with newspapermen who specialize in reporting on various political assemblies. But it has few or none who are competent to give an expert opinion on pensions, health insurance, mothers' allowances, and other aspects of social welfare. It seems to me that a change in pension legislation or educational subsidies can mean more to many of us than a rumor of a change in the federal cabinet.

Or consider an entirely different field, equally important to our sense of community: the arts. To many newspapers, both here and abroad, the whole field of culture remains a hopeless enigma. In most newspapers, literature and the arts are given a few meager columns of material produced by writers who are usually even duller than those who write the editorials. This is not because of a lack of talent but because of an attitude toward the arts which was outdated long ago. The attitude is one of quiet respect for a rather dull old aunt. Newspapers believe that the arts are a habit of the well-to-do. There may have been some truth to this a few decades ago, but it has very little relevance now.

The citizens of a community, who indirectly employ the newspapermen among them, have a right to expect that newspapermen will be more conscious of what is happening around them than the average citizen can be. This is, after all, the newspaperman's profession: Not to know what is happening is probably the only real crime he can commit. But in some fields, it appears to me, the people who work on newspapers lag behind the general community. In the last decade, as we have been remaking and enormously expanding several Canadian cities, architecture has become a more and more important factor in our lives. My own experience suggests that the community as a whole has come gradually to understand this fact, but the newspapers have barely heard of it.

Some of these shortcomings are known all too well to newspapermen, but there is one problem which we find hard to recognize and even harder to understand. This is the frequent breakdown in communications between newspaperman and reader. The newspaper is primarily a medium of communication, and it should be as direct a medium as possible. Yet every newspaperman has had the unsettling experience of meeting an apparently attentive reader who has misunderstood what he has read, or has somehow managed to avoid grasping the central point of a major issue. In the papers major stories are sometimes hinted at first, then blown up to flare headline size, then dropped to minor headline size, then eliminated entirely. The result is that readers can easily be left wondering whatever happened to the Suez Canal, or how the controversy about report cards actually came out, or what, in the end, really did happen during the Commonwealth conference at Accra. It seems likely to me that readers are often left without a coherent view of an important event, even when they have followed it fairly closely and even when there is a coherent view to be had.

Confronted with the fact of noncommunication, and with the blanks in coverage, newspapermen can fall back easily on their inherent difficulties. We can cite the near impossibility of getting out a paper every day, we can tell how the news on some days seems to push the editor around, we can plead lack of space, time, and talent. These are all pleasant rationalizations—that is, evidences of self-satisfaction.

This leaves us with the newspapers we have, and we can either live with them as they are or find ways to improve them. I believe that within the newspaper business itself there is a profound current of discontent, and that this is leading to important changes. Newspapers have seen the need for better writers and editors, and unions have helped them to see the need to pay the salaries which a better class of employees demands. Newspapers, confronted with television, have also slowly come to see the need to provide something more than the facts; the background of a story is more important now than it has been in the past, and in their different ways the three Toronto papers, for instance, have made vigorous efforts in this direction. But a newspaper, like any other institution, can only serve its community if the community responds to it intelligently.

Obviously, the number of people who buy a paper constitute the main response, and there is nothing discouraging in the circulation figures of those papers—here, in England, and in the United States—which have tried to present broader and more searching material to their readers.

Beyond circulation figures, however, a community can respond to its newspaper in forceful and effective ways. The late Albert Camus was pointing in this direction when he proposed a sort of antinewspaper: a paper to come out every day, after all the others have been published, comparing and criticizing their various accounts of the day's news. It seems hardly likely that such an institution could be established; after all, who would pay for it? But Camus' central idea—that there should be some form of check on the press—is still useful.

In this connection I would like to make two proposals. The first is a general one: that more people in the professional and academic communities take a serious interest in the newspapers which are helping to shape the larger community in which we all live, and that they indicate this interest in public. If a newspaper can criticize the president of a university, as it does, then why can't the university president criticize the newspaper? The fact that most editors shriek like wounded bears when anyone suggests they are less than perfect should deter only the faint-hearted.

My second proposal is more specific. In Toronto one organization we cherish is called the Association of Women Electors. The members of this group make it their business to scrutinize carefully the activities of municipal government and occasionally to make recommendations for new legislation. I think it would be very helpful if similar citizens' groups were to appoint themselves to scrutinize the press. It would make all of us pretty uncomfortable at times, but I think we could stand it. A similar organization or committee might function on a national scale, perhaps as part of a larger group. In this way criticism of the press would be rooted in the community rather than limited to occasional magazine articles or TV shows or conferences. The press badly needs disinterested criticism. It is my hope, as a newspaperman and as a reader of newspapers and as a citizen, that we can develop a new critical response to newspapers in which our great daily papers can be viewed at least as critically as they themselves view the rest of the world.

Fewer Papers Means Better Papers

JOHN COWLES [JULY 1951

This article is based on an address at the University of Missouri, which had awarded its 1951 medal for distinguished service in journalism to the Minneapolis *Star* and *Tribune,* published by Mr. Cowles.

Newspaper standards of editorial objectivity and fairness and integrity are immeasurably higher than they were a generation ago.

During the last thirty years, newspaper publishing costs have steadily mounted and at an accelerated rate. The survival of marginal papers has become increasingly difficult and will become more so.

In addition to rising publishing costs, however, it has been the public itself which has dictated the reduction in the number of newspapers. As the public acquired many more sources than formerly from which it received information and news—radio, news magazines, news letters, labor union papers, etc.—the public tended to concentrate its newspaper reading on whatever was the best afternoon paper and the best morning paper in each community. As a result, the poorer and weaker papers simply could not survive.

In a highly thoughtful speech last March, Secretary of Commerce Sawyer said that in 1910 when the United States had a population of 92 million we had 2,600 daily newspapers. Today with a population of 150 million, we have 1,772 dailies.

In discussing the trend toward fewer newspapers, Secretary Sawyer made the following statements: "An examination of the consolidation phenomenon indicates that it is due largely to increased costs of operation—especially the cost of labor and newsprint. In many cases the choice was combination or bankruptcy. In my opinion such combinations as have occurred have not resulted in deterioration of product. Some of our greatest newspapers exist in towns where the ownership is limited to one firm. The Minneapolis *Star* and *Tribune,* the Louisville *Courier-Journal,* the Atlanta *Constitution* and *Journal,* the Kansas City *Star* and *Times* are examples."

Although many people wring their hands in sorrow whenever there is a newspaper suspension or merger, I want to say emphatically that I think the trend toward fewer and better daily newspapers has been clearly beneficial to the people of this country. But, whether one thinks it is beneficial or harmful is immaterial. As a practical matter, there are going to be many more consolidations and suspensions in the next few years, and the total number of daily newspapers in America is going to decline further. But that does not mean that the number and variety of the sources of information and opinion will be reduced.

Actually, I am convinced that where newspapers have combined or suspended and single-ownership newspaper cities or fields have evolved, the resulting product has, in almost every instance, been superior to the newspapers that preceded it.

I say flatly that with only a small number of exceptions the best newspapers in America are those which do not have a newspaper competing with them in their local field. By best I mean the most responsibly edited, the fairest, the most complete, the most accurate, the best written, and the most objective.

The *Milwaukee Journal* is alone in the afternoon field in Milwaukee. With the two possible exceptions of St. Louis and Washington, is there an afternoon paper with local competition anywhere in the country that compares in high quality with the *Milwaukee Journal?* I know of none.

Again excluding St. Louis and Washington, and always New York, which is an exception, there aren't a handful of newspapers published anywhere else in the United States that, in my judgment, are as responsibly and well edited, as complete, as fair, as objective, and which serve the public interest as well as do at least forty or fifty newspapers which are published in so-called monopoly or single-ownership cities.

These newspaper institutions which have no local daily competition are not monopolies in the sense that they control the sole source from which the public gets its news and information and ideas. It is impossible to overemphasize this point. There are dozens of sources—radio, television, news magazines, labor papers, community papers, outside dailies, etc.—which also provide them.

The reasons why the newspapers that do not have local daily

newspaper competition in their home field are superior, generally speaking, to those that do have competition are manifold.

In the first place, the publishers and editors have, I believe, a deeper feeling of responsibility because they are alone in their field.

Secondly, those newspapers that are not in hotly competitive fields are better able to resist the constant pressure to oversensationalize the news, to play up the cheap crime or sex story, to headline the story that will sell the most copies instead of another story that is actually far more important. The daily that is alone in its field can be as free as it wants to be from the urge to magnify the tawdry and salacious out of its importance in the news of the day. The newspaper that is alone in its field can present the news in better perspective and can free the news of details which pander rather than inform.

Newspapers that don't have local newspaper competition are better able to resist the pressure of immediacy which makes for incomplete, shoddy and premature reporting. It breeds inaccuracies which can never be overtaken. It is responsible for a distorted emphasis and lack of perspective. The newspaper in a single ownership city doesn't have to rush on to the streets with a bulletin rumor that Russian troops are invading Yugoslavia if it has reason to suspect that the unconfirmed report may not be true. It does not have to protect itself against a rival in case the story turns out by a long-shot chance to be accurate. Newspapers in single ownership cities can be, and usually are, less inhibited about correcting their errors adequately, fully and fairly.

And if a "monopoly newspaper" is really bad, then it won't last as a monopoly. New competition by abler and more socially moral newspapermen will eventually displace and supersede it.

I referred to New York as being an exception to the condition I was describing. This is because New York has such a huge population that it can profitably support many different types of daily publications. Smaller cities can't.

In my opinion, the great mistake in the Hutchins Commission report on "A Free and Responsible Press" was its assumption that restoration of local daily competition was the only answer to the need for more responsible journalism. I think much in the Hutchins Commission report was excellent, but its basic premise was completely erroneous. As a newspaperman who has had many years' experience in both hotly competitive and in single-ownership cities, I am convinced that an increase in the number of competing dailies would have precisely the opposite effect from the one the Hutchins Commission assumed. Secondly, newspaper competition as it existed in the U.S. when newspapers were virtually the only medium of information and opinion is simply not going to return. There are going to be fewer, not more, newspapers.

I agree thoroughly with the implication contained in the Hutchins Report that unless the press generally manifests more self-discipline and shows more obvious concern for the genuine public interest than some papers show, the dangers of restrictions upon our free press are very real.

Although I accept the view of the American Society of Newspaper Editors that it would be unwise for the ASNE to create an agency to sit in judgment upon the performance of the American press, I think there is a widespread need for more self-examination on the part of American newspapers. I welcome the idea of more critical studies of the press, if made in good faith by competent, independent agencies.

We in Minneapolis have given a lot of thought to the possibility of creating an independent agency that would continuously examine how well the Minneapolis newspapers were performing their functions and fulfilling their obligations to the people of the Upper Midwest. We would be happy regularly to publish the full reports of such an agency, detailing its opinions as to our specific sins of omission or commission. The great difficulty that has so far thwarted our setting up such an agency is the finding of competent personnel in whom the general reading public would have complete confidence and who would, at the same time, know the practical problems and difficulties of metropolitan newspaper operations. If anyone has any constructive ideas in this regard I would be happy to have them.

Can a Yellow Rag Change Its Color?

MAX HALL [MARCH 1964

Mr. Hall, after his Hearst chapter, served the Associated Press in Washington nine years, interrupted by a Nieman Fellowship, 1949–50. He is now editor for the social sciences, Harvard University Press.

During my first ten years after college, 1932 to 1942, I worked on two Hearst papers. Each, in an earlier period, had sought circulation by noisy and sometimes questionable methods. Each, in my time, was trying to build more solidly by winning the respect of the community, especially the portion that buys advertising space. Each paper now is dead. One of them was the *Atlanta Georgian* & *Sunday American,* the other the *New York Mirror.*

Hearst had invaded Atlanta in 1912. A friend of mine recalls a day when a *Georgian* newsboy, "Foots" Guthas (who later became the paper's street-sales boss), sprinted down the middle of Euclid Avenue bellowing "Oh how horrible" in frightful tones. On that occasion a homicide of major interest had just occurred, but the *Georgian* did not require a murder case for its daily explosion of excitement. On a dull day a prowler in the basement of Tenth Street School, who was persuaded to leave by Jackson, the janitor, before he molested any of us children (if indeed he had this in mind), was awarded his Gothic eight-column banner. The city's residential neighborhoods were haunted by the chilling cry of "extra, extra" in the night. People learned that the shouts were often the equivalent of "wolf, wolf"—but, then, one never knew for sure.

In daily circulation the *Georgian* never did catch its two rivals. The figures in Ayer's *American Newspaper Annual & Directory* show that in 1937, the *Georgian* attained 93,000; but by then the other afternoon paper, the *Journal,* had risen to 107,000 and the morning paper, the *Constitution,* to 109,000. True, the Sunday situation was different. The *Sunday American,* powered by Hearst's *American Weekly* and comic section, had an awesome figure of 180,000, far ahead of the other two papers. But in neither daily nor Sunday circulation was the Hearst paper growing as fast as the other two, and it fell harder than they in the newspaper slump of 1938. Advertising revenues, as always, were disappointing, and in 1939 the Hearst organization sold out to James M. Cox of Ohio. He promptly killed the paper and took some of its best people and syndicated features to the *Journal,* which he had also acquired, and which now made a startling leap in circulation. (Governor Cox later bought the *Constitution* too, and by 1961 the *Journal* had 258,000 daily circulation, the *Constitution* 201,000, and the combined *Sunday Journal & Constitution* 499,000.)

A great irony of the situation is that the *Georgian* of the 1930's, under the respected publisher Herbert Porter, who had been hired away from the *Constitution,* had the best staff in town. At least we were in no doubt of it at the time, and, looking back, I am still convinced it was true. Tarleton Collier, Dudley Glass, Harold Martin, and many other gifted people kept the place humming. The sports editor, Ed Danforth, besides being something of a genius at the typewriter, was a one-man journalism school, peopling the paper with his graduates.

But the *Georgian,* despite its talented people and its superior spirit of enterprise, had three major disabilities. First, it printed Hearst editorials and went along with Hearst biases, and therefore found it hard to overcome the stigma of an alien, absentee influence that didn't really "belong." Second, it was weak in news originating outside Georgia, having no wire service but International News Service. And third, it was still commonly regarded as a sensational rag.

The lengths to which the paper went to rise above its past were sometimes amusing. I remember editing a lengthy I.N.S. story about a celebrated murder in Chicago or somewhere. Carrying out orders, I carefully removed the bloodiest passages, toning down the account as befitted the nicest family newspaper. The next morning the conservative old *Constitution* (where Ralph McGill was then sports editor), under a gray little headline on the front page, routinely printed an Associated Press story containing all the gore that I had mopped out of our story. I doubt that anyone accused the *Constitution* of being offensive, or noticed our righteous backward-leaning-over posture. After all, the *Georgian* still had a lively makeup with big clear pictures and readable type. People just wouldn't believe that it had reformed.

In 1937, two years before the *Georgian* was unmercifully put to sleep, I moved to New York. There, I began serving what would turn out to be a five-year term on the *Mirror,* the tabloid morning paper which, from the mid-1930's to its death in 1963, had the second highest newspaper circulation in the country, and yet never really emerged from the shadow of the paper that had the highest, the *Daily News.*

By 1937 the *Mirror,* like the *Georgian,* was trying to make people believe that it was no longer a yellow rag. I was given a "taboo list." For example, the word "nude" must not appear in the paper. "Naked" wouldn't do, either; "unclad" was the word we always used. "Rape" was strictly outlawed in our shop—a special inconvenience in view of the ambiguity of the words we were forced to use, "attack" and "assault." Louis Lyons recalls that another paper where "rape" was in disfavor once reported that a woman was murdered but not "criminally assaulted"; I am sure such absurdities must have appeared in the *Mirror* too. We were also forbidden to use the words "gossip" and "scandal." Even the word "rumor" was scrupulously changed to "report."

The *Mirror* of 1937, of course, had not turned its back on crime, sex, and folly. A slain unclad female was almost as welcome in its columns as a slain nude one had been earlier. "Balm suits" and other misfortunes of flashy persons were chronicled, often in a tongue-in-cheek sort of way.

Nevertheless, the *Mirror* had unmistakably entered a new era. The legendary Arthur Brisbane, who forty years before had been the principal founding father of the crime-and-underwear school of journalism, was gone. He had died at the end of 1936, having anticlimaxed his life during its next-to-last year by assuming personal command of the *Mirror* in a furious unsuccessful effort to achieve a million circulation as a trophy for the Lord of San Simeon. In Brisbane's place, Charles B. McCabe, a different kind of publisher, who had been hired away from the Denver *Rocky Mountain News* at age 36, was trying to make the paper a more attractive advertising medium. Circulation was still passionately desired, but there were fewer stunts, somewhat less sex and degeneracy, and an increasing effort to report the news that happened outside the tabloidal milieu.

It was not until 1941, when Emile Gauvreau published his fascinating book *My Last Million Readers* (E. P. Dutton & Co.), that I had any clear idea of what the *Mirror* was like in the period before I joined it. Gauvreau had organized the *Evening Graphic* for Bernarr Macfadden in 1924 and had conducted it in a struggle against Hearst's *Journal* until 1929, when he quit because, he said, all he could see ahead for the *Graphic* was a long period of financial drain. This paper, generally considered the most contemptible of all tabloids, faced the same problem as other sensational papers whose owners did not want to lose money forever. Gauvreau wrote, "When to tone down its sensationalism with the assurance that the paper still would hold a half-million readers and appease the advertisers was a problem I was no longer able to judge. Pulitzer had accomplished it although he had never aroused the wrath which had come down upon us." Gauvreau then served from 1929 to 1935 as editor of the *Mirror,* which, like the *Graphic,* had started life in 1924 and was a heavy loser.

Hearst had founded the *Mirror* in imitation of the *News,* whose readership had been growing fantastically ever since its beginning in 1919. The *Mirror,* too, grew fast by ordinary standards, but neither Gauvreau's predecessors nor Gauvreau himself could prevent the *News* from widening its lead. Toward the end of 1934, with the *Mirror* nearing 600,000 and the *News* over a million and a half, the Old Master came in with fanfare as Gauvreau's boss. Brisbane, now almost 70, succeeded Albert J. Kobler as publisher. His goal was a million at the very least. According to Gauvreau, he spoke of the circulation records he had broken on the *Journal* during the Spanish-American War, smashed a massive fist on Gauvreau's desk, and said, "By God, if they want slush today, they're going to get it!"

Apparently they got it, but the circulation did not increase very fast during Brisbane's tenure, except temporarily during the kidnap trial of Bruno Richard Hauptmann. Even worse, some advertisers didn't care for the "slush," and Brisbane was caught in the dilemma of trying to appeal to a mass audience and appease businessmen at the same time. Gauvreau reported that Brisbane once told him in a memorandum: "Will you inform the editor of the pink edition that we would make a better impression on business people if we had left out last night's picture of the lady who keeps a 'gay house' in Chicago. At least off the front page. Also she is hellishly ugly. Let us print photographs of as FEW prostitutes as possible unless they commit an interesting murder, or otherwise force themselves into the news, as they are bound to do. I see also that the *News* used the word ADULTERER in a headline. Let them have it. That sort of thing will swing the church over to us. Stories of vice we want to tell coldly. By that I don't mean that we have to leave out the interesting facts, but we shouldn't tell the reader about it as though we were *enjoying* it."

But this virtuous behavior, like our substitution of "unclad" for "nude," must have been lost on the business people. According to Gauvreau, Brisbane later showed him a letter from Kenneth Collins, an executive of Gimbel Brothers, saying: "I was shocked at the preoccupation of the *Mirror* with nothing but cheap scandal, murder and arson." Collins listed some stories of degenerate crime he found in the *Mirror* and contrasted these with the important national and world news he found on the front page of the *Times* the same day. "I have a genuine interest in the success of the *Mirror* and, incidentally, a certain concern over a number of advertising failures we have had in the past few days from the paper. I believe that ideas of cheap sensationalism are still motivating most of your writers."

Gauvreau said Brisbane assumed the attitude of a misunderstood prophet, as follows: "The trouble with these people is that they don't know our problems. I should like to see THEM try to get a million readers with such news as they describe. They ought to know that when I get a million and a half more readers I'll tone the whole thing down, make room for more advertising and be smug like Captain Patterson. Pulitzer did it. He was yellower than Hearst, once, but now they're canonizing him. This is pure hypocrisy!"

In the light of this history it is no wonder that the *Mirror* of the late 1930's had quieted down. But, as the decade drew toward a close, another big reason for the changing emphasis was that even tabloid readers were becoming more interested in news from abroad and from Washington. Hitler's aggressions, Munich, the Hitler-Stalin pact, and the outbreak of war in Europe pre-empted more and more of the meager space in what was, after all, a rather small paper. The *Mirror,* unlike the *Georgian,* had plenty of external news facilities; indeed it was the only paper in New York that could boast of having all three wire services, the Associated Press, United Press, and International News Service. True, the I.N.S. was as often a handicap as a help, for there was a standing order that at least one of the five or six major wire-service stories of the day must be an I.N.S. story. This order was hard to obey, and sometimes was *not* obeyed, for the I.N.S., though it had a few stars, was generally weak on news coverage and furthermore tended to use language like: "Moving swiftly to launch a sweeping drive along a far-flung front." One of its favorite phrases was "in the wake of," and it was always reporting that somebody "moved" to do something instead of saying specifically what *was done*. But we were able to put together from all three sources a good daily account of the war news, concise, exciting, and readable.

An echo of the earlier *Mirror*—an instance of making and manipulating news rather than only reporting it—occurred when the gangster Lepke gave himself up after jumping bail and hiding out for two years. Early in the evening of August 24, 1939, Glenn Neville, our able night news editor, told me that Lepke had surrendered, that Walter Winchell had the news exclusively, and that I was to write the story under Winchell's by-line. We had nothing but two or three facts phoned in by Winchell and some clippings from the files. My lead was:

> By Walter Winchell
>
> Louis (Lepke) Buchalter, ruler of the rackets, abdicated last night. He surrendered to Head G–Man J. Edgar Hoover in New York City and was placed in the Federal Detention Pen.

As Neville took each paragraph from my typewriter and sent it to the composing room, I kept pounding:

> The long-sought racketeer, termed Public Enemy No. 1 by District Attorney Tom Dewey but only No. 4 on Mr. Hoover's list, said he had never left New York State.

And so on. Most of the rest was from the clips, concerning Lepke's career and the charges against him. It was a large beat for Winchell and the *Mirror*. Later that night the other papers got the story when the FBI announced the surrender. But Winchell kept us ahead by writing an insert to my story giving some exclusive details on how Lepke looked and what he said to the G–Men. Hoover at a press conference commented mysteriously that Winchell had been of considerable assistance in leading to Lepke's apprehension. Winchell, when questioned by other reporters, said, "No comment."

Twenty-four hours later the truth came out. Winchell broke another exclusive story telling how Lepke had actually surrendered. The racketeer, fearing that the FBI would shoot him down like Dillinger, had arranged to meet Winchell on a street corner, and Winchell had taken him to Hoover. Thus did the *Mirror,* with the cooperation of Winchell's friend Hoover, get two days' mileage out of one day's exclusive.

Such journalism, however, belonged to an era that seemed practically over, mourned by some newspapermen, not by others. Even the news of Lepke's surrender could not dominate the paper as it would have done earlier. By the final edition the line LEPKE SURRENDERS at the top of page 1 had to share honors with a three-line head in much bigger type: 'NO WAR' F.D. PLEA TO POLES AND HITLER, and still another that said GERMANY POISED TO STRIKE.

The staff of the *Mirror* in the late 1930's was a strange mixture. To me the extremes of the spectrum were occupied by Dan Parker, the brilliant sports writer, and Nick Kenny, the so-called radio columnist, who devoted himself to tin pan alley and put one, two, or three exclamation points after his sentences. The paper had a number of superlative writers and skilled desk men. It also had hacks and phonies and nepotists and persons of the sort that would later write *U.S.A. Confidential* and similar books. There were young men on the way toward better surroundings, older men from the *Mirror* of yesteryear, still older men from pre-tabloid times, cynics, Communists, Communist-haters, and even some (I imagine) who agreed with the paper's editorials. The city room was a place of a good deal of tension and antagonism. It seemed to me that very few of this motley assemblage really had any respect for the paper or its top editors during that period.

Some of my most vivid memories are of small incidents. Once, when I was on the copy desk, perhaps a bit over-aggressive because I knew I looked much younger than my twenty-seven years, I was publicly denounced by Howard Shelley—a beefy red-faced man who wrote the society column under the name "Barclay Beekman"—for changing the word "domicile" to "home." When I argued back he drew himself up and said, "I'll have you know I have two master's degrees!" I also remember coldly ripping to pieces, day after day, what seemed to me the wretched copy of a man named Sam Boal; a few years later, when articles by him began appearing in the *New Yorker,* I wondered whether my pencil had been too heavy. I was again bawled out in the city room, this time by John McNulty during an argument over what I maintained was a grammatical error in Dan Parker's column; but McNulty the next day admitted he was wrong.

After I moved to the rewrite staff, I learned to play chess from Pete DuBerg, a thin young man with a bushy black mustache who told me that he had suddenly become fed up with Yale University while crossing the campus with an armful of books, and had deposited the books in a nearby mailbox and walked away, never to return. I will never forget writing a story that began with the following sentence, spread over five columns: "The astounding Dr. Jekyll-and-Mr. Hyde career of F. Donald Coster, indicted president of the $80,000,000 McKesson & Robbins, Inc., giant drug, liquor and chemicals concern, was exposed last night when he was revealed as Philip Musica, notorious ex-convict and swindler of pre-war years." Nor will I forget being in the first press plane to spot the *Queen Elizabeth* on her secret maiden crossing of the Atlantic; collaborating with Edward O. (Ted) Berkman on a short story which, to our surprise, no magazine accepted; and being sent to the anteroom to represent the managing editor in greeting the angry family (mostly oversized males) of a decedent, not yet buried, whom the *Mirror* had incorrectly identified as a principal figure in a famous police corruption scandal of an earlier era. After I had served on telegraph and makeup and had become night news editor, I was impressed with the unusual talents of our rewrite man named Jim Bishop, who spent his spare time in the back of the room reading Sandburg's *Lincoln;* I thought of this later when his *The Day Lincoln Was Shot* was published.

I know little about the last twenty-one years of the *Mirror* before its death on October 16, 1963; for I joined the Washington bureau of the Associated Press in 1942 and never entered the *Mirror's* premises again, nor even looked at a copy of the paper more than once or twice. Apparently it expired of an aggravation of its old ailment—inability to convince advertisers that they needed to buy large space in both the *News* and the *Mirror*. The second biggest newspaper circulation in American history did not mean very much in terms of profits so long as *the* competitor stayed so far ahead. The million daily circulation that Brisbane had coveted finally came in 1947, but by then the *Daily News* had 2,400,000. In the same year the *Sunday News* led the *Sunday Mirror* 4,700,000 to 2,200,000. Both the *News* and the *Mirror* declined gradually in circulation between 1948 and 1963. The *Mirror* is said to have lost 85,000 in the 1963 newspaper strike; by September its circulation was 834,743 daily.

My experience on Hearst papers in Atlanta and New York convinced me that once a paper dyed itself yellow, it was liable to remain yellow in the eyes of the community, regardless of its efforts to change. Perhaps a really drastic change, a noticeable metamorphosis to a different sort of newspaper, could have erased the old image—but wouldn't the old circulation have fallen away, and could it be replaced?

I do not claim to have made a thorough study of the fate of America's sensational papers, which, as everyone knows, are no longer the factor in national life that they used to be. But at least the hypothesis of fade-proof yellow should be tested by reference to two papers already mentioned, Joseph Patterson's *News* and Joseph Pulitzer's *World*.

Patterson himself has been quoted as saying, "The *Daily News* was built on legs, but when we got enough circulation we draped them." I am not sure at what period this draping is supposed to have taken place, and I don't know enough about the newspaper business in New York in the last twenty years to evaluate the effects of the draping. To the degree that this super-tabloid has freed itself from association in the public mind with crime, sex, and gossip, I suppose it was helped by the excesses—and the names—of its imitators in the 1920's and 1930's. With William Randolph Hearst and Bernarr Macfadden available as scapegoats, advertisers could with more comfort put their money into exposure to the *News's* multitudes. Whether or not the *News* has really overcome its original image, though, is not so important as the fact that its sheer power made draping of the legs not only more feasible but also less necessary. The *News* rushed so fast into so huge a vacuum in 1919, got such a formidable head start, and stayed so far ahead that no rival could compete as an advertising medium to reach that sort of reader.

The case of Pulitzer seems clearer. The *World* unmistakably won much respect in the twentieth century after giving the impression in the middle 1890's—in the words of Don C. Seitz in his *Joseph Pulitzer, His Life and Letters* (Simon & Schuster, 1924)—that it "must be conducted by a combination of ghouls and perverts." Some of the circumstances that enabled Pulitzer to get away with it are, it seems to me, as follows:

Pulitzer, though hated by some, never became the symbol of infamy that Hearst did. Pulitzer, though he can't escape responsibility for his paper's excesses, at least did not plan them so deliberately, and indeed was not personally on the scene when they took place. They were engineered mainly by Brisbane; and Brisbane, after Pulitzer in alarm clamped severe restrictions on him, went over to Hearst, who gave him more leeway. Pulitzer was willing and able to take a cut in circulation and build it back later. The *World's* editorial page excited the admiration of intellectuals and helped to dim the memories of yellow journalism. Pulitzer continued to put out a live, aggressive paper, saying, "No paper can be great, in my opinion, if it depends simply upon the hand-to-mouth idea, news coming in anyhow." But—get this—he took care, especially on the *Morning World,* to reduce the size of the headlines.

In that connection a memorandum Pulitzer wrote on December 5, 1899, as quoted by Seitz, is illuminating: "I think both the bigamy story on Saturday (outside column, first page) and the Beecher story, same place Monday, may be good, but the four column head bad anyhow. It distinctly tends to lower the tone of the paper and to revive the idea of sensationalism, the giving of the foremost place and extraordinary headlines to what is, after all, a salacious story and not an important or serious matter. I think it tends towards the other extreme—sensationalism—and although the wisdom of placing such stories in the most important column is a question, there is no question about the four column headline being *bad.*"

So maybe the real secret of getting rid of old yellow-stain is: (1) publish a good newspaper; (2) change the typography; (3) not be named Hearst.

The Newspaperman

WILLIAM M. PINKERTON [APRIL 1947 TO JANUARY 1948

This piece consists of excerpts from a series of four articles by William M. Pinkerton published in consecutive issues, April 1947 to January 1948. But they were written six years earlier, when, as a Nieman Fellow studying sociology under Professor Talcott Parsons, Mr. Pinkerton explored the sociology of journalism, largely out of his own experience, starting on the *Omaha World-Herald,* and the experiences of friends from all parts of the country on the Associated Press staff in Washington and among his Nieman group. After wartime service in the Navy, he worked for a year on *U.S. News.* He came to Harvard as director of the News Office just as *Nieman Reports* was launched, and lent it a strong hand.

I. THE PUBLISHER AND HIS PAPER

There is little doubt that the newspaper business today is in a condition of change. Evidences are all about: new typographies, new departments, new features. Wirephoto and its competitors, refurbished editorial pages are concrete signs. Newspapermen are alive to the potentialities of new competitors—radio, television, news magazines, picture magazines. Many alert publishers long since have hedged their investments by venturing into the radio field. At the same time, the depression decade left the nation with fewer metropolitan dailies than it had in 1929. Dozens of cities which once supported four or five newspapers are now "one-paper towns." The great chains have displayed their financial weakness in a rapid-fire succession of mergers, sell-outs and close-outs. Inside the newspaper business itself, few persons are not aware of new technological developments which might change the mechanical and financial basis of the business.

Some critics of "The Press" find solace in the thought that new processes, by cutting down the financial factors in publishing, may bring a resurgence of "the personal journal" in a newspaper of comparatively small circulation printed at low cost.

The fact remains that, as of today, a daily newspaper is a financial venture of corporate dimensions. To start from scratch with a brand-new newspaper, even in a rather small city, means financing which runs into the hundreds of thousands. Not only must the enterpriser purchase linotypes, presses, stereotypes, trucks, and quarters, but he also must be ready to meet the awful financial drain of daily rolls of newsprint, weekly barrels of ink, press service assessments and the biweekly salaries of reporters and admen during the long months of getting established.

Finance, then, is a basic fact. And yet many a metropolitan newspaper is not three generations removed from an enterprising youngster who borrowed a couple of thousand, set up a press, hired reporters on half-pay-and-stock and laid the foundations of a great institution. This development parallels, of course, similar histories in other fields of American industry.

I should think that a major question concerning the future of the newspaper business is: Will newer newspapers spring up to challenge these well-established organs, now largely in the hands of the founders' heirs, or may we expect particular newspapers to become dominant and self-perpetuating institutions, such as one finds in the railroad business, in the public utilities, and in banking? I should hesitate to guess the answer.

Nevertheless, the manner in which modern newspapers have come into being—sparked by the genius of a single man—is reflected in the formal organization of the typical newspaper. Typically, the financial interest in a newspaper rests in a rather small group of stockholders—often, for all practical purposes, in a single family. With the exception of Hearst enterprises, the stock of newspapers is not available for purchase on the New York Exchange. It seldom changes hands, and then only in such emergencies as financial difficulty or death. I think it might be inferred that newspaper stock is valued both as an investment and as a vehicle of trust or power.

Because of the nature of stock ownership, I would venture the further generalization that control of a newspaper rests typically in the hands of the actual owners. In such great corporations as U.S. Steel and General Motors control of business policy may be lodged in less than five per cent of the stock—the rest being scattered widely among thousands of small, unorganized investors. In the newspaper, however, control and ownership tend to merge. Usually "the family"—which may include a few associates occupying key positions and deriving their status, not by kinship, but by life-long service to the enterprise—actually owns a majority of the stock.

In this connection, it is interesting to speculate on the fact that the newspaper business largely escaped the tendency toward consolidation into great nation-wide holding companies which marked so many other American industries during the twentieth century. While the Hearst chain and the Scripps-Howard chain might be compared in size with Commonwealth & Southern in utilities or American Airlines in transportation, it is still true that the locally owned, independently financed newspaper remains the most typical management set-up in the newspaper field. Development of the Associated Press, a cooperative enterprise for performing the costly function of "covering the world" for all its members, may have been a strong deterrent on the economic side. This development was paralleled, of course, by the private-owned services of United Press and International News Service. On the social side, the prestige of the publishing family in the community—hardly to be compared with that of a merely industrial dynasty—must be reckoned a factor. There does not appear to be anything in the Hearst and Scripps-Howard experience to prove that an economic advantage attaches to chain operation of newspapers.

A family which does not own a majority of the stock subjects itself to the danger which hounded the railroad tycoons in the days of Jim Hill and E. H. Harriman—the danger that a jealous rival might seize power by a stock-buying coup.

Control is vital. Beyond the financial benefits of newspaper ownership are much larger benefits in the field of public affairs. The publisher of a newspaper is a potent factor, almost per se, in his community. He is a personage; people read "his" newspaper, sometimes they read "his" editorials, they discuss what "he" had to say on a vital issue of the day. Often a publisher's friends will speak in these terms even when they know that the publisher does not write a line of the printed matter appearing in "his" newspaper.

And what "he" says is important. He may rank with the banker, the industrialist and the department-store proprietor in the city's business councils; but in the field of public affairs he outranks them all. The institution which he heads says its say daily, to a large audience, on matters of public concern and public policy.

Still, what the publisher says in "his" newspaper is not always a direct reflection of the views he voices at the country club or at the dinner tables of his friends.

The newspaper enjoys a certain institutional standing in the community, quite apart from the individuals who produce it at any given time. People "swear by the *Globe*" or "always read the *Journal*." (I remember that my father continued religiously to read the *Milwaukee Sentinel*, once the editorial wheel-horse of Wisconsin Republicanism, long after it had become an adjunct of the Hearst chain.) Thus, a publisher—even if he comes from outside the newspaper's organization—is limited in his policies by a force that can only be called tradition. He may order a complete about-face on policy; he may, over a period of years, drastically change the entire nature of the newspaper; but in any decision to do these things he is inhibited, more or less, by the "character" of the newspaper. "Character" is a factor of importance both to financial success and to public influence. Ill-considered change may destroy in short order a following built up by the struggles of decades.

The dead hand of the founder continues to check the reins of newspaper management long after his death. The *Chicago Tribune* in 1928 faced a serious conflict between its tradition of Republicanism, established by Joseph Medill, and its strong editorial policy against prohibition. Tradition won. William Rockhill Nelson's stricture against mentioning snakes in his *Kansas City Star* continued in force long after the man himself had passed on. The family nature of newspaper ownership may be a partial explanation of this phenomenon.

The newspaper's very position in public life is a factor further limiting the publisher's freedom. Rare indeed is the American newspaper publisher who has not paid his respects to the noncommercial functions of his organization—its functions as a servant of the people and an instrument of democracy. Thus, the publisher may well feel a sense of responsibility concerning the public attitudes of his newspaper which he would not feel about his own personal attitudes expressed in private. In this contrast of "public" and "private" attitudes, the publisher is not much different from a doctor, a lawyer, or the governor of a state.

The fact that the publisher occupies a position of unusual prestige in his community—that he is at once the peer of bankers and industrialists and also the peer of ministers, mayors, and professors—does not spring from any inordinate lust for power on his part. It springs from the very nature of the newspaper business.

In the menagerie of modern industry, the newspaper is a strange two-headed creature. One head is a business head, with an eye single for the profit margin. The other head is shaped on the classic lines of a Greek embodiment of Justice. It has an all-seeing eye, an all-hearing ear, and a tongue with which to tell. It has horns which may be used for hanging dilemmas out to dry or for goring the unrighteous enemy of the people. This is the head of Journalism.

The thin nerve center which connects these two heads is the Publisher. His function is to keep the balance between the two parts of his beast. He has power to throw the balance of control now to the business side, now to the editorial side of his newspaper.

By training, most publishers of today are businessmen. They know the technical facts of cost accounting, advertising solicitation, circulation, promotion, and profits. The mysteries of the city hall run, the magic of headline writing and the metaphysics of news judgment they know at second hand, as men who have followed the process from outside. Their bias is toward the business function of the newspaper.

The editorial side has only an indirect connection with the money-making aspects of the business. It is true that an editor may "sell" the publisher on an out-of-town story or a costly campaign in terms of subscriptions. It is true that editors weigh certain news accounts in terms of their possible effect on advertisers or on a large section of the citizenry whose subscriptions have importance to the newspaper's financial success. But such considerations are largely incidental. The major concern of the editorial side is to "get the news," and to get it into the paper; and incidentally to discuss its meaning in the columns of the editorial page.

The editorial worker's interest in the business success of the enterprise is that of any workman who is concerned that his employer will not close up shop overnight. There is little in his position in the newspaper organization to make him think of himself as a businessman performing a business function.

Instead, he thinks of himself as a journalist (though he may balk at using the word)—as a specialist in the techniques of obtaining information, of writing for readers of varying intelligence, of judging the value to readers of various aspects of the day's budget of history. Not uncommonly, the editorial worker will express antagonism toward "the business side," as a nuisance which must be put up with.

That the public reflects this view is a matter of simple observation. The newspaperman of story, stage, and film is inevitably an editorial employee, and never an advertising solicitor, or a circulation manager, or even a business executive.

II. GETTING THE NEWS AND PLAYING IT

The work that newspapermen do usually is described in terms of a rather long series of titles: reporter, special writer, correspondent, feature writer, rewrite, copy reader, desk editor, city editor, telegraph editor, state editor, news editor, managing editor, editorial writer, columnist, editor. The list of titles may be longer or shorter; usually it will center on these.

But newspaper organization is quite informal; the work done by men bearing a given title varies greatly from newspaper to newspaper. On one paper, the city editor may serve mainly as a personnel officer, directing the work of the reporting staff; on another, he may direct both the reporters and the staff of desk men who edit the news articles of local interest. A news editor may be a person of great importance, making major decisions as to the order in which news stories shall appear in the paper—which shall have positions of prominence and which shall be subordinated—or he may be merely a liaison man between the editorial office and "the back shop," directing printers in the mechanical arrangement of articles whose news value has been decided by others.

Most newspapermen recognize a vague hierarchy of positions ranging upward from the "cub" reporter, through the various levels of reporting, editing, and editorial writing, to the managing editor and the editor. But the status of the various positions is so poorly established that a city editor may become in fact the directing force for the entire news-gathering and news-handling staff; a seasoned reporter may scorn, with justice, an extremely responsible desk position; a man may step directly from the position of "star" reporter to that of editor or managing editor; a man may leave the desk editor's chair to take a turn at reporting without losing his standing with his fellows.

The hierarchy is equally flexible on a salary basis. Some reporters will be paid higher wages than some desk editors on the same newspaper. An outstanding reporter or a Washington correspondent may draw a pay check as great as any save that of the managing editor.

For purposes of understanding the kind of work newspapermen do, therefore, it is easier to discuss the processes of newspaper work. These are three: coverage, play, interpretation. To a certain extent, every newspaperman performs each of these functions. In general, however, each function is associated with a group of positions, thus: *coverage* (reporters, rewrite, special correspondents, feature writers, press services) ; *play* (copy readers, desk editors, news editors) ; *interpretation* (editorial writers, political correspondents, columnists) .

COVERAGE may be defined as "getting the news." To this end, each newspaper has its own network of runs, districts, specialists, and general utility men. The press services assume the responsibility for providing the news of state, national, and international interest. For the newspaper, the problem of coverage centers largely on the city and its trade area. The problem is further simplified by setting up various independent departments within the editorial staff. They are responsible for the news in fields of special interest—such as sports, society, financial. These departments operate apart from the general reporting staff, but follow in general the same methods.

The main body of reporters and special writers work under the city editor. His responsibility is to collect, in news form, material on all events within the city which might be of interest to a large number of persons. At first glance, this might seem an impossible task. However, the work has been greatly simplified by what is known as "routine coverage." Whether correctly or not, newspapermen have come to work on the assumption that almost all major events of interest to newspaper readers center on certain official fulcrums of community life—the police station, the city hall, the county court house, the federal building, the business and financial offices. Each of these is staffed by one or more "run men," regularly assigned to visiting the same offices every day. For the duration of their assignment on the run, these men become specialists in the kind of public information with which they deal.

The run man's keenness in spotting the significance of a dull item on a police blotter or a wordy legal document in the office of the clerk of court—and his friendship with persons who might tip him off to good stories—is a major factor in determining what is offered to the editors of the paper as grist for the news mill. While some men are better than others at spotting the importance of the day's dull fact, the factors of insight and intelligence are not alone in determining the run man's success.

The limitations of time and space bear as oppressively on him as on any newspaper worker. For reasons of cost, he is apt to be assigned a rather large number of offices and people to cover. Often, he faces the problem of whom to visit first, or which set of records to dig into first. He must determine how often it is necessary to see certain minor officials. How long can he afford to sit in on a potentially important hearing or trial where nothing seems to be happening? How far can he afford to dig into the legal documents without risk of missing an equally important story elsewhere? These are matters of judgment and intuition. The reporter plays his hunches—he sometimes takes a chance on missing the story at one place to get a better story at another place. When he guesses wrong, he must repair the loss by checking the stories of eyewitnesses and the statements of officials to reconstruct the action.

In the nature of things, much reporting must be of this second-hand nature, rather than the first-hand observation of events. The murder already has been committed, the brief filed, the little courtroom drama enacted when the reporter gets his tip.

With the remainder of his staff—the "general assignments men" —the city editor must fill in the gaps between the runs and catch the unexpected incidents of community life. The measure of a great city editor is his ability to spot the places where a story is lurking unwritten. Because of this, the city editor is ideally the best-informed man on the newspaper staff. His interests are all the scattered affairs of the city and its people; but with this, he needs an intimate knowledge of affairs in general. He must sense when a visit of some outside politician or financier or labor leader may have special significance. He must know what trains or planes or buses might bring a missing gangster or movie star into the city's limits. He must know what clubs men frequent, and who their friends are. He must know who paid for whose election campaign, and why. And he must know what local persons and places are good for a light "human interest" story on a dull day.

Nor does the city editor neglect areas covered by run men. He is answerable for the work of the run men, and he must know when a man is missing a story on his run or when he is shirking his job. A good city editor will sense the fact that a run man has missed part of the story or has mistaken the facts. He advises the run men on possible leads, and coordinates the work of men on separate runs when their fields converge. He will decide when to send an extra man onto a run to devote long hours to a story which the run man cannot handle for lack of time. In short, with a small staff of reporters of varying degrees of training and skill, the city editor must contrive to keep informed of all those events which would interest large groups in the community.

In a way, the city editor must function like the traffic manager of an airline or a railroad. He must sort and shuffle his men to meet the most pressing news demands of the moment. Keeping pace with the changing importance to public affairs of various news sources is part of the job. He must know when a new office needs to be added to the routine daily coverage of the run men. In some midwestern cities the Federal Land Bank suddenly became, in 1933, the major financial institution of the city. The assignment of run men to cover relief agencies in the depth of the depression was a measure of the city editors' alertness to the changing scene. In Washington, similarly, various agencies grow and die in news importance. The early years of the New Deal saw "downtown" Washington—the departments and administrative agencies—eclipsing "the Hill" in news importance. The Supreme Court took on a special importance during the days when the constitutionality of New Deal laws was in question.

Alert general-assignments men, who dig up stories on their own hook, help the city editor keep pace with the ever-changing news picture. Although the top general-assignments men usually will be working on only one story at a time, their problems are similar to those of the run man. The sources of their news are not as neatly catalogued as those of the run man. A general assignments man may find himself in a strange neighborhood, seeking data from informants he has never seen before. Here, as in the run man's work, judgment and intuition are valuable tools.

Obviously, there is selection in the matter of coverage. If the responsible reporter or editor fails to perceive the implications of the changing course of daily happenings, a news center of vital interest to large groups of people may be overlooked. An alert newspaperman must be resurveying and checking his position constantly. This is done, but not by any self-conscious method, not by the keeping of charts and graphs. It is done almost subconsciously by an all-but-mechanical habit of repeatedly asking oneself, whenever one meets a new idea, a new person or a new situation: "Is there a story in it?" "Am I missing a news angle here?"

It is amply clear that "coverage" is a selective process. From the city's thousands, the city editor selects each day a very small number to pursue and interview. From the hundreds of happenings in the city's daily life, he selects a comparatively small number to investigate. His resources of coverage are limited by the size and competence of his staff. The constant ticking of the clock and the daily supply of blank pages to be filled enforce a kind of economy of effort. In the repeated decisions to pursue one story rather than another, he is guided by a ratio of the potential news involved and the expenditure of time and effort needed to get it.

Chance spins the wheel. A happening which might make "a good story" on a dull day may be ignored completely on a day when great events are crowding the paper's pages or on a day when manpower is concentrated on a particular event of moment—a man-hunt, a national convention, or a flood. Unfortunately, newspapers seldom turn back to do justice to an important turn of events once its news-day has passed. It is covered or missed that day.

PLAY is a matter of what goes into the newspaper, and how. Here the mass of data written during the day is formed into a scheme of value—"news value." Here the desk editors, with cold hearts and black pencils, go into action.

The colonial precursors of American journalism displayed a grand indifference to the arrangement of materials in their papers. Today, few metropolitan newspapers would think of inserting the last-minute, latest, or greatest bit of news anywhere but on page one.

Below the big type of page one which marks the day's major news offering in the modern newspaper there is ranged a whole series of news stories, each rated more or less as to its interest and importance. To achieve this rating, the newspapers have evolved an elaborate series of techniques and principles. The varying size of headline type is only one method of rating the news. Mechanically, a major story may be set apart further by being set in two-column measure, by "leading" of the opening paragraphs, by setting significant passages in bold-face, by associating pictures with the story. A lesser story may be set apart by a margin of white space around it, or by a box of black lines. Furthermore, the columns on a page are rated in order of their eye-catching location; the right-hand column is best, then the left-hand column, and so forth. Usually, a two-column headline will claim special notice within this structure. Inside, the right-hand page is considered more eye-catching than the left-hand page. The top of the page is considered more prominent than space "below the fold."

Fitting the day's reams of news copy into this hierarchy of "news value," on an hour-to-hour basis, implies a continuing series of rapid judgments on matters of great moment. The judgments must go even farther. Since the output of a metropolitan news machine is always far greater than the day's advertising will warrant publishing (or the readers read), someone must decide what to throw away, what to cut down, what to let run at some length.

While the executive function of arraying the news in a scale of importance lodges in a small group of newspapermen—sometimes, for all practical purposes, in a single person—every worker in the editorial department of a newspaper is conditioned by the idea of "play."

The reporter "writes for the play." The rewrite man angles his lead paragraph "to get the play." The copy reader checks the story to see that the main news fact is played up in the first paragraph, writes a headline to stress the news value of the story. In hurried conferences during the day, desk editors argue over whether a new development will "take the play away" from the story which has been featured in the first edition.

"Play" becomes the ultimate measure of news value. It is the final answer to the question: What is news? While the grand insult of newspapermen is to say "he doesn't know a story when it comes up and bites him," while any newspaperman will tell you quickly whether a given fact is news, few have any clearly defined concept of what factors govern news judgment.

Various writers have sought to define the elements of news in maxims—"when a man bites a dog, that's news," and "the best news is a good fight"—and in categories of human interest—money, love, humor, the unusual, etc. Dozens of definitions have been attempted; and probably no one has come closer to a fool-proof definition than this: "News is anything published in a newspaper which interests a large number of people."

It is apparent, I think, that "news" is not a scientific term, even in the limited sense that "health" might be in medicine or "legal" in the law. It is apparent that news judgment—play—is not a scientific process even in the limited sense that a doctor's diagnosis or a lawyer's brief might be called scientific. There is no organized body of principle which will explain the varied play of news in such organs as the *New York Times,* the *Chicago Tribune,* the *Cincinnati Enquirer,* the *Daily Mirror* and the *Washington Evening Star.* Certainly, no reporter or editor ever applied any set of principles, in a conscious way, to decide whether a given set of facts constituted "news."

The play of news varies from newspaper to newspaper, and from month to month on the same newspaper. It seems to be a compound of the newspaper's own tradition, the composition of the particular public to which the newspaper is addressed, certain general principles of human psychology, "hunches" and a kind of directed intuition developed within the craft.

There are "big stories" which "would be news in anybody's paper." There is a continuity of practice on each newspaper which any good newspaperman will grasp quickly. And there are stories that are "made" because of an editor's hunch or a reporter's curiosity.

Every American newspaper is concerned first with the coverage and play of news. One way or another, each newspaper tries also to interpret the news for its readers.

INTERPRETATION is the "what it means" of newspaper work. It might be helpful to enumerate the ways in which newspapermen now go about interpeting the news:

(1) Explaining the news. (2) Filling in the background. (3) Forecasting the future. (4) Passing moral judgment.

Moral judgment is the element of the editorial writer's work best understood and most widely accepted by the general public. In the same way, it is the thing which emphasizes the gap between the work of reporters or desk editors dealing with news and the writing of "powerful pieces" in the newspaper's "ivory tower."

The new power of the columnists—a breed somewhere between the reporter and the editorial writer—has brought a demand from some publishers and editors for more "interpretive stuff" from their own staff writers. But the phrase "interpretive writing" is surrounded with just enough haze to make these demands sometimes difficult to meet.

At the same time, a hard core of newspapermen, believing in the values of their craft, are giving renewed thought to the problems which must be solved if our present ideal of news is to be saved. They are seeking solutions which demand a new kind of interpretative writing, divorced both from the moralizing of the editorial page and from the gossiping of the columnists. Their aim is a newspaper written in the language of the average reader, with background folded into the news account itself, with full use of human interest—not to pander to the reader but to coax the reader to the news he needs to know.

If trained newsmen put these ideas to work, the concept of interpretation will affect all aspects of the daily press, just as coverage and play do now.

Why Should News Come in 5-Minute Packages?

EDWARD R. MURROW [JANUARY 1959

This is from Mr. Murrow's address to the radio and television news directors' convention, Chicago, October 15, 1958. At that time the star of the Columbia Broadcasting System, he later headed the U.S. Information Service until his health forced retirement. Mr. Murrow died on April 27, 1965.

It is my desire if not my duty to talk with some candor about what is happening to radio and television in this generous and capacious land. I am seized with an abiding fear regarding what these two instruments are doing to our society, our culture, and our heritage.

I invite your attention to the television schedules of all networks between the hours of eight and eleven P.M. Eastern Time. Here you will find only fleeting and spasmodic reference to the fact that this nation is in mortal danger. There are, it is true, occasional informative programs presented in that intellectual ghetto on Sunday afternoons. But during the daily peak viewing periods, television in the main insulates us from the realities of the world in which we live. If this state of affairs continues, we may alter an advertising slogan to read: "Look Now, Pay Later." For surely we shall pay for using this most powerful instrument of communication to insulate the citizenry from the hard and demanding realities which must be faced if we are to survive.

I am entirely persuaded that the American public is more reasonable, restrained, and mature than most of our industry's program planners believe. Their fear of controversy is not warranted by the evidence.

The oldest excuse of the networks for their timidity is their youth. Their spokesmen say: "We are young; we have not developed the traditions, nor acquired the experience of the older media." If they but knew it, they are building those traditions, creating those precedents every day. Each time they yield to a voice from Washington or any political pressure, each time they eliminate something that might offend some section of the community, they are creating their own body of precedent and tradition. They are, in fact, not content to be "half safe."

Nowhere is this better illustrated than by the fact that the chairman of the Federal Communications Commission publicly prods broadcasters to engage in their legal right to editorialize. Of course, to undertake an editorial policy, overt and clearly labeled, and obviously unsponsored, requires a station or a network to be responsible. Most stations today probably do not have the manpower to assume this responsibility, but the manpower could be recruited. Editorials would not be profitable; if they had a cutting edge they might even offend. It is much easier, much less troublesome to use the money-making machine of television and radio merely as a conduit through which to channel anything that is not libelous, obscene, or defamatory. In that way one has the illusion of power without responsibility.

So far as radio—that most satisfying and rewarding instrument—is concerned, the diagnosis of its difficulties is rather easy. And obviously I speak only of news and information. In order to progress, it need only go backward to the time when singing commercials were not allowed on news reports, when there was no middle commercial in a fifteen-minute news report; when radio was rather proud, alert, and fast. I recently asked a network official: Why this great rash of five-minute news reports (including three commercials) on weekends? He replied: "Because that seems to be the only thing we can sell."

In this kind of complex and confusing world, you can't tell very much about the *why* of the news in a broadcast where only three minutes is given to news. The only man who could do that was Elmer Davis, and his kind isn't about any more. If radio news is to be regarded as a commodity, only acceptable when salable, and only when packaged to fit the advertising appropriation of a sponsor, then I don't care what you call it—I say it isn't news.

One of the minor tragedies of television news and information is that the networks will not even defend their vital interests. When my employer, CBS, through a combination of enterprise and good luck, did an interview with Nikita Khrushchev, the President uttered a few ill-chosen, uninformed words on the subject, and the network practically apologized. This produced a rarity. Many newspapers defended the CBS right to produce the program and commended it for initiative. But the other networks remained silent.

Likewise, when John Foster Dulles, by personal decree, banned American journalists from going to Communist China, and subsequently offered contradictory explanations for his fiat, the networks entered only a mild protest. Then they apparently forgot the unpleasantness. Can it be that this national industry is content to serve the public interest only with the trickle of news that comes out of Hong Kong? To leave its viewers in ignorance of the cataclysmic changes that are occurring in a nation of six hundred million people? I have no illusions about the difficulties of reporting from dictatorship; but our British and French allies have been better served—in their public interest—with some very useful information from their reporters in Communist China.

One of the basic troubles with radio and television news is that both instruments have grown up as an incompatible combination of show business, advertising, and news. Each of the three is a rather bizarre and demanding profession. And when you get all three under one roof, the dust never settles. The top management of the networks, with a few notable exceptions, has been trained in advertising, research, sales, or show business. But by the nature of the corporate structure, they also make the final and crucial decisions having to do with news and public affairs. Frequently they have neither the time nor the competence to do this.

Upon occasion, economics and editorial judgment are in conflict. And there is no law which says that dollars will be defeated by duty. Not so long ago the President of the United States delivered a television address to the nation. He was discoursing on the possibility or probability of war between this nation and the Soviet Union and Communist China—a reasonably compelling subject. The networks—CBS and NBC—delayed that broadcast for an hour and fifteen minutes. If this decision was dictated by anything other than financial reasons, the networks didn't deign to explain those reasons. That hour-and-fifteen-minute delay, by the way, is about twice the time required for an I.C.B.M. to travel from the Soviet Union to major targets in the United States. It is difficult to believe that this decision was made by men who love, respect, and understand news.

Potentially, we have in this country a free-enterprise system of radio and television which is superior to any other. But to achieve its promise, it must be both free and enterprising. There is no suggestion here that networks or individual stations should operate as philanthropies. But I can find nothing in the Bill of Rights or the Communications Act which says that they must increase their net profits each year, lest the republic collapse.

The question is this: Are the big corporations who pay the freight for radio and television programs wise to use that time *exclusively* for the sale of goods and services?

If we go on as we are, we are protecting the mind of the American public from any real contact with the menacing world that squeezes in upon us. We are engaged in a great experiment to discover whether a free public opinion can devise and direct methods of managing the affairs of the nation. We may fail. But we are handicapping ourselves needlessly.

Let us have a little competition. Not only in selling soap, cigarettes, and automobiles, but in informing a troubled, apprehensive, but receptive public. Why should not each of the twenty or thirty big corporations which dominate radio and television decide that they will give up one or two regularly scheduled programs each year, turn the time over to the networks, and say in effect: "This is a tiny tithe, just a little bit of our profits. On this particular night we aren't going to try to sell cigarettes or automobiles; this is merely a gesture to indicate our belief in the importance of ideas." The networks should, and I think would, pay for the cost of producing the program. The advertiser, the sponsor, would get name credit, but would have nothing to do with the content of the program. Would this blemish the corporate image? Would the stockholders object? I think not. For if the premise upon which our pluralistic society rests —which, as I understand it, is that if the people are given sufficient undiluted information, they will then somehow, even after long, sober second thoughts, reach the right decision—if that premise is wrong, then not only the corporate image but the corporations are done for.

Just once in a while let us exalt the importance of ideas and information. Let us dream to the extent of saying that on a given Sunday night the time normally occupied by Ed Sullivan is given over to a clinical survey of the state of American education, and a week or two later the time normally used by Steve Allen is devoted to a thorough-going study of American policy in the Middle East. Would the corporate image of their respective sponsors be damaged? Would the stockholders rise up in their wrath and complain? Would anything happen other than that a few million people would have received a little illumination on subjects that may well determine the future of this country, and therefore the future of the corporations?

TV News: Reporting or Performing?

JOHN F. DAY [APRIL 1956

Mr. Day records here the impressions of his first year in radio–TV as director of news for CBS. This was a talk at the University of Minnesota School of Journalism on February 10, 1956. He later returned to newspaper work, and in 1964 bought the *Exmouth Journal*, a British weekly. Mr. Day was a Nieman Fellow in 1942–43.

I have noticed recently a tendency of certain television newsmen to endorse products and to permit their names and their faces to be associated with the promotion and sale of these products.

Personally, I feel embarrassed when I see these ads. And that is true despite the fact these persons do not work for CBS News and thus are actually no responsibility of mine. But I feel very strongly that newsmen should be newsmen; not pitchmen. And these men carry not only the nomenclature of newsmen, but of television newsmen.

Is television news going to destroy itself in commercialism before it gets out of its swaddling clothes?

Television as it exists today *is* show business. For that reason at least one branch of journalism is trying to adapt itself to a strange new world. In so doing it has taken on some of the elements of show business. Not all of these elements are new, of course, for TV news is in part an extension of radio news, and radio too is in show business. But television is show business with a capital S.

Television news has tried to fit into this glittering show world by a series of compromises which affect both the persons working in TV news and the product they put on the screen.

First, let's consider the effect on the individual.

Journalism has never known such a disparity in pay as exists at the network level in radio and television. The office boy, the news writer, and the news editor make more than the average for their jobs on metropolitan newspapers. Enough more to make recruiting from newspapers practicable, but surely not enough more to make the jobs utopian. The reporter who works with a camera team and develops pictorial stories requires new skill, and his job cannot be compared exactly with a particular newspaper job. But his pay is comparable to what a news writer or editor makes.

It is when a newsman becomes a performer, a director or a producer that things get wild. Here it's what a man can command and what the traffic will bear. It's what he and his union and his agent can get.

To one who worked in newspapers as long as I did, it seems strange to have a news correspondent's *agent* making formal calls upon him to discuss better assignments and fatter contracts. But that's part of the element of show business, and that's the way the system works.

I should explain here that correspondents (men who are reporters but who also appear on mike and camera), as well as directors and producers, have basic contracts calling for staff salaries that are NOT in the high brackets. Thus persons who do not earn commercial fees are paid well but not fabulously. However, on top of the basic contract there is an elaborate fee system which makes it possible for some to soar into the upper five-figure and even six-figure annual pay brackets.

Another element is the fact that television newsmen (and, to be sure, radio newsmen as well) are called upon to deliver commercials. Ever since it has had a news service, CBS, thank heavens, has tried to keep the news and the advertising separate by having persons other than the reporters deliver the commercials. We are not simon pure in this respect. The pressures from advertising agencies, and sometimes from persons within the company, are strong and unrelenting. In the matter of "lead-ins"—introductions to commercials that may in themselves endorse the product—a couple of sponsors have gotten a foot in the door by pressing our newsmen into reading them.

This may lead to the question of whether one can be half a virgin. I'm not positive about the answer to that, but I do believe one can do some flirting around without becoming a prostitute.

Seriously, CBS News strives with continuing vigilance to protect its newsmen from the chore of doing commercials.

Please understand, I have nothing against advertising. I am in fact one of its strongest advocates, because I believe its effect has been immeasurably great in the expanding of the economy. But in this field I believe in segregation. Let someone not associated with the news deliver the sales pitch. It is worse than unfair to ask a man to try to deliver an explanation of some world crisis in one breath and an appeal to his listeners to buy a certain remedy for aches and pains in the next.

Now that I have pointed out some elements of commercialism as they affect individuals in television and radio news, I think it is important that I make this observation: Big as is the money that floats around in electronic journalism, I personally know of not one single case where a newsman has deliberately slanted a story, omitted a story, or added a story because his sponsor asked for it. I have no doubt there have been such cases. But they must be few, for talk of things like that travels fast. I'm happy to say that although electronic newsmen may become prima donnas, they don't become crooks.

I said earlier that because television today was show business, both the individuals and the product have made compromises to adjust to that business. I have talked so far about the individuals. Now to the product.

Television news has been cut to a pattern that says, "Television is an entertainment medium; therefore television news must entertain."

Who says television HAS to be an entertainment medium? Some broadcasting officials act as though they have been handed holy writs saying, "This is your air and your electronic gadget; you're to use them solely for the purpose of making money and amusing the morons."

It's fortunate for all of us that the real leaders of the industry don't assume such an attitude and that the Federal Communications Commission keeps an eye cocked on the industry's obligation to operate in the public interest.

Electronic journalism must hew a path through the jungle if it is to achieve a goal of adding something to human knowledge. While recognizing that most people today regard television as an entertainment medium, electronic journalism must not forget this is a convenient assumption, not an unalterable law of the universe, or even a proved fact. While conceding that news must be presented interestingly if it is to compete and hold an audience, newsmen must not succumb to sensationalism. Just as it is true that a good newspaper doesn't have to be dull, television news can inform with liveliness and vividness. The point is that it must not forget that its primary purpose is to INFORM.

Radio news went through its formative stages in the 1930's; came of age during the 1940's. I am not particularly happy about the trend in radio toward a vast number of five-minute summaries, but the 15-minute programs such as our "World News Roundup," "News of America," and the Ed Murrow news have held their own, and I believe we will soon see the addition of some half-hour news-in-depth shows. So, basically, radio news has achieved stature; it knows what it can do and where it stands.

Television news, on the other hand, is in ferment. It is growing and it is improving—let there be no doubt about that. But it also is groping for answers. No one on the outside has made criticisms of television news that we who are working in it haven't made. I have never known of any craft, trade, or profession so thoroughly self-examining and so unceasingly self-critical; so willing to try to find ways to improve itself.

We at CBS News carry on a continuing study that amounts to intense introspection. We keep asking ourselves such questions as: "What IS television news?"; "What should it be?"; "How can we best present the news each day?"

We have not resolved the basic question of what the television news program should do. The argument revolves around the matter of whether television should use only that news the medium can do best, or whether it should undertake to report ALL the news that is of importance or interest. The news that television can do best, of course, is (1) the event "live" as it actually happens, and (2) the strictly pictorial story on film. But a full report—one designed to make the viewer reasonably well informed by the TV medium alone—requires use of the "ideal" story that is difficult or close to impossible to illustrate well.

I am a strong advocate of the complete news report. I believe that television is a basic medium for conveying information and adding to human knowledge. If we don't use it in this way, we abdicate all claims to its being a basic news medium. I think we MUST not become obsessed with the pictorial and the merely entertaining at the expense of the meaningful. We must find ways to present difficult stories more effectively. None of us who work in news at CBS is satisfied that we are making the best possible use of the visual medium. Too much of what we present is superficial and unimaginative. But we are trying, and trying hard, for better technical and editorial quality. We try incessantly to find people who can THINK in visual terms, who can plan the best possible pictorial coverage of the story which lies in the realm of ideas. We carry on continuing experimentation with and discussion of new types of cameras, film sound-recording devices and other equipment. We discuss the relative merits of sound film and silent film; of animation techniques; of showmanship—roughly comparable to "readability" in newspapering; of the length and type of film clips; of the balance between voice reporting and picture reporting.

And at the same time we must keep an eye on costs. Television news is an expensive product, no matter how you figure it. The viewer hears the newsman say, "Now we take you to San Francisco . . ." and presto: there is a film or a live picture of a California flood. But the picture doesn't just happen. It takes planning and it takes M–O–N–E–Y. In all probability we have had to install loops and connections in the San Francisco station. (When I first made my acquaintance with such figures as, "Installing loops and connections . . . $1,800" I thought those loops must be made of platinum, studded with diamonds. But they're just cables.) Then there is the line charge for the cross-country switch. That runs to another $1,500 or so. And these of course are more or less incidental costs to the covering of the news and the producing of the show. We had to have cameramen and reporters on that as well as many other stories. For the same show that used the transcontinental switch, we may have sent a cameraman and his excess-baggage equipment from Tokyo to Hong Kong to cover a story that runs a minute or minute and a half. Is the show worth all these costs? Well, circulation must be counted here. Some 11,000,000 persons or more see it.

Mention of audience size brings up that bugaboo, "ratings." This is a bugaboo the broadcasting industry very largely brought on itself. Certainly it is important to have as accurate a picture as possible of how many people are watching or listening to a given program. But I am appalled by the importance placed on decimal-point changes by the broadcasting industry, by advertising agencies, and by companies who buy time. Rating systems are valuable as guides. Enslavement by them is tragic. Currently, because it's all part of the show-business system, electronic news can't ignore the rating obsession. If the news doesn't do well against certain competition, it is liable to be moved to another time period or to lose its sponsor. Those are the facts of life. Even so, electronic journalism must keep its balance and remember that a high rating is not the end to which all means must be subjected. There IS such a thing as a quality audience, and there IS such a thing as the growing sophistication of the American television viewer. The late Mr. Mencken notwithstanding, the American public is not uniformly the "booboisie."

Earlier I asked whether television news was going to allow commercialism to destroy it before it really gets out of its swaddling clothes. I have pointed out some of the dangers that make such a fate possible, but I am optimistic that the pitfalls will be circumvented and that television news will, in the not too distant future, achieve the stature of the good newspaper and the good radio program.

To do this it must improve both its editorial and its technical resources. It must overcome or at least lessen its logistical problem. Mobile units are a long way from being mobile. Films can't move with the freedom of words. The biggest newspaper goes to cover a national political convention with perhaps fifteen persons. Television must go to cover a convention with a veritable army of men and machines. In fact, TV requires considerably more men behind the scenes to get a man on camera than the Army takes to get a man on the firing line. It must incorporate into its product the same sort of diligent, intelligent, meaningful, and objective reporting and writing and editing which has characterized the best in American newspapers and in radio and which has given American journalism its high place in the world. And then it must present this product with imagination and taste—yes, and, where suitable, with showmanship.

Certainly a large order; no doubt of that. But so unlimited is the horizon of television that I am reasonably confident these things will be achieved. Recently, in making an intramural estimate for future plans of CBS News, I hazarded a guess that our operation five years from now will have much greater scope and much higher quality in programming and will employ approximately twice as many people.

The technical people tell us that the following developments are here or on the way:

1. Color films, and live events in actual color.

2. Magnetic stripe on film for audio recording. Current sound-on-film quality is, as you know, generally pretty poor. The new process should approach high fidelity.

3. Magnetic tape for recording pictures. This is still some distance in the future, apparently; but eventually there will be a process that will permit recording and instant play-back.

4. Closed-circuit systems that will nearly eliminate moving film about the country by plane. An editor in New York will monitor film on video tape in Los Angeles, choose what he wants, record it in New York, edit it and use it on his next news show.

5. Facsimile machines instead of teletypes for the rapid movement of raw news copy and scripts.

6. Trans-Atlantic, and eventually world-wide, television networks through the scatter system of bouncing signals off the ionosphere.

All these, of course, are merely the tools. But what tools! Given brains, moral fiber, and clearly sighted goals (no small order!) where else can television news go except forward?

III. NEWSMEN AT WORK

John Hulteng, a Nieman Fellow of 1949–50, now dean of journalism at the University of Oregon, once wrote a piece for *Nieman Reports* on "The Genuine Glamour of Journalism" (July 1957). It expressed his own feeling about newspapering, one certainly shared by very many of the craft. Even though some of its glamour has been stolen by the more dramatic medium of television, newspapering holds a special fascination, as Hulteng says: "There are, thank God, some who still go into newspaper work with a sense of excitement and lively eagerness, who see more than a job. The challenge of newspaper work today is dramatic and profound. One of the most immediately gratifying ways to satisfy the creative urge is through newspaper writing. The power that rests in the hands of America's reporters is enormous. There is glamour in wielding such power in the public interest—*real* glamour, not tinsel."

In the final analysis, it is this feeling about the newspaper job that makes it worthwhile to talk about it, fuss over it, criticize it and grouse about it. Here some pieces tell of the feeling of a good newspaperman for his work, hail some of the great newspapermen and present some slices of the rich history of journalism, some of its excitement, some of its bizarre aspects.

There is such a thing as a natural reporter, as there is a natural athlete. We recognize him when we see him at his game. His quality may be hard to define but it can be happily illustrated. A great American reporter of my cub days, Frank P. Sibley of the *Boston Globe,* once defined the most essential quality of a newspaperman as perennial curiosity. That is, a compulsion to find out, a fresh questioning approach, an unjaded interest, a capacity to inquire and to listen and to learn, to absorb, to get at the meaning of things—to acquire understanding.

I once tried to tell students about the requirements of reporting. Some of it (printed in *Nieman Reports* for January 1955) will do for a preface to some pieces of the newsman at his work:

The reporter's first role is to go and find the story. How can one possibly use the precise word for a description if he hasn't observed what he is trying to describe? The words are apt to spring to their task if the writer has received a vivid impression of an actual situation.

The eyewitness report of the disaster is at a premium in newspapers, even though the eyewitness is not a writer. He has something you can't take away from him, and that you can't duplicate if the horror were not seared into your own eyeballs.

Samuel Eliot Morison has more writing style than any other contemporary American historian. It may be only coincidence that he follows the scent of the story himself. He goes out after his own raw material. He outfitted a ship to follow the course of Columbus. He stood on the deck of the *Massachusetts* when it shelled the North African Coast. He was with the ships at Saipan and Kwajelein, indeed on the flagship. He writes both as reporter and as historian.

To a graduate student, studying the New England fisheries, Morison advised one January: "Go out to the fishing grounds with a fisherman. This is a good time to go. It's good and rough."

As to style, Samuel Morison says, in his very practical leaflet, *History as a Literary Art:* "Just as Voltaire's ideal curé advises his flock not to worry about going to Heaven, but to do right and probably by God's grace they will get there; so the writer of history had better not work consciously to develop a style but concentrate on day-by-day improvement in craftsmanship. Then perhaps he may find some day that his industry, which left readers cold, is carried to a large popular audience by something that the critics call style."

Morison's practice and preaching come from sound background. His greatest antecedent as a New England historian was Francis Parkman. Parkman's unique contribution to the history of this continent was that he went all over it. To write of the Indian wars he lived in the forest, tramped and camped like an Indian, explored the sites of their battles, went over the ground. Parkman's *French and English in Canada* is a classic, and also a graphic report. This was true of his earliest journals, and became a part of the writer from his college days, when he spent every summer exploring the forest and reaching toward the frontier and filling notebooks with detail.

The very first of his journals describes a trip up Mount Washington. Read it, if you have ever been up Mount Washington yourself. You will read what you yourself saw, felt, experienced on your trek, as Parkman put it all down a hundred years ago. All of it—the view, the clouds on top, the difficulty of the trail, the burden of the pack, the mountain flowers—all of it. He wrote it down in the freshness of his first experience, and captured every sensation, every fact, every bit of interest, every crumb of information that came out of the trip. It fascinated him. It excited him. It filled him with a new crop of facts. It gave him a zest for the mountains and forests and the life out of doors, and he writes these feelings in his notes.

Now this was a hard chore. He was going all day, and pushing himself to get over the ground. His stops were few, and certainly hot and hungry ones. At night there was no light after sundown. He had to carry everything, even his notebooks. Yet he wrote in the heat and zest and excitement of the trip. Because the words were wrought in the striving of the adventure, they are as current today as in 1854.

Who was it who envied the bards of ancient days who wrote when the words of the language were fresh with dew? But words that tell the sharpened actuality of action are not dulled by usage. It is the fancy word that won't stand repetition, the synthetic word that reminds the reader of your contriving.

You are not conscious of Parkman's words as words. You see them as windows to what he describes.

May I suggest that there is no substitute for great models of writing? To read Parkman's journals is itself a vivid experience.

Frank Sibley of the *Boston Globe* was said by his colleagues to have a photographic mind because he could describe in such faithful precise detail a colorful event—whether a parade, a fire, a shipwreck, or a courtroom scene. He was a great talker too, and what I noted about his writing was that he wrote in the same natural, direct, explicit way that he talked. But he had his models. He once advised me to read Kipling. He said I would find that Kipling never had a character merely walk or run. He leapt, darted, vaulted, sped, swept, skipped, slid, slithered, whisked, loomed, glided, flung, crashed, trod, tiptoed, stole, flitted.

Meyer Berger of the *New York Times* had much the same descriptive gift in reporting as Frank Sibley had,—and the same disdain, let me add, of reporting by telephone. He went to the scene, followed the trail himself. He won the Pulitzer prize for local reporting that way in 1949.

Berger could have got it by phoning the police. Or picked up the notes of the district reporters and woven it together. But he went out on the trail and followed in detail the course of the deranged veteran who went on a shooting spree in Camden and killed the first twelve people he happened to meet. Berger traversed the course of these shootings, talked to people who had been at each spot, oriented himself to the scene of each crime, and reported it with a sense of having experienced it—almost with the impact of an eyewitness. That was reporting. I am sure he had no problem of finding the right word. He needed no thesaurus. The thing was vivid in him; the story told itself because he had made it a part of him.

The business of going and seeing—of experiencing the thing for yourself—is fundamental to everything else. Everything flows from that. You have to know what you are talking about. You have to know what it is, who is doing it, why, what kind of person he is, what he is up to, how he does it, what he feels about it, and everything else. You have to know the situation. You have to ask the questions that can only arise from having first exercised enough curiosity to explore it yourself. You have to ask the questions of the man who knows, who lives with the answers. Doing that you multiply the dimensions of your story. He is a story too. And it is not the same to talk to him on the telephone with the pat little list of questions you noted down on reading the report. You want to spend a day with him in the field, or take the trip yourself, or somehow share the experience. The stuff needs to be dug out if it is to have substance.

If a story is in a person and can only be got from him, the subject needs to be played subtly, almost like a game fish. You need to get him relaxed. If he says he's got only a few minutes, tell him you don't want to be a nuisance; you'll come back at the end of today, or tomorrow, or see him tonight—whenever is best for him.

And then the thing is to ask questions only until you get him launched on his own talk. Let him talk. It's his story you want. Only after he's talked of his own interest enough to feel easy and interested does he tell the anecdotes and details that make the story, and that illumine his personality. Much of this you don't need to write down. You can remember his stories till you get back to your desk. The really vivid or picturesque detail is etched in your impression. You couldn't lose it. He may flow more freely if you use a pencil sparingly. You can soon tell. Or the reverse. A methodical man—an engineer or a scientist—may worry about it if he doesn't feel the details are being set down precisely as he recalls them. You have no trouble catching this mood and adjusting to it. A trained reporter must sometimes do as a diplomat always has to do: remember the conversation till it is over. Then he recalls it in his diplomatic report. This is not really very hard to do on a subject that interests you. Anybody can get total recall of a funny story, for instance. But never hesitate to ask precisely, and check on the essential figure or date or fact that you must have right.

You may need to wait for this till the end of the interview, so as not to break off an interesting recital. But before you go, pin it down. The interviewed will have increased confidence in you because of your care. But there is a difference between care and pettifoggery. Don't bore a man with picayune or fussy quizzing on details that to him are obviously inconsequential. Or if they are essential to you, wait till he's told his story his own way before badgering him on the points he's left out.

You have to have capacity yourself to share his interest to do a good story. That's a large part of Frank Sibley's perennial curiosity. It is the opposite of the blasé. The reporter who's bored with a story is a total loss.

Some of the most satisfying articles in *Nieman Reports* have been by newspapermen describing their jobs. Here are only a few of them selected with an eye to the variety and scope of journalism and some of the qualities it takes.

For That Hole in the Forms

EDWIN A. LAHEY

[MARCH 1963

Mr. Lahey is chief of the Washington bureau of the Knight Papers. He gave this address to the Associated Press News Council in Charlotte, North Carolina, December 8, 1962. Their urgent request for an advance manuscript yielded what is said to be the only prepared text of a Lahey speech in existence. Mr. Lahey was a Nieman Fellow in the first group, 1938–39.

It is a time-honored custom for the out-of-town speaker to tell you what's wrong with newspapers.

Forgive me for flouting tradition—but I don't think there's a goddamned thing wrong with newspapers.

I'm proud of my business, and grateful to it for a satisfying life as a reporter. I'd rather cover a president than be president. I'd rather cover the county courthouse than be the town banker. I'd rather be club editor than president of a country club to which a reporter couldn't belong.

If journalism had not rescued me from the working classes, I would today have about forty years seniority on the Chicago & North Western Railroad. This would perhaps have permitted me to work the day shift in the train yard at Proviso yards in Chicago.

When I need some self-justification for this professional smugness, I recall as my example a man named Jack Burke, a pit boss in a Havana gambling joint. I met him during an investigation of Batista's links with the U.S. underworld five years ago. I asked Burke how he had got into the racket, and he recalled the event with some pride.

"I used to drive a milk wagon in San Francisco," Burke told me. "After a while I noticed that I had to work twenty-nine days to get a day off, but that they worked the horse only every other day. That's how I became a crap dealer."

To belabor the point, I have never for a moment regretted the day that I had a chance to become a reporter. And my most thoughtful prayer at this stage of life is that my bosses will remain solvent and that I'll hang on until it's time for them to give me a gold watch and some matched luggage.

My strong feeling about a business that has been good to me makes me impatient with intellectuals who criticize the American press for its banality, its parochialism, and its imputed failure to keep our people dewy-eyed and well informed.

Frequently these intellectual discussions use the *New York Times* as a measuring rod for the deficiencies of us provincials.

There's always a gaping hole in this presentation.

The *New York Times* is a great institution, everyone agrees. If it did not exist, the Ford Foundation would have to start one. But there's room in this country for only one *New York Times*. God forbid that we could support more than one. If we ever got into an orgy of keeping well informed to the point that everyone was reading the equivalent of the *New York Times*, there'd be no coal dug, no yarn carded, no automobiles bolted together.

Nearly every highbrow discussion of journalism in which I've participated has ignored the dichotomy of the newspaper business. So long as we have a free-enterprise society, newspapering is first of all a profit-and-loss operation, and after that a thing of the spirit.

A. J. Liebling is the most devastating critic of the U.S. press that we know. But read Liebling, and you sense that he is still suffering from a traumatic emotional experience he had back in 1930, when some hard-headed character took a look at the account books at the *New York World*, decided he didn't want to lose any more money, and killed that great institution.

The callous business judgment which killed the *World* also left Liebling with a lifelong bitterness. Why? Simply because Liebling, as an idealistic young man, had overlooked the fact that the romantic life of a reporter in a battered hat is impossible unless some advertising hustler in a hard hat is bringing in the sheaves.

The tiresome discussions about the role of the press in a free society could probably be deflated a little if newspapermen and their critics alike kept in mind the unique and dichotomous nature of journalism in a democratic society resting on a free-enterprise system of production.

Newspapering is a mass-production, assembly-line manufacturing process, first and foremost. And like any other manufacturing process, the assembly line shuts down if the customers don't buy the merchandise.

But there is a slight difference that makes our manufacturing business unique. And you'll pardon me for repeating that ancient story about the debate over equal rights in the French chamber of deputies. When a speaker remarked that there was only a slight difference between men and women, the chamber arose as one man and shouted:

"Vive la petite difference!"

"La petite difference" in our business is this: We are the only commercial enterprise specifically covered by a guarantee in the Constitution of the United States. I refer, of course, to the freedom of press specified in the First Amendment, a simple and well-worn phrase packed both with opportunity and responsibility.

Shaken down, this is what it means:

After we have filled the forms with ad copy, with the crossword puzzle, with Ann Landers or Dear Abby, with the daily bridge hand (where north and south for some reason always get the cards) , with recipes for Lenten meals, with the vital statistics, with the night police report, and with the canned material from New York, Washington, and Hollywood, we find a little hole remaining in the type.

That is where comes to flower the brilliant thought you had in the shower. That is where reporters find space to report an unjust conviction, or some evidence of stealing in high places, or the preposterous utterances of some politician suffering from delusions of grandeur.

It's that little hole in the forms, where we express ourselves, that the First Amendment was written about. The expressions of the spirit that go into that free space, sometimes noble and courageous, sometimes petty and self-serving, are the things that make "la petite difference" between us and all other manufacturing industries.

That freedom of the press of which you are custodians is precious. And editors would be less than human if they were not at times hypersensitive about freedom of the press. They would also be less than human if they did not sometimes overemphasize the privilege of freedom enough to blur their vision of the responsibility that is part and parcel of the privilege.

I do not offer this as serious criticism of the people in our business. When editors are either hypersensitive about their rights, or insensitive to their responsibilities, a better balance is soon restored by time, events, and the pressures of competition.

I think that an editor's sense of responsibility is sometimes blunted temporarily by his personal environment, which can permit a cultural gap to develop between editors and readers. Let me explain this theory. A $20,000 editor will live in a $20,000 suburb; he will play golf and poker with $20,000 people; inevitably he will think $20,000 thoughts; with enough environmental conditioning, an editor could find a cultural gap between him and the people on the wrong side of the tracks. This cultural lag, if it exists, can betray itself in a delayed awareness, on the part of the editor, toward a fresh wave of news affecting groups outside his personal life. I think this lag was apparent in the early 1930's, in the explosive rise of a labor movement which is now almost respectable. It has been apparent in more recent years, among some editors who have forlornly wished that this boring story of the racial crisis would just go away.

Ours is a nerve-racking business. It follows that hypersensitivity about freedom of the press appears more frequently in our ranks than does insensitivity to duty.

In thirty-six years as a reporter, I have had my share of personal experiences with arrogant or corrupt people who took it upon themselves to stop the flow of information. But I have difficulty getting agitated about these characters. Somehow or other the information starts to flow again. You steal it, you keep harping about it, you get legislators on your side who want their names in the paper, and they carry the torch for you.

To me, a much more serious problem than suppression of news by public figures is the selection of news by reporters. I have been aware of this particularly since living in Washington. There's just too much of the world for the human mind to comprehend any more. The reporter or editor who can settle on a news budget on any given day without some secret apprehension about what he's missing is probably a very rare bird.

On many a day when I am afflicted with this problem, I think with nostalgia of a German who was on the night desk of the old *Wesliche Post* in St. Louis. President Harding was on his death bed in San Francisco. Right after the German editor had locked up his front page for the night, the AP bulletin phone rang, and a voice said:

"Flash . . . Harding dead."

"Vee got enuf news already," the editor said as he hung up.

We can all envy the stolidity of that editor. If we had it, the incidence of ulcers in our business would certainly decline.

And with that German's sluggish self-possession, editors and reporters as a group might be slower in their wrath about threats to the freedom of the press.

We've had an uproar in recent weeks about news management and suppression. I hesitate to criticize the brethren in Washington with whom I share the daily burden of futility and frustration. But I think that extended residence in that insidious atmosphere tends to make many of us too touchy about what goes on amongst the federal payrollers behind closed doors.

I derived only one lasting impression from the Cuban crisis—John F. Kennedy, looking very much like Matt Dillon, one of my own heroes, walked up to the mouth of a cave and told Khrushchev to throw out his gun and come out with his hands up. The break in the tension that followed may some day appear to be the most important event of our generation. The fact that the president did this with some clever news management has failed to disturb me.

I think many of you are still upset by the Pentagon order which requires all officials in the Department of Defense to report to the public information secretary the substance of any talks they have with reporters. This sounds like implied censorship. It carries the germ of something that could be contrary to public interest.

But in fairness to Art Sylvester, formerly of the *Newark News,* who is Assistant Secretary of Defense for Public Affairs, another side of this order should be considered. Ever since the armed services were consolidated in 1947, with the statutory provision that the Secretary of Defense must come from civilian life, there have been flareups of guerrilla warfare conducted by the information services of the military service branches against the civilian authority imposed upon them by law. This warfare has been carried on through the leakage of contrived stories behind the backs of civilian information officials. The purpose of these illicit leaks is generally to influence public or Congressional opinion against the decisions or pending decisions of civilian authorities.

The Pentagon directive which has created controversy is quite simply a defense weapon of the civilian authorities against the furtive insubordination of the information officers of the separate service branches. Secretary of Defense McNamara, with a proper concern for morale, does not like to have this discussed publicly, but that's the fact of the matter.

If and when a form of news management like this becomes a vehicle for concealing information to which taxpayers are entitled, I think we can be certain that somebody will break the blockade.

The incidents involving suppression of news are actually conflicts between mortal men and an institution.

You are the institution. You'll be around.

The payrollers are the mortal men. In the long run, they've got to lose.

I doubt that many public wrongdoers have gone unpunished. At some time or another an unexpected shift in the wind topples the screen and reveals them in all their ugliness. Or the voters finally catch up with them, usually after long and painful efforts by newspapers to expose them as fakers. Whatever they do, life eventually closes in on them. And if you aren't around to record the event, your successor will be. The important thing to remember is that you'll have the last word.

Louis Stark's Own Story

LOUIS STARK [JANUARY 1952

When Louis Stark left his long-time Washington labor beat for the *New York Times* in 1951 to join the paper's editorial-page staff, his colleagues and many others joined in a dinner of testimonial to his pioneer work in developing the field of labor as news. At the end Mr. Stark responded with this autobiographical statement, unique in the record of this modest man.

Just for the record, I'm not the pioneer in labor reporting, although you might say I'm one of the pioneers. The *New York World* had a man, John Leary, and he was very helpful to me. It was a lesson that I never forgot. And if I have been of any assistance to any of the men who have spoken so handsomely tonight, it's probably due to the fact that I wanted to be a teacher and did teach school for six months before I gave it up. Maybe there's something about that in my blood.

It's been a kind of dual job that I've had all these years. When I came to know the field of labor fairly well, I had a feeling of responsibility to the fellows who were coming in and didn't know it, because I didn't want them to go off the deep end and make mistakes, which wouldn't have done them any good and wouldn't have done their papers any good. And yet, this is a competitive business. And I really don't know how it is that I did whatever it is that I did. Those were the two things that were working at the same time. And the thing that pleases me, perhaps, above all else, one of the things is, that despite the fact that I've been in a competitive business—and a "beat" is, well, what it is, although it's something that's forgotten about very quickly—despite the rivalry, the men with whom I have worked, by and large, have held me in esteem, and trusted and respected me and have shown how they feel in honoring me on this occasion.

There are many things that I think about, that rush through my head from the early days. They say that I counseled people; perhaps I did at times. I was reminded today, by Bill Lawrence of our paper, of something that I said to him in Detroit about 1937 during the General Motors strike. We were talking about labor news and he was just beginning at that time and he said today: "You told me that when you're writing about the A. F. of L. or the CIO to think out the logical thing they would do and then write the opposite." Well, with due respect to Phil Pearl, Charlie Herrold, and my friends, Green and Meany, there was not only a little truth in that; there was quite a bit of truth in it even though it sounded paradoxical. By this time I had learned that these labor leaders were terrifically shrewd traders. And I knew that I couldn't outsmart them in thinking what they might do. And in collective bargaining, they would, very frequently, just turn the thing upside down. It may have been my facetious way of speaking but Bill told me he hadn't forgotten that.

You've been reminded that I came down here in '33, a greenhorn to Washington. And I like to think of two incidents that occurred on the first and on the second day of my arrival. On the first day, I ran into some railroad people here and one of them told me something about a coordinator of transportation being named by the president soon, a man named Joe Eastman. Well, I thought that was a story the *Times* would be interested in. So I made some notes, and went back. The notes were based on the executive order which had not been published. When I got back to the office, Delbert Clark who was on the desk was rather excited. He said: "We've been looking for this story for a week. Do you think you can get a copy of this thing verbatim?" Well, I said, I copied it from a verbatim thing, but I'll see if I can borrow a copy. I went uptown and borrowed a copy and they sent it verbatim. And Felix Belair, who had been covering the ICC and who knew Joe Eastman like he knew the top of his hand, very kindly and graciously helped me write the story. The next day reporters flocked in to President Roosevelt, into a conference, and they asked him about the story, whether it was true. "Well," he said, "I had a copy of this order here last night and it isn't here now." I don't know what he meant to convey by such an intimation, but he did verify the fact that the story was correct.

Well, that was the first day. The second day I was here, I came downtown from the capitol with Jett Lauck, who was the economist for the United Mine Workers. And he told me something about a bill called the National Industrial Recovery Act. Well, that idea had been kicking around Washington and people had taken a poke at it and he told me the origin of it, what it was to contain, all in the course of this taxi ride. When I got up to the office, I said to Delbert Clark: "Do you know anything about this National Industrial Recovery Act?" He said: "What do you know?" So I told him what Jett Lauck had told me. And he said: "Write it; we'd like to have it." So I wrote it. Well, that was a "beat" like the first one.

The reason I tell this story is the sequel. Ted Wallen was then the head of the *New York Herald Tribune* bureau, and some malicious friend of his ran into him on the second day and said: "Ted, that fellow Stark, he has a contract. He has to deliver a 'beat' once a day."

Well, I don't know how seriously Ted Wallen took that statement but, of course, I couldn't keep up with the record, and didn't.

I think it has been my good fortune—through fate, accident, or what you will—first to be associated with a paper that was willing to have men explore this particular field when other papers didn't see the opportunity in labor news, and to give me a free hand. And in the second place, the idea captivated me when it was first broached in 1923—although as a general work reporter I had reported labor news just as other people had on occasion, having reported my first big labor convention in 1919, the A. F. of L. convention in Atlantic City.

I was fortunate in another way, to which I have alluded. And that was that I had the edge of perhaps ten years on the other papers and so had acquired a background which came in such good stead in 1933, when the National Industrial Recovery Act, and Section 7A, and the codes of fair competition became the order of the day. It was easy for me. All I had to do was to stand on the third floor of the Department of Commerce Building, figuratively hold my hat in my hand, and people would go by and drop stories in it, people I had been cultivating, people I had known for ten years. And by that time many of them knew and trusted me.

It was no particular credit to me but it was a fact that I had had what Arthur Meyer, an arbitrator in New York, once called a monopoly. He said: "The trouble with you, Stark, is, you've got a monopoly." Well, that monopoly didn't last forever, because beginning in 1933 other papers began paying attention to labor news and assigning men to this beat.

Covering the labor movement and labor-management relations has been an unending source of wonder and interest to me from the very beginning. The psychological relation between those who manage industry and those who take orders is a delicate one not yet sufficiently understood.

I was offered the choice of covering Wall Street for the *Times,* at first. And I said: "Thank you very much. I think I'd like to pass it up." I was asked if I would like to specialize in the very important and complicated transportation problem in New York City—which is still a problem and Page 1 news. And I thanked them and passed that up. And why they chose me for the third one, I don't know. But they did. And I'm very glad that they did. It was a pioneer effort. I was not the first one there; but it was a pioneer effort.

And very early in the game, I learned one thing. And that was to take no part whatever, to be under no temptation whatever to take sides in an interunion dispute. I had seen one or two other labor reporters who were very strongly biased in favor of people whom they liked. And I felt that not only were they doing themselves a disservice, but in the long run they would rue the day. I remember one man, whose name I won't mention, who was so biased in favor of the A.F.L. United Garment Workers that when the Amalgamated

Clothing Workers was formed as a split-off and began to make news he would never go up to Sidney Hillman's office. But he would use the stuff in his paper by rewriting the City News Association.

Well, that was such an obvious thing to learn that it didn't take anybody with any great brains to learn it. And I think perhaps I can pride myself on the fact that in all these terrible interunion disputes—perhaps there's nothing quite as bitter as an interunion dispute—I meticulously kept away from offering any advice and from making any suggestions whatever. Not that I have refrained from offering counsel, but only if I were asked to do so. I never volunteered advice to any trade union leader on his problems.

Of course, I have been very timorous for a very good reason. And that reason is a simple one that you will appreciate. No matter how much I myself might know about his particular problem, I could never in the world place myself in his position. And this goes for the industrialists who have asked me for advice, too. I could never place myself in the exact place of the individual who has the responsibility for acting. He was responsible, the trade union leader, to his people; the industrialist to his board, his president, and his associates. I, as a newspaperman, was completely devoid of this kind of responsibility, despite whatever kind of imagination I may have had. I could never really completely place myself in his position. And therefore, as I say, I always approached such a task with a great deal of diffidence.

Yankee on Broadway

An Interview with Brooks Atkinson

DOM BONAFEDE [OCTOBER 1960

When Dom Bonafede did this interview with Brooks Atkinson in the spring of 1960, Mr. Bonafede was just ending his Nieman Fellowship and Mr. Atkinson was about to retire as drama critic of the *New York Times* and become a roving columnist for that paper. Mr. Bonafede was then on the *Miami Herald,* later on the *New York Herald Tribune.*

Justin Brooks Atkinson, who sat in judgment on multimillion-dollar Broadway theater productions for more than thirty years, rendered his decisions from an unregal setting. His office, a cubicle in the huge city room of the *New York Times,* was as neat and spartan as a New England landscape. There was nothing to show that the occupant was a dominant figure on the Broadway scene; there were no signed portraits of stage greats, no yellow theater bills. Instead, a large, colored drawing of three Summer Tanagers by artist Roger Tory Peterson, flanked by two small, green plants, loomed above the desk. Off to one side was a pastel caricature of Joe Jackson, an oldtime clown famous for a zany bicycle routine.

On a pillar behind the desk hung a portrait of H. T. Parker, Atkinson's boss on the old *Boston Evening Transcript.* A wood cut of Walden Pond was alongside.

With a pipe clamped between his teeth, with his short cropped hair and clipped moustache, Atkinson reflected more his academic background than the glitter of the Great White Way. In *The Story of the New York Times,* Meyer Berger said of him:

"The *Times* man who looked least like a potential war correspondent was Justin Brooks Atkinson, the drama critic. He never weighed more than 130 pounds, even in a rainstorm, and was more apt to tip the scales at 115. He was—and still is—the tweedy, spectacled, pipesmoking scholarly type . . . He was New England clear through."

Atkinson was born November 28, 1894, in Melrose, Massachusetts. Except for a year spent as instructor of English at Dartmouth, he has devoted his adult life to newspapering. He has written a half dozen books, mostly collections of contemplative essays, as well as a scholarly treatment of Henry Thoreau. He and his wife, Oriana Atkinson, divide their time between a Manhattan apartment and a country home in the Catskills, where he engages in his favorite pastime of bird-watching.

The interview took place in Atkinson's office amid the hammering and banging of nearby workmen. At one point the mild-mannered critic raised his voice an octave and bawled, "Damn it! You can't hear yourself talk in here." He then returned his pipe to his lips and settled back.

Last December the *Times* in a two-inch item at the bottom of page 55 announced that Atkinson was quitting his seat on the aisle at the end of the season. Told of the news, author and former critic John Mason Brown commented, "I feel as if St. John the Divine had been bombed." Brown, who was speaking for the theater world, spoke for the world of journalism as well.

Interviewer: You have been both critic and a straight news reporter. What would you say are the principal differences?

Atkinson: The reason we have reviews in newspapers is that the opening of a play is news. The review is a news report. Instead of being objective, it is more highly subjective. That is the main difference. Actually, there's an amount of subjectivity in merely determining what is news and what is not news. The stock-market reports and ship sailings and arrivals are the only things in newspapers not subjective.

Interviewer: What in your opinion are the basic qualities which make a good critic?

Atkinson: I think he should have a cultural standard, a cultural background and a knowledge of the history of the theater. He ought to be interested in the theater and be an enthusiastic theater goer. He is writing for newspaper readers and those who read him the most are theater goers. He may have all the necessary qualities but if he is not genuinely interested in the theater he won't be much of a critic.

Interviewer: Does the knowledge that your appraisal of a play goes a long way in making or breaking the production weigh heavily upon you?

Atkinson: I never think of it. And I don't believe it. Our reviews are supposed to have some influence but nobody knows what it is.

People like to believe in demonology. It gives them some security to believe there is a devil controlling their universe. The success of the theater does not depend upon the critics. For example: *The Andersonville Trial* got a negative notice from me and it seems to be doing well. *At The Drop Of A Hat* received good reviews from everybody but me and it's been running since November. I wrote a favorable review of *Greenwillow* but I don't think it will be financially successful.

Interviewer: Then you think talk about the power of the critics is overplayed?

Atkinson: Whether a play gets a good review depends upon what is on the stage. The theory of criticism is that the critic has no power. He translates what he sees and feels to the reader. Nobody says critics are responsible for successful plays: the actors, directors and writers are given credit. So I don't see why reviewers should be blamed for failures. I had a request recently from the *Reader's Digest* asking me if I'd do an article on why plays should not be reviewed the same night the critic sees it, the idea being he should have more time to mull it over. That's like the old assumption that women's votes would clean up politics. Naturally, I refused to do the article. The awkward factor in criticism is that everybody is human. You can't get away from human beings; that's what makes the trouble.

Interviewer: In commenting on the art of criticism in *Once around the Sun,* a book you wrote in 1950, you said: "In the appreciation of drama there is one basic problem, is it good or is it bad? But this is a question that so far has defied systemization and that has to be answered afresh every time a new play opens and by everybody who sees it. In art there is nothing right or wrong but thinking makes it so. There are no concrete rules that specify the virtues and vices of a drama, and there are no authorities learned enough to give the magic word." Would you stick by that today?

Atkinson: Yes, I would. My ideas haven't changed a bit in ten years. I'm afraid I rewrote that same thing for a current *Theatre Arts* piece without even thinking back to it.

Interviewer: Your views seem similar to those of Robert Penn Warren. He claims it is nonsense to assume that any one kind of criticism is "correct" criticism. He says there is no correct or complete criticism.

Atkinson: I agree. There are all kinds of criticism. Newspaper criticism is different from academic reviewing. A newspaper critic should be concerned with what is on the stage and not try to reform the theater. He is primarily a reporter. Of course, he should write about the kind of theater he believes in and on his idea of the ideal theater.

Interviewer: Well, what is it you look for in a drama?

Atkinson: Like any other theater goer, I look for an evening's entertainment. I don't fight a play, at least not consciously. My intention is to surrender to it. Everybody has prejudices. I wouldn't for a moment think I'm a good audience for every theater. In order not to be influenced, I never read any out-of-town notices. I sit in the theater and later comment on it from my impressions. I know it sounds too good to be true and it is too good to be true.

Interviewer: How about stimulation? Don't you look for that in drama?

Atkinson: Yes. If I'm emotionally involved I feel it has something for me. But if it doesn't have emotional involvement, it's not for me.

Interviewer: What are the steps you follow when you leave the theater and return to the *Times* to write your review?

Atkinson: The first thing between the theater and the office I try to get the lead sentence in my brain. I have about an hour to write the review for an eleven-thirty deadline. I write with pencil in long hand. Each paragraph is taken to the copy desk as soon as it is written. When I finish the review I go to the composing room and read proof on it. My intention is to get everything corrected by eleven fifty-five, which is when the paper is supposed to be locked up.

Interviewer: Why do you write in long hand after all your years as a newspaperman?

Atkinson: It's just a habit. The discipline of pencil on paper helps me. I write news stories on the typewriter but comment is more difficult. My Sunday pieces I write in long hand at home. I feel leisurely and grand there, but when I get to the office I feel less leisurely and grand and I rewrite it on the typewriter.

Interviewer: Do you do any revising of your reviews?

Atkinson: No, there isn't time, except to correct typographical errors. I try not to change anything because it puts a strain on the composing room. I might cut a paragraph, as I did in today's review of *Viva Madison Avenue,* because I feel it doesn't contribute anything.

Interviewer: Have you ever had second thoughts about a play and later reversed or modified your original opinion?

Atkinson: No. When I'm in the theater I'm thinking about it all the time. My mind is then made up. If anybody agrees with me, fine. If they don't, I'm not going to change my opinion. You always have people on your side. Like *Greenwillow:* I was the only one to report favorably on it and many people think I'm a hero—but not enough to make it a success. There are always differences of opinion about a play. Some people didn't like *South Pacific* or *My Fair Lady,* and if that's their opinion, it's all right.

Interviewer: Does the critic's mood ever influence his judgment?

Atkinson: I don't know. In my case, on the night of a play my wife and I have dinner alone after which I take a good nap. I never go to a party before a play and then rush to the theater the last minute. I get there early and read the program. I don't ignore the fact that mood can be a factor. I try to compensate for it.

Interviewer: I've heard that you personally know very few of the people you've been writing about for years. Is that the result of a conscious effort on your part to retain your objectivity?

Atkinson: I make a virtue of the fact I'm antisocial by nature. I don't think friendship is a good basis for criticism. I like theater people but I don't make a practice of cultivating their friendship.

Interviewer: The Alsop brothers in their book *The Reporter's Trade* said they shy away from getting too close to important news sources.

Atkinson: That's the way with me. I have only one or two close friends in the theater. It puts a strain on your relationship. Alec Guinness told me he never knew what attitude to take with critics. If he was "upstage" with them people would say he was trying to get in good with them; if he was cool towards them he was called a snob.

Interviewer: How much influence do you believe the New York critics have on the success or failure of a stage production?

Atkinson: Everybody says it's enormous but I'm very skeptical. I wrote a Sunday piece a few years ago called *Cloud of Critics.* I remember the title because it comes from Gibbon's *Rise and Fall of the Roman Empire.* In the article I examined what the critics said and the number of successes for that year. I remember the ratio wasn't black and white. There was a relationship between good reviews and the successes, but after all there are good and bad plays.

Interviewer: You hear much these days of the high cost of the theater. Is this economic hazard likely to strangle the theater in New York and drive it off Broadway and to the hinterlands?

Atkinson: The economic factor is the most destructive element in the theater today. If the same was true of another business it would have gone under thirty years ago. I think the result is that the theater is becoming decentralized. Also, talkies and television satisfy most people today. It's almost like an anarchy. The silent screen, on the other hand, was never a threat to the theater. There are more smaller theaters now, as in Houston, Dallas, Los Angeles, and San Francisco. That seems sensible to me. Cities should invent their own theaters. There is no reason why they should take Broadway plays.

Interviewer: How large is the New York theater audience?

Atkinson: About ten million people go to the theater in New York each year. A lot are duplicates and many are from out-of-town but this is a good, exciting theater town. It has a combination of Broadway and off-Broadway plays to offer now.

Interviewer: Why are you an exponent of off-Broadway productions?

Atkinson: I think off-Broadway has higher literary taste and is more enterprising from an artistic point of view than Broadway. Unfortunately, off-Broadway's resources are not as good. And because of lack of money it can't get as fine actors as Broadway. The real paradox between Broadway and off-Broadway is that off-Broadway can't get good actors but does artistic plays; Broadway could get the actors but doesn't stage the plays.

Interviewer: Is Broadway absorbing any of the off-Broadway talent?

Atkinson: Much of it. Such performers as Ben Gazzara, Geraldine Page, Nancy Wickwire, and George C. Scott came from off-Broadway.

Interviewer: There seems to be a mild revolt against the New York critics these days. Helen Lawrenson in *Esquire* maintains critics of an earlier vintage—such as Nathan, Woollcott, Benchley, and Gibbs—were franker, funnier and possessed of higher standards and greater talent. She claims the present crop of critics are either too old, or too rich, or too stale or too dumb. What do you say?

Atkinson: This woman wants criticism she's not getting. I couldn't give it to her if I tried. What she is looking for, I'm not.

One of the truisms of the theater is that dead critics are the best. I'm not looking forward to canonization after leaving this post.

Interviewer: What was the most memorable evening you ever spent in the theater?

Atkinson: A lot stand out in my mind. Some of the great ones were *Mourning Becomes Electra, Death of a Salesman, Our Town, Skin of Our Teeth, Streetcar Named Desire.* If I went over the list there would be twenty-five or fifty.

Interviewer: At the risk of putting yourself on the spot would you name the best performers you've seen?

Atkinson: The Lunts are the best we've got. I'm a sucker for actors. I like a lot of them. I'm always fascinated with what they do and why they do it. Most are wonderful people, sweet, intelligent, humorous and they have less vanity than you would expect. Most good ones are simple and modest people. Many are very excitable but temperament is an essential part of a good actor.

Interviewer: You won a Pulitzer Prize in 1947 for a series of articles on Russia. Could you say something about that?

Atkinson: After we left Moscow, where I had been assigned for about a year, my wife and I got on a freighter in Odessa. I sat down and wrote an article of about 5,000 words summing up my ideas on why we were having trouble with the Russians and why we'd continue to have trouble. When the story reached the office it was decided to divide it into three parts and run it as a series.

Interviewer: Was it a prediction of things to come?

Atkinson: It was more of an analysis of the situation then. Looking back it seems very routine and commonplace. But it created a lot of interest and mail. People at that time had not yet made up their minds about Russia and were looking for guidance—perhaps, I should say clarification. There was much comment about it, most of it favorable but the leftists were angry, full of wrath and unhappy. My agent was threatened. And my wife had written a book called *Over at Uncle Joe's* describing daily life in Moscow, which put more juice in the stew.

Interviewer: Did you ever sweat harder over a story than you did over your exclusive on Gen. Joe Stilwell's removal as U.S. commander in the China-Burma-India sector during World War II?

Atkinson: That was a message-to-Garcia type of thing. I admired him and still do. He was the most honest and the best general out there, thoroughly American. When this happened I was sick in bed. His adjutant called and said the general wanted to see me alone, something he had never done before, since he was scrupulous in his dealings with the press. When I saw Stilwell he showed me a cable from Gen. George Marshall telling him to get home. I was not as surprised as he was because Ambassador Pat Hurley had told me he was going to recommend it. I told Stilwell it was a hell of a story but I could never get it out of China unless I took it out myself. Stilwell then offered to take me back to the United States with him. We left almost immediately and I left my toothbrush and most of the rest of my belongings behind. I never did find out what happened to the stuff.

While in the air between Kunming and New Delhi I wrote my story, still sick with jaundice. I put it in my uniform and forgot about it. Stilwell stayed behind at New Delhi but made arrangements for me to fly ahead. As yet I hadn't even told the *Times'* office I was on my way home. When we got to Cairo we had to change planes. Before boarding the second plane a G.I. censor ordered us to turn over all our documents. I had a briefcase full of papers and thought there goes the story. I had forgotten it was in my pocket. I finally got back to the U.S. and the censors in Washington withheld the story. I understand Roosevelt gave final approval to release it since I was already in the country and could have written it here. It was my last story from Asia. I went immediately into the hospital. At the time I weighed 114 pounds.

Interviewer: How did you get into newspapering?

Atkinson: My first job after graduating from Harvard in 1917 was on the *Springfield Daily News* for twelve dollars a week. Shortly afterwards I was offered twenty dollars a week to teach English at Dartmouth and naturally I took it. This was during the war. I had been turned down by Plattsburg and then by the draft for hidden diseases which never became prevalent. I got a job on the *Boston Transcript* as a police reporter but soon after was drafted for limited service and I spent three months as a clerk at Camp Upton. I then went back to the *Transcript*. From eight to three-thirty I was a police reporter. After three-thirty I wrote reviews on my own time under H. T. Parker, who was the drama critic for the paper. In 1922 I went to the *Times* and became drama critic in 1925.

Interviewer: After 38 years as a *Times* man you are retiring. What led you to make that decision?

Atkinson: I'm 65 and for a long time I thought that was a good age to quit. I'd rather leave voluntarily than have people say it's about time.

Interviewer: What are your thoughts on leaving the business you've served so long?

Atkinson: Actually, I'm going to stay on the paper. I'll probably do some kind of features. But I won't have any more night work.

The Reporter in the Deep South

JOHN HERBERS [APRIL 1962

All John Herbers' thirteen years as a newspaperman had been in Mississippi when he wrote this in 1962. He was then UPI state manager. Later he served UPI in Washington, then returned to the South as a *New York Times* correspondent. He was a Nieman Fellow in 1960–61.

In *Absalom, Absalom!*, one of William Faulkner's great Gothic novels of Yoknapatawpha county, Quinten Compson goes to Harvard and is questioned endlessly by his Canadian roommate and others: *"Tell about the South. What's it like there? Why do they live there? Why do they live at all?"* Young Compson has some trouble describing the incredible state of affairs back home.

That was 1910. Today, Yoknapatawpha county, after being left alone for more than eighty years, is undergoing rather drastic, externally wrought changes. Telling about it can be fraught with difficulty, if not for the novelist, for the journalist who must live there.

I have found some curiosity among newspapermen about how racial news is covered in the Deep South. Implied in the questioning is this: what strange set of circumstances shapes news coming from the South and how do we know some of it is not being suppressed?

It would be no overstatement to say the Deep South is a unique region and the reporter responsible for writing about it for both local and external consumption undergoes a unique experience.

Circumstances do shape his copy but usually not in the way the uninitiated might suspect.

My purpose here is to explain some of the problems involved and the framework in which the reporter must function. To do so, I must confine myself to Mississippi, still the hard core of the Deep South, and to my point of view as a wire-service reporter. In this way, however, the problems—shared to some degree by all reporters in the region—can be presented in acute form.

It is necessary first to give a brief description of social and political conditions. There is running through the South what is commonly called the black belt. Its characteristics include an agrarian economy, a large Negro population, and ultraconservative opinion in economic and social matters on the part of its white leadership. Virtually the same climate of opinion exists in all black-belt counties whether they be in North Carolina, Tennessee, or Alabama.

The difference in Mississippi is that these counties cover almost the entire state and there is no large urban area or extensive coastline to mitigate the black-belt influence—such as exists in, say, Louisiana or Georgia. Black-belt thinking has permeated all facets of public life and it dominates the civic and business leadership of Jackson, the capital and largest city, as well as most other larger communities in the state.

Neither the federal government nor civil rights organizations such as the National Association for the Advancement of Colored People chose to press for equal rights for Negroes in the hard-core areas of segregation until changes had been made in the border states. For six years following the Supreme Court's 1954 desegregation decision, Mississippi was an anxious spectator while the federal courts slowly brought about integration in some areas of life in surrounding states. With each decision and with each racial incident, white opposition to any change in the status of the Negro hardened. The moderates were neutralized.

Thus, in 1961, when the civil rights front moved into Mississippi in the form of freedom rides, Justice Department intervention in voting, numerous federal court lawsuits, and demonstrations by local Negroes, the resistance was something like dragging an angry tomcat by his tail across a thick carpet.

It would take several columns to describe adequately the climate of opinion existing in the white community at this time. It will do here to state that news reporters are not the most popular people around. The least of the problems for the reporter, however, is the threat of being mauled in places like McComb. The greatest problem is pressure from news sources, officials, and clients of the news service—in effect, pressure to quit seeking the news.

We cover Mississippi from Jackson with a five-man UPI bureau. It is customary to maintain part-time correspondents in most areas of the state to protect us on breaking news. Usually these people work for newspapers or radio stations and are an integral part of their community. The average community is engaged in an all-out drive for industry to stem population losses and bring in much-needed prosperity. More than almost anything else its Chamber of Commerce does not want the name of the town associated with racial strife. As a result we are not likely to be tipped on a story with a racial angle by anyone in the community. (This is not true, generally, in counties where a daily newspaper is published, but they are few and far between.)

Instead, it is likely to come from a Negro leader and usually it has come to him by a devious route. One day last summer an NAACP leader in Jackson called in a report that a plantation hand in a remote county had been lynched by his landlord and his sheriff. He said the report had come from Chicago from a relative of the victim. John Garcia, a staff reporter, spent several hours on the telephone trying to find out what had happened, but no one would claim any knowledge of the alleged incident. The sheriff went so far as to say he had seen the youth who was reported dead "hanging around town" that very morning. But when he was pressed for more information he spouted profanity and ungrammatical denials. Garcia moved a brief story on the basis of what the NAACP leader and the sheriff had said. In it, he cleaned up the sheriff's speech except for one phrase with bad grammar, perhaps to retain some degree of realism. This prompted a call from a client editor who complained that he knew the sheriff to be a college graduate and we were slanting the news by making him appear illiterate.

It was not until later in the day that we found out what the story really was. We sent a staff reporter, Ted Smith, to the scene, 100 miles away. He found that the young man in question was in jail and had been there for three days charged with assault and battery on his landlord.

The defendant's mother told Smith she saw her son severely beaten, without provocation, by the sheriff and the landlord and he had been taken to a hospital for treatment before being jailed. At the jail, Smith found that the youth had been questioned by an FBI agent. But the sheriff would not let Smith interview him and sent Smith away from the jail. By this time people around town were beginning to grumble about UPI "stirring up trouble" and Smith left town under threat.

The FBI reported it found no ground for entering the case and its findings were not disclosed. The story probably rated no more than two paragraphs on the national wires, although we carried the details locally. One news bureau was spent and frustrated.

Southern police usually are cordial to newspapermen. Jackson police were during the freedom rides last summer. Recently, they used police dogs to break up a crowd of Negroes who were protesting segregation of the state fair. Several were chased for blocks, and one bystander, who had nothing to do with the demonstration, was bitten on the leg. A reporter went to the hospital to interview him. Everything was fine, it seemed. The city had bought him a new pair of pants and the mayor, Allen Thompson, had sent his apologies. This seemed nice of the mayor and it was included in the story.

But it had no sooner appeared than the telephone started ringing. One call was from Chief Detective M. B. Pierce to Bureau Manager Cliff Sessions. He said the mayor was upset by the story. He had offered no apologies and owed none. The man should have moved if he did not want to be bitten. We stood accused of irresponsible reporting.

When the Interstate Commerce Commission order against segregated travel facilities went into effect November 1, 1961, UPI checked several cities to see what they would do about it. Most planned to continue segregation but the mayors of Winona and Grenada said they would comply with the ICC order. But they had not reckoned with Citizens Council leaders who leaped into action as soon as the story appeared. The mayor of Winona explained he thought he had been talking to an ICC agent rather than to a reporter. The mayor of Grenada said in a formal statement he was misquoted, and the chamber of commerce and city council adopted resolutions condemning "false" news reports, all of which was carried in full in the *Grenada Sentinel-Star* without explanation. I wrote a personal letter to publisher Joe Lee: "It was perfectly clear that when the Citizens Council people put the screws on your mayor, then came the statements of denial, resolutions, etc. It doesn't matter to us what they do about the bus stations in Grenada, but it is news that has to be covered. And I sure resent being used as a scapegoat for a public official who is forced to back down from his prearranged plan."

Lee agreed and printed the letter in full on page one. We never heard from the mayor.

Usually we don't come out smelling as sweet. In one city we were harassed by the newspaper and both radio stations for reporting some behind-the-scene developments that did not fit the official version of what happened.

These are not isolated incidents. Everyone is emotionally involved. Persons who never before paid attention to news coverage have suddenly become experts on how the delicate subject should be handled. For a long time we were told that the activities and statements of integration leaders were not news because they did not have enough following to give them substance. That is seldom heard now. Most complaints concern the way the news is worded. For example, when Memphis integrated three schools we relayed this abbreviated version on the state radio wire:

(Memphis, Tennessee) —Thirteen children ended more than a century of school segregation in Memphis today.

They romped and played with their white classmates then left for home half an hour early.

The children were accompanied from the schools by their parents and whisked away in automobiles about 2:30 this afternoon. The white students were dismissed at the regular 3 o'clock time.

A policeman reported earlier that he saw two Negro girls skipping rope with some white youngsters at one of the three schools integrated. A Negro boy was seen running hand in hand with a new-found white friend at another school.

The whites and Negroes ate at the same tables in the cafeteria and put away their dirty dishes together.

There was none of the bloodshed and violence that erupted at Little Rock and New Orleans when schools were integrated.

This prompted an "official protest" from a subscriber. "Why can't you report the facts without romancing the Negro race?"

The reporter begins to feel he is in a strait jacket. While he may not acknowledge criticism as justified, he may find himself writing without direction. He is inclined to turn out dead-pan copy when interpretive reporting may be in order.

Newspapers, by and large, understand the problems involved and the reporter's need for freedom. There is considerable sensitivity to the fact that newspapers outside the South frequently play down racial strife in their own cities and play it up under a Southern dateline. There is a feeling that every incident is played nationally. Actually, the great bulk of that reported never goes beyond the state wires. There simply is not room, and probably no demand, for all of it on the trunk wires.

This leads to another problem. We feel a responsibility to report this type of news in some detail. It is used by subscribers, and it is felt that justice is more apt to prevail in the light of publicity. In doing so, however, we load our wires with it and the energy of the news staff is consumed in tracking it down. Taken in large doses it can be pretty dreary stuff. Some days more than half the stories on the wire pertain either directly or indirectly to the race issue.

Dealing with the subject day in and day out the reporter may acquire a strange sense of imbalance. He may become preoccupied by this one issue and find himself a stranger to the larger, more important events in the world today, a provincial fellow.

There is, I believe, a need for a new approach in reporting the kind of social change that is going on in the South today. Certainly dead-pan rendering of facts is not helping to bridge the gap of misunderstanding that exists between races and groups involved. Why does the Main Street banker persist in thinking all integration leaders are wild-eyed Godless radicals saturated by Communism, when many of them are deeply religious and in many ways conservative; why do some liberals always categorize all white segregationists as irresponsible, insensitive lawbreakers, when frequently they are acting in conviction out of a lifetime of conditioning to their "way of life"? Why, unless there has been some breakdown in communications, whether through mass media or otherwise. It cannot all be attributed to blind prejudice.

Obviously, there is a limit to what wire services can do under the most favorable circumstances. Most newspapers seem content to continue under the old formulas. In the summer of 1961, during trial of a lawsuit for admission of a Negro to the University of Mississippi, an unusual opportunity presented itself for conveying some of the deeper meaning involved. The trial was conducted in a federal courtroom under a giant mural painted in the 1930's by a WPA artist. It was meant to depict rebuilding of the South but within the stereotyped framework of the Old South—forward-looking whites working and planning in front of a large columned building with magnolia trees and a steamboat in the background, while Negroes, segregated, pick cotton or strum a banjo.

The scene below was different—a well-dressed Negro youth on the stand asking for admission to Ole Miss, an outrageous request if placed in juxtaposition with the mural, and vice versa; a dark-skinned woman lawyer with a Grecian profile demanding, and getting, a court instruction on the correct pronunciation of "Negro" for benefit of the white attorneys; a gesticulating state attorney with a Tidewater Virginia accent deploying an array of dilatory tactics.

Those two scenes told a lot about the way things are and the way people think they are, about the past and about the future. We moved a story on it. It wasn't a great piece but it was a fresh approach and it told more than any story of the trite testimony in the trial. It drew compliments from other journalists, but that was as far as it got. I had a hard time finding it in print.

Most newspapers from outside the region have played the Southern integration story from the point of view that it—the court-ordered change—is morally right, the law of the land and inevitable. Obviously, the wire services cannot do this and they should not be asked to, any more than they should be asked to write from the point of view of the Main Street banker who looks on freedom riders as the lawbreakers, considers state segregation laws superior to U.S. Supreme Court rulings and looks forward to the day when the courts will return to William Graham Sumner and *Plessy vs. Ferguson.* Wire services can and should maintain a vigilant watch for any violation of individual or group freedoms guaranteed to all citizens of the United States and report the truth as nearly as it can be ascertained. Finding and reporting the truth has become a good deal more difficult than it used to be, and it probably will become worse before it's better. There is a need, as never before, for highly competent, skeptical reporters who can, if nothing else, keep the record straight.

Whaddya Mean, Local?

SYLVAN MEYER [OCTOBER 1954

Sylvan Meyer is editor of the *Gainesville Times* in North Georgia. He was a Nieman Fellow in 1950–51.

Back on my high school newspaper every once in a while we would prevail upon the principal to hold an announcement until the weekly was distributed. That way we could get a scoop.

The small town daily has to get its scoops about the same way. We beat the gossips occasionally, but even when we don't the gossips read the paper avidly. They want to see if we got the story right.

But, then, who cares about scoops? Many of our readers don't see the paper until the next day, anyway, and even that manages to keep abreast of the metropolitan paper in the territory on wire coverage, thanks to the fact that rural mail route carriers only make one round a day. Your papers wait at the post office a long time to catch that one.

Readers forget that one big story, that magnificent campaign. They pick up the paper to read about themselves and their community and the more detail they read, the more interpretation, the more exhaustive analysis of their own affairs, the better they like it.

Every man interprets the universe according to the way it reflects on his own image. Consequently, the first mirror is his own community and its environs. When he understands what he sees there and knows that he is a participant in its life, he is ready to be a statesman and a nation-man and a world-man.

What do we mean, local? I pick up local papers, large and small, and find canned editorials, uncredited; a hodge-podge of syndicated features unleavened by local talent (no matter how lousy); obituaries literally buried in the insides; dull wire stories played high on page 1 with lively local stories played low on the back page. Why do newspapers do this? I don't know. Suppose the ladies' ready-to-wear store on the square put Dior fashions in the window and concealed the prints under empty boxes in the basement?

Readers call up when the paper is late. (The carrier is playing football in a sandlot.) "Where is the paper? We want to read *our* news!"

Nieman Reports, Editor & Publisher, Quill—all the trade magazines print more or less frantic solutions to the television problem. Actually, the solution is easy. No other medium of mass communication now in existence can do what the newspaper can do. Radio and television haven't the time, the staff, nor the facility to disseminate detailed, background news of the local community. Their commentators can wax glib about the four corners of the earth and toss their generalizations concerning Iran and Indochina toward millions of ears and eyes, but they'll never walk into the courthouse at Gainesville, Georgia, or even Chicago, Illinois, and come out with a list of land transfers, or marriage license applications, or grand jury indictments.

The newspapers have an absolute monopoly on detail and vital statistics and I am constantly amazed at how few capitalize on their opportunity to run lists, just plain, old everyday lists, of jurors, court proceedings, building permits, and all the other six-point accumulations that furnish conversation in the drug-store coffee club and at the civic club meetings.

And I'm not talking about country journalism. I'm talking about things that people talk about. I have yet to hear the hardware clerk and the farmer buying fence staples discuss the subtleties of Naguib's coup d'etat.

They're saying, "Did you see in the paper where John Jones, ol' Bob's boy, bought the Smith place up the road to build a corn mill?"

Corny? No, sir. Something they didn't hear on NBC? Yes, sir.

Of course, our readers hear about Naguib. They know almost as much about world and national affairs as they would from normal reading of a metropolitan paper. For the news is in the paper, in less length and detail, to be sure, but national and world news is backgrounded in excellent special features from the wire service and the syndicates. These are promoted and pointed out as worth reading.

By assigning a five-man staff to a beat list of more than sixty separate categories and organizations, suppressing the desire for even finer breakdowns, our local newspaper searches for detail. In a follow-up story, it interprets the detail, in another it features the people who are involved in the detail, and on the editorial page it tries to appraise the detail in a logical opinion.

Will John Cameron Swazey ever announce into the living rooms in your town his ideas on the county commissioners' decision to raise the tax levy two mills?

Neither will he look into the progress of your community's effort to build tourist trade and wrap up the separate projects of the past six or eight months so that people's thinking on the subject will be better organized.

Local newspapering never gains the advantage of anonymity and that may well be one reason why it is sometimes a discouraging trade. News sources are all too aware that the man who writes the front-page article is the same man who writes the editorial, and if they don't like the editorial they can be difficult to deal with. Even in large cities, the distinction between an editorial and a news story burns brightly only behind the brow of the professional. Many readers and news sources don't know the difference and don't care.

So the habit of thorough local coverage becomes important. If you do today what you did yesterday and you do the same thing tomorrow, pretty soon the sheriff becomes accustomed to your poking around his jail docket and the commissioners get used to your sitting in on their meetings. It's the first poke and the first sit that require holding out for your rights.

We have "freedom of information" trouble, but with more staff we would have less of it because we could make routine those checks that now are special and that arouse the justified suspicion that we are checking because we caught wind of special treatment or a cover-up.

Now all of this goes beyond selling papers or pandering to mass tastes.

Unless the local newspaper gives the public detailed and accurate information pertaining directly to the heart-beat of the community, the public will not get it at all. In government coverage particularly, the newspaper's information should be so complete that a citizen who reads it carefully can make up his mind intelligently on a policy decision in that government.

We have high school and college graduates throughout this land who understand the structure of Congress, the cabinet and the Supreme Court, know vaguely of the organization of their state's general assembly and what the governor does, but who don't know how many county commissioners they have or what the city manager is supposed to manage.

Even local government becomes more and more delegated to planning boards, hospital authorities, housing authorities, park and recreation boards, boards of education, and municipal cemetery committees. Thus the effective processes of government drift further and further from the direct control of the electorate. Only complete newspaper information, reported in infinite detail, can fill the gap.

The metropolitan press often does the best it can to cover not only its own city but the smaller cities and villages in its circulation area. But to give them real coverage is an impossible job. State-wide newspapers promote the myth of state-wide coverage. Often no other daily serves their scattered territories. They hit most of the small places with a lick and a promise. Success stories blossom, series after series extoll "progress," Four-H Clubs," etc. If someone is killed or dies, if a school burns or a train is wrecked, they print it.

Some heated squabble, generally due to local misunderstanding resulting from incomplete information and unconfirmed rumor, receives play embarrassingly prominent to the local community and invariably inadequate in terms of local background. But the day-by-day routine of news, the full and detailed treatment of each step the community takes along its way never makes print. I realize how impractical a task it would be for every big newspaper to cover every little incorporated town that nestles beneath the stone wings of its journalistic edifice. But ain't it a shame.

We gasp with horror when the polls reveal that 27.9 of the people in the nation never heard of Bataan; 19.3 never heard of Anzio. How many people in hometown America never heard of their school superintendent, their local judge, their own indebtedness?

The job belongs not to the smaller dailies alone, but to the big ones, the 25,000 and 50,000 and the really great big ones who hold sway as "the" paper in perhaps hundreds of communities known only to the state editor—and to him only as those places where, when he gets time, he must hire a high school boy to string for him.

Community life, save for a thin skin of sophisticates, forms America's foundations. It is the individual's primary contact with all the rest of humanity. His feeling of responsibility to his neighbor and his fellow villager, townsman, or suburbanite comes before his concern for the next town or the next country. World peace is important but he views world peace in terms of his community's part in making it possible. If his newspaper doesn't help him to understand his own community, he doesn't have much hope of ever understanding the larger communities of which he is a part.

People fidget with their newspaper. "Not a thing in this rag tonight," they say. How silly, says the editor. There's an exclusive yarn from Trieste, a brilliant analysis of the world bank, four distinguished columnists, an editorial on autumnal leaf coloration plus a soul-searching essay on our moral obligations to Formosa, with an untold variety of recipes, comic strips, dress patterns.

"Funny thing," says the editor, "this survey says the classified ad page has tremendous readership."

Well, there is a reason, Buddy. Those little ads hit people where they live. And your readers are opening their papers at the back to read those ads before they read your news.

No want ads on TV, eh, Mr. Swazey?

News at the Legislature

RICHARD L. NEUBERGER [APRIL 1949

Richard Neuberger was the Northwest's most notable journalist before he entered politics. He was in the Oregon legislature when he wrote this. He later served in the United States Senate from 1955 to his death in 1960.

State legislatures are the lawmaking bodies closest to the American people. How good is the news coverage of the average legislature in the United States? Do the folks at home really know what goes on under the marble dome of the state capitol?

After having participated desultorily in the coverage of legislative sessions in at least half a dozen Western states, I look at the problem today from the other side of the mahogany rail. I am a member of the Oregon State Senate. My constituency is the 13th district, which comprises the city of Portland. I was elected last November to a four-year term.

The two dominant papers in the state are the *Oregonian* and the

Journal. Both are published in Portland, the only large city. Each has three men covering the session. These include the capital correspondent of each paper, the political editor, and one other member of the general news staff. They file to the two papers a grand total of approximately 7,000 words every legislative day.

Although both the *Oregonian* and the *Journal* have profound editorial biases, the coverage by their correspondents is factual and untinged by opinion. The two papers are conservative in policy—both urged the election of Dewey—but this policy rarely creeps into the news stories about the legislature. Controversial issues such as fair employment practices, workmen's compensation, and Columbia Valley Authority are handled as they occur, with no slant given.

In addition to the coverage of the legislature in considerable detail by the two Portland dailies, the Associated Press and United Press each has two staff men in the Senate and House chambers. The session also is followed closely by the pair of dailies published in Salem, the state capital. These are the *Statesman* and the *Capital-Journal.*

Here, again, the coverage is factual, truthful and unbiased, although the editorials of the *Capital-Journal* are too far from reality to communicate with it by smoke signals. To be candid, the only "policy" material I have noticed emanating from the legislature is that which some senators and representatives send back to their home-town papers. This plays up the local lawmaker as quite a hero. And, because the members from the smaller communities and rural areas are almost invariably conservative, the columns mailed by them to the country press tend to portray the liberals from Portland as a pretty shabby lot.

Of course, this is not serious, for it reaches only a small proportion of the voters. The *Oregonian* and the *Journal* blanket Oregon. One or the other of these big dailies reaches into every remote upland and mountain valley. I have been a guest at ranch houses so isolated that the nearest schoolhouse was too far away for the children of the family to come home except for Christmas. But when the mail arrived, these people got the *Oregonian* or the *Journal.*

Yet despite this blanketing of the state by the big dailies—and in spite of the basically truthful coverage of the legislature by those papers—I find many people uninformed on what is taking place in the carpeted chambers of their capitol building.

As chairman of the Senate Committee on Municipal Affairs, I

talked a few days ago with the mayor of a city of 25,000 people. He knew nothing at all about bills in our committee which vitally affected his community. Perhaps I was even more chagrined that he did not know the identity of the committee chairman!

Yet, in general conversation, I found this man fully acquainted with the progress of the Congressional debate on repeal of the Taft-Hartley Law. He knew who was sponsoring the Columbia Valley Authority bill in Washington, D.C., but not who was sponsoring a memorial backing the bill in Salem, Oregon.

I have wondered a good deal about this, and I have asked quite a few questions. As a result, I have come to the conclusion that, because of one particular reason, many Americans know a lot more about what takes place in the capital of the nation than in the comparatively nearby capital of their state.

That reason is the columnists.

The big Portland dailies are well buttressed with columnists from Washington, D.C., and the East. The *Journal* prints Pearson, Stokes, Sokolsky, Lawrence, and Pegler. The *Oregonian's* repertoire includes Childs, Lippmann, Fleeson, Thompson, Alexander, and Lyons. Thus both papers encompass a fairly wide circle of opinion from national sources.

Yet neither paper publishes a column from Salem, the capital of Oregon. This, in my opinion, is why people in our state often know more about what goes on in the legislative halls 3,000 miles away than in halls a mere 50 miles distant.

The real story is often the inside story. Pearson specializes in revealing the story behind the headlines. Men like Childs, Stokes, and Lawrence specialize in analyzing it from varying viewpoints.

There is no counterpart of this in the coverage of our state government in Oregon. Each of the two big dailies has a whole stable of Washington columnists, but none at the legislature.

Frequently, the very rectitude of the men covering the capital keeps them from going behind the scenes. Some years ago the *Oregonian* and the *Journal* heavily tilted their news columns. Political items inevitably were weighted. But as older staff men were retired, as people became more conscious of journalistic ethics, a new generation of writers was told to "play it straight." The facts were allowed to speak for themselves.

The men covering our legislative session will tell you what takes place, but they have strict orders against opinionated news stories. They need a "news peg" before they can allege that a former governor is lobbying for gamblers or that state school timber has been sold for a fraction of its value. The columnist is held back by no such rules. He can flail out at corruption and chicanery, news peg or no news peg. In some instances, this may be bad *per se,* but it does afford easy access to the "inside story."

Newspapers occasionally shy away from the story close at hand. They are notoriously braver about the skullduggery of the Russians than that of the local real estate board. This may pertain somewhat to the analogy of Washington, D.C., and the state capital. It may be easier to run the comments of a hard-hitting political columnist who operates 3,000 miles away than one whose writings concern people within walking distance of the editor's office.

If we are to give vitality to state government, I am convinced we must cover our state capitals as thoroughly, as intimately, and as revealingly as Washington, D.C., is covered. It does not make sense for each of our big Portland papers to print four or five editorial-page columns from the capital of the nation but no counterpart of these from the capital of Oregon. Nor are potential authors lacking. I am sure the chief political writers of the *Oregonian* and the *Journal* could produce legislative columns with as much vitality as the so-called "inside story" which those papers buy from afar.

The hold of columnists is one of the phenomena of our time. From the gossip in the senatorial lounge over coffee and sandwiches each noon, it is obvious that even many of the politicians acquire much of their knowledge of politics through reading the columnists. The appeal of a straight news dispatch cannot compete with a column which supposedly divulges the "intimate" story. Unquestionably this is not too salutary a circumstance, but it exists and must be recognized.

Most of our newspapers plead for state sovereignty vis-à-vis the octopus of the federal government. But state's rights also must be accompanied by state's responsibilities. One way to begin would be to cover the 48 legislatures with as bright a spotlight as that the press focuses on Capitol Hill.

Newspapers rail against federal dominance, but it is obvious that they themselves have not been immune to it.

Yet whatever shortcomings newspapers may have, they are far superior to radio as a means of political coverage. This was demonstrated to us early in the legislative session, when a pressman's strike closed both Portland dailies. People suddenly were reliant exclusively on radio for reports of the legislature. We found our constituents completely uninformed. The torrent of mail on pending issues dwindled to a trickle. Interest in the legislature all but vanished. A resolution was even introduced in the Senate suggesting that the legislature adjourn until the presses of the *Oregonian* and *Journal* should roll again.

Topics considered under the dome of a state capitol, whether they involve school bonds or the comparative merits of using a river for salmon or water power, often are too complicated for the staccato of radio. Furthermore, labor leaders and League of Women Voters officials said that a roll-call read over the air made scant impression on listeners. Only in type on the printed pages, where it could be studied and analyzed, did the tally of *yeas* and *nays* acquire any real significance.

The Thalidomide Story

ARTHUR E. ROWSE [DECEMBER 1962

Mr. Rowse is a news editor on the *Washington Post,* and the author of *Slanted News,* an analysis of the handling of the "Nixon fund" story in the 1952 presidential campaign by the thirty-five largest newspapers.

"Who can exaggerate the importance of a single person speaking?"

These words, spoken recently on television by Archibald MacLeish, no doubt were intended to embrace things written as well as spoken. Their truth, as applied to the press, has never been more amply illustrated than during recent months.

History is spotted with examples of the tremendous power of the press. One can point to just one article in a tiny Texas weekly and its effect in blowing down Billie Sol Estes' multimillion-dollar house of cards. Or, on a broader scale, one might consider a more recent newspaper article about a certain little-known doctor and drug that caused a national furor.

Since the middle of July 1962 the nation's communications media have been basking in the knowledge that they alerted the American public to the frightening menace of a seemingly harmless sleeping pill that has been blamed for horrible deformities in thousands of babies the world over. Widespread public attention to the thalidomide story undoubtedly has saved many mothers-to-be in this country from taking the suspected drug.

The impact on government has been equally great. Before July 15, the outlook for Congressional passage of an effective drug-control law was extremely dim. A Senate committee had pulled almost all the teeth out of a bill submitted by Senator Estes Kefauver after a series of hearings dating back to 1957. Even the toothless bill was given little chance of survival. The cumulative effect of pharmaceutical-industry pressure on the press and Congress was considered too great to change the status quo despite all the evidence of drug profiteering that had emerged in the Kefauver hearings.

Then came the explosion. On July 15, the *Washington Post* printed a story by reporter Morton Mintz describing how Dr. Frances O. Kelsey, a medical officer in the Food and Drug Administration (FDA), had resisted persistent industry forces for more than a year in blocking the public sale of thalidomide in this country.

The dramatic account was flashed around the nation. The revelations were made even more stunning by the subsequent disclosure that while Dr. Kelsey was blocking public sale, more than two and a half million tablets were being distributed to unsuspecting human guinea pigs by 1,267 doctors. Through a loophole in the law, drug firms were allowed to offer new drugs to doctors for what is called "clinical investigation."

Reactions to the story were rapid. A frantic search of medicine cabinets gripped the nation. Further drama was added by Sherri Finkbine's transoceanic quest for an abortion to prevent the birth of what she feared might be a deformed child as a result of her use of thalidomide pills during early pregnancy.

President Kennedy, recognizing the sudden change in atmosphere, sent an urgent appeal to Congress requesting that such loopholes in the pending drug bill be plugged and the bill passed.

Senators were quick to comply. The diluted bill that had already been reported at the time of the president's request was restored almost exactly as he wished, and it sailed through the Senate by a vote of 78 to 0. A similar bill passed the House, 347 to 0. The measure signed by the president on October 10 grants the FDA greatly expanded powers to regulate drugs.

Few stories in recent years have so decisively demonstrated the power of the press, once aroused, to change the course of events—in this case, thankfully, to the public benefit.

But the extensive coverage, coming after so much human damage had been done, also left some provocative questions. For one thing, could a more alert press have recognized the news any earlier and thus prevented some of the infant deformities still being attributed to the drug in this country?

Thalidomide first aroused suspicions of the medical world back in February, 1961. That was when Dr. Kelsey chanced to read a letter in a British medical journal suspecting the drug of causing nervous tingling sensations in some people. Thalidomide, under the trade name of Contergan, had been marketed in West Germany since 1957. It became known for an ability to relieve morning sickness in pregnancy and for being suicide-proof even in very large doses. Distribution soon spread to other countries.

One of the first articles about the drug in the general press appeared in the August 16, 1961, issue of the widely circulated German newsweekly, *Der Spiegel*. The full-page article described the drug's suspected nervous effects. By this time, Contergan had become the most popular sleeping pill in West Germany.

At the same time, an Australian gynecologist, Dr. W. G. McBride, was beginning to raise the first suspicions that thalidomide had been the cause of an outbreak of baby deformities in Australia. But his letters and articles failed to cause a stir.

It was not until November that a much larger outbreak of phocomelia was linked to the drug in West Germany. Phocomelia, the Greek word for seal flippers, is the term used to described the very rare phenomenon in which infants are born with stunted and distorted limbs on abnormally large bodies. Dr. Widukind Lenz, a Hamburg pediatrician, made a survey of mothers of deformed babies and reported that at least half of the women had used thalidomide in early pregnancy.

In the face of Lenz's evidence, the pill was immediately withdrawn from the market by the manufacturer, and the German Ministry of Health issued a warning about use of the drug by pregnant women.

Immediately the issue became top news in European newspapers, magazines, radio and television. But for some reason, American mass media did not pick it up. At the time, few people knew that the drug was already being circulated in this country by the Wm. S. Merrell Company of Cincinnati and by persons who brought the drug back after buying it abroad. A routine check by a competent reporter could have turned up this information and provided the basis for a news story. About the only American reaction, however, came in the offices of the Merrell Company. The firm sent a warning letter to doctors.

In February 1962 the controversy landed closer to home. On February 22, the day after a second warning letter from Merrell, the Canadian Department of Health and Welfare reported the situation publicly. This set off widespread reactions in the Canadian press. But still no news of the international sensation reached the readers, viewers, and listeners of American mass media except in *Time* magazine. The issue of February 23 carried an article entitled "Sleeping Pill Nightmare." On March 30, the magazine made another reference to thalidomide and mentioned "a sharp-eyed woman doctor on the FDA staff" whom it did not name. Even *Time,* however, did not follow up its own lead on Dr. Kelsey's epic struggle.

In reporting new drugs, American news media generally have been ecstatic in praise and exact in parroting publicity handouts. In controversial cases, the media traditionally have sided with the manufacturers. Senator Kefauver, whose persistent efforts toward stricter drug controls culminated in unanimous passage of the drug bill, has been a frequent target of the press.

All this makes one wonder how many other news stories of this kind are lying around right now waiting to be recognized.

It was left to another alert woman doctor to present the first full medical report on thalidomide in this country. This came on April 11 when Dr. Helen Taussig, a pediatrician at Johns Hopkins University, revealed results of a European research tour at the annual meeting of the American College of Physicians in Philadelphia. In describing the tragic developments in West Germany, where an estimated 7,000 babies have been or will be born with grotesque deformities, she warned that a similar outbreak could happen in this country under existing drug laws.

In her talk were elements of a good story of potentially great interest to Americans. Her speech was covered at length by the *New York Times* and a few of the papers taking the *Times* news service. The Associated Press also sent out a story, its first on the subject. But a random check of large papers across the country showed that few printed anything.

A high point was reached six weeks later, on May 24, when Dr. Taussig testified at an open meeting of the House Antitrust Subcommittee headed by Rep. Emanuel Celler. She showed color slides of deformed infants she had seen and revealed the existence of several cases in this country.

Certainly by this time, thalidomide had become of major news significance, not only for what Dr. Taussig actually said but also for what a diligent reporter might have turned up with a little effort. Yet, according to one committee staff member, there was no specific reference to this hearing by any general newspaper, magazine, radio or television outlet in this country for eleven weeks, long after the *Washington Post* broke the story about Dr. Kelsey.

The issue of *Science* magazine dated the next day, May 25, carried an editorial by Dr. Taussig mentioning the role of Dr. Kelsey. And the June 30 issue of the *Journal* of the American Medical Association carried a long article by Dr. Taussig with photographs and a reference to Dr. Kelsey. Although both of these publications are closely watched by the mass media for story ideas, they apparently caused no stir with these articles. Nor had a brief reference to thalidomide in the May 5 issue of *America* magazine.

By early July, several large papers were known to be tracking down tips from high offices about a possible news story lying around the FDA. Mintz found that he was not the first reporter to have interviewed Dr. Kelsey on the subject. But no details of her long struggle reached print until his story in the *Post*. Mintz himself was acting on a tip received by another *Post* reporter who had covered some of the Kefauver drug hearings.

His story broke the dam. Saturation coverage soon made Dr. Kelsey and thalidomide household words. The thoroughness of coverage testified to the news value of the story. But it also posed further questions. For example, are the American news media so somnolent that they must be prodded before they recognize news? Are they too producer-oriented to be aware of the kind of information that American consumers want and need?

The thalidomide story showed both the failure and the power of proper communication of vital public information. For months, the most highly developed mass media in the world failed to recognize a sensational news story. Yet all it took to tell it, and completely reverse the course of plodding government and public health, was one good reporter.

Crusading in a Small Town

ERNEST H. LINFORD [FEBRUARY 1947

This article from volume I, number 1 of *Nieman Reports* was written by Mr. Linford when he was editor of the *Laramie Republican-Boomerang*. An energetic independent editor, he succeeded in increasing circulation and profits of the paper and in bringing reforms and improvements in Laramie. He also learned the pitfalls of crusading. Later he became chief editorial writer of the *Salt Lake Tribune*. Mr. Linford was a Nieman Fellow in 1946–47. After appearing in *Nieman Reports* this article was reprinted in *The Press and Society*, ed. George L. Bird and Frederic E. Merwin (New York: Prentice-Hall, 1951).

The *Laramie Republican-Boomerang* which Bill Nye founded three quarters of a century ago as an outlet for his budding humor has been identified with some successful campaigns, but it has lost many a fight.

For many months our paper campaigned against smoke and cinders which make life hazardous and unpleasant on the leeward side of the Union Pacific railroad tracks. Cash prizes for letters brought torrid comments and proposals. Prize-winning letters were published and matched with pointed editorials, causing a mild sensation in a town noted for knuckling down to the Union Pacific, the payroll of which plays a tremendous part in community economics.

As the campaign neared its climax, Union Pacific engineers met with community committees to discuss what to do about roving cinders. But the marked clearing of the Laramie air, figuratively and actually, came not from a spirit of cooperation but by effects of John L. Lewis's "no contract, no work" enterprises, and as transportation fell off, fewer engines spewed unpleasant carbon over the business district.

In a blind retrenchment campaign, the Union Pacific all but closed its Laramie shops, furloughing about 300 family heads, some with a 25-year seniority. One has to live in a railroad town to realize the effects of such layoffs, be they seasonal or at the height of depressions. Rumors run wild; men curse the company and predict dire economic repercussions for the community. Business men are drawn into the dark psychology resulting in their own retrenchment programs.

When the layoff list was posted at the roundhouse the editor of the *Republican-Boomerang* was caught off guard by a sugary feminine voice on the phone which asked, "Would you like to have an item for your cinder campaign?" When he replied in the affirmative she snapped: "They're closing the shops today. I hope you're satisfied."

Editorials on cinders were not popular during the rest of last summer. Laramie friends wrote this winter that the cinder nuisance was at its height again and many of the furloughed shopmen were back at their machines.

Seventeen years in small-town newspapering, twelve as an editor, have taught me that success is sometimes more troublesome than failure, journalistically speaking. Professional and personal jealousies often take the edge off satisfaction of a job well done. I have learned through experience, at the end of a campaign, to bow out in favor of the Chamber of Commerce and other civic organizations which keep the ball rolling; to lie low while others take the bows.

At the end of a successful campaign a newspaper editor often learns that his work is just beginning, that he has a responsibility to guard and defend the new project. When the newness wears off a program comes up against hard realities.

In 1942 my newspaper brought to a climax a spirited campaign for council-manager government. Laramie citizens voted in the first city manager setup in Wyoming. Many factors contributed to success of the drive. The old mayor-council (second class city plan) had become outmoded, unwieldy, and illegal. The out-going city administration, locked in bitter rows, was unpopular and some members under suspicion. The town had outgrown its ancient charter. We hit while the iron was hot and helped convince the voters that they should not only turn the rascals out but bring in an entirely new setup.

But the sponsors of the radical change, including the editorial writer, were not prepared for such sudden success! When the council-manager system was voted in we found ourselves in a dilemma. The state statute governing the system was full of bugs. Nobody had had any experience with the new plan. The constitution forbade hiring anybody outside of the state and the state had no city managers.

Our No. 1 problem was to buck the machine which had picked mayors and councilmen for years and to institute a council of nonpartisan residents. Since the city treasury was sadly in the red, it was thought best to get as many business men on the council as possible. We were successful but not without a great deal of finagling which would put the old party ward heelers to shame.

A national city officials' magazine gave the *Republican-Boomerang* credit for securing the new government setup, but nobody knows better than the editor that it took more than a newspaper campaign. You can't shove a proposition down the throats of the people unless they are ready for it. You can help to make them ready but you must not move too rapidly. In most of our successful campaigns we worked hand in hand with civic organizations and in some cases have had the impetus appear to come from others.

Our campaign for better government started five years before there was any hint of success. We published stories on government in other towns. We ran series of articles on plans available under Wyoming law and discussed their merits and faults. When the time seemed propitious the editor took the project to the Lions Club, whose civic betterment committee he headed. We held a number of panels, discussing municipal governmental problems, and climaxed the series with the organizing of a Lions Club study committee. The Chamber of Commerce, which often coordinates the work of civic groups of the community, then absorbed the committee, adding other members. After several months of investigation the commission presented a report at a well-publicized mass meeting. The body recommended the council-manager form of government for which we had been thumping for a long time.

The recommendation was placed on the ballot at the general election that fall and then we accelerated our campaign.

One of the things I have learned about newspaper campaigning is that the job can be overdone.

What I considered our best campaign, utilizing all we had learned through the years, backfired. Yet by going "underground," we finally won a compromise. I refer to a campaign to secure a new municipal water system.

To understand the obstacles we encountered one has to be acquainted with the psychology of the high and dry, windswept western town. I hope that some day a psychologist makes a study of the effects of high altitude (Laramie is over 7,000 feet), a continual wind, and aridity on thinking and acting of human beings. In our town people act toward water as women do during war shortages when soap or nylons are offered for sale at a store.

Actually there is plenty of water for household and industrial uses and it is especially good water, but there isn't enough for the householders to pour on lawns twenty-four hours a day. Yet rugged individualism in Laramie is blended with a psychosis about growing plants. Every one has an attractive lawn, trees, and an abundance of shrubs and flowers which will grow in the cool climate.

Laramie's water problem is complicated further by the fact that the Union Pacific railroad owns first right to the flow of the main city springs. (It was traded to the company in the early days by an extremely weak-kneed city council. This is just one of the many acts of kowtowing to the Union Pacific in our community.)

The story of the many ambitious, varied, and expensive programs to explore the underground water resources is far too long to be recited here. But the street-corner experts refused to believe the geologists and engineers who said the problem couldn't be met by simply sinking another well. And when the city announced that it would be necessary to go to the river (Laramie) for an auxiliary supply, it was like waving a red flag at a herd of bulls! The bond issue was defeated by a whopping majority in 1937 in spite of a threat of parched lawns.

The drouth continued and temporary emergency measures were taken to keep the city and the railroad supplied. The war brought the real crisis.

A desperate city council proposed a new bond issue. A planning commission had made another investigation, hired a nationally known engineer. His report was read at a mass meeting. There was no alternative. The city must go to the river for water! Since it was doing that it might as well cut loose from the railroad, which owned the spring, reservoir and some of the pipelines. The cost was to be almost a million and one-half dollars.

Little was said at or after the mass meeting. But that silence we mistook for consent was shock!

Assisted by the planning commission, city officials, and interested citizens, we launched our most ardent newspaper campaign. We turned the newspaper over to the program of proving that if Laramie was to avoid drying up and blowing away the bond issue must pass.

We gained momentum as we went along. We went overboard! The people seemed to be with us. The mayor, city manager, and chairman of the planning board said we were doing a wonderful job. Letters and telephone calls backed up the assumption.

Then one day, toward the final week of the campaign, a chronic letter writer who had opposed most municipal proposals in the past, brought in a letter for publication in the morning paper (the *Daily Bulletin,* under the same ownership).

The letter was turned down on grounds it libeled city officials. The action was unfortunate. Word spread that the papers were refusing anything critical of the water plan. (The *Republican-Boomerang* had received no such letters.)

Suddenly, like a horde of locusts, came a barrage of mimeographed handbills carrying scurrilous, vicious charges. Some of the attack was aimed at the newspaper monopoly of the community and personnel.

We endeavored to answer all questions and refute all accusations. We conducted a question-and-answer column which oftentimes took up a great deal of the front page.

What hadn't been clear at the outset, gradually took form. It became a battle between the people who called themselves "the working men," against the "privileged class." Business men, who would have paid a large part of the bill, were generally for the plan, supported by most white-collar people, including university faculty members. But the railroaders, cement workers, and timber workers were violently opposed.

And at the election the opposition won by a margin almost as wide as it had seven years previously.

We had lost more than an election. We had imagined ourselves allied with working men; we had now become anathema to them.

Recriminations came thick and fast. Some who had said we were doing a good job passed the word along that we had overplayed our hand. By campaigning so ardently we had lent credence to the suspicion that the bond issue meant more to the paper than community betterment.

The discouraged, confused city council submitted the same water program again at the regular November election. The disillusioned *Republican-Boomerang* was relatively aloof this time. The campaign took the form of a battle of the throw sheets! The Water for Laramie Committee tried to outdo the Citizens Water Committee in invective, appeal and propaganda. A confused electorate voted the plan down again but paradoxically elected the city councilmen who sponsored the unpopular program.

Water became a topic not to be discussed in polite circles, and regulations on irrigation were tightened to near prohibition. The thirsty locomotives, pulling war goods across the continent, increased their demands. Springs were pumped, with the city realizing it was using capital for living expenses.

During the next few months a wise and sober little circle of city attaches and others decided that the crisis was very real and nothing would be lost by another election. After all, a million and a half dollars is a lot of money for a town of 11,500. Maybe some items could be pared. Maybe the river water bugaboo could be eliminated. The compromise plan, when it emerged, was a unique one. Emotions had burned themselves out in the community by this time. The *Republican-Boomerang* supported the plan strongly in editorials, but they were dispassionate, objective pieces. The vote was small at the new election, but the victory decisive. A "lost cause" had been turned into a compromise after long campaigning. It was much better than nothing, maybe better than the original program.

Between water elections, while trying to patch up our fences, we enlisted the assistance of the Lions Club and established a community service award by which we honor a local citizen each year. It is a nice ceremony with the *Republican-Boomerang* furnishing the plaque on which names are engraved. Annually we sponsor an essay contest on community betterment.

Years ago we campaigned for a unified city garbage collection system. The service was established at long last but because of the heavy drain on the general fund every administration has sought ways to curtail the program. We have steadfastly resisted any such move. The housefly problem was alleviated by the program. Likewise we have watched over Laramie's municipal skating rink, one of the finest of recreation centers. It also is a "white elephant" and unpopular among the city's budget makers. But it furnishes grand recreation, free, to hundreds of children. And there's hardly a youngster in Laramie who cannot and does not skate.

Years of crusading have convinced me that the small town newspaper's leadership should not be too obvious. And when a campaign is won, silence or passing the credit to others is a good way to ensure success in the next campaign.

One of our main handicaps today is the suspicion on the part of a number of citizens that the newspaper is trying to "boss" the town. Needless to say, we haven't always been bosom buddies of some mayors, city managers, and Chamber of Commerce officials.

An editor has to keep in mind the long-term project, the campaigns which cannot be won in a few months or years—the drive that is never fully successful. His responsibility is to jog the community conscience, to keep ever vigilant, to promote honesty and responsibility. If the political officeholder knows that the press will fight him if he is dishonest or does something which is not for community benefit, he will be more cautious at least.

It would be more comfortable to sit on the moon, and raise hell in complete objectivity when hell-raising was indicated. But the editor who plans to live in the community the rest of his life has to think of the long-term results and his future effectiveness.

It is a hard job to trample on the toes of a fellow citizen in the editorial column and meet him socially that evening or the next. Small-town residents take the editorial column seriously. It takes courage to jump on the police department—even demand that the chief be fired—and go around the next day in search of news.

Newspapermen and Lawyers

ANTHONY LEWIS [JULY 1960

At the time of this article Mr. Lewis was in the Washington bureau of the *New York Times,* covering the Supreme Court. He had devoted a Nieman Fellowship in 1956–57 to studies in the Harvard Law School. This is from a talk to the *Harvard Law Review* dinner, April 23, 1960. His reporting won a Pulitzer award in 1964, and in that same year his book *Gideon's Trumpet* appeared. He is now London bureau chief for the *New York Times.*

I propose to express myself on a moderately pretentious topic, the public responsibilities of newspapermen and lawyers. It may seem surprising that the two professions—if profession is not too high-flung a term for my business—are in any way comparable. It seems to me that newspapermen and lawyers share at least the basic attribute of being generalists. One of the great joys of my brief experience at the Harvard Law School was the discovery that teachers were, on the whole, not trying to drill particular facts into reluctant student memories. In the first-year course I took, Procedure, much of the year seemed to be taken up with persuading the class that there were no absolute facts to be learned. Of course the aim of the Law School is to awake a process, a way of thinking that can be applied to any situation in life. Although many lawyers do become specialists, the essential quality of the lawyer to me is that he is a non-expert, a generalist, a *whole man* in a world made up increasingly of half-men or quarter-men—experts on narrow, specialized problems whose immersion in their own field makes it hard for them to see its relation to life outside.

Now something of the same requirements of broadness, of adaptability, exist for newspapermen—or ought ideally to exist, at any rate. The reporter is constantly being thrown into new situations. He is expected to write knowingly one day about interest rates and the next day about the humane slaughter of animals. As life becomes more complicated, there is a tendency on newspapers as in law offices to create more experts—science writers and legal writers and so forth. But at heart the real newspaperman, even while he ponders whether a maritime tort for jurisdictional purposes arises under federal law, is ready—eager, I should say—to cover the presidential campaign.

I do not want to leave the impression that I overrate the similarity in approach of lawyers and newspapermen. They may both be generalists, but the lawyer has to dig deeper into any problem he is handling. There will be published next month a book of reminiscences by Justice Frankfurter, and in it he recalls working on a financial manipulation case for months while an Assistant United States Attorney in 1907. He writes: "When I think of what I then knew about brokerage accounts! But I know nothing now. A lawyer becomes an expert in so many fields for so short a time."

The newspaper tradition is very much against becoming even a short-term expert on anything. In the past, at least, the reporter was expected to be the jack of all trades and master of none. One reason for this may be the well-founded fear that the more one learns about a subject, the harder it is to write a good simple story about it. Every sentence you put down cries out for qualification—and there is no space for a qualification. I am sure you all know how much easier it is for the visiting correspondent to write the complete story of Soviet Russia today in 1,000 words after he has been there a week than it would be if he stayed a year. In the same way, newspapers tend to present all issues in blacks and whites. A lawyer's training is to see how many sides there really are to a question, but the newspaper may feel it does not want to see all the possibilities because it can't afford to; that might just confuse it and its readers. I think the two qualities of the legal profession which I mention—the drive to master each subject as it comes along, and the ability to see problems in all their complexities, not in black and white—are needed on newspapers, and I think, hopefully, that the trend is in that direction.

As my concern is public responsibility in our professions, I want to focus especially on Washington. In that city, I think, lawyers and newspapermen do share a basic motivation and joy in life. Charles A. Horsky, in his book, *The Washington Lawyer,* called it "an intimate sense of participation in significant affairs." Douglass Cater, in a book which referred to the press in Washington as "The Fourth Branch of Government," spoke of correspondents having a "heady sensation of power and participation."

Turning first to the press, I have no doubt that a feeling of participation in great events is the life force of many Washington correspondents. Perhaps a heady sense of power, Mr. Cater's phrase, is more accurate. I really hate to see the press taking itself so seriously that it begins writing books about itself as a fourth branch of government. But that the press in Washington has an influence on public affairs, that it is to some degree a participant, is surely true.

A former president of the *Harvard Law Review* has said to me that reporters are different from lawyers because they are not, or need not be, men of judgment. They are accountable to no one, he suggested, and so they are without responsibility. I agree that the reporter ordinarily does not bear the lawyer's responsibility for decision; he writes for an anonymous and remote audience, while the lawyer determines the course of action to be taken by human beings immediately present. I agree also that I would trust the judgment of the best lawyer over that of the best newspaperman to decide the fate of the nation, or my own fate. But the suggestion was that reporters really make no judgments at all, that they just write and the editors make the decisions.

If that is anyone's impression, it is incorrect. I start with the proposition that news stories are much more significant in shaping public opinion than editorials. Even editors will admit this, perhaps because readership surveys show that only a small portion of the subscribers ever reads the editorial page. And in my experience the reporter has very much more to do with the shape of the news story than any editor does. For the Washington correspondent, editors are a group of anonymous people at the other end of a telegraph wire. Of course they retain their power to cut the point out of a story. But usually this is done by inadvertence, because of the demands of space, rather than by design. The real decisions—what facts to report, and in what light to report them—are made by reporters, in my opinion.

As an example consider a recent story. William R. Connole is a member of the Federal Power Commission whose term expires on June 22. On April 19 Senator Prescott Bush of Connecticut disclosed that the White House had told him Connole would not be reappointed. I wrote a story in which the bare fact of Senator Bush's disclosure was the lead. There followed the statement that Connole has been regarded as the one member of the Power Commission concerned about the consumer and determined to hold down natural gas rates, and that his being dropped therefore was causing a political fuss. Then the story noted that a month ago it had been learned that Mr. Connole and two other Power Commissioners had had private visits from a lawyer in a pending case at the F.P.C. Mr. Connole was to explain this to a Congressional committee on May 2. But the story concluded that this possible impropriety on Mr. Connole's part had nothing to do with his failure to win reappointment, since Senator Bush had been informed of the White House decision before this question of impropriety had arisen. I am sorry to go on at such length about that story. I do it simply to contrast the version of the same events written by the Associated Press. Its lead went something like this: "William R. Connole, who has admitted to off-the-record contacts in a controversial natural gas case, will not be reappointed to the Federal Power Commission."

I need not belabor the point that the two stories gave a very different impression of the significance of the reported White House decision on Mr. Connole. And it was the reporter who determined the shape of the story. Many, perhaps most, Washington events are not simple facts about which only one objective account can be written. The facts can be given more than one interpretation, and the "truth" depends on one's point of view. I do not suggest that newspapermen live like characters in a Pirandello play, chasing elusive and changing truths. I say only that judgments are involved in writing even what purport to be straight newspaper stories.

There are many examples that could be given, but the most telling is probably the whole McCarthy situation. During much of Senator McCarthy's career the Associated Press as a matter of high-level policy kept all interpretation out of its stories about the Senator. The stories were supposedly objective, factual, dead-pan presentations of the Senator's activities. But after a while some of the more sophisticated members of the A.P. began realizing that objectivity may be a little more complicated. Was it objective to report a speech by Senator McCarthy without pointing out his own internal contradictions? Was it objective to report his account of the spies uncovered at a closed session of his investigating committee without checking others who had been in the committee hearing and had seen no spies unveiled? The McCarthy issue deeply troubled American newspapers because, I think, it drove home to them the necessity of interpretive reporting. The idea of reporters exercising judgment worries many editors, just as some judges prefer to find absolute commands in the texts of statutes and constitutions because, they say, it is inappropriate for judges to weigh these things in the balance. I am not going to get into the judges' disagreement, but it seems to me that there is no way for newspapermen to escape making judgments.

I have been talking about the process of deciding what goes into a story—setting the facts in the necessary framework of interpretation. There is also the simple question of what is news. It is said, I think correctly, that the most important decision made within the *New York Times* is what to put on page one. Although these are much more editors' decisions, reporters have a hand here, too. When the Supreme Court hands down a half dozen or a dozen decisions on a Monday, our editors rely to some extent on my advice as to which cases are significant. When Lyndon Johnson makes a speech, our political writers are likely to be asked: "Is there anything new in this, or is it more of the same?" To a surprisingly large extent, what the Washington bureau of the *New York Times* files over the wire to New York each day depends on the judgment of the staff members. Of course certain stories obviously must be covered; we would hardly ignore General de Gaulle's visit. But if you read the *Times* Washington coverage carefully, you will observe that much of it is not so obviously big news. How prominently we play an antitrust suit, for example, depends in part on the significance seen in it by the man covering the beat. The *Times* may ignore a week of testimony by scientists on nuclear testing, and then carry a prominent story because a member of the Washington bureau thinks certain threads in the testimony add up to a significant shift in scientific thinking.

To some extent the newspapers themselves create news. Let me go back to the story about the Power Commission and Mr. Connole. Mr. Connole's reputation as a protector of the consumer, I said, was causing some political fuss to be raised about his reappointment. But it could fairly be said that the newspapers were at least an instrument in raising that fuss. I had written a story saying that the heads of seven state utility-regulating commissions had urged Mr. Connole's reappointment. A columnist had written two pieces purporting to disclose how the "gas lobby" had blocked his nomination. Until these and other stories were written, there may well have been no public issue over the appointment at all. Mr. Connole could have been quietly dropped with almost no one noticing.

The other day Senator John F. Kennedy accused the press of creating the religious issue in the presidential nominating campaign. He argued that hordes of reporters combing through Wisconsin and West Virginia, asking the citizenry whether it would support a Catholic for president and then reporting the existence of religious bloc-voting, had in effect made the citizens think of religion for the first time as a factor in politics. I believe there is some accuracy in the picture; the press has at least sharpened the religious issue. But given history and the political realities in this country, could the press really have failed to wonder whether primary voters would cast ballots along religious lines?

My examples should suggest that these newspaper judgments may involve moral considerations. Nothing raises more acute problems here than the leak. The leak is the great weapon of the Washington politician. Most of the stories that are called scoops probably result from a calculation by some official that publication of the material at this time will be advantageous to him and the interests he supports. The idea may be, for example, to start building public support for a program which has not yet won approval within the administration. Or it may be a leak designed to frighten Congress out of heavy spending by, say, painting a horrifying picture of the gold outflow from this country. Sometimes the reporter's initiative is vital; many good stories are obtained by asking the right question at the right time. But other stories are presented on a silver platter. In both cases there may be ethical concerns.

I am as critical of newspapers as anyone, but I do not think the Washington press corps is predominantly irresponsible. Individually, and collectively with his editors, the reporter does tend to impose on himself the restraint, the responsibility of concern for the public interest.

Finally let me raise the most difficult question of all for Washington newspapermen, the extent to which they can properly become participants in events—doers instead of observers. Reporters, like lawyers, have opinions. They are naturally interested in public affairs. They are not eunuchs. Almost inevitably they find themselves rooting for one side or another. Along with this comes the frustrating feeling that they could do things so much better than those who are the participants. Every reporter who covers Congressional committee hearings finds himself full of questions that the Congressmen don't have the sense to ask.

But there are limitations on newspapermen. I do not know precisely what they are, and so I shall simply raise some questions.

What about a reporter who was praised by the Senate Rackets Committee for bringing in adverse information on Jimmy Hoffa? How does his position compare with that of the reporters who fed tidbits to Senator McCarthy? If they were wrong, what about the reporters who opposed Senator McCarthy, discussed strategy with his enemies and, I think, had a good deal to do with bringing him down?

There is no sure guide for all situations, but I think it is clear that the reporter must not become entirely committed—an obvious special pleader. His instinct should be all the other way. If he has a concern for the public good, as I think most Washington reporters do, he must reconcile himself to satisfying that urge by uncommitted reporting. Justice Frankfurter has put it that the reporter is an educator, not a reformer. I accept that definition, with the proviso that the educator be allowed to harbor within him just a little of the spirit of reform.

Which brings me, at long last, to the public responsibility of lawyers. A little over a year ago I heard Judge Wyzanski say in a memorable speech that the bar does not live up to its responsibility for public service. I am afraid I agree.

How many law offices encourage their younger men to devote time to public matters? I fear the number is not large. How much have the practicing lawyers of America done during the last dozen years to bring reason and fairness into loyalty and security proceedings? A few have done a great deal, but the record of the bar as a whole does not seem to me adequate. What has been the reaction of the country's lawyers to the barbarian attacks made on the Supreme Court in recent years? On the whole, I think, silence.

A few years ago Dean Acheson wrote to a friend about the reasons for going into public service. He spoke of the *exhilaration* of public life, of the scope it gives a man that private affairs cannot. A newspaper reporter can sense this exhilaration, but he can never really be a participant. Perhaps the fact that he must remain an outsider makes the newspaperman believe that lawyers should seize the opportunities for public service given them by their training and status. If there is one thing the legal profession might borrow from journalism, it is a touch of the romantic and impetuous. Newspaper reporters are becoming stodgier all the time, but they are not yet as stodgy as lawyers. Perhaps lawyers need a bit more Don Quixote in them to fulfill the public responsibility I think they have. If you would borrow that from us, I hope we might borrow from you the thoughtfulness of lawyers, the concern for longer-range values, the sense of accountability and responsibility.

All the Same Face

LOUIS M. LYONS [JULY 1950

From the Don Mellett Lecture for 1950, given at Pennsylvania State College, May 21, 1950.

William Allen White, when I encountered him once in Boston with my friend Charles Morton of the old *Transcript,* both seeking an interview with the sage of Emporia, put his arms around us both and said, "We all have the same face. It is not an acquisitive face."

It is important that newspapermen should share that face. To any students going into newspaper work, I suggest one standard to set for their own future satisfaction: work for a newspaper that is run by a newspaperman—not a banker or industrialist. I don't know that we can prove that journalism is a profession. But the important thing is that the men in it act as if it were. The professional attitude is simply the feeling of responsibility toward the news, of an obligation to the reader; that the reader is their only client.

Feeling so, they need to give themselves a chance by selecting an employer who understands that feeling and shares it—who has "the same face" as William Allen White—the newspaperman's face. There are never enough such men running newspapers. But there will be more. There must be. The times demand it. If the reader has any rights—and I hope he will learn to assert them—one is that his newspaper be in the hands of a professional newspaperman, who is not using it for any other interest but to serve his readers.

It is a healthy thing for newspapers that the public is as critical as it is. It means that the institution of the press is important to them.

The press is by its nature a critic of other institutions, but it does not receive its own due of criticism. That is one of its difficulties. Who is to police the policeman?

The Hutchins Commission is a landmark in the history of American journalism. Its assignment was to examine the freedom of the press. Its report lifted the assignment to a higher level. It added Responsibility. Its title was "A Free and Responsible Press." It held that only a responsible press can remain free. It considered the adequacy of the press to inform citizens on public affairs and found it wanting. It criticized sensationalism and triviality not so much for themselves as for crowding out the necessary information for the citizen to determine public issues. And it deplored the lack of an adequate forum in the press for the presentation of diverse views.

One of its reports—by William Ernest Hocking—particularly criticized the lowering of public taste by the failure of standards of the press.

It is notable—and depressing—that after a half century of unparalleled spread of education to ever higher levels, the tendency for much of the press appears to have been to tap new lows in taste and intelligence. Always with distinguished exceptions, the headlines are more garish; the selection of stories more sensational; and the comics more vapid and intrusive, in the bulk of the press. A publisher of a very good newspaper confessed recently that he found he could gain more circulation by adding four pages of comics than by putting the same money into more staff reporters.

The decline of the reporter—and so of the individual quality in newspapers—is a notable trend. Not only comics replace reporters but a multiple production of canned goods—columns, features, syndicated news and commentary. It is cheaper by the dozen. So papers buy canned content by the dozen and the gross. So right across the country there is a stereotyped sameness to most newspapers—the same columns, features, comics, fixtures. And a reduction in the individuality that comes from extensive reports of regional news by an adequate staff.

This is the trend of the times. It goes with reduction in the number of papers and with a sameness of news and views in most of them. It goes with a reduction of individual enterprise. Scoops are less valued. It is surely no accident that the greatest record for enterprise among our newspapers is the *New York Times,* which has resisted the trend to stereotyped canned products and has maintained and expanded energetic, independent staff reporting. It produces a paper out of its own initiative, without dependence on the syndicate salesman.

The syndicated material that fills so much of the insides of our newspapers has reached almost the proportions of the old boiler plate or patent insides of the most meager country weeklies. Most of it comes from New York or Washington. These are dynamic centers and produce good copy. But they are not all of America and the monotonous sameness of the published product is an unreal reflection of America.

A major lapse of the U.S. press at mid-twentieth century is its failure to report America to America. We do not have even as many regional correspondents in the U.S. as foreign correspondents. True the wire services are highly organized to spread the standard news of disaster, strikes, politics, or crime. Indeed a rape in any corner of the country is apt to be front-page news from coast to coast. But between sex trials and strikes what news flows from one region to another to picture the vast varied activity of America? You get it only on the stock-market page because basic crops move in a speculative market.

The *St. Louis Post-Dispatch* is a distinguished exception. It reaches out into the national currents to take frequent soundings for its unique editorial title page. The *New York Herald Tribune* has a reporter in Chicago to cover the Middle West. The *New York Times* has also one in the Old South, one in the Southwest, one in Hollywood, and a few more spanning the continent. But that is about all. Even the far-flung correspondence of the Sunday *Times* appears to be written usually more in response to general queries from the New York office than from the correspondents' sense of the interest of developments in the region covered. By and large the immense variety of American life flows on without reporting to interpret one region to another. In fact the job of reporting on America to America was more comprehensively and purposefully done in an earlier day when the traveling correspondent, often the editor himself, sent descriptive articles to his metropolitan paper on the richly diverse hinterland he discovered.

This is so far a thing of the past that when the *Christian Science Monitor* tried it a few years ago, bringing home a foreign correspondent to report on America as he had done on Europe, it was a unique feature.

Some papers have developed weather forecasts into bright, interesting reports that take account of the seasonal changes, the lateness of blooms, conditions of foliage, etc. But such developments have not been carried very far.

In a paradoxical reversal of the tenses, it is the American historian, not the newspaperman, who has plumbed the stream of the common life to tell the story of everyday America in between wars and presidential campaigns. That is the new history. It has made the fame of our Turners, Schlesingers, Commagers, Merks, Parringtons. And in history it is already two generations old. We like to say of news that it is history in a hurry. But is the accent to be, forever, so on the hurry that there is nothing out of Iowa but a sex trial, and nothing out of California but the love affairs of actresses? The story of America is bigger than that. And the resources to tell it are there to be tapped. Any newspaper could find in a dozen small-town newspaper offices in Kansas a splendidly equipped regional correspondent. The news magazines have exploited this indigenous talent—often in peculiar ways—but with more enterprise than the newspapers. Richard Neuberger has shown what can be mined out of a sparsely covered region.

I suppose we will all agree with the *New Yorker* that the first duty of a newspaper is to survive. But the biggest news about newspapers recently has been of their deaths. Invariably the stated cause of death was the economics of publishing.

It is a depressing thing that in this great age of communication the number of places for professional journalists is declining with the diminishing number of newspapers, and young men, earnest and able to report and interpret, students of America with independent minds and alert intelligence, are having to turn for careers to those fringes of journalism that come under the head of public relations. We know the coal mines controlled by steel operators as "captive mines." Public relations is captive journalism. Much of it serves a useful purpose. But it is all controlled by the special interests it serves and the immense expansion of it has so tipped the balance of information available to readers that a great source of all our information is this "captive journalism." It all has an axe to grind. It may be a fine axe and worth grinding. But it is not independent reporting and if the field for independent reporting diminishes while captive journalism grows apace, it throws our total communications out of balance. Too much of what we read is pre-digested, to sell us something.

It is an unhealthy symptom of the national psychology that sees a diminishing of the market for independent reporting while the field of public relations expands. It pays better too. But many and many a young journalism graduate would reject the better pay for any kind of newspaper job where he could have a free mind. Of course if it is the kind of newspaper that does not harbor free minds, one might as well take the higher pay for honest axe-grinding.

It may be that a community is no more entitled to a good newspaper than to a good airport or a good art museum. But these latter it may build for itself. In our society it must take its newspaper as it finds it. It is the great good fortune of New Yorkers that an Ochs came there from Tennessee to run a newspaper, and of St. Louisans that a Pulitzer came there to run a newspaper, and of Louisvillians that both a Bingham and an Ethridge serve their journalistic needs, and of Clevelanders that Louis Seltzer works there on the *Press*. Few Americans are more deserving of monuments—or need them less—than the rare newspaperman who has built a newspaper into a great institution of public service. It must be much easier to be a great banker or a great industrialist, for great newspapermen are rarer.

There is nothing rational about it. It is just the good fortune of domiciling a great personality who chose a newspaper career. Every great newspaper we have had has been the projection of a distinguished personality. And we have had very few instances yet of the institution's continuing its distinction much beyond the life of its builder. Not all cities have been able to keep a tradition of a great newspaper.

Whether the character of so sensitive an institution can be continued in other hands is still a great question. A favorable answer appears to be in prospect for the *New York Times* after fifteen years of Ochs' successor, and it is time to suggest that Arthur Sulzberger must have other qualities than his great modesty.

The dismal demands of economics have probably fated us to fewer papers, all seeking a common denominator of mass sales.

But there remains a wide variation in the content and character possible to such a paper, even after priority is given to successful purveying of advertising.

Is it to have responsible direction of its news production by a professional journalist, or by a hack who follows the whim or policy of a business manager? Is it to have a vigorous presentation of views on public affairs, or be a colorless reflection of the prevailing prejudices of the most cautious downtown merchants? In short, is it to have any character of its own?

The *New York Times* conducts an instruction course of lectures for teachers on the newspaper and public affairs. In one of its lectures this season its news editor asked the schools to produce better readers.

Dartmouth College, undertaking to teach Great Issues, found it had first to teach students how to read newspapers—with discrimination and sophistication—so as not to be sucked in by propaganda and prejudice; so as to be able to follow the main threads of events and to find reliable and adequate sources for reports on the issues of the times.

They worked out a technique for this. And it is worth copying. Few things are more important than that people know how to read a newspaper so as to know what is really going on.

As the Hutchins Commission pointed out, the citizen's need is for more than surface facts. He needs, often more than the report of the event, an interpretation of it: the truth behind the facts, as the commission well said. He needs to know the meaning of events.

In an increasingly complicated world this suggests increasing use of specialists to explore and explain. The press has done little with specialists. Yet it can easily be shown that the most competent job of the press is in the few fields in which specialization has either been forced on it or has come naturally. Politics, for instance, which is the oldest and most complete specialization in the press. It has responded very little to the more recent needs of specialization.

Science has come to demand specialists. But even here and even under the compelling impact of the atom bomb, the newspaper market for science specialists is very thin and very precarious. Yet here specialization definitely pays off.

The Nieman Foundation has been proud that of the half dozen newspapermen who specialized as science writers on their fellowships, three have won the Westinghouse award for science writing in the last three years. (Another I might add has just won one of the first Lasker awards for medical reporting.) But two of these three have left the newspaper field, which proved inhospitable. One is associate editor of a great national magazine. He had done a science column in a newspaper. But he was disappointed and finally frustrated with what he could get into the paper. No solid content of the steady progress of science could find an outlet there. That is a very common experience of science writers.

One of the other two went all the way with his specialty into medicine. That is one of the hazards of developing specialists for journalism. If they go too far with it, journalism loses them to the special field itself. But surely the problem here is to make the journalistic specialty attractive enough to compete for the ablest men.

It is true I believe that the immense diversity of journalism, the unpredictability of news, the universal dimensions of the scope of newspapering, require that the bulk of a staff be mobile, adaptable people, alert, intelligent, possessed of perennial curiosity that permits them to become temporary specialists in many fields consecutively. Such a reporter may be required to know more than anyone else in town about a certain subject this month and to become equally absorbed in a quite different field next month. That is part of the fascination and attraction of newspaper work. But, for competent background of the most complex matters, the office needs some specialists. They need not even be writers. They can be consultants. They may have other tasks, in research, statistics, polling, special columns. But they should be fully available and on call when the news desk needs them.

The future belongs to those who make it. I believe that the bell tolls in journalism only for those newspapers that fail to fulfill their high function.

The zest and satisfaction of good newspaper work carry their own reward. I have just scanned 100 applications for Nieman Fellowships and have felt, as often before, the earnestness and faith of the best of our young newspapermen. They have as much to offer their institution as any generation. They can serve the press as greatly as its men of yore. They aspire to have it pull its full weight among the institutions that serve our society. All of us who feel pride in membership of the Fourth Estate have an obligation to join our voices in insistence that the conditions of the press of our day permit it to fulfill its vital function—that it render a true report of our times and serve as a true interpreter of man to man and of man's world to himself.

How Best Prepare for Newspaper Work?

Nieman Fellows Answer the Question

EDWARD A. WALSH [OCTOBER 1951

Professor Walsh of the Department of Journalism at Fordham University asked the Nieman Fellows of 1950–51 for their views on education for journalism and reports the results in this article.

Educators in the field of journalism need to take a "new look" at their objective. That was one of the many interesting comments from the Nieman Fellows of 1950–51, polled by the writer to get their ideas on what is the best education for journalism.

The Nieman Fellows were selected for the poll because they are all members of the working press, on leave of absence while pursuing studies in their fields of interest. It was felt that because they had newspaper experience and must have had outstanding ability to be named Fellows, their reactions would be of special interest.

Briefly, the questions asked were: Do you think a liberal arts education is the best preparation for journalism? Liberal arts education with electives in journalism in junior and senior years? A four-year course at an accredited school of journalism? A college degree supplemented by a year of graduate study such as the Graduate School of Journalism at Columbia University? What do you think of such a plan as Fordham's where a Master of Fine Arts degree is given for 18 hours of graduate work in a special field such as Psychology, Sociology, Labor Relations, etc., and 12 hours of journalism or creative writing?

The questionnaire said the questions were in the nature of suggestions and the Fellows could, if they liked, write a general letter giving their views and experiences, some of the pitfalls they met, what they have found to be valuable or useless in their training.

Some of the replies have been condensed, others are in full. Care has been taken to give the salient points.

The writer, a former newspaperman, has often been troubled by the question of what is the best education for journalism. He took up teaching to give students the benefit of his twenty-odd years of experience, and found many students who would not take journalism because editors or other teachers told them the straight liberal arts course was the best preparation. He found many newspapermen in his own experience who felt the same.

Newspapermen, of course, are not cast from any single mold. Some excellent men never went to college. Some have done graduate work in journalism and others have not. Some cannot be put in any specific category so far as education is concerned. The question is absorbing, and, the writer feels, still unsettled, especially in view of the impact of the social sciences on journalism education. The views of the Nieman Fellows were interesting to him, and he thought others might find them as thought-provoking as he did. The comments follow:

Roy M. Fisher *Chicago Daily News*

. . . I feel educators in the field of journalism need to take a new look at their objective.

I do not mean that journalism schools should be abandoned, a belief that is held by a number of my colleagues. There is, I think, considerable value in maintaining the journalism schools as the administrative framework covering those students who intend to make journalism their life work. It gives them an opportunity to rub shoulders with those of similar ambitions, to meet faculty members who often are experienced newspapermen, to attend seminars which enable them to meet face to face with the leading newspapermen of the day, and to work effectively on school publications. Those are benefits that I believe can be best administered through the organization of a school of journalism.

Beyond that, however, I think much of the present journalism curriculum is a waste of time. At least, it does not represent the maximum use of time. Men who intend to work on newspapers the rest of their lives should make full use of their short college years to acquire a knowledge of history, government, economics, science, and the other subjects upon which they later will be expected to hold a working knowledge. Not that I believe the courses in journalism subjects should be completely forsaken. I think they should be telescoped into less space. It is enough if they give the student a general idea of what working on a newspaper means in terms of the hour-to-hour routine. He can refine the skills later.

Edwin Guthman *Seattle Times*

I have mixed feelings about the value of journalism schools. For my money, the most effective would offer a limited number of journalism courses for upper classmen.

It is essential, I believe, to have a small, experienced journalism faculty to advise promising newspapermen and to weed out the ill-fitted and also to serve as liaison with the newspapers of the area and to assist students in finding employment. All journalism students should be urged to work on the college paper—one that is entirely free of faculty guidance or control. I believe the journalism faculty should offer courses in newswriting with heavy emphasis on a critical analysis of present newswriting standards. Courses in the history of American journalism, libel, freedom of the press, the mechanical processes of getting out a paper, and the responsibilities of a free press are other musts.

Journalism students should not be required to take a prescribed list of courses, but should be urged to get the broadest type of education possible. They should be on their own to follow their interests wherever they lead. A deep understanding of American history is the most important, I believe.

The most important thing to attempt to instill is a realization that newspaper work requires continued reading and study *after* graduation. It is all right if newspapermen doze in this respect occasionally, but if they ever fall asleep, they're through as understanding, balanced reporters or editors.

Malcolm Bauer *Portland Oregonian*

Basically, in my view, the best possible liberal arts education should precede any specialization in journalism techniques. My experience (at journalism school) two decades ago was that classes in trade subjects (proofreading, printing, copyreading) took up much of the time that should have been devoted to study in literature, languages, social sciences, or other subjects in the general arts and sciences curriculum. This overemphasis of training in the trade makes for a serious limitation in the study of basic subjects that seem to me to be indispensable to the proper understanding and interpretation of the day's news.

If time and resources of the individual permit, I should strongly advise that the liberal arts education be pursued through a master's-degree level at least. It is not necessary, of course, that a minimum amount of technical training be excluded from study, but emphasis should not be placed upon that which is purely preparation for the newspaper trade.

An indispensable supplement to the liberal arts course, in my view, should be active participation in a publication of school or community. In most cases, such activity will take the place of any technical training that might be offered in less practical form in the classroom. It is difficult to conceive how anyone really drawn to journalism could refrain from active participation on the school publication. Should he so refrain, that would seem ample proof that journalism is not for him . . . full and responsible participation on the staff of the school paper is not only training, but the degree of success achieved will be a dependable measure of the success that can be expected in that field after completion of formal education.

Angus McLean Thuermer — Associated Press, Chicago

By choice, I am not a graduate of a school of journalism. I still am to be convinced of their value. I subscribe to the proposition that a broad general liberal arts education is the best training for newspapermen. The more education a man can get, of course, the better. I think that the more graduate work that is done the better. I cannot see what good the technical courses in writing news stories, learning how to count heads, and page makeup, are when stacked up against other courses that could be taken in the time spent on these subjects. When you come into a newspaper office, you have to learn how to write news style and you have to learn how to count heads, etc., etc., and if you don't pick that up in a couple of weeks under a good city editor, you better go back and sell bonds.

A young man planning on entering newspaper work should, I feel, soak himself in American history, economics, and political science. I am particularly hep on the idea that broad cultural study courses of other civilizations should be taken . . . I daresay my views on schools of journalism are not popular with employees of same. More and more good men are coming from schools of journalism, it is true, but I weep to think of all the broad courses that could be taken in place of copyreading. Though far from a scholastic shark, I passed five hours of journalism proficiency tests without cracking a textbook just by working on the old college daily and listening as hard as I could in the composing room.

Sylvan H. Meyer *Gainesville* (Ga.) *Times*

Journalism courses are simple as pie to anyone with the aptitude for news writing and they are simply impossible for people without that aptitude. Courses in libel, history, etc., are important. Grammar, which is as important as everything else put together, is generally neglected. Even the professors know little grammar these days.

I guess a liberal arts course with some journalism electives plus some practical experience would be best. I think the college daily on which student writers, editors, and managers have a maximum opportunity to learn by trial and error and to get the "cuteness" out of their systems offers the best field for training in newspaper work. This was the way I learned; so I admit possible bias.

Reading newspapers is good training. I'm repeatedly amazed by newspapermen who never read anything except what they write themselves. Small wonder they never improve. On my small daily I insist that everyone on the staff read every word in the paper . . .

My two pet theories are: (1) journalism schools overlook training in newspaper finances and management; (2) journalism schools overlook the fact that eighty per cent of the newspapers in this country are under 25,000 circulation and that these papers require all-round people who have curiosity, which can make local stories from apparently insignificant information, who are versatile and can handle, in one day, an editorial, a book review, a political story, a legal story, the press wire, headlines, layout, and, in the meantime, peddle a couple of ads.

Wellington Wales *Auburn* (N.Y.) *Citizen-Advertiser*

I can only speak from my own experience. I went to a liberal arts college (Dartmouth) where there was little or no instruction in journalism, and followed that with a year at Columbia University, *after* I had worked two or three years. Columbia at the time seemed ineffectual, but the longer I am away from the place the more I appreciate what it had to offer.

In any case, to my way of thinking, the best means of acquiring journalistic proficiency is to supplement school with work on a *small* paper where one has a chance to do all sorts of news work, cover all sorts of assignments. This suggests a sort of work-instruction program of the sort they have at Bennington College for women and a few other places.

Your system at Fordham sounds excellent; I hope you give your undergraduates plenty of instruction in the intricacies of the composing room.

Dana Adams Schmidt *New York Times*

For my money the best preparation for journalism is a four-year liberal arts course followed by a postgraduate year at a school of journalism such as the one at Columbia. Or such a plan as you have at Fordham would serve the purpose equally well. I do not believe in four years, or even two years of undergraduate journalism courses. Journalism is not a body of knowledge like law or medicine; it is primarily a technique. And one year should be plenty of time to master the technique in so far as it can be mastered at school.

My observation is that good newspapermen are usually men with good general education. But very good newspapermen are usually men who have in addition developed a specialty about which they know a lot. Developing a specialty is a very personal thing. It ought to start in college if not earlier. A school of journalism cannot be expected to help much in that respect, except in so far as you have provided for it at Fordham. Sounds like a very good idea.

Hugh Morris *Louisville Courier-Journal*

Is a liberal arts education the best preparation for journalism? I can only answer this question by confessing that my technical education in high school and college left me seriously one-sided and handicapped in my news job. This is the principal reason why I sought a Nieman Fellowship—to have an opportunity to study courses I missed earlier such as history, government, economics, social sciences, etc.

I don't want to convey the notion that engineering training was wasted on me. I find it particularly valuable in covering state government. It helps me plow through statistics and uncover "cover-up" techniques so often used by public officials. Also I feel that my scientific-mathematical background tailored my thinking along logical lines: how to approach a problem and how to reason through to a solution.

I believe that a solid grounding in English fundamentals is a serious need in present-day journalism . . . To my way of thinking every reporter should know and understand the principles underlying the development of Basic English if his own writing is to be understood by this "average reader" who, surveys tell us, has only a seventh-grade education . . . Most colleges have operated on the assumption that an entering undergraduate who passes entrance examinations has sufficient grounding in English. I believe this assumption is fallacious, especially if the undergraduate intends to go into journalism. Undoubtedly my own experience leads me to lay such stress on *mastery* of the techniques of using the language.

Simeon S. Booker, Jr. *Cleveland Call-Post*

I believe that a well-rounded liberal arts course in college is the best background for a prospective newspaperman, especially on the editorial side. After the college degree, he may want to take a year, getting a Master's at a journalism school. I would think that any course in journalism would be a combination of practical experience (working on a newspaper, preferably a live one) and real down-to-earth theory.

I think journalism schools, as yet, have made no great impact on the American newspaper . . .

Journalism schools will never change the American journalism field at the top brass level, but by producing young men who have vision and character and ideals they will infect the field with new fresh blood and vim. And we may grow stronger and healthier in journalism morally . . . I make two points: (a) future journalists should have strong, all-around college backgrounds, and (b) journalism courses should include a certain apprenticeship program with work on live newspapers.

Bob Eddy *St. Paul Pioneer Press*

The "ideal preparation for a career in journalism" that you mention would seem to me to be a four-year program in an accredited school of journalism where a good liberal arts background is required and is available, and where practical experience on a good college daily is offered. But, wait, that's not all. After this minimum preparation our "ideal" would include at least three class hours a week, either in special projects in journalism or in arts or science courses related to our student's work (we are assuming he got a job after his four years' course). This classroom-and-workshop would continue until he died or got too rich and fat to work; the former eventuality is more probable in journalism. In other words, I don't think a journalist is ever completely "prepared" in the sense that his background is perfect for each new task he faces . . .

Hoke M. Norris *Winston-Salem Journal*

Certainly one should be taught the mechanics of journalism if he's going to be a newspaperman. He should know the framework of a news story, an editorial and a feature story, as well as something about staff organization, type and composition, covering a beat, rewrite, and, perhaps, the business management and financing of a newspaper. However, I believe these subjects can be covered in a very short time—perhaps in a single course of half a year. The major emphasis should not be, I think, on how to write, but on what to write, lest the prospective reporter become like an empty flask, all form no content . . . I do think the liberal arts education is the best preparation for journalism. Journalism electives in junior and senior years might be just what I have in mind, except they should be brief courses, as brief as possible . . . I certainly wouldn't devote an entire four-year college course to journalism. When an editor hires a reporter, it is assumed that he can write. Writing aptitude can be sharpened by schooling, but if the basic talent is lacking, nothing in the world can make a newspaperman of one. A man who has the talent doesn't need to learn how—he needs to learn what . . . The best school of journalism in my opinion is the city room. Why not let the student go to work in one?

* * * * *

Louis M. Lyons, Curator of the Nieman Fellowships, gave his views, which the writer felt were of particular interest. He said, in part:

"In general, I am for providing the maximum chance for studies of a general nature, history, literature, economics, sociology, etc., and a minimum time on techniques of journalism. But just what that minimum should be I would not attempt to prescribe for varying conditions. If you ask, a minimum for what: I should say a minimum for getting a job; for I am sure that techniques are best learned, and most rapidly, on the job under most conditions. If a student has a good general education, as for example, in the case of one already having completed a liberal arts program, then I see no objection and some advantage in concentrating on techniques as in a graduate year like Columbia's.

"My impression is that journalism programs are tending toward a greater concern for educational background and a lesser time for techniques, and that this is, in most instances, good. But I can imagine situations in which an able team of technicians might put up a better educational experience for the student than the general-education curriculum, and I have a friend teaching journalism who insists that his journalism course is the strong thread that ties together all the content courses of his students because he makes them read and write so as to report on what they are learning, and turn it all into good journalism. That is splendid, but, I suspect, exceptional . . ."

IV. THE WRITING

Writing is only one of the tools of journalism and not the one that is commonly rated highest by newspapermen. When they speak with proper respect of "a natural newspaperman," they are apt to have in mind other qualities, beginning perhaps with Kipling's "insatiable curiosity," and are as likely as not to forget even to mention that instinct that Philip Gibbs described as "a feeling for the quality of words." Gibbs was English and of a generation ago, and on both counts given to more concern with style than can be claimed for the current run of American newsmen.

It is characteristically American to care more for the matter than the manner and so more for facts than the form of presenting them. That is not to be deplored. Yet finally the effectiveness of the reporting is capped by the writing. Its quality may lift a good story to a great one or reduce it to run of the mill.

But our great news services confess a good deal when they employ "readability" experts to show their staffs how to write sentences that make sense to the readers. One of the first troubles the experts diagnosed in news writing is what they aptly called "fog." That is, the writing gets in the way of its own meaning. Under the tutelage of the word-doctors, our news services and some leading newspapers have been making progress toward the fundamentals of clear, concise, and simple sentences that use words to mean something. It was high time. "Journalese" had earned a place of reproach in the language as a synonym for slovenly writing. This despite a notable list of writers developed from journalism, including Mark Twain, Bret Harte, Stephen Crane, Damon Runyon, and Henry L. Mencken, and also much distinguished contemporary writing in the press.

The pressure of time in newspaper work has been too glibly assigned as the cause of bad writing. The late President Charles W. Eliot of Harvard once told a young newspaperman: "You are in the worst business in the world." He explained that the necessity of haste prevented painstaking work. The public widely accepts this excuse, which indeed legitimately accounts for a great deal. But it is a fair question whether its effect could not be minimized and largely overcome (as it is overcome by the most skilled practitioners in the newspaper craft) were it not for certain practices on newspapers. These are discussed in a very practical symposium by the 1949–50 group of Nieman Fellows at Harvard that made up the April 1950 issue of the quarterly.

The circumstances of this group enterprise are described by Professor Theodore Morrison in his article challenging the form and quality of newspaper writing. The only other article space permits from that symposium is Max Hall's on the traditional form of the newspaper story (the inverted pyramid) and his justification of it.

My piece on writing is a by-product of lectures at the Bread Loaf Writers Conference, then directed by Theodore Morrison, which made two *Nieman Reports* pieces, October 1954 and June 1955.

A Reader Unburdens

THEODORE MORRISON [APRIL 1950

Now Professor of English at Harvard, Mr. Morrison at the time he wrote this piece was director of the freshman English course known as English A. He is the author of *The Stones of the House* and other novels, and of *The Dream of Alcestis* and other books of verse. This article was the introduction to the special issue of *Nieman Reports* entitled "Reading, Writing and Newspapers."

I am a rank outsider to the newspaper business. By exposure to several groups of Nieman Fellows, a little of my innocence may have been rubbed off, but I remain an outsider, without any direct experience in the production of news. Anything of value that I may have to say about the project presented herewith will come from the very fact that I am an outsider, a totally unprofessional reader of a few newspapers and a somewhat more professional observer for the last six years of the copy offered to an informal seminar by volunteer groups of Nieman Fellows at Harvard.

The history of the in-and-out Nieman Fellows seminar in writing which I have conducted is incidental to the present project, but some readers of *Nieman Reports* may be interested to hear a word about it. In the fall of '44, A. B. Guthrie, Jr., had the idea that Nieman Fellows while at Harvard might well devote some study to the craft of writing. He and others of his vintage offered me the flattering but alarming privilege of presiding over a shop course. Besides Guthrie, Robert Bordner, William H. Clark, Edward Edstrom, Kendall Foss, Ben Holstrom, Nathan Robertson, Charles Wagner, and Houstoun Waring took part. I can remember that we considered magazine articles, editorials, short stories, and verse, with other kinds of copy. Undeniably the lucky excitement of this first seminar was the chance to hear a succession of chapters of Guthrie's novel, later published as *The Big Sky*. Guthrie's extraordinary talent for fiction, a talent as natural as water finding its level, has been widely recognized; he has permanently enriched the record of America in his novels. But I should like to pay him a tribute on another score, too, as a generous human being, interested not only in his own success but in the success of others, notably newspapermen. The Nieman Foundation exists "to elevate the standards of journalism." I don't know how one man can do more to accomplish this end than by watching out for ways to open gates and enlarge opportunities for younger men in the business in whom he has perceived talent and imagination.

In later years the fortunes of the seminar that began with Guthrie's generation have been variable. Once it petered out. It hasn't always been a seminar. Sometimes a few Nieman Fellows have joined my undergraduate course, and have not met as a separate group. Such was the case in '46–'47, another high point of productivity for Nieman Fellows who submitted themselves to my critical idiosyncrasies. Out of that Nieman generation came William McDougall's two volumes, *Six Bells off Java* and *By Eastern Windows,* recounting his escapes and imprisonments as a correspondent, and Henry Hornsby's novel, *Lonesome Valley,* which at its best is almost more natural than water finding its level.

Of course, only a few of the total number of Nieman Fellows

have offered themselves to my ministrations. Many others have written valuable books and articles without my interference. Some even of the few have written much more successfully on their own than when they tried to satisfy me. What I did for those who succeeded under my nominal direction, if anything, was to help clean some rust out of the tap so that the reservoir in them could run freely and clearly in its own way. Most of this rust, I think, was journalistic corrosion. But if a man becomes a better writer, does he necessarily become a better journalist? The answer to that question, it seems to me, depends in good part on the conditions that govern writing in the newspaper business. Hence the present investigation.

Early in my acquaintance with the writing of newspapermen I began to receive on my nerve-ends a sharp impression. I was wisely timid about expressing it. Presently one or two Nieman Fellows themselves put into words the conviction I had been forming, or came close enough to expressing it so that I felt confirmed. Now I have become less timid and no doubt less wise. I'm willing to say it straight out.

Newspapering, from the *writer's* point of view, is a highly conventionalized business. Many of its conventions and rigidities obstruct and prevent good writing, that is, writing planned and expressed in the way most appropriate to making the given facts and ideas, their relations and their importance, readily available to the understanding and memory of the reader. But in their effect on the writer, newspaper conventions and rigidities are sometimes even more profoundly destructive than if they merely prevented him from exercising a skill he might otherwise use. They destroy that skill, or overlay it with thick accretions of wrong habit until it is as good as gone.

One can sometimes very sharply perceive the crippling effects of journalistic habit when a newswriter tries to write a piece of fiction or a magazine article. A journalist with a novel or an article on his mind thinks that though he may not have tried that kind of thing before, his professional experience as a newspaperman at least puts him a long jump beyond the amateur. Just give him a little more time than he is used to, he thinks, and his years of practical operation as a journalist will count in his favor. They may not do so at all. They may count against him. He may first have to see what journalism has done to his writing habits, then slowly learn or recover quite different habits before he can go ahead. But it doesn't matter, you say, whether a journalist writes a novel or an article. It's a pleasant success if it happens to him, but he should stick to his profession of journalism. I should say that his helplessness in the face of his story or his article is a *measure* of how journalistic convention has affected his mind, a measure of the difference between writing cut to the conventions and rigidities, and writing that thinks only of the best way to transmit the material and the intended effect to the mind of a reader.

I have put the matter sharply, no doubt extremely. Many newspapermen write admirably; many papers are earnestly experimenting and studying ways of escaping conventions and rigidities where it is possible. Still, the conviction I have expressed has enough general truth, I believe, to be worth exploring. At any rate, I suggested to this year's Nieman Fellows that they consider, in the light of their own experience and knowledge, the *specific conditions of the newspaper business* that obstruct good writing or make it more difficult, and that they report their findings.

No definition of "good writing" will be found in these papers. Such a definition could only be abstract at best, a useless verbalism. We have construed the term "writing" liberally, perhaps even loosely. We have not attempted to isolate something called "writing" and free it from entanglement with content or moral choice. If it is a condition of the trade that a writer must sometimes blow up a news story out of nothing, then to that extent he is injured as a writer—and his reader is injured, too, whether he knows it or not—for any purely literary skill that makes one piece of emptiness more adroit than another is too unimportant to bother about. The same may be said about editorial writing. If a man is put to the moral choice of expressing views that he regards as false or dangerous, or asked to take a heroic stand on an artificially manufactured and unreal issue, his problem as a man is the same as his problem as a writer. We think of newspaper writing as the responsible and skillful transmission to a reader of what the reader needs to know or has a claim to be told for his enlightenment or his interest. Hence the recurrent emphasis throughout these papers on a need for greater opportunity to supply interpretation and background with the news, for bolder and more skillful copy-desk work toward this end, for more time and more facilities by which the reporter or editorial writer could post himself on topics requiring special knowledge. Conditions that affect the choice of one kind of content rather than another, and affect the strategy of presenting the content, are conditions that very importantly affect *writing*. Writing is words, but skill in words comes into play only after the writer has digested his material and found its appropriate method of presentation.

Enough has been said, I hope, of the origin and purpose of this project. I should like to end by carrying further my outsider's view of the worst traits in newspaper writing as they appear to me. Four points, all of which obviously overlap, call for attention.

1. *Organization*. The competent expository writer follows one simple but absolutely cardinal principle, and follows a second principle up to the limits of his skill and his opportunities. The first principle is to group related ideas together. The second principle is to keep the reader reading ahead with a sense of expectancy akin to suspense in fiction. What's coming next, or, even better, I can guess what's coming next, but how is it going to affect what I have already been told? These questions are the very definition of interest in the mind of the reader. They are questions as important for the expository writer as for the fiction writer. The newspaper writer often seems to feel forbidden to use these two principles. Compelled to give the main news in his lead, uncertain how much of his copy will be printed or where it will be cropped, he crowds what he thinks is most important at the top and trails off with the rest of his material in diminishing order of importance. Along the way, ideas, facts, quotations that are closely related and ought to be grouped together are shuffled and dispersed, for the principle of organization is not determined by logic or craft, but by the supposedly necessary conventions of daily journalism.

2. *The hugger-mugger sentence*. Closely related to the organization of the story as a whole is the form of the sentences in which it is cast. *Why* should the hugger-mugger sentence be so prevalent in journalism, and why should it take the form it takes? For I am convinced that it takes a characteristic form. Writers who aren't newspapermen write just as disorderly and asthmatic sentences, but they write them in a different way. No one can write worse than some academic writers; but their entangled sentences belong somehow to a different species of entanglement from the journalist's and

come from different mental habits. In composing a sentence, the good writer feels for its natural subject and its natural predicate, and tries to build the sentence as a whole in a shapely and economical fashion around these two elements. I suggest that a writer is not likely to accomplish this end if under joint pressure of time and conventional newspaper organization he is trying to crowd his main news into the top of the funnel and dribble the rest out the bottom, expecting that the spout may be torn off and thrown away and the top sealed and delivered to the public by forces beyond his control. The organization of the whole affects the organization of the parts. Though the hugger-mugger sentence is an outrage on rhetoric, the man who writes it doesn't necessarily lack respect for rhetoric, nor is he necessarily ignorant of it. What happens, I think, is that he falls into a habit of mind bred by the conditions in which he works. More of this later.

3. *Suppression of transitions.* A good prose writer can be defined as one who has learned skill enough to get along with a minimum of formal or conspicuous transitional sentences or phrases. But the minimum is indispensable. Good expository writing is a tissue of general and particular, principle and fact, thesis and illustration. A skillful and needed transition is not a mere formality. It distributes emphasis, makes a distinction, sets relative importance in order, puts a rib in the skeleton, or generalizes the particulars and illustrations. In a good deal of newspaper writing, transitional sentences seem to be forbidden. Anyone who has watched a reporter trying to recover the lost art of transition will understand what I mean by the effect of his working conditions on him as a writer, will understand my emphasis on the *habits of mind* apparently bred by the business as the source of much lamentable newspaper expression.

4. *Fake emotion, false color.* A writer is concerned with two things, with his data, material, facts, news, his content of any sort, and with its *importance*. What does it matter, and to whom? Toward the material itself, his relation is intellectual. He tries to encompass it, analyze it, understand it. Toward its importance, his relation is at least in considerable part emotional. It follows that a good writer must be emotionally responsible. He will not want to palm off a fake emotion on his reader; he will not believe that it can be done except by a few successful cynics operating on especially vulnerable clients. Most men are not successful cynics.

It is easy enough to see why the newspaper often forbids normal expository organization. Unfortunately, there are cogent reasons why. The careful and thoughtful article on organization in this series explains the reasons, but goes on to suggest how the tyranny of the "inverted pyramid" could be reduced and how greater coherence could often be gained in the body of a news story after the lead. The reasons for fake emotion and false color also seem obvious enough. But what are the reasons for the hugger-mugger sentence and for the suppression of transitions?

I suspect that they often spring from a false idea of conciseness, whether in the writer, or in the editor who gives him his orders and his standards, or in both. The characteristics of the hugger-mugger journalistic sentence all come, if my guess is right, from trying to stuff as much into one packed lump as possible. Syntactically, the hugger-mugger sentence uses all the connective resources of our loose and sturdy English grammar to glue as many pebbles together as it can—and uses them badly, so that all logic and subordination are destroyed. It uses conjunctions, participles, appositions, and every kind of rhetorical yoke, in the effort to wad in between the initial capital and the full-stop as many facts (and sometimes as much "color") as possible. The result, in a way, looks concise. A lot of items have been huddled together between the terminals of the sentence. But just to the extent that the reader has been confused by the violent conjunction of things that should be kept apart, just to the extent that the sentences ride roughshod over fundamental relations of time sequence, cause and effect, main statement and subordinate statement, the result is not conciseness, but its direct opposite, *wasted space*. The same can be said of the suppression of a transition. It saves space to leave out transitional sentences or phrases, guidepost sentences, general statements that sum up groups of facts or relate paragraphs or sections of a story with other sections. Or does it save space? What is space for? To the extent that the omission of a really needed transitional statement blurs the reader's view of the structure and relations of a news report, I should say that space is not gained, but lost. The space given to the story as a whole is by that much wasted.

Writing for the paper, that is, for the physical sheet on which words are typed or printed, is one thing; writing for the mind of a reader is another. I think that the hugger-mugger sentence and the suppression of transitions are ways of using printed symbols with an appearance of economy, but it is only economy on the physical sheet, not economy when the reader tries to translate the symbols into meaning. And to the practicing journalist who insensibly falls into the habit of the pebble-and-glue sentence and the suppression of transitions, this habit becomes profoundly corrupting.

If this discussion of sentence and transition has any value, it will raise the whole question of the attitude of the press toward the reader. The newspaper business, I gather, is acutely conscious of the reader. It surveys him, polls him, studies him as if he were a rat in an experimental maze. It discovers that his education and mentality remain on the average at the "level" of the eighth grade or twelfth grade, or whatever the point may be. It listens with respect to experts who define "readability" in terms of freedom from affixes and suffixes and number of words per sentence. All knowledge derived from such sources is relevant and welcome, to the extent that it is knowledge. But in all such approaches to the concept of the reader, I cannot help thinking that an attitude is wrong and an element is missing. How does a writer learn to judge his reader, how does he learn how to write in order to be read? *From his own experiences in reading!* Not by thinking of his reader, surely, as an average on a chart, high or low, an abstraction to be approached by rules about affixes and suffixes and word counts. Dr. Flesch himself, I am confident, would never say so. A man can only write for a reader with whom he himself feels that he has some natural and human link, and I believe that one important way in which a writer gets a sense of this link is by watching himself as a reader, or by intuitions unconsciously derived from his own experiences in reading. Newspapers apparently think and worry a lot about the reader, but I sometimes feel that in doing so they forget the *act of reading.*

Without being a psychologist, I will hazard one or two simple propositions about the psychology of reading. In the first place, people forget, but they don't want to forget, and are ashamed when they are caught out in any really humiliating lapse of memory. When we read, we want to remember, *at least till the end of the story.* We want to remember from paragraph to paragraph, we want to remember the beginning when we get to the end, we want to remember the important parts and subsections; if we don't, we can't see them as *related,* and hence can't *understand* what we are reading. People also want to understand. Confusion, bafflement, is not a satisfying state of mind.

Memory, in reading, is helped by two conditions. It is easier to remember if we are led by the writer along a path of expectancy which is progressively satisfied. Also it is easier to remember a structure with related parts than a succession of mutually exclusive items the relations between which are missing or obscure. If these propositions about reading are true, their bearing on organization, hugger-mugger sentences, the use of transition, and false color should be obvious. False color? Yes, because it is a form of disorder and irrelevance, like the other vices in the list.

There will always be a place for a press that tries to report news of fact and news of opinion, tries to interpret and to judge both, and to put its findings and judgments in the form most accessible and effective for understanding. In order to do this, the press must surely take every advantage it can of all the known and proved methods of organization and expression that best convey fact or judgment to the mind of the reader.

The Shape of the Story

MAX HALL [APRIL 1950

This was one of the articles in "Reading, Writing and Newspapers," the symposium of the Nieman Fellows of 1949–50. Its author was then on leave from the Washington bureau of the Associated Press.

The White Rabbit put on his spectacles. "Where shall I begin, please Your Majesty?" he asked.

"Begin at the beginning," the King said, very gravely, "and go on till you come to the end: then stop."

This passage from *Alice in Wonderland* has been turned into a rule of writing. It has been called the greatest rule of writing that was ever laid down. Newspapermen might agree with the rule if they could define the terms. To them, the beginning is whatever statement spills the beans in the most precipitate manner. The body of the story is an inventory of additional facts, usually listed in the diminishing order of their value. The end is that portion which can be rubbed out with the least regret. And the total result is a top-heavy composition that is shaped like nothing else in the literary world.

Now, there are good reasons for this method of organizing an important news story:

First, it enables editors to throw a newspaper together faster. If an edition is going to press—and one usually is—the editors cannot wait for all stories to be complete. Often they can get only the first part of a story in type, maybe only the first paragraph to use as a bulletin. So they demand that in writing important news the main facts be placed near the top. Besides, they are constantly forced to cut stories to fit certain holes or to make way for other stories. The easiest and quickest method is to lop from the end upward. So they demand that in writing important news *no* main facts be placed near the bottom.

Second, it enables people to read the paper in a hurry and still be fairly well informed. Hardly anyone has the time or the endurance to read the whole paper. So each reader acts as his own editor, glancing from story to story, cutting short the ones he cares little about, reading to the end those that interest him the most. No matter where he stops reading a top-heavy story, he still has learned the gist of what's in it.

Third, it is the natural method by which one person breaks important news to another. When telling news, as distinguished from anecdote, he comes straight to the point: "It's a boy." "The Dodgers lost." "A plane just crashed in Main Street." "President Roosevelt is dead." "The war's over."

So it is clear that the standard top-heavy form—sometimes called the "inverted pyramid"—is firmly imbedded in the habits and needs of writers, editors, and readers. It is a condition of the newspaper trade. We may as well consider that it is here to stay.

At the same time, this condition of the trade exerts a serious influence upon the quality of writing. The method of beginning a story with its climax, so admirably designed for fast news-telling, is not so well adapted to effective story-telling.

The top-heavy method does not make good prose impossible.

But how it limits the opportunities! It nearly kills any chance of structural unity, or any structure at all, because the writer cannot build toward a high point of interest or carry the action along toward any particular destination. It cuts down on his use of narrative. It goes far toward depriving him of suspense, as a means of holding the reader. Because of these deprivations he finds it very difficult to exercise what is usually called the "art of story-telling." True, he is skillful in the "art of news-telling." But the price he pays for his skill is the limiting of his opportunity to offer incentives for the readers to read on. The newspaper industry, by making it *unnecessary* for busy people to read an entire story, has also made it more *unlikely* that they will do so. The news writer, when using the standard form, is hardly ever able to "begin at the beginning" and go on to relate one happening after another until he reaches a natural stopping place.

This handicap is not the only effect of top-heaviness. The top-heavy form, by its very nature, focuses attention on the beginning of the story. Therefore news writers, by extra effort, often lead off with good prose; but sometimes they try so hard to be exciting that the first sentence is shrill with adjectives. Moreover the top-heavy method has caused many a story to begin with a monstrosity—a bulging, dangling sentence that summarizes all of the important and some of the trivial facts of the story. Happily, this extreme form of top-heaviness and bad writing is becoming obsolete, as we shall see later. But it is not yet entirely gone.

In the body of the story, the standard form reduces a writer's ability to be coherent. This is because facts, or groups of facts, are often recited as separate units, in the order of their capacity to excite. They are rarely developed in a smooth, connected manner, as ideas might be arranged by an essayist who knew in advance that the whole essay would be printed and that all his readers would read till the last word. The news writer, who manifestly cannot have those comfortable assurances, must busy himself with packing all the essential facts as close to the top as possible. He is reluctant to allow anything to push an important piece of information downward toward the precarious tail-end. So he sometimes neglects to place high in the story the background material which the readers need in order to understand what the information means.

Further, his efforts to be smooth and coherent may be hindered by the need to return a second or even a third time to facts that he has already mentioned. Suppose him to be covering the coal labor case on a day like February 11, 1950. On that date came the following developments: a board of inquiry reported to President Truman; a judge issued a restraining order against John L. Lewis; Lewis ordered an end to the strike; Lewis informed the mine owners that he was ready to resume bargaining; and miners in Pennsylvania seemed ready to defy the government. Each of those developments needs elaborating. But good news-telling requires that all of them be told in the first few paragraphs. So the explanations and details must come below. With skill and a little time, the strands can be woven together in a neat manner. But it is absurdly easy to confuse the readers during the process of backing and filling. And the least skillful reporters fall victim to repetitions and paraphrases of their own previous statements.

So now the problem is squarely faced. We have shown that the standard form of the news story is here to stay. We have also shown that the standard form is to blame for much of the bad writing that appears in the daily papers. It remains to show—or at least to suggest—a few ways in which the problem can be attacked. For in spite of all that we have said, reporters can do much to reduce the bad effects of the "inverted pyramid."

One progressive step that a reporter can take is to recognize that the standard form does not rule the whole newspaper. There are areas where the reporter may deviate from it or ditch it altogether without committing a crime.

Almost everyone would agree that in writing an editorial, or a book review, or a column, or a feature story, there is rarely a blazing need to sum up the whole piece in the first few sentences. Of course the writer tries to make a good beginning—to get the reader interested—and that is true even in a short story or a novel. But he has no compulsion to make a clean breast of things with indecent haste. Therefore he has more freedom to arrange his material in a clear and effective sequence.

Now this is also true of certain news stories. Especially is it true of news that has little "importance" but much "human interest." When there is less need for fast news-telling, there is more room for good story-telling. Many newspapermen have learned the trick of relating an episode from life in unorthodox narrative style. Here are the openings of three different stories found in the *San Francisco Chronicle:*

> Robert T. Grace is shy. Particularly when it comes to nudes.
>
> * * *
>
> "You're pretty nice for a cop," said James Hayes to Officer Edward Naughton as he puffed at Naughton's cigarette and waited for the patrol wagon. "I might as well confess and let you get the credit."
>
> * * *
>
> The Case of the Conscience-Stricken Car Thief was added to the files of the Oakland Police Department yesterday.

Sometimes, if the story is brief, the climax can be deferred until the very last line, with forceful effect. This practice has limitations: it requires the re-education of headline writers, who usually spoil the fun, when you delay the point, by putting the point in the headline; it also places an additional strain on makeup editors because of the difficulty of cutting such a story once it is in type. But it can be done, and is being done successfully on some papers. The practical difficulties only emphasize this valuable truth: that the improvement of writing is not a matter for writers alone; it is a cooperative enterprise.

On December 14, 1942, a story in the *Chicago Daily News* began as follows :

> SOMEWHERE IN AUSTRALIA— "They are giving him ether now," was what they said back in the aft torpedo rooms.
>
> "He's gone under, and they're ready to cut him open," the crew whispered, sitting on their pipe bunks cramped between torpedoes.
>
> One man went forward and put his arm quietly around the shoulder of another man who was handling the bow diving planes.
>
> "Keep her steady, Jake," he said. "They've just made the first cut. They're feeling around for it now."

This was the start of George Weller's story of how a 23-year-old pharmacist's mate and other crewmen performed an emergency appendectomy aboard a submerged submarine in enemy waters, with the nearest competent American surgeon thousands of miles away. Weller could have told all that in the beginning, and could have disclosed at once whether the patient lived or died. He had a better way. Incidentally the story got a Pulitzer prize.

A story does not have to be tragic, or terribly funny, or loaded with drama, to get unorthodox treatment. Many "routine" stories can be lifted out of their dullness by an imaginative approach. Suppose a railroad engineer retires. Some reporters would, by habit, begin by reporting the retirement—a news-telling approach—and only the engineer's family and friends would be much interested. A reporter on the *New York Times* had a better beginning:

> Ernest Evans pulled his motorman's cap down tight on his head and turned to the photographers.
>
> "If you want to take my picture," he said, "you'll have to do it with my cap on. Without it I look 100 years old, and I really won't be 70 until next November."
>
> The flash bulbs popped. Mr. Evans grinned, pulled the throttle, and train No. 75 pulled out of Pennsylvania Station yesterday for Philadelphia. It was Mr. Evans' last run after fifty years of service with the railroad system . . .

We skip now to the last paragraph of the story:

> "I've got only one hobby," he said. "That'll be playing with my little grandson when he starts running his electric trains around the house. I just love those electric trains."

So there are stories—more stories than some reporters realize—which need not be under the tyranny of the top-heavy form. We have no formula for determining precisely when the top-heavy form must be used and when it may be rejected. News is infinitely various, reporters are individuals with different capacities and tastes, and their editors are individuals with different demands. But we do believe that if a reporter understands the *reasons* for the standard form, and uses it only on stories where a good *reason* applies, he will find more freedom for good writing.

On the other hand, when it comes to news of urgent interest, the top-heavy method can hardly ever be avoided. We have heard of no better way to tell such news than to tell it forthwith, and put all the most urgently interesting facts in a conspicuous position. When a passenger plane catches fire in mid-air and crashes in a city street, it may be effective for a news magazine, days later, to start its account with the takeoff of the plane and describe what happened as a connected narrative. But the daily paper's function is to report the news in a form that enables the reader to see immediately what happened. When the Senate votes on an important bill, there may be scores of afternoon papers that barely have time to rush one paragraph into the next edition. It would be inconvenient if that paragraph omitted to say whether the bill was approved. And even a morning paper, which does not go to press until several hours later, assumes that its readers still want a clear, quick picture of the event. The assumption is correct. Very few subscribers at their breakfast tables the next morning would wish to read a thousand words about the Senate debate, even though well written, before arriving at the outcome of the vote. Their reading habits are not geared to that sort of thing, and anyhow most of them lack the time. They would rather read first about the outcome and what it will mean to the country, and if possible to *them*. At that point they will decide whether to read the details.

So the question is this: when a reporter writes a story in which he *must* use the top-heavy form, how can he hold its bad effects to a minimum?

One way is to avoid being *too* top-heavy. There is no need to tell everything in one sentence.

Now the newspaper lead, or introduction, has been getting shorter in recent years. The term *lead* has several meanings: it can mean the first sentence, the first paragraph, or the first few paragraphs; or sometimes it means a complete story, like the "night leads" of the press associations. Here we shall use the term to mean the first sentence only. Leads have been getting shorter, as we said, and this shortening is one of the most noticeable changes in news writing that has taken place in the twentieth century.

We cannot supply a list of all the forces that have brought the change about. But there can be no question that the press associations have given the movement a great push. It is not the first time that these agencies have influenced the writing techniques of the press. Indeed, they had much to do with bringing the "inverted pyramid" into general use; for it was (and is) quite impracticable for a press association to send important news to a large number of papers in any other form. And then, in the 1940's, the United Press and the Associated Press embarked on readability campaigns to simplify all their language and particularly their leads. Many papers, too, hired experts to advise them to take pity on the readers. Other papers joined in, not wishing to be out-simplified by their rivals.

The result has been fairly obvious. But we wanted further evidence, to satisfy ourselves that the new custom of shorter leads has really penetrated deep. We resolved to make an investigation of the *New York Times*. We figured that if the *Times*, with its aversion to perceptible alterations, has shortened *its* leads, then the movement must be far more than a fad.

So we looked up the *Times* for January 1940, and counted the words in the leads of all the page-one stories by *Times* staff writers, throughout the month. And we did the same for January 1950, ten years later. Sure enough, the leads got shorter. The average lead shrank from 39 to 32 words.*

The *Times* had a more tolerant attitude toward gargantuan opening sentences in 1940. Three leads in January of that year exceeded 70 words. Ten leads exceeded 60 words. Fifty-two leads ran 50 words or longer.

* Editor's note: Ten years later, in January 1960, it had shrunk to 24 words, Hall reported in *Nieman Reports* of October 1961. Here is a summary of his word counts of all the page-one opening sentences by *New York Times* staff members during four months spread over thirty years:

	Number of opening sentences	Average wordage	Percentage of opening sentences: Under 30 words	40 words or over
January 1930	358	38.82	28	47
January 1940	291	38.97	20	45
January 1950	305	31.92	40	18
January 1960	377	23.67	83	1[a]

[a] Actually 53 hundredths of one per cent. Only 2 of the 377 opening sentences had 40 words or more. The longest of the month had 42.

In January 1950, by contrast, there were no leads over 70 words. There were no leads over 60 words. And there were only 11 leads of 50 words or longer. By 1950 you could find quite a few leads that were lean and bare and did not need to be read twice to be comprehended. For example:

> WASHINGTON, Jan. 20—The House, by a vote of 236 to 183, refused today to restore to the Rules Committee its old powers to pigeonhole legislation.
>
> * * *
>
> LONDON, Jan. 10—Britain's election was fixed today for Feb. 23.
>
> * * *
>
> The New York World-Telegram announced yesterday that it had purchased The Sun and would merge the two papers under the title The World-Telegram and The Sun, beginning today.
>
> * * *
>
> WASHINGTON, Jan. 31—President Truman announced today that he had ordered the Atomic Energy Commission to produce the hydrogen bomb.

This change is illustrative, in a general way, of what has happened throughout the American press.

One of the foolish ideas of the past was that a lead was supposed to answer the questions who? what? where? when? why? and sometimes how? At least the textbooks of journalism said it was. And most newspapermen of fifteen or twenty years ago followed the general idea of the "five w's," though they may not have thought of it in those terms. Some of those wide-spreading leads could be aptly compared with a shotgun blast, peppering the whole target. The kind of lead that is considered fashionable nowadays is more like a rifle shot. It still is designed to make a big noise, but it seeks the bull's eye with a single bullet. Leads as short as this are not unusual in newspapers now:

> Traffic Judge J. E. Hutchins was fired today.
>
> * * *

> Alger Hiss was sentenced today to five years in a federal penitentiary.
>
> * * *
>
> The home front became the only front today.
>
> * * *
>
> The Reverend Francis J. Maddock went into brisk training today for a bout with a ghost.

Of course most leads remain longer than that, and most leads have to be, in order to make sense. We oppose rigid rules that limit the number of words to 14, or 30, or any other particular figure. We do not believe that good sentences are made by brevity alone. A given sentence of 50 words may be incomparably better than another of 20.

But in general it is vastly more difficult to compose a good long sentence than a good short one; and we think the present movement toward simpler leads is a healthy one and should continue.

The lead having been written, what about the rest of the story? How can it be well organized in spite of the fact that it tapers?

It seems to us that the central problem here is one of *connections*. The reporter, when he sits down to write, has certain items, or "angles," that he wants to get in the story. Let us suppose that he is reporting a fire, and that he has already written his lead, in which he has said that flames driven by a hard wind destroyed a row of seven tumble-down houses and a lumber yard in West End last night. Many other items are in his mind, jockeying for position. Among them, perhaps, are things like this: name of lumber company and exact location of fire; three firemen injured; estimates of property loss; the number of alarms and amount of fire equipment on the scene; thousands of spectators; theory as to origin of fire; investigation planned; 43 people forced to leave homes. Some items can be told in one sentence. Others require many paragraphs. How is he going to arrange the items? He will arrange them according to the value he places on them. Therefore, as we have seen, he is not likely to build an artistic unified structure. But at least he can furnish connections between the items, and connections within items. Better connections help make better writing, because they bring smoother reading.

Connections are sometimes visible. When you end a sentence

with a colon, you connect it with what follows. When you line up a group of parallel ideas or happenings and number them 1, 2, 3, you connect them with one another. When you begin a sentence with "But," "And," "Then," "Next," "Later," "At the same time," "Meanwhile," "On the other hand," "Besides," "Therefore," or some such expression, you connect the sentence with what went before. When you write a sentence like "But not all Republicans opposed the President's policy," you are connecting it with what went before and also with what is coming next; thus you are bridging a gap from one item to another. When you write "This was important because . . . ," you are connecting a single item with the subject as a whole.

Such connections can be of the greatest value; yet they are often edited out on the ground of wordiness. We believe that such editing should be done with caution. It may sacrifice more in clearness than it gains in space. When a writer consistently omits—or an editor consistently knocks out—the words, phrases, and sentences that act as connecting links, he is likely to produce stories that look as if all the items have been written separately, then sorted and pasted in order. Unfortunately, that's the way many news stories *do* look.

But not all connections are visible. The most effective connections are created by the momentum of the story itself. In other words, by the use of narrative.

We have already suggested that the top-heavy form be discarded, on occasion, in favor of a simple narrative treatment. Now we suggest that even where the top-heavy form is unavoidable, there is usually room for narrative. Take our story of the fire in West End. The use of narrative is *limited* because all the events cannot be told in the order in which they occurred; the reporter cannot give one connected account moving in a line from beginning to end like a short story. But narrative is not ruled out altogether. Many of the items in the fire story deserve narrative treatment. The story is not a mere bundle of accomplished facts—charred wreckage, lost wealth, firemen in the hospital. Things happened: flames advanced from house to house; the occupants fled; crowds gathered; firemen struggled. These happenings should be told in a way that makes the reader "see." They can be told this way regardless of what order the items are in.

Narrative not only makes the reader "see"; it also keeps him interested. Suppose a baseball game is broken up by a home run in the ninth inning. The writer reports that fact in his lead—the top-heavy treatment. But somewhere in the body of the story, he makes a detailed narrative out of the events in the ninth inning leading up to the climax. And if he handles it well, there is a certain suspense about it. It is not the "whodunit" kind of suspense which would exist if the reader were in the dark as to the outcome. It is the kind of suspense that has been aptly called "waiting for the expected." Here, truly, is a formidable weapon for resisting the domination of the "inverted pyramid."

Now for a few words about the tail-end of the standard top-heavy news story. The end is usually the least interesting part. Ideally, it should not be. Granted, few readers ever get that far. But those few customers would come away better satisfied if the end were more interesting. Perhaps they would even begin reading to the end of more stories, if a small reward sometimes waited there.

We are not suggesting that the reporter can save one of his really important items for the conclusion. But we do suggest that if he has a less important item that would make an appropriate ending, he should not hesitate to use it. An "appropriate ending" might be one with a chuckle in it, or one that returns with a twist to the main theme of the story, or that leaves the reader with something to reflect upon. If this ending gets lost in the shuffle of sending the paper to press, no tragedy has occurred. If it rides through into print, the story is better organized. Such endings, however, are hard to find. If they give the appearance of being contrived, the copy desk should kill them. Here is an example of a good ending to a news story in the *New York Times* about the restoration of the White House:

> William H. Kelley, Government project manager, shares the admiration of many of the builders for the carpentry, masonry and plastering of 1817. However, he observed today that, for all the fine hand work, the building only lasted about 150 years, and he expects the new interior to be standing firm at the end of another 500.

We have considered the organization of the news story from its rifle bullet beginning to its unsatisfying end. The standard top-heavy form is the best way to tell important news. Yet it causes many of our literary defects. Thus newspapermen who are interested in good writing are caught in a dilemma. Probably they can never completely reconcile the top-heavy form with story-telling excellence. But they can go far in that direction. They don't have to use the top-heavy form in all stories. And when they do have to use it, they can avoid some of its pitfalls. They can begin with a clean and solid statement; they can take care to provide connections so that the reader will move smoothly along; they can use narrative whenever it is consistent with accuracy and the news-telling function. And maybe, occasionally, they can hit upon a pleasant ending that will see the light of day in print.

The Business of Writing

LOUIS M. LYONS [OCTOBER 1954

This is from a series of lectures at the Bread Loaf Writers Conference in August 1954.

Journalese has a bad name. It is a bad name.

But the best journalistic style is superb for all narrative purposes—I almost said for all practical purposes.

It is lean economy of language, moving on active verbs in a simple structure that is effortless to read, and is given life, vigor and color by a sound ear for the needed word.

This is, I say, at its best. We recognize it when we see it.

Meyer Berger on the *Times,* at his best, has it—a lively pace all the way. James Morgan on the *Boston Globe*—all too rarely now, but New Englanders have enjoyed him all their lives—uses an almost Biblical frugality of words, to gain the strength of simplicity. Tom Stokes in Washington is a plain blunt man like his sentences. Ed Lahey of the *Chicago Daily News* has a pungency in choice of words that saves him acres of description and explanation. Homer Bigart in the *New York Herald Tribune* has a penetrating force in his hard sentences.

We remember the strong individuality of Heywood Broun's light but devastating sentences. E. B. White's books were first journalistic pieces.

Any vigorous writer you will find uses direct rather than indirect sentences, active rather than passive verbs. He makes his story move. And it moves on verbs. The verbs are the dynamic parts of speech. They get you there.

Adjectives have their place but not every place. A lean, muscular style will do with few adjectives. They can easily become excess baggage. They ought to earn their way like the articles in a knapsack that has limits to its capacity and can easily weigh you down with anything not indispensable.

Brisk movement then is a desirable characteristic of good journalistic style.

It means telling the story efficiently, with no waste motion. It is lively. It is active. It doesn't drag or turn off into blind alleys, or pause for irrelevant observation, or pull in extraneous matter. It gets over the ground without stopping to moralize or reflect on the meaning of the universe or to gaze aimlessly around at the scenery or conjure up pretty images of details not visible to the eye.

In short, it sticks with its task and carries the reader along through a terse, cohesive recital.

At its best, I say, this is the most economical form of writing—an economy of the reader's time and of his attention. For it keeps to the point and does not tax or dissipate his energies in following the trail through a diffusion of language.

The disciplines of journalism are despotic as to time and space. These are the great limitations. They may be oppressive. They can be destructive and are certainly discouraging to fine writing. The journalist speaks slightingly of fine writing. He means fancy writing, and his medium affords no chance for it. It gets in the way. It intrudes into space needed for facts. It is discouraging to the young writer, self-conscious about style and bursting to express himself.

The journalist most of the time is not expressing himself. He is merely an agent chronicling an event as it occurred, as nearly as he can approach that actuality. He must repress his urge at self-expression, and restrain his flights of fine writing.

This curbs if it does not repress the instinct for creative writing—for imaginative work. For the imaginative writer who has real literary talent for literature with a large L, as McGregor Jenkins used to put it, newspaper work can be disillusioning and possibly destructive. He is a misplaced person in journalism. And so I often feel he is. Ever since young graduates in literature began coming to see me about getting onto newspapers, I have had some mighty misgivings about the literary fellow who wants to start on a newspaper. He may find its limitations frustrating.

But for the fellow whose ambition and talent are for literature with a small l—the everyday writing of reports, articles, editorials, topical magazine and book writing—the exactions of daily journalism may be a valuable training, a discipline in a craftsmanship that is peculiarly adapted, I suggest, to our times—to our needs, which I would describe in brief as the need to be informed. A compelling need in a complex world when there are too many things we need to know and most of them coming too fast for us and too complicated.

We need clear, crisp reporting, so presented as to be capable of our use—within the limits of our time, energy and grasp.

It is a hard job to be informed—never harder than now—never more important than now.

The complexity of events increases. The difficulty of getting at the facts behind the news grows greater. All our time we have been befogged one way or another by censorship, secrecy, security, the new science of propaganda, the Iron Curtain, to say nothing of the murkier fog of demagogic distortion of the facts.

Some of our most responsible magazines, recognizing this need, have increasingly sought out the topical article to interpret the background of the most timely and important and complicated events. This means they have turned more to reporting—reporting in depth—to pick up from where the daily headline left it and go on from there. For this very essential purpose, the reporting style I have been describing is truly functional.

We value efficiency in the writing of the things we need to read. With our leisure we may choose to devote our time to reading imaginative works, philosophy or art. But for our need of information, for our bread and butter reading to keep up with events, whether by book or magazine or newspaper, we require direct, simple economy of statement, an informed report. It must arrest our attention to the compulsion of knowing the score, and it must hold our interest to the essentials of what is happening. If it is wordy and diffuse or difficult, we lay it aside as something we ought to read when we have time; but in the competition for our attention, the chances are against our going back to it. We find other material less demanding of us.

You can scold us as intellectually lazy. But we have a right to economize our time. We can argue for the necessity, with so many demands on our attention. And as President Conant said in a wry criticism of culture for culture's sake, "Some people would rather go to the ball game."

In a very real sense all topical magazine and book writing is reporting. It stems from the same need. It deals in the same requirements: to inform the reader. A rock-bottom imperative in all such writing is that it deal objectively with the facts. Objectivity is *the* ultimate discipline of journalism. It is at the bottom of all sound reporting—indispensable as the core of the writer's capacity, of his integrity.

When I was a cub reporter I had a story to do on the quarterly report of the old Boston Elevated system, the present MTA—the transit system, whose history then as now was a nearly unbroken record of deficits. This time they were in the black. I knew just enough to know how extraordinary that was.

I wrote:

"The Boston Elevated had a remarkable record for January—It showed a profit—etc."

The old night editor brought my copy back to my typewriter. He knew I was green. In a kindly way, quite uncharacteristic of him, he spelled out the trouble:

"Remarkable is not a reporting word," he said. "That is an editorial word. We just tell the facts. Tell the story so that the reader will say, 'That's remarkable.' "

Objectivity is the primary lesson of journalism. Complete objectivity may indeed be unattainable, as our friends on *PM* used to plead when caught violating it. But the striving for it is the grail of journalism, and what gives it character. Many never attain it. Some are incapable of understanding it. These are forever inept, out of place in the job. A reporter without it is like an artist who cannot draw. You can never be sure of the shape of things with him.

Objectivity is a hard discipline for the young. It means losing yourself in absorption in the facts. It means keeping yourself and all your whimsies and idiosyncrasies out of the way of the story to let the facts make their own impact on the reader. This is a mature concept. It takes most people a long time to learn to submerge themselves in the report and let it be wholly factual. It is more than a matter of style. It is a habit of mind, even a trait of character.

I don't mean that a story tells itself. The journalist needs great facility, a ready vocabulary, a sense of precision in choice of words, of accuracy in phrasing, a definiteness of statement, a sense of the concrete. But his is *not* self-conscious writing. The reader should never have to be conscious of the writing at all. It should be so transparent as to leave the reader's attention free to follow the unfolding narrative.

The enemy of efficient writing is obscurity. Journalists have a word for it—fog—which means just what it says. Fog gets in the way of clear, definite statement. It has to be rigorously edited out and the sentence thinned down and straightened out to say what it means without any fuss or blur or uncertainty. There isn't any room for argument as to which is the antecedent. There shouldn't be any *which* there in the first place if there is a chance of question as to whether it means this or that. The newspaper reader isn't going to spend any time figuring out how to parse the sentence. All that side of it has to be second nature to the reporter who is going to hold his reader long enough to tell him anything. Very often the quick answer is to cut the sentence in two. It is amazing how many sentences gain in clarity and also in vigor just by putting a period where that comma was.

While we are down to details like commas, it is worth noting that another enemy of clarity is the self-conscious effort to avoid repeating a word. If you have to hunt for a synonym, the safe rule is, don't. It is no sin to repeat a word. If the word, as often happens, is a key word in the report, possibly the subject of it, repetition may be necessary to make sure it is intelligible. The sense of the sentence always comes first. The absolute essential is that the reader have no chance of failing to understand it. If there is any chance that your "it" or "he" or "they" or "those" may be construed as referring back to anything but the word you want to avoid repeating, then repeat it.

The New Yorker of August 7 had as one of its ironic items, this:

"Who Should We Educate?"—title of an article in the California Teachers Association Journal.

The New Yorker replies:

"Golly, don't ask little we."

The English language is so full of booby traps that we can't afford to take any chances with it. Americans never really learn grammar, to handle it safely. The least you can do with its fine points is to avoid getting involved with them at all. If you aren't sure of who or whom, avoid them. They are usually best avoided anyway. Who clauses are usually cumbersome. If you don't know *that* from *which,* use them sparingly. That-which situations are safer than who-whom, because most readers can't discriminate that from which. Subjunctives for most are as lost as Atlantis.

But anybody making a living by writing ought now and then to get hold of a grammar and spend some time with it. It is an interesting exercise.

Fowler's *Modern English Usage* is a joy to read and full of sound sense and instructive hints for avoiding bad English. One has a right to certain prejudices in usage—like Mr. Churchill—but not to very many—not to a point of eccentricity—not to a point where the form intrudes on the reader's attention.

I was taught, and thoroughly shared the view, that it is weak, pointless and indirect to start a sentence with "It is" or "There are." In general I believe it is true, and that these forms are to be avoided in favor of a more direct, active opening. But on reading Eric Hoffer's strong article "The Workingman Looks at His Boss" in *Harper's* for March, I find he starts his article with "There are" and as he uses it, it lends weight to the sober statement which he makes his text:

"There are many of us who have been workingmen all our lives and, whether we know it or not, will remain workingmen till we die. Whether there be a God in heaven or not; whether we be free or regimented; whether our standard of living be high or low—I and my like will go on doing more or less what we are doing now."

That is surely no weak opening. I would not change his "there are"; rather it changes my prejudice.

That happens to all of us. It is an indication of the flexibility, even fluidity, of our language that prejudice gives way to usage when it proves itself. When I was young, A. Lawrence Lowell was a name of great authority. I remember an English teacher who urged against using "couple" to mean other than a married pair, until in an annual report as president of Harvard, Lowell used "a couple of years" and, such was his stature, that ended the hostility to such use of "couple" with great numbers of English teachers.

What saves us is that English is a flexible vehicle and usage is tolerant with the writer who is interesting and has something to say.

The abuses of journalistic writing are many—largely traceable to incompetence and near illiteracy in some of its practitioners. But in the hands of a craftsman, it has efficiency, vitality, the interest of sharp clear statement and the accuracy of precise and plain language. It can also have a pleasant ease of natural manner and a happy association of sound with meaning if the writer has a good ear for a well-chosen word: what Philip Gibbs calls a feeling for the quality of words.

Such an ear is a natural gift in a writer as in a musician. But its effective use is an art worth cultivating.

The modern mechanics of communication makes us more aware of this sense of sound. Increasingly in our time the written and spoken word approach each other. Radio has transformed reporters into broadcasters. The news all has the same source in the great news agencies. They rewrite it for radio, and commit many sins in the process. The purpose is obvious: to adapt the sentence to easy listening. This is the less needed if it is a sound sentence to start with.

Most people make hard work of writing. Perhaps all of us do at least part of the time.

This, I think, goes with a tendency to overwrite.

When I speak of hard work of writing, I do not mean to deprecate or minimize the drudgery of redrafting, of polishing, of refining. There can never be too much of the perfecting of a manuscript.

But I refer to the first draft, to the beginning of the operation, of getting it started. The warm-up—the striving for a striking lead.

A very wise editor once suggested that the best result comes from throwing away the first page of a manuscript. What he meant was that so many writers have about that much fluff or froth or superfluous excitement, or nervous uncertainty about the shape of the story, that they have to work off before they get down to cases and begin their story.

You see feature writers—indeed any kind of writers—tearing off one trial after another of a lead—sweating it out—doing a paragraph—throwing it away—trying another, using up their nervous energy, just on the first sentences.

I suggest this is usually the wrong approach. That the thing is to get your notes organized—shipshape—lean back and think about them a bit, and then just start to tell the story in a natural fashion.

After it is written you may come upon a better start. You may even want to turn it end for end. But that is a second part of the job. Also it often suggests itself. After you've written it a while, so that it begins to flow, so that the story is telling itself, a much more natural opening may turn up. After you're done, you may very well want to reshape it to start with that.

But it can be an awful waste of time and energy to do over and over the opening merely for the sake of a smart opening. Meantime you are losing steam for the whole job, and very likely getting tired of it all.

I think this overstress on the opening comes from newspaper work and is one of the evils of newspaper work—the terrific emphasis on the lead. Of course, in writing for a deadline, you may have to complete the lead and let it go on the wire or to the copy boy before you finish the story. That is one of the limitations of newspaper work from which you are blessedly freed if your medium is a weekly, monthly, quarterly, or for no deadline at all—something to do when you have the mood and leisure to do it right.

Another curse of the journalistic habit is the tradition that everything goes into the opening. The what, why, and when, how, where, who, Rudyard Kipling's six honest serving men. Important, true—but not necessarily all to be packed into the lead. That is for the reader who is suspected of never turning beyond the first page—or getting much below the headlines.

One of our most successful newspaper editors, Basil Walters—"Stuffy" Walters—used to have a conviction that most writers overwrite. To get them out of it he required a reporter returning from an assignment to come in and recite the story to him before he wrote. In his oral report, the reporter tended to give a natural, rapid narrative, leaving out nonessentials. Then Walters would tell him to go and write it just as he'd talked it.

Time, Inc., whatever else it is guilty of, deserves some credit for discovery that the best way to report a story, usually, is to follow the prescription of the King of Hearts, in "Alice." "Begin at the beginning and go till you come to the end; then stop."

What difference would it make how or where Dickens opened one of his Pickwick stories? Or at what point Mark Twain began talking of life on the Mississippi?

Edith Sitwell, writing a moving, intimate recollection of Dylan Thomas in the first *Atlantic* to come out after his death, starts simply: "Dylan Thomas is dead."

Jacques Barzun in "America's Passion for Culture" (*Harper's* for March 1954) opens with as nondescript a sentence as one well could:

"Whatever department of life one thinks of today . . ."

Yet it is a provocative article, and lively all the way. One almost concludes it makes little difference how you get into a piece that can make its own way.

We have all had an experience of picking up a book or an article and finding our eyes caught by a passage well into it, feeling held by it, and going on with it—and then out of interest turning back to see where it began and who did it. But we didn't need any artificial stimulus of lead or title—it was all interesting; it attracted us by its own quality.

It is the same as with a talk. You hear a speaker. He opens with a funny story—he hopes. Then, having done his duty by the tradition of after-dinner speaking, he drones on laboriously for his half hour. You would escape if you could. Another speaker just starts in and holds your attention by his own keen interest and grasp of the subject. You feel you are getting something new and fresh or interesting or different all the time he talks, and you want to hear more.

We encounter both kinds of writing. The article that opens with an artificial device to sell it to the reader is most apt to sag into a desultory recital after it gets past the contrived lead.

The mere fact of so much contrivance of writing—so many articles on how to write—so many gimcracks about arresting attention—such a science of the word-doctors—as to how many words to a sentence and how many syllables to a word—all this suggests that the field of writing is attracting many people who have no natural capacity for it and would probably be more effective and happier doing something else.

Peter Abraham, colored South African author of a fine novel, *Tell Freedom,* says:

"I read the Bible and I saw." He credits the simplicity and strength of his prose to an instructor at a teachers college who, "whenever I used big words or made clumsy and almost meaningless sentences, sent me to the Bible."

James Stern, reviewing the result in the *New York Times Book Review,* August 8, says:

"In *Tell Freedom* there is not one big word, not one clumsy sentence."

It seems to me it is time for resistance to the props and patterns that yield so much ersatz writing. To the writer who hasn't got it and never will have, this can't do any harm. He has no talent to bury in slick processing. But to the writer with a promise of development, the only road to growth is to be yourself, and that requires you to tell your own story your own way.

V. FOREIGN AFFAIRS

Nieman Reports has carried many articles about the foreign correspondent, most of them field reports from former Fellows describing conditions and problems of reporting in far places, Algeria, Korea, the Congo, Vietnam, China, the Middle East, Africa.

Among the most illuminating and thoughtful of all were two articles on "Reporting in the Far East" (January and April 1954) by Christopher Rand, who had extensive experience as a correspondent for the *New York Herald Tribune* in China before the Communists took over, and later roamed the earth and wrote what he saw, felt, and smelled, for the hospitable, uninhibited columns of the *New Yorker*. These two are telescoped here into one. In Rand's experience Americans as foreign correspondents are limited by their subjective American bias.

Henry Shapiro's criticism of reporting on the Soviets comes out of a quarter century as a UP and UPI correspondent in Moscow. Henry Tanner of the *New York Times* encountered the nightmare of the Congo after covering the war in Algeria. Stanley Karnow was a correspondent for *Time* and *Life* when he wrote about reporting on China from Hong Kong. Blair Bolles describes the work of a traveling correspondent exploring the "grass roots" in Europe.

Reporting in the Far East

CHRISTOPHER RAND [JANUARY AND APRIL 1954

Mr. Rand, formerly with the *New York Herald Tribune,* now with the *New Yorker,* was a Nieman Fellow in 1948–49.

A main vice of reporters in the Far East is the tendency to view the reporting trade, or the Far East, or the two combined, as merely an interesting background for one's personality. This is a form of egotism—perhaps "romanticism" in a sense of that vague word. With Americans it goes back, apparently, to what a friend of mine calls the bower birds—a generation of men who collected Asiatic trinkets as adornments to their nests—who cluttered their studies with gongs, idols, war clubs, model junks, lacquerware, chinaware and other bric-a-brac. I associate this vogue with Theodore Roosevelt's contemporaries. In those days, I gather, a man who visited Asia and returned with gongs and idols not only got prestige from it but established himself as an expert. It was a cheap way of buying a diploma, and it seems to have worked. Americans who had any link with the mysterious East were deemed authorities on it by themselves and others. The spell could even be inherited. One hears that Franklin Roosevelt thought he knew a good deal about China because an ancestor of his, or distant uncle, had once done some trading round Hong Kong. It all went with the Golden Age when we had a small, parochial upper class whose members could approach anyone or anything through personal friendship and correct introductions. When that age was wiped out by our runaway commercialism and mass production, the bower bird, one might say, gave way to the trained seal, a less attractive creature because less amateur. The phrase trained seal can, with a little stretching, apply to anyone who lives by self-laudatory accounts of his adventures while crossing forbidden Tibet or eating bullets in a no-man's-land. Anyone who has spent much time in Asia knows that almost any piece of this literature is a fake; he can tell by internal evidence, by the style; he doesn't have to check the facts. Indeed writers seem to have fewer adventures than other people as a rule. Those interested in doing good work lack the time for them, it seems, and those interested in writing adventure stories lack the fortitude. The bad taste of the latter is usually too flagrant to be harmful and the misinformation too self-centered to cloud much of the waters.

But at times a sentimental liking for the picturesque makes trouble. In 1949, for instance, when the Nationalists were nearly through on the Chinese mainland, the world press suddenly began touting a group of Moslems in China's Northwest as the people who would stop the Reds. It is true that the Moslems' boom was much encouraged by Americans engaged in business with them, and true also that anti-Communist reporters and papers were clutching at straws then. But apart from this the Moslems found takers on their romance-appeal. They lived in a dry, barren, remote part of China, on Marco Polo's silk route. They were great cavalrymen, and their leaders, a clan named Ma—the Chinese word for horse—were dashing, adamant, and tyrannical in an exotic way. Their territory had sheep, deserts, nice rugs, and delicious melons. The press went into ecstasies about this set-up—wholly justified ones, I thought—but then it traveled a step further and deduced that because the Moslems were strange and exciting they would therefore stop the Communists. This leap of reasoning didn't prevail. When the Reds got round to them the Moslems collapsed and the bigger Mas fled with much of their region's gold, though by then America had got well into a debauch of wishful thinking about them.

Personal romanticism is an ill motive for anyone choosing to be a Far East reporter, because it loses its drive as one's hair thins and may give way to cynicism. The saying that reporters have fun because they "meet such interesting people" is true up to a point. Spokesmen of strange oppressed nations come and go through the reporter's hotel room; doors open to him that stay closed to his equals in other trades; he may even have a way with the girls. But these advantages seldom grow with time. As Far East reporters get older they become repositories not only of tropical diseases or alcoholism, but also, if they are sensitive, of a heartbreak peculiar to observers in the East-West borderland, where inhumanity is violent and shows little sign of abating. They reach a dead end, and there are not many escapes because reporting lacks the natural progression of other careers. Some foreign correspondents reach the top of the ladder, more or less, in their thirties. They become staff reporters for good daily papers, and that is that. In the years following this stage a reporter can gain in prestige and usually get some small raises in pay, but he can seldom move up to become vice-president, president, chairman of the board, etc., as in a proper industry. To the extent he has become a good reporter he has stopped being a businessman and has disqualified himself for the few lucrative front-office jobs on the paper. Perhaps he can work as an editor or editorial writer, but this isn't really a step up even if it pays better, and it requires an abandonment of his free-and-easy ways. Good reporters who don't like such alternatives—and there are many of these—may find themselves condemned to weary roaming amid dreams of settling down with a country paper somewhere. They are like Lennie and George, the drifting barley-buckers in *Of Mice and Men,* with their wistful talk of the rabbit or chicken farm.

II

Romanticism can be lumped with some other reporting vices under the larger head of distractions.

Distractions of all kinds lie in wait for reporters, and they are often subtle and well camouflaged. A few years ago I tried taking up photography in a part-time professional way. I reasoned that my work as a reporter thrust me against strange sights that if preserved on 8-x-10 glossy prints would yield extra money and pleasure. I was right about this; for a year I had a reflex camera, and much help and advice from my friends, and during that time I snapped a few hundred dollars' worth of pictures. I did especially well on a trip to Chinese Turkestan, a desert region in Central Asia where the air was so thin, and the sun so bright, that a blind man could point a well-stopped-down camera in any direction and get results. My series on the Kazakh nomads of Turkestan—with their felt tents, fiery horses, and incredible customs—was peddled far and wide, even to obscure European magazines. I had other successes too, but as time went on I discovered that the camera was doing to me what the tar-baby had done to Brer Rabbit. My hands were so full of it I could rarely take notes at crucial moments. Whenever something noteworthy happened at a gathering, I found, I was off in a corner changing the film. When I traveled I was so burdened with responsibility for films, filters, bulb-releases and other tricks that I had scant time for the wool-gathering one must do in the reporting game. Finally, I believe a reporter should be an unobtrusive element in the scenes he covers—should pad about in the background, speak in murmurs, and leave all noisy, conspicuous behavior to his victims; yet in photographing groups of personages I always found myself in mid-stage, with eyes focused on me; I can't deny that my clumsiness entered into this, but I believe the problem is there for a deft man too. Anyway, I allowed the photography a fair run through the year, exploring its tarbaby side all the while, and in the end I gave my camera to a Chinese widow.

The rage for curios is another distraction. I once flew with colleagues to a remote but newsworthy town deep in China that also produced a few celebrated lines of crude handicraft—let us say pottery and brassware. Some of us were keen collectors, and when the plane touched ground we were off like colts from the barrier. The rest of the party hardly saw us again in the day or two we spent there; we were buried in the shops, though there was much to be learned in the town through interviews and the like.

Of course no one should try appreciating a country without learning something of its arts—that study should perhaps be the first step. But it is one, I see now, that needn't involve the care and feeding of objects, a pursuit sure to take a reporter's mind from his work.

It seems the worst distractions of a reporter come from personal ties—from a wish to be like the neighbors and share their conventions. I have never seen a reason why newsmen should be proper members of society, though I have seen plenty why they shouldn't. One hears that the noted editor O. K. Bovard refused to make friendships with his St. Louis neighbors, at least on their terms, and surely this had good results. Monks have their celibacy. On a different level artists have their bohemianism; I think for a kindred reason. It seems we reporters (in our humble way) should go in at least for a touch of the hobo spirit—of nihilism and disrespect for persons. Many of the officials and others we deal with regard us as they would cobras, and sometimes we resent this and try to prove them wrong. I think we are mistaken.

The power of the press is a snare. Even at home it is used constantly for things like getting reporters let off traffic tickets—I have used it that way myself when I could. This gives the press an interest in good relations with cops and politicians—groups it pretends to judge and keep watch on. Of course it subtracts from our freedom, as the tycoon social life of publishers does from theirs. Overseas the problem is a bit different. Since favors there come from aliens instead of our own people, we reporters are more carefree about the obligations they entail. On the other hand the favors themselves are often bigger.

III

I think, too, that the crusading or bellicose tradition of U.S. journalism goes badly with foreign reporting. One of the ablest of our reporters in China used to specialize in exposés. There was much corruption among the Nationalists in the late 1940's and this man went to work on it, baring the malpractices of high Chinese in detail, and I think irrefutably. But he touched on little else, I gathered from an incomplete reading of his stories, and gave little indication of what was happening to China as a whole. If my impression was correct—it may easily not have been—I should say he had not quite crossed the gap between work in America and work abroad.

In America the American reporters are spread thick; between them they supposedly cover everything of note many times over, and it is fitting to have some of them confined to narrow specialties. Besides, press crusading is a historical requirement of our politics. There was not such requirement in Chinese politics, though, and the American reporters were spread thin there—we were kept busy just watching the general scene. By role, it seems, a foreign correspondent is a commentator or annalist, not a crusader. Experienced men say that to be a good reporter at home one needs facility in digging, in piling up evidence—needs to be a sort of detective. This doesn't seem true of foreign reporting, or didn't in China. What you needed there was judgment and a broad interest in the field. You needed to know that various officials were grafting, and you needed to say so at the right times and in perspective, but it seems you didn't have to make a sensation of it, as it was only a detail in the chaos of the times. The standings of high Chinese politicians were ephemeral anyway, and hardly worth assailing. If one developed too much interest in the assault it hurt one's objectivity.

Besides the question of perspective there was that of taste—of whether our reporters should presume to expose China's faults in such detail. We were eager to find and describe what we considered mistakes in the Nationalist way of doing things—no one was more so than I, I fear—but in looking back I think we were ill mannered. The reader might imagine his reaction should the Chinese press dutifully bare the evils of Chicago in the same way.

What I saw later at the Korean War led me to think that our crusading tradition had gone rather sour as a whole—that the crusaders had become more eager to put on an act than to right wrongs. Or perhaps they had fallen into mere hostility for its own sake. Korea drew reporters of all kinds from all quarters—a great many young ones, of course, as they were looked on as the cannon-fodder of the trade, but also a mixed bag of older foreign reporters, Washington reporters, police reporters and so on. This gave us all a chance to see how the other halves worked. It seemed to me that some reporters out from the States were happiest when they had a devil to chase—when they could see a story in terms of someone's malfeasance. At one point in the war, I remember, a medium-high American officer was relieved of his command for what, so far as I could tell, was incompetence and nonperformance on a blatant scale, but some of the homeside boys took this up and made him a martyr, ranting in paragraph after paragraph about the sins of the "top brass." It seemed plain that these particular sins, whether or not they existed, had given the reporters a chance to work out in a familiar, time-tested way. I thought it was a perversion, or stylization, of the old spirit. I thought there was an air of needless controversy—professional hostility—about those reporters that seemed to shed light on the all-around cat-throwing now prevalent in Washington—though I know little of this matter and have doubtless generalized on it too much.

Our perfunctory muckraking, or imitation of crusading, if it is fair to use these terms, gets into our foreign reporting a good deal. This may have something to do with the ill temper we have developed against other countries since the war. We do not like the Chinese Reds and we do not like the Chinese Nationalists. In Indochina we do not like the colonial power, the French, and we do not like the anticolonial force, the Vietminh (or in other words we don't like the Communist force, the Vietminh, and don't like the anti-Communist force, the French). In addition we have little but scorn for the compromise we have inspired in Indochina, the Bao Dai government. In effect we like no movement or party there, and this seems to be our tendency in most countries. Since we are also vocal and judgmatical about our dislikes, one can hardly imagine a worse tack for us to be on diplomatically.

IV

Our press couldn't have understood China, of course, just by an effort of good will and a reform of our habits. There was also the outside task of interpreting between East and West. Perhaps this was impossible to do well. Language alone was a formidable bar. In China many of our reporters could speak a bit of working Chinese—enough for ordering meals and being superficially polite—but almost none could hold an abstract conversation or read a newspaper. We stood automatically apart from the people we were expertizing on, and we had to try bridging the gap by the means available, none of them too good.

The use of paid interpreters was a good device in the war, when alliance against the Japanese made Chinese intellectuals glad to serve with, or under, Americans. After VJ Day this relationship failed, I thought. The interpreters of foreign correspondents play a humiliating part in general. Their salaries are only a fraction of what their bosses get; they do the dirty work and are trusted with little responsibility; they have almost no chance of rising to the top; they are a secondary caste. With postwar nationalism running strong, it seemed, few well-integrated young Chinese cared to debase themselves in such a role—unless, of course, they had political reasons for wanting to influence the news. So we reporters sometimes got the weaker and more twisted production of the Westernized universities, places whose effect on Chinese minds was often unsettling.

I think many of our interpreters were unhappy working for us—at least they rarely got into the spirit of it. Sometimes they deliberately mistranslated the statements of Chinese we were interviewing. They told us what they thought we wanted to hear. Or, to keep us quiet, they put off our questions with fantastic explanations of things. I once crossed South China with a young interpreter who repeatedly made me (and himself) miss trains and meals by giving wrong answers about schedules; he was too embarrassed to enquire. I was new to China then, and rudely inquisitive, and I gave him a bad time with idle questions.

The Chinese friends of nearly all Americans came from the more Westernized slice of the population: the English-speaking officials, traders, and professional men from port cities like Shanghai, many of them returned students from the U.S. This was inevitable because of the language problems, and because the Westernized clothes and manners of such Chinese were not repellent to a newcomer, or vice versa. It had a bad effect, though, on the press. Many of our reporters took these Westernized friends as true spokesmen of Chinese thought, a subject that some of them probably didn't understand well. The leading example, perhaps, was T. V. Soong, whom some Americans deemed an oracle on China, but who was rated a virtual Westerner himself by many Chinese. It was as though a British reporter had come to America, had talked with only the keenest Anglophiles in the banks and drawing rooms of the Atlantic Seaboard, and had thought he had thereby taken the country's pulse.

The idea that the Chinese wanted America to take a strong hand in their affairs got impetus from this relationship. Mr. Soong and others like him told Americans constantly that the Chinese were praying for such a strong hand.

One of the best aids we had in China was personal observation, which was done by riding through the country in buses, wandering in alleys, consorting with soldiers and waiters, drinking with generals, sleeping in small hotels, and watching what people did all the while. For fun and education there was nothing like it. Floating from province to province, one learned where the peasants were in rags and where they were well clothed; which troops were disciplined and which oppressive; what the merchants were buying; what the students were saying; and so on. One couldn't begin to learn these things by sitting at a desk.

By observation in the late 1940's it was easy to see how the Nationalists had cut themselves off from the people. One winter's night I and a friend, a young editor on a quick trip from the States, were riding through Peking in pedicabs, the three-wheeled bicycle rickshaws the Japanese had promoted. We reached a corner and were halted there for some reason by two policemen, and they started capriciously beating one of our drivers out of hand, and kept it up till we stopped them. Their performance, though not extraordinary for those times, amazed my friend, and it told him things about China that words could not have conveyed.

Again, one heard much about Chinese mistreatment of the border peoples around them, but none of this was so real to me as a sight I saw one nightfall on the edge of the Tibetan plateau: a bent old Tibetan woman trudging along and leading a horse on which sat a Chinese soldier taking his ease.

It is no wonder that travel is limited in Red countries.

To work from observation in reporting is to go from the particular to the general, to use induction. You see a thing happen, and think about it. In time you see other things happen that are like it or different, and you think about them too and combine them with the first. Thus you create an image of the matter you are studying—say the condition of China—which you keep remodeling as you go along—adding, subtracting, changing. Meanwhile you keep going back to the particular again, using the large image to enlighten your stories about the subject's different aspects. Then the stories are not at random but in a pattern, however dim.

How firmly should a reporter cling to his native viewpoint and prejudices?

I have known Americans to decry the water buffalo and call it ugly without reservation. They were right, I suppose, by the standards we use on movie queens or even cows, but I think they were wrong in claiming grounds for judging. Buffaloes have their nature, and it is best appreciated by the impartial eye. The old Chinese landscapists made a point of impartiality, and I doubt if anyone who examines buffaloes in their paintings can think them ugly.

Judged by our American standards, again, the Chinese are traditionally unpatriotic, unkind to animals, undemocratic in politics, dishonest in bookkeeping, physically uncourageous, and disdainful of individual rights (the Reds are trying to change some of these traits). A reporter who clings to the home prejudices will judge the Chinese unfavorably because of these things, and many of us have done it. By showing their deficiencies in filling our ideal we have made them seem less than men, and we haven't noted the many virtues they have outside that ideal. We have misled our readers and encouraged our national wish to make others imitate us.

I fear that most of us were bound by the subjective American bias.

The cure for this fault, I believe, is for a reporter to be as detached as he can, not judging anything by preconceived values, neither the looks of a buffalo nor the wisdom of a Chinese idea. To reach such a state the reporter must learn to float free and almost de-nationalize himself. It is an attitude that has been much studied by Asiatic sages—Buddhists, Taoists, and others. The Buddhists say the pairs of opposites so common in human thought must be done away with—there must be no "good" compared with "bad," no "we" compared with "they." The Taoists believe a man should empty himself of notions and let impressions come in unhindered. Christ said the same thing, more or less, in "Judge not that ye be not judged." A reporter who can practice these teachings, I believe, will be more able than most to recognize truth and convey it. He needn't constantly declare that others are right or wrong. He need only open his senses, float from place to place and say, as best he can, what the people there are up to. His readers can make the judgments if they must.

Yet I feel a reporter who reached this stage would be in for a bad time with readers and editors both. If he de-nationalized himself, subdued his American prejudices, he would be accused of being "more Chinese than the Chinese," "more Afghan than the Afghans" or something like that, and would be rushed home so he could see again what America was like—be re-indoctrinated. If he learned detachment his readers would think him cold and negative, unmoral. They would be disappointed not to be stirred up one way or another about things, and the reporter would be lucky to survive. So reporters are probably no more to blame than the man in the street, who above all values his dream world and wants others to help maintain it. Reporting, indeed, may not get better till everything else does.

Interpreting the Soviets

HENRY SHAPIRO [JUNE 1964

Mr. Shapiro, UPI bureau chief in Moscow, has been reporting from Russia for twenty-five years. This is based on a report to the meeting of the International Press Institute at Stockholm in 1963. He was a Nieman Fellow in 1954–55.

Since the fateful day of November 7, 1917, when Lenin's Red guards stormed the Imperial Winter Palace in St. Petersburg, the Soviet Union has dominated the headlines of our press and still claims the lion's share of our newspaper space.

With all allowance for the Chinese inroads on the once monolithic Communist camp, Signor Togliatti's plea for polycentrism, and Marshal Tito's so-called revisionism, Moscow remains the epicenter of international Communism and we have had the opportunity of studying it for almost half a century.

Yet forty-six years later the Soviet Union to the average newspaper reader, despite the revolutionary advance in our communications facilities, largely remains a terra incognita, a veritable darkest Africa of the time of Dr. Livingstone and Stanley.

In the past two or three decades the Western world has been astonished and jolted, unnecessarily I submit, by a succession of events which *could* and *should* have been anticipated by any serious student of Soviet affairs.

To name just a few: the Red Army's effective resistance to the German onslaught, Stalin's postwar political offensive and the economic recovery of the Soviet Union, the significant domestic reforms of the Khrushchev era, the pioneering achievement in space, and the veritable explosion in Soviet education and science—not really an explosion but the end result of a cumulative process set in motion in the early days after the Revolution.

A recent example of fallacious interpretation of Soviet events which flies in the face of elementary facts is the speculation that the Wynne-Penkovsky espionage trial was merely a prelude to an extensive purge in the Kremlin, which would involve the falling of many key military and political heads.

Such speculation disregarded the simple fact that public trials in the Soviet Union are not the beginning but the end of any given case, not the prelude but the epilogue of a story. The trial, to the extent that it made certain public disclosures, did not reveal anything to the Soviet authorities that they did not know half a year earlier when Penkovsky was arrested. Chief Artillery Marshal Varentsov, a major-general and two colonels who were demoted for associating with Penkovsky, were not degraded as a result of the trial but many weeks earlier. The public airing of facts and views in the Soviet Union takes place after decisions and policies have already been framed and approved by the top leadership.

This illustrates a common temptation to rush into print with inadequately considered comment and speculation on Communist events—a disservice, I submit, to the citizen of a free and democratic society.

Let me state it dogmatically, if not provocatively. The Western image of the Soviet Union is, in some respects, no less false than the Soviet image of the West. And with much less justification or no justification at all. Closed as Soviet society may be, it is not hermetically sealed. The Western journalist's critical faculty has not been blunted. He has access to an endless variety of materials covering the whole spectrum of political life from the extreme right to the extreme left. He rejects the Marxist concept that news is a weapon. And he can freely test his ideas and information in the marketplace of fact and opinion.

In attempting to interpret the Communist world he may well ask himself "what is the function of a reporter?" I mean a reporter or commentator, as distinguished from an editor or a professional propagandist.

Is he to be a crusader for Western civilization, a cold-war warrior, a one-day historian and mere chronicler of events, or a political scientist, or a combination of one or more of such functions? How can he function in a Communist capital?

I need not restate the well-known obstacles to the free and unfettered collection and transmission of news and comment from the Communist area—the frustrations, the deceptions, and even the dangers to which foreign correspondents are exposed.

But I shall take the liberty of indulging in a bit of what the Russians call "self-criticism." It seems to me that Western journalism has not taken full advantage of all the available opportunities to serve the reader a complete, balanced and accurate report of the Soviet Union, so essential to the moulding of public opinion in a democratic society.

The great newspapers of Europe, Asia, and America, with some notable exceptions, followed the policy of their governments and for a long time refused to establish "diplomatic relations" with the Soviet Union. For many years the report on Moscow was based to some extent on rumor and gossip compounded with wishful thinking from some of the capitals on the Soviet periphery, Riga and Warsaw, for example. Some of the reporters lacked the necessary background of Russian and revolutionary history and did not always relate the day-by-day events to the social and political significance of the transformation occurring in one sixth of the world.

There was an understandable reluctance to recognize *one somber fact of life*—the existence and viability of the Soviet regime. There was the common temptation to simplify the convulsive conflict, for example, between Trotsky and Lenin and later between Khrushchev and the Molotov group, as struggles for naked, personal power, and not as functions of the fateful political issues which shook the Communist world. And the picture was compounded by the uncritical and adulatory reports of fellow-traveling and pro-Communist writers who survived to write the story of "the gods that failed."

It was an attitude of neglect and of what a distinguished leader of the International Press Institute has described to me as *defeatism*. It was illustrated by the fact that on the day Hitler marched across the Soviet frontier on June 22, 1941, an event which the entire world had predicted almost to the minute, only four Western news organizations, aside from the Germans, were represented in the Soviet Union—Havas (the French agency), Reuters, the United Press, and the Associated Press.

Similarly, when Stalin died in March 1953, making the advent of a new era in international Communism, the only reporters present in Moscow were the representatives of the two American wire services and France-Presse, Reuters, and the *New York Times*. The great newspapers of Scandinavia, of Germany, of Italy, France, Great Britain, and Japan were conspicuously absent. No wonder that although the pseudo science of Kremlinology or demonology was then at its apex, a not quite accurate journalistic quip had it "there are no experts on the Soviet Union, only varying degrees of ignorance."

I submit that there is no more dangerous concept in our effort to interpret the Communist world than what might be called the frozen concept of Soviet history. Soviet history does not begin when a particular reporter arrives in Moscow and it does not end when he leaves, or in some cases when he is expelled from the Soviet Union. Khrushchev's Russia is as different from Stalin's as Stalin's from Lenin's or as Lenin's from that of his imperial predecessors.

Given certain almost immutable basic premises, Soviet society is in a state of flux and in similar flux is the attitude of the Soviet authorities toward the foreign correspondent and the opportunities for adequate coverage and sound interpretation.

The death of Stalin and the subsequent 20th and 22nd Party Congresses opened new vistas and new opportunities for the foreign observer in the Soviet capital. It will be a long time, or perhaps we shall never see the day, when Moscow or Peking will be as open as any normal Western capital, as Stockholm, Rome, Paris, or Washington, for example. The door which Peter the Great opened to the West some 300 years ago was closed by Stalin. It was reopened, although not quite fully, by Khrushchev, who is now waging an intensive campaign against ideological coexistence with the West.

There have been significant improvements in the more than a quarter of a century since I began my career as a Moscow correspondent. There have been welcome changes even in the last five years. The highlight of improvement has been the lifting of preliminary censorship of our dispatches. New sources of information, still inadequate by our standards, have become accessible.

The academic world has been the first to take advantage of the new opportunities and an impressive volume of scientific works have come out of the great universities and research centers, out of Oxford and Munich, Harvard and California. The press has been rather slow in exploiting the new possibilities but the new era is reflected in the fact that instead of the few correspondents who were on hand to cover Stalin's funeral, there are about fifty Western reporters in Moscow now.

The occult practice of Kremlinology is now becoming a respectable political science to which Moscow correspondents are now able to make increasingly worthwhile contributions. In many respects we are still making bricks without straw, still waging an uphill fight for the free flow of information and comment, but to paraphrase a Stalin phrase, "there are no fortresses which journalists cannot take."

The Churchillian phrase which defined Soviet foreign policy as a riddle wrapped up inside an enigma has lost, I believe, some of its validity. The situation was better expressed a few years ago in the words of the distinguished American diplomat, Charles Bohlen, formerly ambassador in Moscow and now in Paris: "Russia is a country of many secrets but no mysteries." The challenge to the Western press is the extent to which it is possible to probe and unravel the secrets of the Kremlin.

Congo: Reporter's Nightmare

HENRY TANNER [OCTOBER 1961

Mr. Tanner, a Nieman Fellow in 1954–55, was *New York Times* correspondent in Algiers when the trouble began in the Congo, and was one of the first correspondents to reach the scene. He later went to Moscow for the *Times*. He sent this article from Leopoldville in September 1961.

The Congo is a reporter's nightmare—mostly because the English language is woefully inadequate for describing Congolese affairs.

Words like "strongman," "general," "minister," "offensive," "Communist," or "civil war" all have a generally accepted meaning and presumably evoke a fairly precise image in the reader's mind. Well, let the reader be disabused. Any resemblance between the things he visualizes, when reading such words in a dispatch from the Congo, and the things the reporter has seen is strictly coincidental.

"General" Mobutu once was the Congo's "strongman" and is still to be reckoned with. But take the quotes off his titles and what remains? A general in the sense of West Point? A strong man? Certainly not. He was a noncommissioned officer in the Force Publique, the pre-independence army, serving in the "department for secretaries, accounting and stenography." For a while he worked on the fringe of journalism. He is a personable young man with an intelligent face and an attractive ready smile. And lately, especially when he has had a glass of champagne or two, he has been effecting a carefree military swagger.

But a year ago, when he held the Congo's fate in his hands, he was forever bemoaning his ill-fortune, complaining about overwork and ill health. "Do you want to kill me? Can't you see I am sick?" he asked reporters who went to see him at his heavily guarded residence. Then, having set the tone, he dropped onto a sofa and held an hour-long press conference. Recently, as the capital was buzzing with reports of another "Mobutu putsch," the general held a meeting with reporters in his headquarters when Adoula, then defense minister, stormed into the room and curtly ordered the general "to terminate this conference." The "strongman's" reaction? A nervous giggle, then silence.

The evening of Mobutu's putsch on September 14, 1960, the Telex broke down earlier than usual, while Mobutu was still talking. There was barely enough time to type out a few lines on the live line to London. That night I woke up in panic, remembering my lead: "The army took over the Congo tonight." Of course the army had done no such thing. Mobutu had climbed on a table in a local cafe and there, to the surprise of the assembled guests, had *said* he was taking over the country. Once the announcement was made he went home and callers were told that the colonel had retired for the night and that further inquiries should be made in the morning. How could an experienced reporter be stampeded into confounding the colonel's statement with an accomplished fact? But a few days later the putsch seemed real enough. Mobutu was taken seriously, on even flimsier evidence, by the world powers. While standing on his cafe table the fledgling "strongman" had proclaimed that the "Russians must leave the country." Three days later the Soviet and Czech ambassadors staged a disorderly, hasty exodus, taking with them scores of "technicians," a dozen-odd planes and tons of radio and other equipment that had been intended to help Lumumba stay in power.

Or take parliament. Newspapers have always made politicians look more intelligent than they are by improving their grammar and compressing their rambling statements. But what do you do about a senate which solemnly decides that "the events of the last three days are void and have not occurred," and where a member gets up in the middle of a crucial debate and announces that he has to leave the chamber because he "has something to do."

What do you write about a prime minister who holds clandestine press conferences in private homes and reporters' apartments as did Ileo during the crisis last year?

Or how do you report the economic policies of a government, whose working habits are these: A minister calls in his adviser and tells him that a plan must be worked out to give employment and decent salaries to 100,000 unemployed. The adviser promises to mobilize the experts of various ministries and to have a detailed project ready within two or three weeks. "You don't have two weeks," the minister replies. "I need it by three o'clock this afternoon; I have a ministers' council and must submit the project."

How can you explain, in the single paragraph that such an occurrence merits in a news story, that the project was submitted that afternoon; that of course it was totally unrealistic; that the minister, who is a highly intelligent man, knew it was unrealistic; but that the fact of having a project in writing and being able to adopt it in a formal meeting solved the entire problem of unemployment in the country and disposed of it, because the government had "assumed its responsibilities" and that was all that was needed.

"To assume one's responsibilities" is a favorite phrase in the Congo. It means that an official, a minister or a general, has recognized the existence of a problem and has perhaps discussed it with other ministers or generals—and that therefore the problem is taken care of.

How can a reporter write about the "Cold War" and "Communism" in a country where the representative of the Ford Foundation hears a furtive knock at the door of his hotel room one morning? The man who enters wears the well-pressed dark suit and white shirt that is the uniform of the successful politician and, of course, carries a briefcase. He identifies himself as a political leader from the interior and explains that his purpose is to solicit financial assistance from the United States and particularly from the enterprise directed by Mr. Ford. When the man from New York asks what the funds would be used for, the provincial leader, unfazed, answers in an urgent, conspiratorial whisper: "To establish Communism."

Or, how can a reporter make it plain that a "coup d'etat" in Leopoldville is not like a coup in Algiers? Why? One day a prominent foreign diplomat makes a routine call to the residence of one of the highest-ranking men in the country. "Tell me," the host says after the preliminaries, "you have been here several months now. How many provinces do you think we should have?" The foreigner answers that if there were a request from the Congolese government a team of experts might be organized to make a survey and come up with a solid answer. The high-ranking Congolese has lost interest. "More urgent," he says, "how do you go about making a 'coup d'etat'?" The visitor, knowing his host's sense of humor, answers easily: "Well, you'd get hold of the airport first, then the radio station, the post office of course, and you might want to . . ." Then he sees the gleam of keen and totally un-humorous interest in the questioner's eyes and breaks off the conversation. Next day the Congo is front-page news. There has been a "coup d'etat." Kasavubu has dismissed Lumumba and Lumumba has deposed Kasavubu, and the airport, the post office and the radio station are focal points of the power struggle.

So it's all a comedy—a Marx brothers movie in an African setting. Or is it? I have heard it argued, before censorship on outgoing news was lifted in the Soviet Union, that in fairness to the American reader every dispatch from Moscow should be preceded by a box saying that it had been passed by censor. Perhaps, by the same token, every dispatch from the Congo should be preceded by a box to this effect: "When the Belgians left on June 30, 1960, this country did not have a single Congolese officer or a single Congolese physician. There was one Congolese lawyer and perhaps half a dozen young men with some training as economists, administrators, and technicians. These men had to run a country as large as the United States East of the Mississippi."

Whenever the dispatch contained a reference to "rampaging soldiers," the box might well include a passage like this: "These Congolese soldiers belong to the Force Publique which lost all but a dozen of its officers, all Belgians, at the start of its mutiny immediately after independence. Before that the Belgians kept the Force Publique like a good police dog on a short leash but lean, mean, and hungry. Whenever there was trouble in the villages, they let it loose to deal with offenders in its own unceremonious way." The box might add that what happened after independence was that the dog broke his leash and jumped his master in the way he had been trained to attack others.

Furthermore, if the dispatch referred to people being kicked and beaten with rifle butts upon being arrested, a bracketed insert might explain that beating a prisoner, whether he is guilty or innocent, a thief or a political offender, is a reflex that in this country comes as automatically to the arresting soldier or policeman as the pangs of hunger came to Pavlov's dog when the bell rang. The insert might add that Congolese soldiers and policemen got their training before independence.

There are many more contradictions and incongruities in the Congolese story. In South Kasai a group of us saw a charge of Baluba tribesmen, eighty or one hundred of them, emerge from the bush and bear down on us across a field brandishing spears and bows and arrows. The tribesmen were not naked, not wearing feathered headgear, weird masks, or rings in their noses, but dark pants and white shirts which, had they been clean, pressed, and mended, would have looked every bit as proper as the traditional garb of a U.S. office worker out for a coffee break.

How could one make it plausible, in a few well-chosen words, that many of these "savages" hundreds of miles from the nearest urban center actually were young office workers who a month or two earlier had been employed in the administration of the principal capital, where tribal and family ties had over the years given the Balubas a near-monopoly on office jobs, and had left the city in obedience to the orders of their "King" who wanted his "nation" regrouped in a separate state?

How could we explain that the handful of tough and reasonably well-trained Congolese soldiers who were with us failed to fire a single shot from their modern rifles and submachine guns to halt the charge of spear-wielding tribesmen. How does one describe the terror in the eyes of these soldiers as they scrambled aboard our truck to seek safety from the tribal charge? We couldn't ask the soldiers why they were paralyzed with fear. They spoke Lingala only, and even if they had understood our questions, they would not have known the answer. We could only guess that an attack like this, a band of tribesmen caught in an outburst of mass anger and mass hysteria, was to these Africans an elemental force like lightning or a tidal wave. One doesn't argue with the elements; one doesn't fight them; one runs and seeks shelter.

So there you have the picture of these Congolese who kick and beat their prisoners, who burn villages and push their tribal enemies back into the flames of a burning hut, who massacre each other and maim women and children when caught in a frenzy of tribal hatred. Here are the "savages" of whom Conrad wrote only fifty years ago that the "worst of it (was) this suspicion of their not being inhuman."

How, having reported this picture, can one explain to the reader that these same Congolese are one of the gentlest, most sensitive people you ever met; that to an amazing degree they are capable of human kindness, of graceful generosity, and that in their reactions toward strangers they are thoughtful in a way that Europeans like to attribute to "breeding" and to good manners being taught in kindergarten?

How can one explain that the tape recorder carried by a radio reporter might cause a group of soldiers to panic in fear and then to attack with rifle butts and bayonets, just because the gadget which looks mysterious and therefore dangerous, trips a mechanism of fear and, hence, aggression? How does one explain that the soldier approaching you with his finger on the trigger is actually trembling with fear even though you are not armed, and that he doesn't know yet, as he steps forward, whether he will shoot at you, crash his rifle butt against your ribs or pump your hand in a friendly welcome? How can you explain that moments later, having overcome his fear and his urge to attack you, he will thank you earnestly for having talked to him so kindly and explained the business that brought you here?

So, old Congo hands among reporters are inclined to refer the reader to the one writer who did justice to the Congo—Conrad, in *Heart of Darkness*—who described the "general sense of vague and oppressive wonder"; who felt the "great demoralization of the land" where "there is no joy in the brilliance of the sunshine"; who traveled "back to the earliest beginnings of the world when vegetation rioted on the earth and the big trees were king"; who glimpsed "a burst of yells, a whirl of black limbs, a mass of hands clapping, of feet stamping, of bodies swaying, of eyes rolling, under the droop of heavy and motionless foliage"; who knew he was "cut off from the comprehension of our surroundings"; who felt the "great silence" and who summed it up as "the stillness of an implacable force brooding over an inscrutable intention."

Snaring the Dragon from Afar

STANLEY KARNOW [OCTOBER 1960

Mr. Karnow, formerly with *Time,* now with the *Saturday Evening Post,* was a Nieman Fellow in 1957–58.

In Hong Kong not long ago, a group of correspondents and diplomats were studying a recent photograph of Mao Tse-tung and his aides, measuring rank by position in the line-up. "Wait a minute," one reporter interrupted, "Mao's wart is on the right, not the left side of his face. That picture has been reversed."

There was a dramatic moment of silence as everyone mentally turned the picture around. The significance was obvious. Premier Chou En-lai would now stand at Mao's right, and thus Liu Shao-chi, the supposed heir apparent, had been moved down a notch. Lively discussion ensued, reportedly followed by some speculative stories on the "new changes." Later, someone complimented the perceptive reporter—who shall remain anonymous—on his astonishing knowledge of Mao Tse-tung's facial features. "To tell the truth," he confessed, "I haven't a clue where Mao's wart is. I just tossed that out to see what would happen. How was I to know anyone would take it seriously?"

But just such trifles as Mao's wart and its location are serious business for the thirty-odd correspondents covering Red China from Hong Kong. Few reporting jobs in the world, I believe, are more important, and not many are as fascinating. Yet none that I know can be so chronically frustrating.

Like a good reporter anywhere, the Hong Kong operative must be studious without being academic, patient but not docile, imaginative yet not dreamy. Above all, he must be skeptical and humble. But in Hong Kong, he must use the tools of his craft in a particular and peculiar manner. He cannot apply them to a subject he can see, touch, or smell. He is forced to observe by intermediary, like an art critic attempting to judge paintings from second-hand description. With this handicap, he must estimate, calculate, synthesize, and speculate. Sometimes he is wrong; sometimes he is remarkably accurate. But he never enjoys the satisfaction of working with his own senses.

Whether he begins at midnight—as do correspondents trying to meet New York deadlines—or at eight in the morning, the Hong Kong man's day starts with the file of *Hsinhua,* the New China News Agency, monitored by Reuters and Agence France-Presse. This material, usually thirty or forty pages of single-spaced prose, can be as tedious as, say, *Pilgrim's Progress.* But it is essential reading. Here one follows the movements around China of Mao, Chou, and other Chinese leaders. Here are the lists of Cuban, Congolese, Algerian, Japanese, and assorted other African, Asian, and Latin American delegations which seem to be visiting China with significant frequency. Here is "news" of mining developments, apple production, steel output—some of it, through protestations of success, perhaps denoting economic setbacks. Here is Peking's version of foreign news, usually couched in irritating stereotypes (e.g., "The US propaganda machine, UPI, in a Washington dispatch yesterday . . ."). And equally important is what the daily radio transcript omits. Khrushchev's warning against war, made in Bucharest in June 1959, was all but ignored by the Chinese who have been speaking out against "peaceful coexistence."

One of *Hsinhua's* most important contributions to the world's knowledge is its broadcast of editorials from *Red Flag* or the *People's Daily,* which in effect lay down the Party line. Scanning an editorial requires special skill that can be acquired by anyone with perseverance and grade-school competence in grammar. The method consists of first getting the gist of the article—usually apparent by the fifth or sixth paragraph. Then run the eye quickly through the rest to find the conjunction—the inevitable "but" or "however" or "nevertheless"—that introduces the oppositional passage, or "nullifying amendment." Examples abound. On the summit meeting in the spring of 1960, to take a random sample, the Chinese considered it "a good thing that the heads of the governments of the USSR and the USA have decided to call upon each other." Only deeper in the editorial could the oppositional passage be found: "But one can no more hope to get the US to give up its policy of creating tension than one can expect a cat to keep away from fish." Hence the safe and significant conclusion that Communist China was cool to a summit meeting in which she herself would not participate.

It is desirable to follow a couple of hours with the *Hsinhua* by a short but intensive session with the "Survey of China Mainland Press," an admirable collection of translations from Chinese Communist periodicals, compiled by the United States Consulate in Hong Kong. Here are articles from Chinese magazines and provincial newspapers covering almost every imaginable subject. Some are fanciful tales of the exploits of Mao Tse-tung, evidently aimed at creating a cult around his infallible personality. Others are labyrinthic ideological expositions, and there are pieces on child care, illiteracy and its cure, grain production in Hunan province, and poems for Ho Chi Minh's birthday. However tedious the task, keeping up with this background is necessary. For into it, daily reports may fit like moving figures against a broad landscape.

Peking's sources, however ample, are never enough. Just as a doctor follows medical journals, the conscientious Hong Kong reporter feels it necessary to keep up with specialized publications—the *China Quarterly,* the *Problems of Communism, China News Analysis,* the *Far Eastern Economic Review,* the annals of various academic societies—and he can hardly afford to ignore the vast bibliography on China, from the *Selected Works* of Mao Tse-tung to the latest first-person-singular report by a visiting writer.

Although isolated diplomatically, Communist China is still very much a part of this world. Viewing it in the international context is also part of the job. An eye must be kept on Moscow and other Communist capitals, and not long ago, in the midst of the running Sino-Soviet ideological dispute, many of us devoted an inordinate amount of time to reading the Russian and Eastern European press, available in translation through diplomatic channels. Equally important is China's impact on the underdeveloped countries. Many Hong Kong correspondents travel frequently into Southeast Asia, where China's shadow looms large. At the same time, we try to maintain some familiarity with trends in Africa and Latin America, where Peking is attempting to exert influence.

Getting honest human reaction, feeling, and information on

China is another task. The opportunities in Hong Kong for picking people's brains or taking their pulse are limited by time rather than opportunity. There are European or Asian businessmen who travel in and out of mainland China. There are diplomats who may have reports from Peking. There is, occasionally, a British or Italian or Swiss journalist who has been "inside." There are ordinary Chinese—the friend's houseboy who has been visiting his relatives in Shanghai or the refugee fisherman lately landed in Macao. If one wants sterile clichés, there are Communist "public relations men" available. Chinese Communists of any importance, however, shun the Western press.

No single one of these people is, naturally, able to reflect more than what his own narrow, subjective vision has seen. The businessman who returns from the Canton Trade Fair may be knowledgeable on the subject of Chinese export goods, but it's a fair bet that he's totally ignorant on, say, a textile worker's diet. The diplomat's information, never totally imparted if at all valuable, is often conjecture picked up at a cocktail party in Peking's "ghetto" of non-Communist embassies. The lucky journalists who have seen for themselves are often as divergent in their impressions as a group of witnesses at a police court. Individually, however, each of these sources contributes a quote or a sentiment or a figure. The bits and pieces may fit into a pattern which must be checked and double-checked against a general trend. And the "general trends"—the drive for urban communes, increasing the militia, or backyard steel production—must themselves be constantly referred back, if possible, to what people may have seen inside China.

Each reporter in Hong Kong may have his special pipeline, his private tipster. Some believe that Chinese Nationalist intelligence in Taipei is helpful. Others claim that the Japanese, some of whom visit the Mainland, are good sources of information. But by and large, nobody comes up with news about Red China that is not available to his rivals. Victory, in the form of a more accurate and well-balanced story, goes to the patient, dedicated, and reasonably imaginative student of the subject. There are no spectacular scoops in store for the correspondent covering China from the outside.

Because the Hong Kong press corps cannot intimately cover China with its own five senses, there seems to be a tendency in some editorial offices back home to question or perhaps minimize the authority of its copy. Obviously there are shortcomings in what might be called "reporting by proxy." But it is also important to consider the limitations of covering China from Peking. The two Western correspondents there—Bernard Ullman of Agence France-Presse and Ronald Farquhar of Reuters—are heavily restricted in their travel, limited in their relations with the Chinese, and if not actually censored, very much at the mercy of a sensitive Communist Establishment. (Despite coverage generally sympathetic to the regime, for example, Frederick Nossal of the *Toronto Globe and Mail* was expelled last June.) Peking-based reporters even have great difficulty obtaining Chinese periodical literature, a problem they solve by having packages of translated press material sent to them from Hong Kong. For all the glamour of a Peking date line and the veracity of an eyewitness account, day-by-day reports out of Communist China are perhaps likely to contain less real substance than better-documented, more reflective stories from a more liberal vantage point. The *New York Times,* to take the best available barometer, has noticeably reduced its use of Reuters files from Peking in favor of its own correspondents' "second-hand" stuff written in Hong Kong.

This is, of course, no argument against entering China. The ideal, many of us in Hong Kong think, would be to visit the Mainland frequently, as some of our British colleagues were able to do until two or three years ago. We—and the U.S. public—are victims of blunders that are too familiar to rehash. But whatever the State Department's past rulings in prohibiting American correspondents into Communist China, the present block to entry lies in Peking. Late in 1959, Washington removed the sanctions against travel from the passports of thirty-one correspondents. Not a single one has been given a Chinese visa, and there seems no likelihood of visas being delivered in the foreseeable future. But—here I am, making the mistake of predicting what Peking might do, when experience should have taught me that only Peking's unpredictability is predictable.

The Grass Roots Foreign Correspondent

BLAIR BOLLES [JULY 1956

Mr. Bolles, after long experience in Washington, was European correspondent for the *Toledo Blade* from 1953 to 1957. He later became a corporation executive in Washington.

The way to cover Europe in these times is first, to spend half of every month of every year away from the great capitals, and second, to leave the capitals by conveyances where you are likely to meet the undistinguished people. Go in second-class or third-class train coaches, or in a car with enough jalopy flavor not to awe hitchhikers and discourage them from talking frankly. The Europeans you meet under these circumstances are the Europeans who in the long run decide what way the political news is going to run. As individuals they are seldom quotable, but a few words with many plain people are essential to give a balance to the many words a reporter exchanges with the few "important people"—prime ministers, foreign ministers and such.

One reason is that politicians in the capital are often out of touch with their publics in the provinces. The success, for example, of the followers of Pierre Poujade, the anti-tax rebel, in the elections in France in January 1956 took government officials in Paris by surprise. Reporters who left the glamour of Paris and carefully combed the grass roots caught the trend first. At a luncheon of politicians in Paris the day after the government called for elections, the name Poujade was not once mentioned. But the name Poujade never failed to appear in the course of fifty talks with fifty people along the banks of the Loire 140 miles southwest of Paris where two correspondents headed a week after that luncheon. On December 17, more than two weeks before the election, the *Toledo Blade* was able to run a story under the head, "Poujadists Are the Group to Watch." Yet while it was obvious outside Paris that Poujade had large popular support, in Paris he continued to be regarded as powerful only because he had tremendous gall. Even when Paris papers began to report that Poujade possessed an unexpectedly sizable following in the country, Paris experts to whom foreign correspondents occasionaly talk dismissed the news as unsound. Disagreement between capital and province about what was going on in France did not end until January 2, 1956, when the French elected 54 members of the Poujade parties to the National Assembly.

Late in the winter of 1955 I took the four-cylinder family car on an 1,800-mile trip around West Germany. Almost the last point of call was Bonn, the capital, where, at the beginning of the trip, the German government and the American high commissioner's office were showing real satisfaction because the Bundestag, the lower house of the German parliament, had approved the London-Paris agreements which joined Germany to NATO and authorized Germany to rearm, up to twelve divisions. Officials made two assumptions which created news—one, that with West Germany in NATO, Russia would no longer raise objections to West German union with East Germany under circumstances that would safeguard freedom; two, that the new German army would soon exist.

But away from Bonn it was difficult to find a citizen who shared the government's interest in arming, and one could not help meeting dozens of citizens willing to make the kind of concessions to the Communists that might put West German freedom in danger if only the concessions would bring unity. Businessmen, bricklayers, women who were mothers, women unattached, students, and retired old men said arms were a bar to unity and that unity would make arms unnecessary. They did not share the government's confidence that for West Germany to ally itself with its neighbors would destroy Moscow's interest in East Germany.

They gave other reasons for objecting to the twelve divisions. Remembering Hitler, they suspected the raising of an army was inevitably the first step toward the outbreak of a war, instead of an action to prevent war. They did not want a military program to get in the way of prosperity. These opinions were impressively universal, expressed in the Black Forest and in Hamburg, in Frankfurt and the Schleswig peninsula. Despite the public sentiment, it seemed unlikely Chancellor Adenauer, with his tremendous authority, would not get his way in his policy of arming. Yet a year later the new German force he wanted to create consisted of only a few volunteers, and the Bundesrat (Senate) had approved a conscription bill only after cutting the period of service to twelve months, less than the time required by any other NATO member, a time so short it created doubt whether Germany could maintain an army of twelve divisions without dislocating its industry. A year after approving NATO membership, the Bundestag had yet to approve the creation of a real German military force within NATO. And a year later Russia had refused to permit the unification of the two Germanies on any ground but grave concessions from West Germany to East Germany. Chancellor Adenauer had proposed, but the public both foresaw the future more clearly and affected its character more certainly than he had.

The practice of getting the clue to the reality in the news from simple people is vital (although not always possible) in dictatorship countries, where governments are even more inventive and more outrageously optimistic, than they are in democratic countries. Cyrus Sulzberger caught Poland for the readers of the *New York Times* when he quoted a French Pole who had gone back to his native land. The Pole said he missed France. "Why?" he was asked, "for its wine? for its food?" "For its liberty," he replied.

Poland is easier to get around in than the buffer between it and the Western world, the Democratic Peoples Republic of East Germany, but East Germany is accessible at the time of the Leipzig Fair (twice a year). By luck, it was possible to go to Leipzig in February 1956 from East Berlin via the East German railways and thus to ride the way the East Germans themselves have to ride. The police checked on the passengers three times in a journey of 120 miles, all of which lay within one sovereign area, about the distance from Boston to New London but no state lines crossed. The return train, reserved for western travelers to a destination not in East but in West Berlin, had only one simple police check, when it crossed the East-West boundary. In Leipzig the East German government was offering a Potemkin-type show of a happy population in a burgeoning city. But Leipzig citizens, courteous to all and talkative to those they trusted, told a different story.

"Dead," said one man, "Leipzig is dead between fairs."

In contrast to government reports on improving standards of living, a housewife described the difficulties of feeding her family with meat rationed (four pounds a month), potatoes rationed and milk rationed ten years after the war in what once had been a principal agricultural region of an earlier Germany. An old man wept when he described the police's vigilant discouragement of get-togethers by friends. When those police are not listening, the irreconcilables in the lands of tyranny take off their masks for Americans. Officials talk often to the press also, but what they say is different.

Such reporting produces little spot news and no great exclusives. But it adds richness and trueness to the reporting of spot news, and sharpens even the best reporter's judgment about the merit of exclusive news thrust into his hand. For the foreign correspondent must perform a service which is less important at home. He needs to put the news abroad into its setting abroad. The reader of the paper at home is part of the home setting and has a feel for it. He can spot political insincerity or hot-air wishfulness because he knows what political acts reflect or distort the reality he sees around him. But on the shores of Lake Erie he cannot easily see the reality around events across the Atlantic Ocean. He needs more than explanation or interpretation of the foreign news. He needs to have laid bare for him the roots of the news. Public pronouncements sometimes deserve a skeptical, even a cynical, reception, but the skepticism ought to rest on experience and knowledge. The plucking at the grass roots gives reporters experienced judgment which adds to their readers' knowledge.

Our Foreign News

LOUIS M. LYONS [JANUARY 1954

This is a review of *The Flow of the News,* a study by the International Press Institute, published in Zurich, 1953.

Counting coverage of the Korean War and the United Nations as foreign news, the average American paper prints about four columns of foreign news a day. The news from Korea is about all that gets on the front page. The average reader reads only about 12 inches a day of this news from abroad and gets very little out of this. But he is not conscious of wanting any more and wouldn't want more at the expense of his local news. Or so he says, when asked. The editors, by and large, are satisfied with this. Two thirds of them say a good job is done on foreign news. This degree of complacency is perhaps about what you'd find in any institution. The one editor in six who is dissatisfied will find a vast amount of suggestive information in this elaborate study of the movement of foreign news into the newspapers of the United States. On him the American public must depend to set the pace in any improvement in information about the parts of the world to which our taxes flow in support of the interests of the United States as the leading world power.

The International Press Institute, headed by Lester Markel of the *New York Times,* made this study with $250,000 from the Ford Foundation. It is put out rather tentatively as the first stage of a continuing study in foreign news presentation. It was concentrated on daily newspapers in the United States. The work filled a year. Staffs were set up in New York, Zurich, and Madras. They had the cooperation of a committee of editors, and of the wire services and a group of foreign correspondents.

Researchers in ten journalism schools set up a random sample of American dailies—105 papers in the sample—and a system of coding and measuring the foreign news in these. They made daily measurements of the various kinds of news from abroad in one week of each of four months—October, November, December in 1952 and January 1953. This yielded the total scores on what the wire services supplied, from what sources, and how much of it the papers used. They tried also to get a qualitative value of this by submitting the clips for analysis to 22 foreign correspondents, each appraising the coverage of his own country. Finally the reader was surveyed as to the impact on him, which was "quite low."

The result is a vast compendium of information and appraisals and suggestions. The 70-page appendix is loaded with raw data from which reader or editor can draw his own conclusions. Indeed he will have to, for the report avoids doing the job for him. It appears to lean over backwards to avoid critical findings.

This, I suspect, is no accident. It is rather the canny approach of Lester Markel, who inspired the study and who believes in foreign news. He doubtless expects by this cautious suggestion to persuade some editors to venture a little further with it. He had to depend on the cooperation of quite average editors, and depended heavily on the wire services, who certainly weren't going to be taken for a ride in this if they could help it.

The $250,000 study inevitably suggests comparison with that other $250,000 spent seven years ago on the Hutchins report. That is as far as the comparison goes, except that the resistance of the newspapers to the criticism in the Hutchins report must go far to explain the cautious approach of this effort. The Hutchins Commission was made up of scholars independent of the newspapers and they aimed at the readers, over the heads of the editors. This job was kept in the hands of newspapermen all the way.

The indeterminate tone of the report is spelled out in the opening of the chapter on "The Value of News."

"How good is the flow of news into the United States? How accurate is the picture it makes of foreign countries? This study has turned up different answers to these questions . . . A majority of American editors reached in this inquiry believe the American press is doing a good job in the presentation of foreign news. News agency executives are reluctant to assess the job being done by the newspapers; generally however they believe the job is adequate. Foreign correspondents analyzing the picture of their own countries in the American press find that picture either inadequate or unbalanced or both."

That is a masterpiece of objective reporting of the attitudes found. But what does it tell you compared to the response you would get from any out-of-town reader who has experienced the pangs of famine during the first week of strike on the *New York Times?*

"In gathering the arguments the Institute has merely served as a channel for an exchange of views." That is the key to the report. Fair enough. Whether it is worth $250,000 Mr. Hutchins will have to say. This time it was his role to provide the money. The material is all here for anyone who wants to carry the argument further. Those who do are invited to hire their own hall.

The Associated Press delivers about 22,000 words a day from abroad. This is five times as much as the average client uses. In fact only the *New York Times* uses that much and it gathers most of it itself.

Three fourths of this flow came from Korea, England, France,

Germany, Italy, Japan, and the UN. The war accounts for Korea, the occupation for Germany and Japan, the Vatican for Italy, and England and France are the traditional stations of foreign correspondents. The UN has a novelty factor; also it is in New York. The novelty of India as a new nation did not bring its news above one per cent. Canada, next door to us, accounted for only 4.6 per cent of the foreign news flow. Korea and England each accounted for about 13 per cent. France came next. It took pretty close to a revolution to bring South America in, and a movie actress or an athletic king to get a dateline from Scandinavia.

Two thirds of all the foreign news dealt with war or politics—"official news." This was a main criticism of foreign correspondents and readers.

Disasters, crime, sports and the inevitable "human interest story" accounted for 22 per cent. Broader, more general news about how people live in other lands got only 12 per cent.

The *New York Times* carried 32 columns of foreign news a day. The *Oklahoma City Times* carried 3.8 columns a day—this cited evidently because it was close to the average. Two thirds of all dailies receive AP foreign news. A little less than half get UP (245 papers have both). One fifth have the INS (174 papers have all three). Reuters serves 36, Overseas News Agency 25, Canadian Press 3. North American Newspaper Alliance and Scripps-Howard Newspaper Alliance also supply foreign news material.

The *New York Times* foreign service goes to 31 papers, the *New York Herald Tribune* news to 21, the *Chicago Daily News* service to 45 and the *Chicago Tribune's* to 38. These services do not send the full foreign file of their papers. They send clients about 15,000 words a day of the more important stories. This of course supplements the file of the wire services, or vice versa.

As to the proportion of the news used in the member papers, one Midwest afternoon paper that was receiving 447 columns in a week from four agencies, used 15 columns that week. Ninety-five per cent of what it used was from one agency. A Southern morning paper used 41 columns in one week out of a total of 61 columns received from one agency, and 6 per cent of the file of a second agency. A more typical Southern paper used 27 columns out of 200 columns received from two agencies, about 14 per cent.

Of 155 editors queried about how good a job is done, 105 thought good, 23 fair, 27 poor. Half of those who said "good" explained they meant only in the larger papers and only in terms of space limits and costs and conditions of foreign coverage. But the other half put no qualifications on their satisfaction with the job done. How complacent can you get?

What the 27 say is obvious enough. News is insufficient from South America, India, Southeast Asia, Canada and other areas, including the Soviet bloc. Foreign news is too largely official news. Foreign correspondents lack background to produce informed reports. So do the news editors handling the foreign news.

The foreign correspondents, asked to make what they could of the news samples from their countries, were unhappy. "The coverage may be accurate as far as it goes and still be shallow. It may be detailed and still not be explanatory." They complain of "the habit of trimming all but the first few paragraphs from dispatches." The report sums up the appraisal of the foreign correspondents. "In the average American newspaper the picture of other countries is generally objective but spotty and incomplete."

The editor defending his scant news file from abroad can point to the readers as shown by surveys to read very little of what is printed and to get very little out of that. Most don't want any more, or not at the expense of local news. Of course most have no way of knowing how much they would like of a more interesting, more informed report.

The data on reader ignorance, though familiar, is always appalling. Barely half could recall any recent news in which Secretary Dulles figured. Less than half could recall reading anything about Syngman Rhee or Tito. Less than half could name more than one Soviet satellite.

But even so, the arithmetic of the reader surveys shows the average reader going through 12 column inches a day of foreign news. This suggests that an informed wrap-up of half a column a day done in the office from the foreign file might be serviceable.

Asked what they wanted to make foreign news more interesting, readers suggested: (1) News written in a more simple understandable way; (2) more pictures; (3) more accurate news ("a surprising number of readers hold the foreign news in their newspapers is not accurate or truthful. They believe it is propaganda."); (4) more human interest (about the way other people live);

(5) better presentation of foreign news. (Foreign news is "scattered all through the paper," "hard to find.")

The most persistent question raised in the report is whether the amount of foreign news printed could be made to mean more to the reader. This would mean explanations to give meaning to remote and complex affairs. The wire services insist that they are providing more of such informing background reports than their clients care to use.

Besides the news flow to the United States, the study examined the flow between India and the West and the flow between West Germany and the rest of Western Europe. These I must omit, except to commend them to foreign editors and all students of foreign relations as helping to explain many things.

India is a very special problem. In no other country perhaps is foreign news given such importance. They give great attention to the UN, as well they might in view of the caliber of their leaders there. The orientation of their journalism to Western Europe, notably England, is much criticized by their nationalist editors who are hard put to it to find ways to cover India. It is a jolt to an American to discover that the sources of news of the United States are neither American nor Indian. Chiefly Reuters. This sharp limitation is aptly described by Robert Trumbull, analyzing its results, as "not a happy circumstance." This alien screen of information between two countries applies to many other areas and is of course a problem in the promotion of peoples' understanding of each other. It puts a large responsibility on the United States Information Service which, in India, is the chief American source of news.

VI. GOVERNMENT AND THE PRESS

Douglass Cater's book, *The Fourth Branch of Government,* deals penetratingly with the relation of government and the press. This is perhaps the most strategic relationship of an institution whose most essential role is the reporting of public affairs. It is a continuous relationship, often complex, full of difficulties, raising issues both practical and ethical. It includes censorship, security, "news management," and much that is more subtle and less classifiable. These problems, various as they are, have a common ground in the reporter's confrontations with officialdom. So they seem to run together. Let us start them with one of the stickiest and most controversial—"news management."

There is a natural conflict of interest between government and the press; any administration seeks to put its best foot forward in public view, and the press insists on uncovering both feet. In war the government asserts the right of censorship. But cold war and atomic secrecy imposed an era of security, classification, and Executive Order which put varying degrees of restraint on the "full disclosure" which the press traditionally holds as its function. This gray area is peculiarly a Washington problem. The government handling of news in the Cuban crisis of October 1962 brought to a head the issue of what correspondents had come to criticize as "management" of the news.

One of the most militant critics of "news management" was Clark Mollenhoff, Pulitzer-prize correspondent of the Cowles papers, a Nieman Fellow and a contributor of a number of hard-hitting articles in *Nieman Reports*. His Harold L. Cross Memorial Lecture to the National Conference of Editorial Writers in November 1962 sharply raised the news-management charge while the issue of the Cuban-crisis story was still in active controversy. This Mollenhoff piece ran in our December 1962 issue, a vigorous polemic. But we had published only one side of a hotly debated question. The 1963 Nieman Fellows, then in Cambridge, proposed making a survey of representative Washington correspondents on the issue. With as many as fifty former Fellows serving in Washington, it was possible to round up rapidly the views of some fifteen serving major publications and these were published in the next issue, March 1963.

This enterprise yielded a good deal more than a sampling on the "news management" question. It proved an illuminating discussion of the work and outlook of the current generation of Washington correspondents. Some of their contributions are reprinted immediately after the Mollenhoff article.

Managing the News

CLARK R. MOLLENHOFF [DECEMBER 1962

This is from the Harold L. Cross Memorial Lecture delivered to a national gathering of editors in St. Louis, November 16, 1962. Mr. Mollenhoff, a Nieman Fellow of 1949–50, represents the Cowles papers in Washington. His Pulitzer prize came in 1961.

The Cuban crisis has resulted in one of our most dramatic examples of the high-level handout. For a period of several days in late October, our knowledge and our coverage were largely limited to the facts that were fed to us through the Pentagon, the State Department, and the White House. There was no power to go behind the self-serving declarations of the Kennedy administration, and for the time being most of us were willing to put up with it.

Assistant Secretary of Defense Arthur Sylvester frankly admitted that the Kennedy administration engaged in an almost total management of the news during those days of crisis. Since the peak of the tension, there has been much serious re-examination of the Cuban-crisis period for purposes of determining if it was all handled in the best way possible. There are many questions that have been asked by reporters and editorial writers. There are many questions that should be asked if we are to do our job as a free press.

It has been encouraging to see the nation's newspapers voicing a general concern over the "news management" during the Cuban crisis. It has been stimulating to hear the Pentagon reporters speak with almost a single voice in opposing the Sylvester directive to control the interviews and telephone conversations between reporters and Pentagon personnel.

The military-affairs reporters contend that there is no question but that the Sylvester directive has the potential for reducing the Pentagon coverage to canned handouts and monitored interviews. Examine the simple one-paragraph directive to Department of Defense personnel:

"The substance of each interview and telephone conversation with a media representative will be reported to the appropriate public information office before the close of business that day. A report need not be made if a representative of the public information office is present at the interview."

Only the naive would take seriously the assurances of Sylvester and Defense Secretary Robert McNamara that the directive is for the purpose of making more information available in "an expeditious and equitable manner." Veteran Pentagon reporters, such as Mark Watson, of the *Baltimore Sun,* and Jim Lucas, of the Scripps-Howard newspapers, comment that the Sylvester directive is a "Gestapo" tactic. Their sharp criticism is echoed by almost every other military-affairs reporter.

This is not a case in which the Pentagon writers have some long-standing bitterness against Defense Secretary McNamara. To the contrary, most of them express considerable admiration for McNamara as an administrator of the department. They simply feel that the Sylvester directive, if implemented, will have the potential for shutting off legitimate dissent on policy matters that have nothing to do with national security. Even if the order is not fully implemented, it is felt it will be a club over the heads of military and civilian personnel. It is a formal order, and can be used as a basis for disciplinary action at the times when the McNamara team wants to use it to curb dissent.

The men who are now leading our nation did not want us to

accept the self-serving declarations of the Eisenhower administration on our defense posture. Are we now to assume that we have finally found that infallible team composed of men who will instinctively know what is best for us? Are we to assume that McNamara, less than two years in the job, can produce the right answers without the benefit of dissent or public debate?

The effectiveness of the press in opposing the directive will depend upon its persistence. While it is encouraging to see the nation's press irritated over the Sylvester order and the attitudes that surround it, it is not unreasonable to express some doubt as to whether the fury will last. If there is sharp and continued criticism, I have no doubt the Sylvester order will eventually be modified or withdrawn.

However, if the nation's newspapers follow what is a more characteristic pattern, the fury will soon give way to a few mild protests, and these will in turn give way to a whimpering acceptance of the chains. The short attention span of many newspapers will mean that the Sylvester directive will be forgotten, and the high-level handout collecting that goes with it will become an accepted part of the news-gathering picture.

It would be appropriate here to bring a reminder of some recent history that set the stage for the Sylvester directive. It was less than ten months ago that the newspapers of this nation gave an overwhelming endorsement to McNamara's use of arbitrary secrecy.

I refer to the so-called "muzzling" hearings by the Senate Armed Services Subcommittee. The chairman was Senator John Stennis, of Mississippi. There was no controversy on many major points. It was a properly authorized committee. It was operating within its jurisdiction. It was headed by a responsible chairman. Members of the subcommittee were orderly in their conduct, and there was no abuse of witnesses.

After establishing the basic pattern of speech censorship, the subcommittee asked for the testimony of the persons who did the actual censoring to determine the reasoning in a program found filled with "inconsistency, caprice, personal judgment, and even irresponsibility."

Defense Secretary McNamara refused to allow the censors to testify, and obtained the support of President Kennedy to claim an "executive privilege" for doing so. McNamara said he was responsible for the operations of the Defense Department, and he would do all the explaining that was needed.

It was as if Agriculture Secretary Orville Freeman had appeared before the McClellan subcommittee investigation of the Billie Sol Estes case to bar that group from questioning subordinate officials in the Agriculture Department. Such a position by Freeman would have caused a roar of outrage, but McNamara was praised.

McNamara declared that the subcommittee would have to content itself with his self-serving declarations—his high-level handouts—and would be prevented from going behind his assertions. His claim was essentially the same as the Defense Department asserted in its "news managing" program during the Cuban crisis. There were some differences. When McNamara was before the Stennis committee he could not and did not contend national security was involved in the "muzzling" investigation. Also, he was defying a Senate subcommittee that had a legal right to have its questions answered.

The editorial cheers for McNamara were deafening. But the reasoning behind the editorials had nothing to do with principles that supposedly guide us in our editorial judgments. McNamara was cheered because he was defying Senator Strom Thurmond, an unpopular Senator from South Carolina. Thurmond claimed that Pentagon censorship was being used to incorporate a "no win" policy in the speeches of high-level military officers.

The question of whether Senator Thurmond was right or wrong in his conclusion was not important. He had fully as much right to ask questions as any member of the press, and he had a right to expect answers that were truthful.

However, principles were forgotten for the moment in the interest of kicking a Senator who held an unpopular view. The press also forgot its own long-time self interest.

McNamara was arbitrary, he was defiant of the power of Congress, and he was crowned a hero. Was it any wonder that he and Sylvester were confident in seeking the maximum in their recent news-managing ventures? Was it any wonder Pentagon officials and the White House believed it was possible to adopt the Sylvester directive to control press contacts at the Pentagon?

If the press of this nation is interested in remaining free, it will be necessary to pay more attention to principle and less attention to expediency or personalities. You do not suggest abandoning normal rules of jurisprudence to jail someone you consider to be a bad influence on society, for you recognize the damage such action could cause.

Neither should you let your judgments on the conduct of a governmental proceeding in Washington be governed solely on the impact of your heroes or on those with whom you disagree.

If you have lost your capacity for balanced independent thinking, then you are a likely candidate for the title of "high-level handout collector."

The real test is this: Have you become the tool of some political figure or pressure group? Do you challenge facts and conclusions of your sources? Are you an independent thinker, or are you a rubber stamp?

The test can and should be applied to your city hall reporters, county courthouse reporters, statehouse reporters, labor reporters, or science writers. It is well to remember that handout collecting is not a disease that is limited to Washington, D.C.

It is certainly handout collecting of the worst kind when reporters or editorial writers accept erroneous conclusions that are whispered by an administration. This is particularly true when legal decisions dealing with the issue are available for examination.

But, isn't it also handout collecting if you support programs you do not understand? Isn't it handout collecting if you endorse the grand concepts and the clever political slogans of a political party or an administration, and never go to the trouble of digging out the facts?

A balanced judgment requires that you know which foreign aid programs have been successful and which have been failures. It requires that you know enough of the details to do your own analysis of projected programs, so you are not merely a rubber stamp for an administration's view—a high-level handout collector.

The public will not expect us to conduct a full audit of the $50 billion defense budget or the $6 billion Agriculture Department budget. However, the public should be able to count on our newspapers' pointing out the symptoms of waste and mismanagement in government.

The reading public should be able to rely on editorials that are the product of clear and independent thinking, rather than a weak imitation of a popular trend.

The public should be able to rely on our newspapers to fight vigorously against the directives under which any administration seeks to stifle dissent. Above all, our newspaper reporters and editors have a responsibility to themselves and the profession to do the study necessary to know when press freedom is at stake. We cannot erase past mistakes but we should be determined that these mistakes will serve as effective warnings for the future.

Symposium: Reporting from Washington

[MARCH 1963

Because of continuing interest in the subject of "news management" by government officials, *Nieman Reports* queried former Nieman Fellows in Washington and published the views of fifteen of them. Not unexpectedly, the replies covered a broad spectrum of complaints, from grievances against specific official behavior to introspective alarm about the complacency of newsmen themselves. Only five of the fifteen are printed here.

P.I.O.: NATURAL ENEMY

By Richard Dudman *St. Louis Post-Dispatch*

The Kennedy administration may try to manage the news a bit more than some of its predecessors. In large part, this is a reflection of the increased articulateness and individuality—some might call it gabbiness and egotism—that characterizes members of this administration.

The big difference here is that the Kennedy administration admits it manages the news and tries to justify it. Kennedy himself spoke along that line after the Bay of Pigs invasion in 1961, and Arthur Sylvester more recently has tried to make it sound honorable and patriotic for newspapers to serve as public relations organs for the government in time of stress instead of printing all the news they can get.

In the Eisenhower administration, officials were hard or impossible to see, and when you did see them they often wouldn't tell you much. I doubt that Kennedy has matched the circumstances of the Eisenhower illness as an example of management of a news event of top importance at the White House.

Some of the complaints about managed news are by reporters who seem to hold the naive belief that government Public Information Officers have the job of providing information to the press. Actually, their work is to promote the good and conceal the bad and put the best possible face on all news concerning their agency. They are natural enemies of newspapermen, and any other assumption is a dangerous delusion.

LOOK AT THE PRODUCT

By John L. Steele *Time* bureau chief

Quite frankly, I believe that in our profession there is entirely too much wailing at the wall on the subject of press freedom and the so-called "management" of the news. I am disturbed lest newsmen become so obsessed with this subject that they forget their own jobs, that of "managing" to tell the news in a meaningful way. In the main, I have found that governmental news policies have not inhibited us to any great degree, and I find important sources somewhat more available than at certain periods in the past.

On balance, I find the current crowd exceedingly interested in what is written about governmental activities, perhaps a little too "image conscious" to the point where they risk overemphasizing the matter of "how things look," rather than "how things are." They do read the hell out of us, and, after all, that's the highest form of flattery in our profession.

Regarding your specific question of accessibility to President Kennedy: that is a matter of presidential discretion and on this score I have no complaints. My concern is not with any special consideration given this journalist or that, but with the outcome of such consideration. Is the product good or bad, mature or immature, realistic or self-serving? I submit that these kinds of judgment lie at the heart of journalistic performance and that, as always, newsmen rather than bureaucrats remain the masters of their fate and the keepers of their professional conscience.

HARD, UNGLAMOROUS WORK

By Julius Duscha *Washington Post*

It has always been the job of public relations men, whether they work for the government or for private industry, to manage the news. On the other hand, it is the job of reporters to tell readers not only what the public relations men claim is happening but to go beyond the handouts to get the full story.

I think that Washington needs fewer reporters who go around bleating about the management of the news and more reporters who are willing to do the hard, unglamorous work of digging out the news.

I seldom cover the White House, the Pentagon, or the State Department, but I have had considerable experience covering the Agriculture, Interior, Commerce, and Labor Departments as well as some of the regulatory agencies. The significant stories in these departments and agencies seldom come from handouts or press conferences. More often, they are developed by reporters who know their subjects, know their way around the agencies—and on Capitol Hill—and are willing to work at their beats.

Despite all of the reporters who are in Washington, the city is actually poorly covered. The reporters tend to swarm to the most glamorous assignments—the White House, the State Department, the big congressional hearings. There is all too little day-to-day coverage of the other departments and agencies, and even the coverage of the big stories often consists of duplicating stories regurgitating the obvious.

There is no question that the Kennedy administration has tried to manage the news, but so did the Eisenhower administration. A favored reporter gets an occasional beat on his rivals, and perhaps even an occasional invitation to dinner. But the beat usually is nothing more than a "puff" for the administration. Significant stories that go behind the official statements seldom come from administration sources. They must be developed from such sources as lower-echelon employes, Senators and Representatives and their aides, and lobbyists.

No big scandal can be hushed up for long by an administration. The Billie Sol Estes scandal, which I spent much of last year covering, is the latest example. I know of Agriculture Department officials who hoped that the Estes case could be hushed up and who advised Secretary Freeman not to talk about it. But in this instance the press would not let Freeman sit on the case.

Not all of the fault with Washington coverage lies with the reporters, however. Many editors are unwilling to provide the space that is needed for comprehensive coverage of Washington. Other editors are only concerned about the big stories on which the pack of Washington reporters converges like yelping foxes for a few days and then drops.

My plea, then, is for more real reporting in Washington. If all of the newspapermen in Washington who call themselves reporters would get out of their offices and the National Press Club bar more often, and look with more skepticism on every official pronouncement, there would be less need for anyone to worry about freedom of information and management of the news.

NATIONAL SECURITY FIBS

By David J. Kraslow *Los Angeles Times*

I think the entire debate over "managed news" is getting out of hand. I am not even sure any more as to what we're talking about. We are scattering our shot at a whole variety of issues. They are somewhat related, to be sure, but I fear we may miss the mark on what, in my view, really counts and we may wind up confusing the public, as well as ourselves.

Executive privilege, White House leaks, excessive secrecy, management of news (name me one politician in all history who did not attempt to manipulate the flow of news to best serve his cause or himself). All of these, and other questions, have come into the debate.

I am inclined to accept Ed Lahey's long view of such matters. We have always lived with such problems. We fight them instinctively—and relentlessly. We gain a little ground; we lose a little ground. But in the net, I think, we manage to stay on top.

There is a "new" and very basic issue on which we should be concentrating our ire and our fire.

It is one thing to speak the magic words, "national security," and then tell the citizens nothing. It is quite another to tell them something ain't so, when you know it is so. And then, when what happened becomes painfully obvious, you explain you had to fib for the sake of national security. The "you," of course, is the national government, or any agency or official thereof.

We ought to be raising hell about doctored news, not managed news. We ought to be raising hell about an official mentality which seems too ready to tamper with the credibility of the United States government for the sake of alleged short-term gains.

The U-2 business of 1960, the Bay of Pigs in 1961, the Cuban mess of 1962 (and I'm not overly concerned about the President's diplomatic cold in the latter instance). Three times in less than three years the American people were misled by their own government on matters of major import. This is a fact, period.

We lost a lot more than a propaganda battle when the United States told a whopper about Francis Powers and his U-2. We have not yet paid the full price for that lie (only last month Eisenhower said he has all along regretted not obeying the instinct that told him it would be better to say nothing than to lie).

I wonder, for example, how the textbooks are going to handle the U-2 affair.

Are they going to say that a government which must have the consent and confidence of the people found it necessary to lie to the people?

If it's all right for government to lie sometimes, the student asks, how can the people know when government is not lying?

I grew up believing that when Uncle Sam said something, you could pretty well depend on it. Prof. Ernest May, a Harvard historian, tells me it's out of character for American governments to lie. That's what we ought to be worrying about.

Obviously, I haven't tackled directly any of the questions suggested in your letter. They are all worthy of discussion, but if I took them on I would be doing precisely what I complained of at the outset.

I might say that the presidential press conference can be a most useful method of helping to keep an administration honest in its handling of news.

As I noted in a *Nieman Reports* piece a year ago, other than newsmen, there is no one—in or out of government—who can examine a president on the record.

Sure, the instrument is far from perfect. But it's all we have. Improve it—don't kill it. And Mr. Kennedy's record on press conferences is still almost as spotty as it was when I wrote the piece.

NO PROBLEM FOR REAL REPORTER

By John J. Lindsay *Newsweek*

The Congress, rather than the Executive, has been my beat most of the past six years, first on the *Washington Post,* and in recent months for *Newsweek.* But there is a good deal of interplay in assignments.

No reporter in Washington with the slightest talent, capacity for hard work, ordinary curiosity, and insight need feel himself left out or conspired against in covering the Congress. With 535 individuals, about 20 per cent of whom exercise real power and have connections with sources of information inside the administration, there should never be a blast about news management on Capitol Hill. Most reporters have to admit they can get as much "inside" information as their brains can absorb.

Now the executive branch is different, but it is a difference of emphasis, rather than anything else. Here's the sharp contrast between the Eisenhower administration's "news management" and that of the Kennedys:

Unless a reporter was with the "in group," that tight little coterie of reporters and correspondents that springs up with each change of administration, it was all but impossible to break through the service of Jim Hagerty under Ike. For instance, if a reporter wanted to talk with Emmett Hughes or Bryce Harlow four years ago, he had to call Hagerty first. After sparring with him for five or ten minutes, he either got the green light or he didn't and frequently he got nothing more than a run-around. Recently I had occasion to need information from Wiesner, Schlesinger, and Larry O'Brien in one afternoon. Calls were placed directly. Schlesinger was out of town but his secretary gave me the name and telephone number of the person he was visiting. Wiesner's secretary said he was out but would be back. O'Brien was in but was tied up. Before two hours had passed, O'Brien was on the phone with a completely candid response to my question.

Wiesner called back, and with a titanic forbearance—for the question I had to ask was piddling—carefully explained his position to me.

The big difference between the Eisenhower administration's news handling and this one is the availability of those who know what is going on and, in most circumstances, their willingness to discuss it candidly. This doesn't mean there are not limitations. The reporter who refuses to accept a response unless it is completely on the record will fill little news space. This is a shibboleth of the business anyway, in my judgment; it is a question of whether you really want to report what is going on or whether you want to demonstrate to reader and employer alike that you scored big by talking to the top man and nailing him down for direct quotes. Frequently, the direct quotes say nothing that any good high school publication couldn't elicit and your readers go begging for the really significant story: what does it all mean?

Not infrequently, when the heat is on, as it was during the second Cuban crisis, your best sources will clam up for three or four days. This in itself is a tip that something big is happening. Rather than sit around with thumbs in ears moaning about it, the able reporter will try to get behind that happening, too. (It is no great surprise to me that despite the red herring dragged across the trail, cover stories and other devices used, two newspapers nailed the story of the administration's plan for the handling of the introduction of Soviet missiles into Cuba. That they sat on this at the request of the administration may be news management but if it was, the precedents are clear and unassailable. No reporter worth his salt here muttered about the ability of those reporters to smoke out a big one. Personally, I was green with envy, but I know how it was done: curiosity, imagination, boldness and the insight to put together extraneous, seeemingly unrelated, scraps of information, stab at the truth and pin somebody down with the evidence. It sure as hell wasn't magic and nobody "leaked" that story. It was obtained, despite one of the most effective security screens ever thrown up.)

The administration personnel are much more sophisticated about handling news than their counterparts under the Eisenhower administration. They are acutely aware of the damage that can be inflicted by the reporter who, in a huff over rebuff, rushes into print with a half-baked story. They also read the newspapers, an example set by Mr. Big as contrasted with the example set by Eisenhower.

There is no reason why any reporter who wants to go after it and can handle it professionally, should be shut out of the sources of news. Those who are content with handout reporting, generally speaking, are those who bleat the loudest when they get their ears pinned back by enterprisers. The fact that the *Herald Trib* is down-beat at 1600 Pennsylvania Ave. N.W., has not noticeably prevented their good reporters from coming up with good, solid, exclusive stories.

There is probably more backgrounding going on in Washington today than at anytime in the past ten years. Is this bad? Background dinners and other such affairs have a limited value, however, for producing news. Any reporter who depends upon them won't be around long to report. Obviously, except in rare instances when the guest fills reporters in on the thinking of his department or agency on a problem to peak sometime in the future, the interview ranges over things past.

This, in a sense, may be "managed news" in that only a handful of reporters are present at a time and place, generally, of the guest's choice. There is the implication likewise, of shutting out other reporters, and, in effect, battening hatches on use of information that might otherwise come out in the course of events.

I am inclined to think, however, that much of the news broken by these backgrounders will come out one way or the other. And because they are conducted on a "nonattribution" rather than "off-the-record" basis, the enterprising reporter has no difficulty shaping things in hard form.

There are unfortunately many Washington correspondents who, although highly successful themselves, blast incessantly about "managed news."

Summing up: I believe the management of news is going to be with us forever. I think there is less of it now than four years ago. Policy makers are more readily available at the highest levels than ever before; they not only know what is going on, they talk about it.

Reporters personally, by and large, carve out their own futures here and no man need feel left out if he is competent, energetic and can handle what he gets like a pro.

Washington correspondents, generally speaking, today are head and shoulders above their predecessors. They are better educated, more aware, more energetic, less inclined either to liberal or conservative dogma, and deeply unimpressed by the panoply of the "big men" in Washington.

My personal view is that even if confined to wire services, the newspapers of the United States are getting more and better reporting than ever before. With the advent of the individual news services promoted by such papers as the *Times; Herald Trib; Washington Post* and *Los Angeles Times;* Chicago *Tribune* and *News,* to mention a few, there isn't a paper in this country with any pretensions to excellence that has the slightest excuse in the world for not turning out a much better newspaper than most of them do.

The Press Lives by Disclosures

JOSEPH PULITZER, JR. [JULY 1961

This discussion of President Kennedy's proposal of voluntary censorship was given by Mr. Pulitzer, editor and publisher of the *St. Louis Post-Dispatch,* in a panel on the press during his twenty-fifth reunion at Harvard, June 14, 1961.

A century ago when an external threat to the survival of the nation was undreamed of, Wilbur Fisk Storey, editor of the *Chicago Times,* declared: "It is a newspaper's duty to print the news and raise hell." This incisive judgment on one journalistic purpose was questioned recently by President Kennedy when he expounded before an audience of American publishers the problems of a free press in the cold war. Mr. Kennedy proposed a voluntary censorship of news on matters involving the national security. He called for more self-restraint or self-discipline in such matters by the press. At the same time the president recognized the responsibility of newspapers to inform the public, in his words, "to arouse, to reflect, to state our dangers and our opportunities, to indicate our crises and our choices, to lead, mold, educate and sometimes even anger public opinion." The dilemma, as he defined it, concerns "a free and open society in a cold and secret war." Speaking of the monolithic and ruthless conspiracy which confronts the free world, Mr. Kennedy said:

> Its preparations are concealed, not published. Its mistakes are buried, not headlined. Its dissenters are silenced, not lionized. No expenditure is questioned, no rumor is printed, no secret is revealed. It conducts the cold war, in short, with a wartime discipline no democracy would ever hope or wish to match. Nevertheless, every democracy recognizes the necessary restraints of national security—and the question remains whether those restraints need to be more strictly observed if we are to oppose this kind of attack as well as outright invasion.

The occasion for suggesting consideration of voluntary censorship was the ill-fated Cuban invasion, in which operation some newspapers, as you know, disclosed active participation by the Central Intelligence Agency. While one may sympathize with the busy public servants who were harassed by newspaper reports of CIA activity, one must weigh against such inconvenience or interference the traditional safeguard of press freedom, protected by the constitution as a fundamental bulwark of our free society. One may respectfully assert that the editor in Chicago uttered a cogent and wise maxim when he declared that "it is a newspaper's duty to print the news and raise hell."

Admitting the roughness of the language, this is not a frivolous conception of a newspaper's responsibility to the public it serves. On the contrary, the statement implies the essence of a free, inquiring, critical press. It recognizes, I suggest, a newspaper's obligation to print a full and accurate account of the news, to interpret its significance or meaning in the broader context of the issues of the day, and to comment on events with vigor, sound reasoning and moral purpose irrespective of the popularity of the views expressed or any denunciations that might thunder from high places of authority.

"The press lives by disclosures," as the London *Times* observed in a wise assessment of the role of the press. More than a century ago, 1851, British officials were agitating for censorship after Lord Palmerston had been disclosed as backing a clandestine operation by Louis Napoleon to become emperor of France. In reply, the *Times* disagreed that the purpose of a newspaper is "to share the labors of statesmanship, or that it is bound by the same duties, the same liabilities as Ministers of the Crown."

> The purposes and duties of the two powers are constantly separate, generally independent, sometimes diametrically opposite. The dignity and freedom of the press are trammelled from the moment it accepts an ancillary position . . . The press can enter into no close or binding alliances with the statesmen of the day, nor can it surrender its permanent interests to the convenience of the ephemeral power of any Government. The first duty of the press is to obtain the earliest and most correct intelligence of the events of the time, and instantly, by disclosing them, to make them the common property of the nation . . . The Press lives by disclosures.

If the foregoing consensus means that the press must serve no master but the public interest, and that the disclosure of the truth is indispensable to an informed public opinion on which rest sound public policies, it is my view that editors can best contribute to the public welfare by the exercise of each individual conscience in covering the news and commenting on it. If the editorial opinions of a newspaper are to be sound, meaningful, and influential in shaping the great potentialities of American life in a free society, those declarations of opinion must rely on the most complete, unrestrained, accurate account of the consequential events of the day. Self-imposed censorship, voluntarily agreed to—conformity to a code of suppression designed to protect the general welfare—would warp the integrity of the news on which sound opinions rely.

Voluntary censorship has been accepted during periods of war as a temporary abridgment of a protected right in order to safeguard American lives engaged on the fighting fronts. But wars have involved a controlled press for only a limited duration. The competitive challenge of the Communist world, it is widely accepted, may threaten the nation for decades. Not with open war but with covert means, our opponents may be expected to test the foundations of freedom.

An ever-widening circle of news suppression over an extended period would merit the people's loss of confidence in the press, deepening as the suppressions or distortions inevitably came to light. Could we accept the decline of an informed public opinion after editorial debate had become an empty ceremonial dependent on a pale replica of the facts? Voluntary censorship in the cold war under government tutelage would, in time, I suggest, stifle the initiative, the curiosity, the skepticism which goad responsible editors to ferret out the facts of important news situations. Valid interpretations and informed discussion of the issues would falter. Enlightened public opinion would languish in a twilight of half-truths. The "collision of adverse opinions," in John Stuart Mill's phrase, would no longer supply the "remainder of the truth" which men must share with their government to ensure that sound decisions are taken and constructive policies are supported.

The press is a tribune to defend the undefended, a chronicle to record its times, an examiner of controversies; it monitors the economy and the social progress of its age, it is a journal of man's successes and failures, a fighter for progress and reform; it is a herald of events, an observer of the tides of change, a commentator on the great issues confronting the nation, a reporter of happenings in public life, a review of the policies—good and bad—of its leaders; the newspaper is a challenge to the policy makers, a guardian of man's liberties; it is a mirror of man's aspirations; a sentinel to protect the public. If the press is all these things—if it offers enlightenment to guide a free society toward a more noble destiny—could it serve unimpaired for long under the restraints of even self-imposed censorship? Would not the honored institution become enfeebled and decline in its capacity to support the nation's struggle against tyranny or, conversely, to challenge decisions which, in a climate of moderation, might be recognized as inimical to America's best interests? A free institution would slowly lose its character and abandon its tradition. If "the press lives by disclosures," a muted journalism would debase the truth and be undeserving of the trust imposed in it by the writers of the constitution.

Surely nothing involving human judgment is absolute or perfect. Flaws of character, errors by prejudice, weakness, unconscious bias, any of these would prevent perfection in the exercise of sound news and editorial judgment in deciding what facts an editor who is also a patriotic citizen should suppress in the interest of military security. If we can agree that no responsible editor would deliberately injure the nation's security, would it not be wise to accept the damage caused by a mistaken judgment rather than acquiesce in a code of censorship administered by men of good will but no less fallible? Mr. Kennedy recognized the need for vitality in public discussion of national affairs when he told the publishers, "Without debate, without criticism, no administration can succeed—and no republic can survive . . . that is why our press was protected by the First Amendment."

In May the president conferred with a group of newspaper executives at the White House. It was reported that the government and the press will continue to study the objective of protecting security without censorship and will meet again in several months.

In conclusion may I quote from an editorial carried in the *St. Louis Post-Dispatch* which summarizes the problem we have been examining:

> In the case of the Cuban affair, many newspapers of Florida agreed among themselves to say nothing about the training of refugees for the invasion. The *New York Times,* on the other hand, sent Latin American experts to Miami to obtain and publish as much information as they could obtain from refugee leaders.
>
> Obviously, the editors of the New York and Florida papers differed in their judgment, as was their right. But it seems also obvious that if all of the newspapers had agreed to conform to a code, in cooperation with a government agency, the American people would be less able to evaluate the Cuban adventure and use its lessons to decide their future course. They might never have learned of the failure; they might not be in a position to demand an accounting.
>
> There is no doubt that the existence of an aggressive and inquiring press is and will be an inhibiting factor in the sort of operation the CIA attempted in Cuba. But it would be better to conclude that maneuvers of this sort should not be undertaken by an open society than that our society should become less open. Perhaps a choice need not be made. This much, however, is quite clear: a free, aggressive, inquiring and above all pluralistic press is indispensable to a free society. In full knowledge that some newspapers may abuse their trust, the free society must rely upon the discretion and sense of responsibility of individual editors and publishers instead of trying to impose upon them all a monolithic uniformity like that of the totalitarian press.
>
> Mr. Kennedy himself gave a partial answer to his own argument for considering press restraints. He said: "Even today, there is little value in opposing the threat of a closed society by imitating its arbitrary restrictions. Even today, there is little value in insuring the survival of our nation if our traditions do not survive with it."
>
> With that we fully agree.

The Newsmen's War in Vietnam

STANLEY KARNOW [DECEMBER 1963

Mr. Karnow, a Nieman Fellow of 1957–58, transferred to the *Saturday Evening Post* in the summer of 1963 after serving as a *Time* foreign correspondent for more than a decade.

Until a *coup d'état* overthrew the Ngo Dinh Diem regime, there were two wars going on in South Vietnam. One was against a Communist guerrilla enemy. The other was against foreign correspondents. The anti-Communist struggle continues; but the revolt that toppled Diem has, at least for the present, given the newsmen peace with honor.

For years, correspondents trying to cover the Diem government's two-way fight against the Communists and its own domestic opposition were plagued by physical violence as well as persistent, invidious efforts to manage their news and discredit their reporting.

They were maligned by the late President Diem for "poisoning American public opinion," and accused by his termagant sister-in-law, Madame Ngo Dinh Nhu, of being Communist-infiltrated.

Observing "guidance" directives from Washington or inventing their own lines of conduct, American officials in Saigon fed them propaganda and limited their movements to such an extent that a Congressional subcommittee recently charged that "the restrictive U.S. press policy . . . unquestionably contributed to a lack of information about conditions in Vietnam which created an international crisis."

As if these obstructions were not enough, the Saigon-based newsmen were also subjected to internecine abuse from fellow journalists. Predictably, the bitterness of their criticism was directly proportional to their unfamiliarity with the situation in Vietnam.

Thus columnist Joseph Alsop, though acknowledging that Diem's press relations were "idiotic," still accused Saigon's resident reporters of carrying on "egregious crusades" against the regime. Less knowledgeable visitors to Vietnam, like Hearst editor Frank Conniff and Miss Marguerite Higgins, then of the *New York*

Herald Tribune, were more hostile. "Reporters here would like to see us lose the war to prove they're right," said Miss Higgins.

The most vitriolic tirade, however, was launched by *Time,* which last September charged the Saigon press corps with "helping to compound the very confusion that it should be untangling for its readers at home." According to *Time,* the journalists presented a distorted picture of events in Vietnam because "they pool their convictions, information, misinformation and grievances" and, in short, were in conspiracy against the Diem government. It was a fascinating thesis. Hardly had it appeared in print than *Time*'s Southeast Asia bureau chief Charles Mohr and Saigon reporter Mert Perry quit their jobs. "That piece," explained Mohr, "was concocted entirely in New York and based on no dispatch sent by a correspondent here."

The target of the offensive was a band of young, hard-working, passionate reporters. The youngest of them, 26-year-old Cornelius Sheehan of the United Press International, sleeps in a windowless room adjoining his office and, as a U.S. army officer once described, "he is bent on beating his typewriter into scrap metal." The oldest of them is 32-year-old Malcolm Browne of the Associated Press, a lean, determined ex-chemist to whom working in Saigon is a "never-ending wrestling match" to extract facts from mysterious sources and laconic officials.

The most proficient among them is tall, dark David Halberstam, 29, of the *New York Times.* A Harvard graduate who served his newspaper apprenticeship in Tennessee, he won the American Newspaper Guild's Page One award for his reporting from the Congo, and has been operating in Saigon since May 1962. In Washington, where wags sometimes call the Vietnam conflict "Halberstam's War," State Department insiders often get more information from the *Times* than they find in government cables. "David is an excellent reporter," a U.S. diplomat says with a mixture of admiration and irritation. "But how he lays his hands on so much confidential material is astounding."

In a paradoxical way, the official freeze on fraternization with correspondents increased rather than diminished the reporters' sources of first-rate information. Many lower-echelon functionaries, in disagreement with high-level policy, did not hesitate to provide reporters with news. This was particularly true within the Vietnamese establishment, where the disaffection against Diem's rule before the *coup d'état* had expanded to such proportions that some astute correspondents were able to build up a network of official native informants throughout the provinces. Sheehan, Halberstam, and Mert Perry had advance notice of the military revolt against Diem—a message reading: "Please buy me one bottle of whiskey at the PX."

U.S. reporters also depended heavily for news on American military and civilian advisers in the field, many of whom were frustrated by the refusal of their superiors in Saigon to listen to reports that deviated from the rosy "party line." One such officer was Lieut. Col. John Paul Vann, formerly the senior U.S. military adviser in a key area of the Delta. His criticism of the way the war was being waged was so systematically ignored that he recently quit the service to be able to speak freely. In an interview with *U. S. News & World Report* last September, he said: "There has been a lack of firsthand information [about Vietnam]. High-ranking people are sent there from Washington and told to get results. It becomes a kind of consuming desire on their part to show some palpable results. I believe this causes a tendency to play down the real picture."

Correspondents who listened to Vann and other officers like him did not purposely seek out military men with criticism to voice. On the contrary, these responsible officers were the best available news sources. To suggest that they performed for the benefit of reporters would be to undervalue the stature of these soldiers.

To suggest, as some critics have, that the Saigon correspondents behaved irresponsibly, is to miss the mark. They have been reproached for their "emotional involvement" in the Vietnam situation, and they do not deny the charge. "I defy anyone to spend six months in Saigon without becoming emotionally engaged," one of them explains. "After all, we're human beings, not jellyfish."

But to a larger, deeper, and more complex degree, their subjective reaction to the situation was a natural reflection of the American conscience confronted with Vietnam's "dirty, untidy, disagreeable" war, as Secretary of State Dean Rusk once called it. In aiding South Vietnam to fight its Communist threat, the U.S. took the politically uncomfortable step of allying itself with the ineffective, unpopular, and tyrannical government of Ngo Dinh Diem and his family. A leading American diplomat termed it "a medieval, oriental despotism"; as a high Vatican representative put it recently: "It was a regime that could have become Communist overnight—they'd have had only to change the flags."

When the U.S. commitment to South Vietnam began to take shape a couple of years ago, it became part of American policy to camouflage the shortcomings of the Diem oligarchy. The U.S. could not, of course, knock a government it was boosting. Also displayed, as George Kennan described it, was "that curious trait of the American political personality which causes it to appear reprehensible to voice anything less than unlimited optimism about the fortunes of another government one had adopted as a friend and protégé."

Thus American policy makers and practitioners, fearful of ruffling Diem's sensitivities, urged American reporters to avoid pessimism and criticism. U.S. generals told correspondents that "bad news hurts morale." Frederick E. Nolting, Jr., then the U.S. ambassador to Vietnam, once said: "Why don't you newsmen give Diem the benefit of the doubt?"

Early in 1961, a special effort was made to create an attractive public image for the Diem regime. One day, a pleasant, Uruguayan-born American named Jorge Ortiz turned up in Saigon as representative of the New York advertising firm of Kastor, Hilton, Chesley, Clifford and Atherton, and he rapidly transformed the atmosphere. He arranged interviews for reporters with government officials and organized airplane tours of the "fighting front." He hired pretty Vietnamese girls to guide visiting correspondents, loaned them Olivetti typewriters, and facilitated the movement of their cables at Saigon's archaic post office. For these services, Diem paid Ortiz and his employers $100,000 per year and expenses.

But no public relations man, whatever his ethics or his acumen, could do much to beautify Diem's image. For Diem did not desire only the "benefit of the doubt," as Ambassador Nolting suggested he be given; he wanted total subservience. *Newsweek*'s Francois Sully was expelled from the country for supposedly slighting the Women's Solidarity Movement, and NBC correspondent James Robinson was declared *persona non grata* for referring to the Ngo Dinhs as a "family clique." On occasion, displeasure with the U.S. press reached shrieks of hysteria. In September 1963, after the *New York Times* unintentionally omitted ten words from one of her letters, Madame Ngo Dinh Nhu cried that the paper belonged "to an international Communist-inspired conspiracy aimed at slandering Vietnam."

To Diem, his brother Ngo Dinh Nhu, Madame Nhu and the rest of the family, the press was an instrument of the state. Their country's twenty-odd newspapers operated entirely under government control. They were told what to print in regular "guidance" memoranda, and some actually had their editorials written for them by officials. All submitted their page proofs every morning to a team of twelve censors, and the penalty for deviation from official doctrine was severe. Last August, for example, a Saigon daily called *Tu Do*—which, ironically, means "freedom"—was closed down for "compromising the security of the state," and five of its staff members were jailed.

As a result, Saigon's newspapers completely lost their credibility. Educated Vietnamese read them largely for their serialized fiction. For news, a great many listened to the Vietnamese-language broadcasts of the Voice of America (which, Brother Nhu declared, "is not the voice of the American government but the voice of a group of capitalists who control it"). Arriving in Saigon last summer, I recall being asked by a customs officer if I had any foreign newspapers. "I'd like to read one," he explained, "so I can find out what's going on in this country."

With their monolithic mentality, President Diem and his ruling relatives sincerely believed that American journalists should also accept some kind of control. Indeed, during a revealing interview in 1961, Madame Nhu candidly submitted that the Western press might well emulate the Communist press by deciding on a common line to follow. Her idea was a sort of press "policy planning committee" headed by Joseph Alsop, who then had nothing but praise for Diem. When the interviewer politely replied that neither he nor his colleagues always concurred with Alsop, Madame Nhu snapped: "Well, if you won't be convinced by people who know the truth, then I can't help you."

Gradually, as the U.S. became more identified with the Diem regime, American officials in Saigon began to behave towards their own press like the regime itself. As Halberstam put it, "The U.S. Embassy turned into the adjunct of a dictatorship. In trying to protect Diem from criticism, the Ambassador became Diem's agent.

But we reporters didn't have to become the adjuncts of a tyranny. We are representatives of a free society, and we weren't going to surrender our principles to the narrow notions of a closed society."

And therein lay the rub. Former Ambassador Nolting, a charming Virginian, never quite understood that American reporters could not be made to tailor their articles to conform to a government policy. He may have had no illusions himself about the nature of the Diem government, but he was under instructions to appease its whimsies. For reasons that even his closest associates still cannot clearly delineate, he expected U.S. correspondents to go along with this strategy. "Fritz Nolting is one of the finest human beings I've ever met," says one of his former aides. "But he didn't have the foggiest idea of how to deal with the press."

To an incredible extent, Nolting underestimated reporters' abilities to unearth stories, and he was constantly being surprised by their knowledge of facts he thought to be confidential. He failed to realize that, while he sedulously withheld information, correspondents were getting their details, sometimes distorted, from Vietnamese officials or out of Washington. During a delicate period of negotiation with Diem in late 1961, for example, Nolting refused to see the press for three weeks, even to give them "off the record" background guidance. Yet Washington was leaking like a sieve with accounts of the same negotiations, and reporters in Saigon found themselves in the peculiar position of being scooped on events occurring in Vietnam by their colleagues back home.

At the same time, Nolting tried valiantly to persuade the press that Diem and his family were much better than they appeared to be. He would tell visiting editors, for example, that Diem was really a popular man "because his picture is displayed everywhere." With reporters who had some experience in Vietnam, however, this line fell flat. "The first time I saw Nolting," recalls the veteran CBS correspondent Peter Kalischer, "he told me that Diem's real strength lay in the countryside. After hearing that, I figured there was no point in questioning him again."

Efforts by U.S. military brass to control the news were even more flagrant. Until early in 1962, they tried to deny that a war was going on in Vietnam. This position may have been motivated by the consideration that, by shipping weapons to the Vietnamese army, the U.S. was violating the 1954 Geneva Accords, which it had hitherto respected but never signed. Observance of this technicality led to comic exchanges. When a huge aircraft carrier steamed up the Saigon River laden with helicopters, a U.S. military information officer was forced to say: "I don't see any aircraft carrier."

Similarly, U.S. troops in Vietnam held only advisory capacities, and attempts of all sorts were made to give the impression that they never engaged in combat. For a long time, reporters were barred from helicopter missions lest they observe Americans pulling triggers. On occasion, U.S. military spokesmen also endeavored to deny that American soldiers ever encountered Communist guerrillas. One evening, for example, a reporter learned from excellent sources that a GI had been kidnapped by the Communists. Checking with the U.S. military information officer, he received a flat denial. "Well, I'm filing the story anyway," challenged the reporter. "In that case," replied the officer, "I suppose we'll have to release the news."

In several cases, however, correspondents were inexcusably wrong. A few months ago, for instance, some of them reported a battle between Buddhist and Catholic troops that really never took place. Last August the Associated Press reported that a jeep carrying Ambassador Nolting had killed a little Vietnamese boy when, in fact, it was an army vehicle that slightly injured a girl. Some top U.S. military men contend that such stories derived from reporters' emotional desire to paint as black a picture as possible. More experienced journalists, while deploring such reporting, attribute it to the fierce competition between news agencies that frequently results in half-cocked accounts.

A more serious difference between the U.S. military command and American journalists lay in their divergent interpretation of how the war should be reported. American generals in Saigon have frankly stated that pessimistic newspaper articles lower morale and adversely affect public opinion at home. Besides, they themselves take an optimistic view of the situation in Vietnam, and they support their opinion with charts and statistics showing the numbers of enemy weapons captured or the number of Communist guerrillas killed.

The bitterness between the U.S. military and the press brewed to a boiling point in January 1963, after a battle at the village of Ap Bac, in the important southern delta. According to American military advisers in the region, the fight had been a blistering government defeat. The Vietnamese army had surrounded the Communist guerrillas on three sides, but declined to carry through their attack. The guerrillas escaped after knocking down five U.S. helicopters and killing 65 Vietnamese troops and two American officers. The UPI's Neil Sheehan, Nick Turner of Reuters and others took night taxi rides into the area to get the story, and in the midst of the confusion they were caught in the accidental fire of the Vietnamese artillery shelling its own men. As a leading American officer in the field said, "It was a miserable performance, just as it always is."

At U.S. military headquarters in Saigon, however, the battle was considered a victory because, the brass pointed out, the Vietnamese army had gained its objective: they captured the village. Admiral Harry D. Felt, U.S. Commander in the Pacific, repeated this thesis when he arrived in Saigon a few days later. And to Neil Sheehan he said, "You ought to get out into the countryside and speak to the people who have the facts."

Early in 1963 the displeasure of the U.S. mission chiefs in Saigon against American reporters knew no bounds. At one stage, when an important VIP was scheduled to arrive from Washington, Ambassador Nolting and General Paul Harkins, the U.S. military commander, commissioned a high U.S. Embassy official to write a memorandum describing the American correspondents. When they saw the memo, Nolting and Harkins ordered the official to rewrite it and make it tougher. And they weren't satisfied until he had characterized American newsmen as inexperienced, unsophisticated, and malicious individuals whose "irresponsible, sensationalized, astigmatic reporting" had damaged the U.S. interest in Vietnam. Inevitably the secret document leaked back to the reporters themselves, and the official pleaded guilty to having submitted to pressure from above. "That memo was the stupidest thing I ever did," he now confesses. "Once I was forced to rewrite it, I should have never signed my name to it."

But that memorandum was no sloppier than the kind of directives being sent from Washington to Saigon regarding news management. The author of one of them, then Deputy Assistant Secretary of State for Public Affairs Carl Rowan, was a former newspaperman who had contended that "this so-called concern about the public's right to know is really concern about the fourth estate's right to make a buck." Advocates of the principle of public access to information, he once stated, "often engage in eager self-deception." Accordingly, he drafted an order to the U.S. mission in Saigon advising that (1) news stories which criticize Diem "increase the difficulties of the U.S. job"; (2) newsmen be told that "trifling or thoughtless criticism of the Diem government" would hinder cooperation between the U.S. and Diem; and (3) newsmen should not be exposed to military activities "that are likely to result in undesirable stories." In short, as a Congressional subcommittee later analyzed the directive, facts were being hidden from the American public.

Actually, Rowan's directive was designed to improve American press relations in Saigon, but it had little effect. Finally, last May, the U.S. Information Agency chief in Vietnam, John Mecklin, went back to Washington and pleaded that official dealings with the correspondents had become so bad that the need to repair them was more important than "security and everything else." A former correspondent himself, Mecklin made no progress until he saw President Kennedy, who instructed his Press Secretary Pierre Salinger to tell officials in Saigon to "take reporters more into your confidence." For some odd reason, the message was sent on White House stationery but was not signed by the president.

But personal relations between the U.S. mission chiefs and the press in Saigon had become so bitter that not even a presidential order could patch them up. Caught in the crossfire of official clumsiness, recriminations, and distrust, Mecklin was ready to hoist his own white flag and surrender. "You can't begin to comprehend this mess until you've seen it from the inside," he sighed. "When I resign I'm going to write a book called *My Two Years in a Squirrel Cage.*"

It wasn't until after Nolting had departed and his successor, Henry Cabot Lodge, arrived that a noticeable change took place. As he descended from his airplane at the Saigon airport, one of Lodge's first questions was: "Where are the gentlemen of the press?" It was, of course, a politician's question, but it cut with a double edge. It served to assure reporters that, having been a newsman himself, he was on their side. It was also calculated to remind the Diem regime that he had no intention of playing its press agent.

Lodge's arrival in Saigon did little to ease the friction between U.S. military chiefs and the American reporters, however. While Lodge moved to get closer to correspondents, the U.S. military establishment imposed tighter restrictions on them by prohibiting their travel on aircraft except with special authorization. This difference in attitude towards journalists between Lodge and the military was more than a matter of public relations technique. It reflected a deeper disagreement about the state of the war. Like the correspondents, Lodge did not share General Harkins' optimism. Nor did he feel, as the military did, that much progress could be made as long as Diem and his family remained in power.

This divergence revealed itself sharply last September, when the U.S. military headquarters in Saigon barred reporters from flying to the site of a crashed American aircraft. "We're not going to risk an airplane and crew so that reporters can take pictures of a crash," declared a U.S. general. "Nonsense," replied an American Embassy official. "The military doesn't want photos of a crashed plane because it contradicts their optimistic line."

When Diem's internal fight against his country's Buddhists developed during last summer, the war of words between officials and journalists entered a new phase. Reporters were now charged with being overly sympathetic towards the Buddhists, whose leaders cleverly used the press as a weapon. Again, amid the complexities and confusion of the Saigon situation, this argument was a matter of interpretation. Correspondents certainly responded to the Buddhists, partly because Americans have an undeniable affinity for the underdog, largely because a burning monk makes news. The Buddhist spokesman adroitly made their case because their press relations were excellent, and they did indeed use the press because international opinion was the only weapon at their disposal. The contention that the Buddhist crisis would not have erupted if the foreign press was not present is dubious. "Diem and Nhu would have cracked down just as hard on the Buddhists," says a Western diplomat in Saigon, "but the world would have never known anything about it."

Critics of the press also belabored correspondents for "overemphasizing" the religious aspects of the ruction between Diem and the Buddhists. Reporters did indeed refer repeatedly to the fact that the ruling Ngo Dinh family were Roman Catholics. Judging from many of their articles, however, they were quite aware of the nature of the dispute. By mid-July, for example, Halberstam was writing in the *New York Times* that "the controversy between the Buddhists and the government . . . has become increasingly political." UPI correspondent Sheehan was even denounced by the Buddhist leaders for stressing the political side of their protest.

Fundamentally, however, Diem's appalling mishandling of the Buddhist issue vindicated the reporters who had claimed for years that South Vietnam's regime was hopelessly inept. In an overwhelming change of outlook, Washington adopted this view. But as *Newsweek* pointed out: "Nowadays, the journalist . . . is still abused for spreading unhappy truths. And indeed, by some curious twist of logic, it has even become the fashion to hold him responsible for the very events he describes."

Censors and Their Tactics

JACK NELSON [DECEMBER 1963

Jack Nelson of the *Atlanta Constitution* won a Pulitzer prize for his investigative reporting in 1960. He and Gene Roberts, while they were Nieman Fellows in 1961–62, wrote a book, *The Censors and the Schools,* which was published in 1963 by Little, Brown. This paper by Mr. Nelson was delivered at the Freedom of Information Conference, University of Missouri School of Journalism, November 7, 1963. In 1965 he joined the *Los Angeles Times* as Atlanta correspondent.

In this age of exploding knowledge, when man is reaching for the moon and we talk about brinkmanship and a nuclear war that could devastate civilization, we still publish high school history books that refer only to the War between the States, a euphemism to please Southern ears. For that matter, many Southern newspapers eschew the name "Civil War."

Shortly after the Civil War, a New York publisher advertised: "Books prepared for Southern schools by Southern authors, and therefore free from matter offensive to Southern people."

But times have changed and regional texts have given way to books competing for a national market. So now the trick is to offend as few people as possible. The result is that many books lack vitality and are too dull to interest the students. Controversial subjects are treated superficially or not at all.

An American history text, complete through the 1960 election, deals with the Southern resistance to the Supreme Court in a single sentence. It is little wonder that the Negroes' rebellion against second-class citizenship catches many Americans by surprise.

To read many textbooks you would think Americans are all white, Anglo-Saxon, Protestant, white-collared and middle class. Two university professors, after perusing a number of social studies books, concluded that students would get the impression that "all Americans live on wide, shady streets in clean suburban areas, occupy white Cape Cod style houses, drive new automobiles, have two children (a boy and a girl of course) and own a dog."

Problems of non-English-speaking migrant workers, smog, water shortages, crowded housing, slums, poverty, crime and disease are glossed over in many texts.

Now textbook publishers do not avoid publishing information about controversial subjects because they believe this is the best way to promote education. They do it because in some cases it is not only the best, but the only way they can sell their products.

The publishers face a dilemma. Every time they show the courage to explore controversial subjects in depth they risk economic setbacks caused by censorship forces. Even relatively minor matters can cost them sales. For example, in Bastrop, Louisiana, recently the school board, learning that Macmillan planned a new line of readers in 1965 which would ignore an old taboo and show white and Negro children playing together, banned the books and urged the rest of the state to do likewise.

In our research for *The Censors and the Schools,* Gene Roberts and I found that the pressures for the elimination of censorship of "unpleasant" ideas or facts often come from diametrically opposed forces. This has been a big factor in the treatment of the Negroes' plight.

On the one hand segregationists clamor to keep out of books pictures of Negroes and whites together or any mention of an integrated society. Some extremists go so far as to find "subtle integrationist propaganda" in the pictures of white and black rabbits. In Alabama a textbook was attacked for including a picture of former Secretary of State Christian Herter shaking hands with the President of Nigeria.

On the other hand, the National Association for the Advancement of Colored People has demanded that facts it considers objectionable be excluded from books.

The high rates of crime and disease among Negroes should be discussed in textbooks as well as in the press. Not to justify opposition to integration, but to help explain it, to help show what suppression in a segregated society has done to the Negro. As the NAACP has said, the outstanding accomplishments of many Negroes should be dealt with factually and truthfully in schoolbooks. But the plight of a majority of Negroes, the discrimination they still face, also should be related with all the "unpleasant" facts included.

Are we to alter or ban American classics in literature because they contain Negro stereotypes? Or are we to teach them in the context and times in which they were written?

After NAACP pressure the New York City Board of Education dropped Mark Twain's *Huckleberry Finn* as a reading text in elementary and junior high schools. And all because of a central character in the classic, "Miss Watson's big nigger, named Jim."

In the words of the *New York Times*, "The truth is that *Huckleberry Finn* is one of the deadliest satires that was ever written on some of the nonsense that goes with inequality of the races."

Now while the NAACP, and, on occasion, other minority interest groups have campaigned for censorship of books, by far the greatest pressure today emanates from right-wing sources and is based on political ideology. The ultraconservatives are better organized and better financed than in any period in our history. In recent years their campaigns for censorship have forced the alteration of many textbooks and have resulted in the banning of hundreds of books from school libraries.

Unlike the NAACP and other crusading organizations which, for the most part, work independently of each other, the right-wing groups distribute each other's propaganda and carry out concerted campaigns.

In San Antonio, Texas, in 1962, a legislative committee investigating schoolbooks for "subversive" contents heard from a score of witnesses armed with propaganda which had originated in Washington, D.C., and at least six different states—from the Watch Washington Club, Columbus, Ohio; the Teacher Publishing Company, Dallas, Texas; America's Future, New Rochelle, N.Y.; the Independent American, New Orleans, Louisiana; the Church League of America, Wheaton, Illinois; and Education Information, Inc., Fullerton, California.

Not long before the Texas hearing, materials from the same sources, plus literature from the Daughters of the American Revolution, the Parents for Better Education in California, Coalition of Patriotic Societies in Florida, and other groups were used in an attack on books in the schools of Meriden, Connecticut.

While some of these groups have different axes to grind, they all find a common cause in the Communist menace as a domestic threat. So you find a Southern segregationist juxtaposed with a Northern industrialist in a campaign for censorship.

A segregationist equates integration with Communism and obligingly includes in the same category the income tax, social security, organized labor and other irritants of the ultraconservatives.

An industrialist sees a Red hand in federal taxes and control of industry and business, and he obligingly ascribes the same danger to the Supreme Court decision outlawing segregation.

You find a physician worried about socialized medicine, a minister troubled by "obscenities," and ordinary citizens concerned about the patriotism of other citizens. And they all blame it on Communism and together put up a solid front for their demands to censor and ban texts and library books.

One day in 1962 a reporter investigating the activities of censorship groups in Texas called on a news-service bureau at the state capitol to ask what it had on file on J. Evetts Haley, leader of a militant, right-wing organization called Texans for America.

The blasé answer was, "Nothing. You can't take Haley seriously. He's not worth keeping a file on."

Yet Haley and his Texans for America led successful censorship campaigns against texts and school library books and helped spark a legislative investigation that turned into a witch-hunt. Professors, authors, and publishers of texts were smeared as dupes and willing conspirators of the Communists.

Like the news-service bureau, most of the Texas press gave Haley relatively little attention. Perhaps they thought a man who publicly advocated "hanging" Chief Justice Earl Warren, punched a professor in an argument over the movie "Operation Abolition," and smeared Southern Methodist University as being "tainted with left-wingers," should not be taken seriously.

Whatever the reason for the scant attention given to the Haleyites and others who have clamored for censorship, the result has been that well-organized forces attacking books in Texas have operated with little organized opposition, free of public scrutiny. And they have forced alterations in many textbooks, the banning of others, and the banning of many school library volumes.

In many other states the same thing has happened to some degree in recent years. During the past five years schoolbooks have come under fire in nearly a third of the state legislatures.

In Mississippi, after a campaign by the DAR, the State Farm Bureau Federation, the White Citizens Council, and the state American Legion, the Mississippi legislature voted to put the selection of textbooks virtually in the hands of the governor, Ross Barnett. In the fall of 1963, Governor Barnett demanded that the state textbook selection committee, which he controls through appointments, remove from Mississippi high schools a book called *English in Action, Course No. 2*. Gov. Barnett condemned the book on the grounds it taught "world government" and he cited one quote from the book which he said was harmful to youths: "I think world government is necessary and attainable."

In California, a breeding ground for groups that attack books and the system of public education, numerous book battles have been fought. In one case an entire chapter on the United Nations was deleted from an eighth-grade civics book.

In Florida the state superintendent of schools assured protesting "patriotic" groups that publishers were deleting from several volumes "phrases that might have been considered objectionable."

In Texas scholars described as "shameful" the extent to which the State Textbook Committee and publishers of schoolbooks bowed to the demands of censorship forces.

In Levittown, New York, in 1963 the board of education banned *The Subcontinent of India* by Emil Lengyel on the grounds the author once belonged to some Communist-front organizations. This is a favorite tactic of censorship groups, attacking a book not on the basis of its contents but on the author's past and present affiliations with organizations the groups dislike. An interesting footnote about the Levittown banning of Lengyel's book is that another of his works, *1000 Years of Hungary,* was banned by the Communists and all of his writings were banned by the Nazis.

When the censors fail to document an "objectionable" affiliation for the author, they urge that the book be banned because the authors listed for collateral reading are "objectionable." Some boards of education, under pressure from censorship forces, have voted to buy no textbooks whose authors have not been "cleared" by the FBI or the House Un-American Activities Committee.

In Alabama, the DAR currently is pressuring the legislature to ban textbooks the Daughters believe to be "un-American" and "pro-Communist." Among "objectionable" authors the Alabama Daughters cite are John Steinbeck, Ernest Hemingway, Archibald MacLeish, Allan Nevins, Henry Steele Commager, Carl Van Doren, Eleanor Roosevelt, and Arthur Schlesinger, Jr., all of whom also are on the national DAR's blacklist.

Unfortunately, some newspapers have editorially acquiesced in, and even supported, some of the book censorship campaigns. When Amarillo (Tex.) College and four Amarillo high schools withdrew from libraries ten novels, including four Pulitzer Prize winners, the *Amarillo News-Globe* lauded the move in a front-page editorial and proclaimed its own guide for censorship: ". . . sentences too foul to print in the *News-Globe* are too foul for school libraries."

The *Los Angeles Herald and Express* (now the *Herald-Examiner*), in a series of articles opposing the adoption of thirteen schoolbooks, warned that many phrases and terms were un-American and pro-Communist. It even found a subversive music book. "Swing the Shining Sickle," which it called "a ditty from behind the Iron Curtain," was found to have replaced, of all things, "God Bless America," in the new edition of the book! The truth was that the song was composed in 1897 as an American harvest song relating to Thanksgiving. The *Herald and Express* attacked one history text because it contained *only* two pictures of the American flag and devoted only one paragraph to "Washington and his comrades." The newspaper put "comrades" in capital letters and commented that it was a "key word in designating members of the Soviet Party."

The *Jacksonville* (Ala.) *News,* supporting the DAR's current book-banning campaign in Alabama, printed an editorial which, at first glance, I thought must be poking fun at the Daughters. The *News* noted that the DAR, and I quote, "exposes to Alabama parents a sample of socialism, first-grade style, which appears as a story in one of the basic first grade readers . . . *Our New Friends* by Gray, published in 1956 by Scott Foresman." The *News* said the story called "Ask For It" contains "an objectionable and destructive lesson" about a squirrel named Bobby who was not willing to work.

It seems that Bobby watched a nut roll out of a birdhouse every time a Redbird (the *News* set "Redbird" in bold-face type) would tap on the door. Bobby tried the Redbird's trick and it worked and then, in the words of the story, he thought: "I know how to get my dinner. All I have to do is ask for it." The *News* was shocked. It very soberly asked its readers: "Have you ever heard or read about a more subtle way of undermining the American system of work and profit and replacing it with a collectivist welfare system? Can you recall a socialistic idea more seductively presented to an innocent child?"

No state escapes the effects of attacks on schoolbooks. When censors in Mississippi force a publisher to alter a textbook, that book is sold, as altered, in Missouri and other states.

More important, perhaps, is the impact that widespread attacks, when left unchecked, have on textbook publishers, who are highly competitive. Wherever possible publishers try to avoid controversy and avoid offending special-interest groups in order to sell books. Works by widely acclaimed novelists, poets, and playwrights are disappearing from the texts and compliant publishers are not solely to blame. Teachers have been fired for putting such novels as J. D. Salinger's *The Catcher in the Rye* or George Orwell's *1984* on classroom reading lists.

Last year the Texas State Textbook Committee told a publishing firm it could not market its history book in Texas schools if it did not drop Vera Micheles Dean's name from a supplementary reading list. The committee, under pressure from ultraconservative organizations, complained that the author "is on a list of persons who are extremely well-listed as to their Communist and Communist-front affiliations by various government investigating committees."

The publisher agreed to this forced censorship and commented: "Imagine objecting to Vera Dean. But in a case like this, we will have to sacrifice her name in all books. It would be too expensive to make a special edition just for Texas."

Publishers also have deleted references to other authors in order to compete in the big Texas textbook market, and one publishing firm went so far as to say it was "not only willing but anxious to delete any references" to the names of authors whose loyalty might be successfully questioned by the Texans for America, J. Evetts Haley's militant right-wing organization.

Gene Roberts and I, in researching *The Censors and the Schools,* found that in most cases where teachers and librarians fought back and the press adequately covered the controversy, censorship efforts were thwarted. The same is true, of course, in textbook battles; censors score their most notable successes when they operate with little public exposure.

In Georgia recently a high school teacher with a zeal for stimulating his pupils to read was dismissed for making available to them John Hersey's war-time novel, *A Bell for Adano,* a Pulitzer Prize winner.

The press gave the matter full coverage and the teacher fought back. John Hersey was interviewed and quoted as saying the teacher "has been done a grave injustice by self-appointed censors of the type who are not interested in what a book tries to say as a whole, but are only interested in words taken out of context."

In a page-one column in the *Atlanta Constitution,* publisher Ralph McGill, defending the teacher and the book, wrote: "The school children deprived of this book likely had fathers or older brothers in the Italian campaign. These will testify there isn't a false note in Hersey's book and no language that wasn't heard every day and night."

The issue of Hersey's book and the Georgia teacher was debated editorially and at education meetings.

The teacher was reinstated.

A newspaper survey showed that, unfortunately, school librarians in three other Georgia cities removed the book from their shelves to avoid possible criticism during the controversy. And one public librarian said she had not withdrawn the book, but added: "I've put it in a special place and haven't told anyone about it. Isn't that a good way to handle it?"

However, librarians, educators, and the press did overwhelmingly defend the book and those who removed it have now returned it to the library shelves. The point is that in our pursuit of the truth we need to operate with full exposure. Too often a librarian or a teacher quietly discontinues the use of a book—or never begins the use of it—because of pressure. Those who exert these pressures and who are, in fact, perverting freedom of the press, would wilt under public scrutiny.

The dominant forces that bring this pressure today include the Daughters of the American Revolution, the John Birch Society, the New Rochelle-based America's Future, and many smaller groups. These organizations, through pressure, have managed to force restrictions on what students may read. And the public still is largely apathetic about such pressure.

The DAR, which regularly mails out a list of almost 170 textbooks it has determined to be "subversive," operates as a respectable patriotic organization whose own values seldom are publicly examined. In 1959, when the DAR first began mailing out its incredible blacklist of books, the American Library Committee warned of censorship activities and declared: "Of all the programs by organized groups, the DAR textbook investigation, at both the state and national level, was the most specific . . . and most threatening."

The Daughters' attacks on books need to be evaluated in light of their constant concern about Communist infiltration in religion, mental health programs, public schools and colleges, the federal government, metropolitan government, urban renewal, Christmas cards, and all international activities, including cultural interchange.

It also should be taken into account that the DAR circulates a long list of literature from other ultraconservative groups attacking fluoridation, the U.S. Supreme Court, the Peace Corps, immigration, the UN, the National Council of Churches, the public school system, the National Education Association, and other aspects of American life.

Pressure groups are an integral part of our society and I am not suggesting that any steps be taken—even if such were possible—to restrict their censorship activities. But these groups and their charges need to be put in perspective for the public.

When America's Future literature is used in an attack on schoolbooks, it is important for the public to know of this organization's fears that the public school system, not just textbooks, is purposely subverting the nation's youth. An official of the organization has written:

"No one who has watched closely what has been going on in our public school system in America these past two decades can escape the feeling that something drastic—and rather terrible—has happened to it. What is more, it is rather difficult to believe that it has happened by accident, that there has not been a planned, slyly executed, and almost successful attempt to deliberately undereducate our children in order to make them into an unquestioning mass who would follow meekly those who wish to turn the American Republic into a socialistic society."

The public, in evaluating these attacks, should be aware of their basis in order to determine whether the group is judging a book on its merits or on the basis of its own fears and prejudices.

Why Diplomats Clam Up

JOHN KENNETH GALBRAITH [MARCH 1964

Former U.S. ambassador to India, author of *The Affluent Society* and much else, J. K. Galbraith used to be a journalist himself (*Fortune*). This was a talk to the Nieman Fellows on returning to his post as professor of economics at Harvard.

The resident American press corps during my time in New Delhi (1961–1963) was comparatively small—the two wire services, the *New York Times, Time,* the *Baltimore Sun,* NBC, *U.S. News & World Report,* and, toward the end of my tour, the *Washington Post*—and very good. The members, with scarcely an exception, liked India and worked hard to understand the country, its culture and its problems. All were by way of becoming experts; at least three, Henry Bradsher of AP, Paul Grimes of the *Times,* and Selig Harrison of the *Post,* were first-rate scholars. At the same time, all the members took a detached view of official pretense and mendacity which, both in volume and self-righteousness, is roughly on a parity with Washington.

Relations with the Embassy were on a similar level. I met with the members who were in town for an hour each Wednesday and more frequently if something were stirring. I tried to be liberal with information that could be used; I am persuaded that, with rare exceptions, what must be said off the record had best not be said at all. The questions on State Department or Mission policy, or what passed for it, were informed and sharp. The questioners were sufficiently resistant to evasion, rotund generalities, or misinformation to protect me from temptation. The flow of information was in both directions. I relied on these meetings for knowledge of what Indian officials were saying in their press conferences, background briefings, or press leaks; for the rumors that were making the rounds of the parliament and press gallery; and for knowledge of the stories that members of the press corps were going to play. Members also kept me advised on spot news. Perhaps three or four times a week someone would call me—I remember Phil Potter of the *Baltimore Sun* with special gratitude—to say "I think you ought to know . . ."

I don't want to give the press a completely clean bill of health. From time to time high-level visits and especially the Chinese invasion brought to New Delhi the fire brigade that goes out with all great people or to all great events. It did much less well. Few were well informed on the country. Some rose above information to intuition. Not many put the event they were covering in proper perspective. All were, of course, relentless in their demand that I reform the public relations or security procedures of the Indian government and (in the case of the military correspondents) get them immediately to the front line or a few furlongs beyond. But my comment here is on the resident correspondents with whom my relations were personally most agreeable, valuable as a source of information, and (I think) useful as an avenue of information on our public activities in India to the American people. It also provided a sharp illumination of the press problems of the State Department. In principle, the Department supports a liberal policy toward the press; those professionally responsible work hard and intelligently to further it. In practice, a policy such as the one followed in New Delhi runs into strong headwinds.

The first difficulty is the surviving conviction that diplomacy is a privileged occupation into which the press and the public should not really be allowed to obtrude. This is a minority attitude but it exists and it is not confined to career officers. Some of the New Frontier appointees have reached extremes in stuffiness and even outright constipation in their press relations, partly in the conviction that this is the way diplomats are meant to behave. Fear is also a factor and the feeling that the press, like the Congress, exists largely to louse up foreign policy. In American diplomatic practice, the current policy becomes to a remarkable degree an article of belief. We are not cynics. So if the policy is to present the Nhu family as the arch-paragons of democracy or blame everything that goes wrong in Latin America on Castro, a differing view by a newsman seems not only wrong but willfully perverse. Better ignore the bastard.

But there is a more persistent if less visible source of restraint. Anything that comes in over the press wires is scrutinized by the score or more of people in Washington who are concerned in one capacity or other with that country. There is not much that can be said that will not strike someone as out of line even when the location of the line is known only to God. A bland comment on the advantages of peace or the need for better weather will be thought by someone to have hit the wrong note. This alert officer then tucks the clipping or tape in his pocket and, at the next meeting with his Assistant Secretary, says: "Did you see, Sir, what came out of Pnom Penh yesterday? Going a little far, I think . . ." In all organizations, the cultivation of executive vanity is a considerable industry. The State Department is up to average. Officials are rather easily persuaded that their prerogatives are being prejudiced. Out goes a telegram of warning. "We note with some concern . . ."

The danger that any politically experienced person will say anything really damaging is slight. In the course of two and a half years, I found myself in hot water only once. (That was a careless and somewhat disputable endorsement of one part of Pakistan's claim to Kashmir made at a press briefing in Washington which was relayed back to New Delhi at something greater than the speed of light. And like the rest of last year's headlines it had no permanent residue.) I also found that an ambassador can stand off this nitpicking as, I am sure, many do. My formula was to ignore it except for an occasional very rude response. In the end, it stopped. But quite a few less securely situated people would have clammed up. As a result, they would have denied both themselves and the country valuable information. They would have a perfect record of no errors and no indiscretions at the price of a much reduced understanding both at the post and at home.

The remedy is scarcely novel. It is to see the problem of press relations as one of maintaining a high score. The man who seeks to avoid all error, all misinterpretation, will say nothing and do the worst job. He will live, as do a surprising number of our officials, in a mentally crippling fear of his own tongue. The man who consistently puts his foot in his own mouth and that of the press should obviously be retired or loaned to Barry Goldwater. The man who maintains a steady flow of sound guidance and information should know that he is allowed an occasional error or mishap. Washington must, of course, also know this and restrain itself accordingly.

VII. BOOKS AND MEN

The quarterly has made a special effort to report on newspaper biographies and newspaper histories as they were published, and we had some luck on this. The few selections here are representative of many that reflect the vitality of great figures in journalism.

Irving Dilliard contributed his personal portrait of O. K. Bovard, the legendary managing editor of the *St. Louis Post-Dispatch.* It was Bovard who put up on the city room bulletin board, after the 1936 election had seen Roosevelt carry all states but Maine and Vermont, "Country 46, Country Club 2." The paper had editorially supported Landon.

I have described in the general introduction the circumstances that brought us A. J. Liebling on Harold Ross as a bonus of a Nieman seminar by Liebling.

"The Enigma of W. J. Cash" was a piece of research by Tom Dearmore, then a Nieman Fellow, into the mystery of this rare newspaperman who is remembered for his one book. The occasion for it was the reprinting of *The Mind of the South.*

Richard Strout's appreciation of Tom Stokes is a profile of one of the most conscientious and dedicated reporters of his generation. Barry Bingham's letter to his son expresses the concern of a publisher for the standards of journalism. The history of the *Times* of London tells of the epic struggle for survival of the character of a great journalistic institution.

The Enigma of W. J. Cash

TOM DEARMORE

[APRIL 1960

Mr. Dearmore, a Nieman Fellow in 1959–60, is editor of the *Baxter Bulletin* in Mountain Home, Arkansas.

February brought publication, for the third time, of *The Mind of the South,** and the enigma of its author is resurrected again.

William Joseph Cash spent about five years in the actual writing of his widely acclaimed book, but, counting the time spent for its conception, it probably represents the work and thought of the last ten years of his life.

The original publication was in February, 1941, by Alfred A. Knopf, Inc. It was later produced in paperback by Doubleday Anchor Books, and is now on the racks in a new paperback edition published by Vintage Books.

The Mind of the South has been accorded monumental stature by students of the social-historical factors shaping Southern life, but the writer himself has been largely enveloped in mystery. The years—almost two decades of them—have closed around the memory of Cash, but he deserves to be remembered.

This book was a labor of passion, but also of laborious study, of reflection, of commonplace experience which stamped itself into a sensitive mind. His is the restless spirit of cramped liberalism, bursting for expression, determined at all cost to puncture the illusions and pomposity of its time.

Cash, contemplating his native area with rare perspicacity, laid bare the greatness and anguish, the delusions and realities, of the pre-World War II South. His text rolls with a unique and exquisite fluency.

In any library catalog the researcher will find only one volume listed under the name of this author. Who was this W. J. Cash, whose book is being republished twenty years after it was written and who is being quoted by eminent historians?

Why did his productivity end abruptly in 1941 with the publi-

* W. J. Cash, *The Mind of the South,* paperback reprint (New York: Vintage Books, 1960).

cation of this one vibrant testimonial which the *Atlantic Monthly* called "a literary and moral miracle"?

Cash's biography is a story of brilliance, of depression, and finally, of tragedy. His life ended in suicide on July 2, 1941, six months after the first edition of *The Mind of the South* came off the presses. The forty-year-old author received a Guggenheim Fellowship in March, to write a novel with a Mexican setting, and ended his life in Mexico City.

He was born on May 2, 1901, at Gaffney, where the last ramparts of the Blue Ridge dip down into South Carolina, and not far from the Catawba River country of which Thomas Wolfe wrote with affection. In fact, Cash's career spanned almost exactly the same period of time as Wolfe's.

The best available insight into the nature of W. J. Cash is furnished by the short autobiographical sketches he wrote for his publisher, Alfred A. Knopf, in April, 1936, and April, 1940. Knopf provides mimeographed forms on green paper for use by authors in setting down a few pertinent facts about themselves. In 1936, the form did not prove large enough for Cash. He seemed compelled to tell about his innermost thoughts, his habits, and his philosophical ideas. The sketch spilled over and covered the back of the form as well as the ruled section on the front.

One fact seems obvious—that Cash had every earmark of the romanticist he described in his book as being typical of the South. But this quality was undershot with something else—a high-voltage curiosity—a searching after something which led him to many excursions of the mind and to travels in France, England, Germany, Italy, and Switzerland.

Into eighteen years, from 1923 to 1941, he packed an exceptional number of activities. During that period he was a student, a teacher of languages, a foreign traveler, a reporter, an editor, a free-lance writer, and an author. His life's story is one of movement which seemed to belie some of his own estimates of himself.

His family left South Carolina and most of his "growing up" years were spent in the village of Boiling Springs, just across the line in Cleveland county, North Carolina. He learned to read at the age of five, was immediately captivated by books, and recalled being absorbed in literature at the age of six as his mother called him "to bring in stove wood."

"After that I read everything I could get my hands on," he wrote,

"Alger, Henty, Mayne Reid, Clark, Russell, Scott, Dickens, Hugo, Milton, Bunyan . . . with impartiality. At fourteen I discovered the girls and so abandoned the Harvard Classics somewhere in the middle, spent the next fifteen years contemplating them—the girls, not the classics—, often painfully."

At college, Cash said he read sporadically, edited the college paper, won a short story prize, but "mainly sat on the benches under the magnolias and thought about the girls."

His efforts at college football, he wrote, "failed ignominiously," the college newspaper always came out late and sometimes not at all, and he "was always in hot water with the authorities" at the college.

He paints a picture of inconsistency in scholarship, but nevertheless his cherished reading list covers virtually the whole range of the classics. In 1918–19 he attended Wofford College at Spartanburg, S.C., and received his A.B. degree from Wake Forest College in 1922. After attending the law school at Wake Forest during the 1922–23 term, he accepted a post as English instructor in 1923 at Georgetown (Ky.) College. During 1924–25 he taught English and French at the Blue Ridge School for Boys, Hendersonville, N.C.

For a brief period in 1923 he served on the staff of the *Charlotte* (N.C.) *Observer,* and in 1924 he traveled to Chicago for a reporting job on the old *Post.* In 1925 he was a free-lance writer in Chicago; then he returned to Charlotte for a position on the *News* staff in 1926 and 1927. In the latter year he traveled in Europe, then edited a weekly newspaper, the *Cleveland Press,* in Shelby, N.C., in 1928. He was listed as a free-lance writer from 1929 to 1937, contributing to the *American Mercury* when it was edited by H. L. Mencken. He served as associate editor of the *Charlotte News* from 1937 to 1941.

During World War I he was unable to enlist in the Navy but got into civilian work at an Army cantonment by "fudging" on his age. Summer employment as a youth included working on his grandfather's farm, driving a truck to haul lumber and brick and working in a hosiery mill headed by his father (twelve hours a night in the latter).

Collection of books and phonograph records "a good deal faster than I can afford" was one of his obsessions, with the accent always on the classics. He read "heavy old books almost exclusively" and thought "Beethoven's C Minor Symphony is still the greatest music ever written." The only sport he ever liked was golf and the happiest time he spent was while riding a bicycle across Europe, with hikes in the Pyrenees, the Swiss Alps, and along the Riviera.

Cash termed himself a shy fellow; yet he liked to talk better than anything else, he said, and drank beer with old friends until the late hours.

He stated that his family and forebears were "never rich or aristocratic" but were "good upcountry farmers" with property in proportion to most of the neighbors. As a young man, he said, he had the attitudes connected with the Old South, and he stated that people "often wonder at my sympathy for any Southern underdog at all." At twenty he was "a thorough Bourbon" in his outlook, but "then a newspaper sent me to cover a strike—and after that I began to look around me."

If there is any doubt that he was a Southerner to the core, this paragraph from his personal sketch should dispel it:

"Reared an intense sentimentalist to the South, my favorite dream as a boy was the fighting over again of the Civil War, and myself leading the charge on the cannon's mouth with the Confederate battle flag. My blood still leaps to the band's playing of 'Dixie,' and to such flourishing phrases as 'the sword of Lee.' And before militantly sentimental ladies who don't like my opinions, I am sheepish and dumb."

Disliking both intolerance and affection intensely, he said, he quite often indulged himself in both. Five years before, he wrote in 1936, he was "a complete neurosthenic" but had since largely cured himself.

About his views of the mysteries of life, he wrote: "I have developed a great interest in the sciences, though in college I hated a laboratory so much that I rarely ever went—and so was in constant difficulties with the authorities. Yet, for all my belief and confidence here, the universe seems to me to be ultimately an impenetrable mystery. And though I have no time for creeds or theological constructions of any kind, I sympathize fully with the awe which is perhaps the primary source of religion."

He was interested in anthropology. And he added: "I think La Rochefoucauld and not Karl Marx laid his hand on the true primary key to human action—that vanity and not economic interest prevails. But even that is only a half-truth." Illness had given him insights into some things, he noted.

His indictment of himself was brief:

"I am hopelessly lazy, and, efforts to convince myself that it is really a virtue having proved unavailing, I am constantly depressed by the knowledge of it."

His ambition, still more brief, is summarized in the final sentence:

"And I want above everything to be a novelist."

No one, it seems, and Cash least of all, suspected that in the magnolia-scented breezes of South Carolina, in the city room above downtown Chicago, in the thin air of the Pyrenees, in various Southern newspaper offices, a book of near-classic proportions was taking shape. His varied life was moving toward an achievement which would assure him lasting renown among the writers of the twentieth century.

There can be little doubt that he was greatly influenced by the emerging progressive colleges of his area—Duke and the University of North Carolina in particular—and by Mencken and Southern scholars such as Howard W. Odum.

It was at Mencken's suggestion that he started work on *The Mind of the South.* Cash's iconoclastic articles undoubtedly appealed to the old master of satire.

Cash, in the early 1930's, saw a deadening vacuity in the life of his region, and in the April, 1933, issue of the *American Mercury* he delivered a scalding indictment against the city of Charlotte.

He called it "an old Tory town, a citadel of bigotry and obscurantism . . . a Gargantuan blue-nose posed on the face of North Carolina." The flow of civilization in that great state, he wrote, could be charted by the device of conceiving it "as a thundering field of battle whereon the justly famous state university at Chapel Hill gallantly defends the standards of intellectual integrity against the ferocious assaults . . . almost wholly, of this very town of Charlotte." Cash called the city, to which he was to return later in an editorial position, "the chief enemy of civilization in the Near South."

He was not entirely unkind to the city, however, and he acknowledged that others in the state, including Greensboro, had changed. And the cities of Raleigh and Wilmington were passive. "In them," he wrote, "is a great defeatism. The Goth, they know, is upon the Flaminian way. The Hun swings southward from the infidel universities of the North and makes himself at ease within the tarheel gates." But these towns "cultivate serenity" and thank "an inscrutable God that the day of wrath is at least not yet."

It is difficult to believe that his final, desperate decision in 1941 could have been due to anticipated criticism in his home sector. For he had been lobbing salvos in that direction for too many years to have been much affected by adverse comment there, and his book was much less caustic than his magazine articles of almost a decade earlier.

The book came out during a boom time for publishers, during a time when the thoughts of Americans were in Europe. Russia was reeling under the strokes of the German army that summer, and an avalanche of both novels and nonfiction about the war was pouring into book stores.

The nation was swept up in a world-wide drama, but seldom, if ever, has a book about the American scene received such enthusiastic reviews as did *The Mind of the South*. The accolade came in a groundswell from newspapers and literary journals.

It won quick recognition from the *New York Times Book Review,* which stated that "certainly no one else has succeeded in writing the ideological and social history of the South from colonial times to the present in such a philosophical and illuminating manner . . . In fact it would seem that there is no important ideological or social factor affecting the life of the South which Mr. Cash has overlooked . . . He has brought to his task a deep knowledge of economics, genealogy, institutional history, psychology and law, and something else without which his book would have been a dull performance—a constructive, historical imagination and a gift for fresh and lively phraseology."

The New Yorker said that it was "probably the most readable and penetrating general treatment of the subject we've ever had." The *American Historical Review* said: "Mr. Cash has written a brave and critical book about the South which deserves a wide circle of readers, including the effective political and social leaders of the South today."

Time magazine declared that "Cash is honest, temperate, eloquent and kind, and he is definitely in command of his subject," and concluded: "Anything written about the South henceforth must start where he leaves off."

Although the book does not deal with recent events, its pertinence is far from being lost as the 1960's begin. In fact, Cash's rare perspective is probably being utilized as never before in this period when the South is, to the amazement of many, exhuming ancient arguments and remembering long-dormant bitterness.

Roosevelt's wartime FEPC and the series of civil rights decrees, which started with outlawing of the white primary in 1944 and reached high-water mark with the school desegregation ruling ten years later, were still in the future when Cash was writing. As the regional mores came under judiciary and legislative assault from Washington the South reacted, and why it reacted as it did is better understood after reading *The Mind of the South.*

But Cash sensed that a time of trial was coming, as he wrote of the South in his final paragraph:

"In the coming days, and probably soon, it is likely to have to prove its capacity for adjustment far beyond what has been true in the past. And in that time I shall hope, as its loyal son, that its virtues will tower over and conquer its faults and have the making of the Southern world to come. But of the future I shall venture no definite prophecies. It would be a brave man who would venture them in any case."

No one, reading the book, can escape the impression that Cash was motivated by a consuming love for his section. True, he assailed the Cavalier aristocracy legend as none other before him, describing the "Proto-Dorian pride" it helped produce, and pointing to a "savage ideal" which gripped the area after the Civil War. The hedonistic "hell of a fellow" was a dominant personality, he said, in a sector where the frontier lasted longer than anywhere else, and there was deprecation of authority and processes of law. He told of racist demagogues with their continued "appeals to such vague shibboleths as states' rights, and heroic gasconade of every sort." He said that there was a "core of tragedy" in the fact that "intellectual leaderships are by themselves always helpless."

But the better nature of the South is there, too, the "sweepingly splendid fellows . . . a kindly courtesy, a level-eyed pride, an easy quietness, a barely perceptible flourish." Some, in the early days, went even "beyond the kindness of the old back country" to set "an impeccable example of conduct and sentiment."

It was "the conflict with the Yankee," he concludes, which really moulded the mind of the South in the way he pictures it, and he said: "The mind of the section . . . is continuous with the past." He calls the South "a tree with many age rings, with its limbs and trunk bent and twisted by all the winds of the years, but with its tap root in the Old South."

So it was in 1940. Who can say how nearly the Southland approximates that description twenty years later, when the winds of a new storm are whistling through it?

His summary is full of feeling:

"Proud, brave, honorable by its lights, courteous, personally generous, loyal, swift to act, often too swift, but signally effective, sometimes terrible, in its action—such was the South at its best. And such at its best it remains today, despite the great falling away in some of its virtues. Violence, intolerance, aversion and suspicion toward new ideas, an incapacity for analysis, an inclination to act from feeling rather than from thought, an exaggerated individualism and a too narrow concept of social responsibility, attachment to fictions and false values, above all too great attachment to racial values and a tendency to justify cruelty and injustice in the name of those values, sentimentality and a lack of realism—these have been its characteristic vices in the past. And, despite changes for the better, they remain its characteristic vices today."

So reasoned a man who wrote briefly and brilliantly, vanishing in his moment of triumph. Strangely enough, this admonition appears in his book as he writes of his fellow Southerners: ". . . the South must not be too much weaned away from its ancient leisureliness—the assumption that the first end of life is living itself—which, as they rightly contend, is surely one of its greatest virtues."

Harold Ross: The Impresario

A. J. LIEBLING [APRIL 1959

Mr. Liebling, a staff member of *The New Yorker* for nearly thirty years and the author of many books, died on December 28, 1963.

It is hard for a writer to call an editor great because it is natural for him to think of the editor as a writer *manqué*. It is like asking a thief to approve a fence, or a fighter to speak highly of a manager. "Fighters are sincere," a fellow with the old pug's syndrome said to me at a bar once as his head wobbled and the hand that held his shot-glass shook. "Managers are pimps, they sell our blood." In the newspaper trade confirmed reporters think confirmed editors are mediocrities who took the easy way out. These attitudes mark an excess of vanity coupled with a lack of imagination; it never occurs to a writer that anybody could have wanted to be anything else.

I say, despite occupational bias, Ross, the first editor of *The New Yorker*, was as great as anybody I ever knew, in his way. He was as great as Sam Langford, who could make any opponent lead and then belt him out, or Beatrice Lillie, who can always make me laugh, or Raymond Weeks, who taught Romance Philology at Columbia and lured me into the Middle Ages, or Max Fischel, who covered New York Police Headquarters for the *Evening World*, and was the best head-and-legman I ever saw. The head helps the legs when it knows its way around.

Given the address of a tenement homicide, Max would go over the roofs and down while the younger men raced down to the street and then around the block and up. They would arrive to find him listening sympathetically to the widow if the police had not already locked her up, or to a neighbor if they had. People in jams liked to talk to him because he never talked at them.

Ross was as great as Max, or as a man named Flageollet who kept a hotel with eight rooms at Feriana in Tunisia and was one of the best cooks I have known, or another named Bouillon who had a small restaurant on the Rue Sainte-Anne in Paris. (It is odd that I should have known two great cooks with comestible names.) He was as great as Eddie Arcaro, the rider, or General George Patton or Bobby Clark and Paul McCullough, or a number of women I have known who had other talents. Ross would not have resented any of these comparisons, and the ones with Max and Patton would have flattered him particularly, because he was a newspaper and Army buff. One thing that made him a great editor was his interest in the variety of forms greatness assumes. He saw it in the entertainers he hired, as cheaply as possible so that they would work harder, to appear in his Litterographic Congress of Strange (Great) People of the World. The Greatest One-Gag Cartoonist, the Greatest Two-Gag Cartoonist, the Greatest Cartoonists Waiting for a Gag; the Greatest One-Note Male Short-Story Writer, the Greatest Half-Note In-Between Short-Story Writer, the Greatest Demi-Semi-Quaver Lady Short-Story Writer Ending in a Muted Gulp; the Greatest Woman Who Ever Married an Egyptian, the Greatest Woman Who Ever Married a Patagonian, the Greatest Woman Who Ever Married a Dravidian Pterodactyl. These latters' stories always began: "My mother-in-law could never get used to my wearing shoes," and still do, although sales territory is becoming rapidly exhausted; the only franchises still available to marry into are the Andaman Islands and Washington Heights. Ross cherished half-bad Great talents too; he knew there will never be enough good ones to go around.

E. B. White once said to me that the relation between Ross and him was like that of two railroad cars—they met only at one point. White was with Ross from the beginning of the magazine in 1925, but he admits he knew only one Ross personally and a couple of dozen others by intuition, hearsay, brag or reputation. Ross had some raffish friends I envied him and some stuffed-shirt friends I wouldn't be seen dead with. He was equally proud and I think equally fond of all of them. He liked anybody who had a lot of money or a good story to tell, and since these are minerals seldom found in conjunction, he prospected around. *The New Yorker* he made reflected this idiosyncrasy, but not what the kids now call dichotomy. He just had more interests than most people. I think that a number of men who knew Ross underrated him because, coming up on him always from one direction, they found him sometimes preoccupied with what was going on in another ring.

It was as if a wire-walker expected a ringmaster to be as exclusively interested in high-wire acts as he was. Of course Ross couldn't write as well as Thurber or Joe Mitchell, or draw as well as Steinberg. He didn't know as much as Edmund Wilson is supposed to, and there were at any given period of *The New Yorker's* existence eighty-four people around who knew more about France or the East Side or where to buy a baby bottle with an aquamarine nipple for Christmas. But he had his own greatness—he put the show together. Why he wanted to I don't know. What made Arcaro a jockey?

Early in December, 1951, when Ross had been ill since the previous April, I said to Bill Shawn, who was doing his work and has since succeeded him: "If I knew he was going to die, I'd put my arm around his shoulder and say I'd always liked him. But if he recovered he'd never forgive me."

That was at a time when the doctors had not admitted his condition was critical, but when the length of the illness had made us all suspicious. He died about a week later, but I think he knew that I liked him, in a way, and I know he liked me, in a way, and that's about as close as I ever got to him in an acquaintance of eighteen years, sixteen of them on *The New Yorker.*

The only letter of his I have chanced to preserve is one I got in Reno, Nevada, in the summer of 1949. He felt there was a great story in Reno, but did not know just what it was. He wrote, "But of course you are a better reporter than I am. (The hell you are!)" He couldn't give a compliment without taking it back in the next sentence—afraid you'd get a swelled head, I suppose. I disappointed him with a slight report on Reno I wrote then, but I took East the seed of a much better story, which germinated until I went out to Nevada again in the fall of 1953 and reported and wrote it. He never saw it, of course.

He was a great hunch man, which is part of being a great editor. Many aspects of life entranced him imprecisely, and he knew that where there was entrancement there was a story, if he could just bring the right kind of man into its vicinity. Like a marriage broker, he could bring together a couple, writer and subject, who ought to hit it off. But sometimes not even Ross could make them go to bed together.

He was also good at sensing a mismatch. Immediately after the end of the war I told him that I would like to travel in the unknown—to me—interior of this country and write about the Midwest as I would of any other strange land.

"You wouldn't like it, Liebling," he said. "You wouldn't like it."

I spent the winter of 1949–50 in Chicago, and he was dead right.

Later in my Nevada summer he came to Reno with some of his Hollywood pals—Chasen and Capra and Nunnally Johnson—on a holiday. He was very happy, happier than I have seen him in any other setting. He liked the West (as distinguished from Mid-) and pretending to be a Westerner. (He had left the West when a kid, and by the time I knew him was an indefinitely urban type, though never a New Yorker.) He got me to sit in with him at the open poker game in the Bank Club, together with the old sheepherders and railroad pensioners. There are always at least three one-armed men in that game—brakemen who fell under trains. I played a half-hour, lost $20 and got out. He stayed an hour and said he won $60. Later he went back, played until five in the morning, and returning to the Riverside Hotel, cashed a check for $500. I heard about it at breakfast from the night manager of the game room, who was just going off duty. At lunch Ross told me he had cleaned up, but I knew better.

When he was young, vaudeville was the chief national entertainment industry, and I often thought he would have made a first-class booker for variety shows. This is no faint compliment, for I adored vaudeville, which lasted well on into my own youth. So must Ross have done; he had a great affection for old comics like Joe Cook and Chasen. He put on a weekly variety bill of the printed word and the graphic gag—always well balanced and sufficiently entertaining to bring the audience back next week. He booked the best acts he could, but he knew that you couldn't get the best specialists in every spot every week. When he had no headline comic he built the show around a dancer or even a juggler. One week he might have a cartoon that people would remember with pleasure for years. The next it might be a good Profile, and the week after that the Fratellini of prose, Sullivan and Perelman, or a tear-jerking fiction turn by Dorothy Parker or O'Hara. Vaudeville, too, had its sacred moments; next to a good laugh there is nothing so nice as a sniffle.

Ross tried to polish old acts or develop new ones, but he never let his notion of what he wanted get in the way of his clear apprehension of what was to be had. In the late Thirties, when all his new writers came from newspaper staffs where they had sweated through the Depression, he said to me:

"Liebling, I wish I could find some young conservative writers who could write, but there aren't any." He was by inclination a kind of H. L. Mencken conservative himself, but he wouldn't book a dancer who couldn't dance just because he liked the shape of her *derrière.* This is a higher integrity than either Right Wing or Left Wing editors possessed in those days. The writing in the *New Masses* was as bad, in a different way, as the writing in *Time.* (The transition, as Whittaker Chambers found out, was easy.) Ross's loyalty was to his readers. He treasured Alva Johnston, an earlier convert from the newspaper fold than we were, who wrote excellent Profiles and at the same time held that stupid Presidents were best, because they let big businessmen run the country, and businessmen had brains.

Alva's only objection to Herbert Hoover was that he was too bright. He was a hard man to satisfy; it is a pity he did not live to see Eisenhower. Ross relished Johnston's concurrent political opinions as *lagniappe;* he wouldn't have given a hoot about them if he hadn't esteemed Alva's technique of defining character by a series of anecdotes on an ascending scale of extravagance, so that the reader of the sixth installment wolfed yarns that he would have rejected in the first.

Nor did Ross insist on playing types of acts that had lost their vogue. During the late Twenties and very early Thirties *The New Yorker* frequently ran a type of Profile of rich and successful men that was only superficially distinguishable from the Success Stories in the late *American Magazine.* (The difference was that *The New Yorker* writer might attribute to the protagonist some supposedly charming foible like wearing crimson ties although he had attended Princeton.) The hallmark of this kind of Profile was a sentence on the order of "Although Jeremy P. Goldrush is as rich as rich, you would never think from his plain old $200 suits that he was more than an ordinary weekend polo player."

After a couple of these heroes had landed in State Prisons, Ross became receptive to portraits in a less reverent style. Although Ross loved the smell of success, he was emotionally irreverent and always enjoyed learning that a fellow he had accepted as a monument to society was in fact a sepulchre with a runny coat of whitewash.

He made the same good adjustment to World War II as to the Depression. He would have preferred not to have it, but he didn't deny it was on. That got me a break. He sent me to France in October, 1939. I attracted the assignment by telling McKelway how well I could talk French. McKelway could not judge. Besides, I was a reasonable age for the job: 35.

Ross was 47 then, and in the newspaper world we came out in different decades; twelve years is a great gap. When we talked I called him "Mr. Ross." I was never an intimate of his—just an act he booked and learned to appreciate, though never highly enough in my opinion. I think that all the reporters of my *New Yorker* generation—Mitchell and Jack Alexander and Dick Boyer and Meyer Berger and I—had the same classical ambivalent son-to-father feeling about him. We were eager to please him and cherished his praise, but we publicly and profanely discounted his criticism. Especially we resented his familiarity with the old-timers—the Companions of the Prophet—and his indulgence for them. Our admiration for their work was not unqualified or universal. (I still think *The New Yorker's* reporting before we got on it was pretty shoddy.)

I find it hard to admit how jealous I was one day in 1946 when Wolcott Gibbs, who was very ill, called up while Ross and I were working over proofs. Ross told him to take care of himself and said: "Don't worry about money." That was white of him, I thought, but he had never said that to me. It was a true sibling emotion. In fact, Ross thought that a healthy writer wouldn't write unless he had had to emit at least two rubber checks and was going to be evicted after the weekend. It was an unselfish conviction, a carry-over from his newspaper days. He reminded me of a showman I knew named Clifford G. Fischer—the impresarial analogy pops up constantly when I think of Ross. Fischer spoke to actors only in a loud scream, and when I asked him why replied, in a low conversational voice he used on non-actors: "Because they are abnormal people. To abnormal people you got to talk in an abnormal voice."

Ross liked writers, but he would no more have thought of offering a writer money than of offering a horse an ice-cream soda. "Bad for them, Liebling," he would have said. But you could promote a small advance if you were in a bad jam. What continually amazed me about Ross, and convinced me of his greatness, was that he took the whole show seriously—from the fiction, which I often cannot read, to the fashion notes that I never try to. He knew no more of horse-racing than a hog of Heaven, but he knew how to find and keep Audax Minor, G. F. T. Ryall, whose tone is precisely right for *The New Yorker.* Here again he had the instinct of a showman, who wants the whole bill to be good, while I have that of an educated seal, who thinks that when he plays "Oh, Say Can You See," on the automobile horn, it is the highspot of the evening. After that the crowd can go home.

A lot has been written about Ross as an editor of manuscript, as distinguished from Ross the editor-impresario. There should be different words for the two functions in English as there are in French—*directeur* for the boss and *rédacteur* for the fellow who works on the copy. Ross did both, but he impressed me less as *rédacteur* than as *directeur.* His great demand was clarity. This is a fine and necessary quality, but you can go just so far with it. You cannot make subtlety or complexity clear to an extraordinarily dull reader, but Ross in editing would make himself *advocatus asinorum.* He would ask scores of marginal questions, including many to which he full well knew the answers, on the off chance that unless all were pre-explained in the text some particularly stupid woman in a dentist's waiting room might pick up a *New Yorker* and be puzzled. Out of the swarm of questions there were always a few that improved the piece—on an average, I should say, about $2\frac{3}{4}$ per cent, and none that did any harm, because you could ignore the silliest and leave Shawn to talk him out of the rest.

I never thought this quest for clarity naive. It was part of a method he had thought out for putting his "book" across in the early days. If the silliest *New Yorker* readers could go through a piece on a "sophisticated" subject and understand every word, they would think themselves extremely intelligent and renew their subscriptions. But there are subjects not susceptible of such reduction; the only way of making clear pea soup, is by omitting the peas. Ross continued his queries compulsively long after the time when *The New Yorker* had to recruit readers. A point had been reached when the silly ones would pretend to understand even if they didn't. This vestigial reminder of the "book's" early hard times was exasperating, but not serious. The writer got his way in the end. Just because he was a great editor, Ross knew when to back down.

I have heard that he made a fetish of Fowler's *English Usage,* a book I have never looked into. (It would be like Escoffier consulting Mrs. Beeton.) He never suggested the book to me, nor told me how to write that mythical thing, the "*New Yorker* style." What is affected as a "*New Yorker* style" by undergraduate and British contributors is, to judge from specimens I have seen, a mixture of White's style, Gibbs's and S. J. Perelman's, but as none of these three is like either of the others, the result is like a "Romance Language" made up by jumbling French, Portuguese, and Roumanian. It is not a satisfactory medium of communication. I don't know anybody who has written a good story for *The New Yorker* in "*New Yorker* style."

Personally, I had a tough first year on *The New Yorker,* from the summer of 1935 to the summer of 1936, because I brought to it a successful newspaper short-feature method that was not directly transferable to a magazine, especially in long pieces. It would have been like running a mile in a series of hundred-yard dashes. I rescued myself by my reporting on a Profile of Father Divine. I found out more of the inner inwardness and outward outerness of that old god in a machine than anybody else had. The machine was a $150 Rolls-Royce acquired during the Depression when nobody else wanted a car that burned that much gas. The old newspaperman in Ross came to the top; he stopped my salary of sixty-five dollars a week and gave me a drawing account of ninety. I have never been out of debt to *The New Yorker* since.

And still, that isn't the whole story. It is hard to be entirely kind to Ross, and he found it hard to be entirely kind to others, as I recalled earlier on. But through five years of war I liked to know that he was behind me, unashamedly interested in what I was doing and seeing, like a kid watching a high-wire act, and that my copy would run as I wrote it. He never usurped the right to tell me what I saw, or to turn my report into a reflection of an editorial conference in Rockefeller Plaza strained through a recollection of Plattsburg in the First World War. That used to happen constantly to the collective journalists. He appreciated a good story, too. He seldom gave unqualified praise to a person—and who deserves it?—but he once cheered me with a note about the "unbelievably high quality" of a piece. He was a ham and understood them.

I wish I had told him once how much I liked him.

O. K. Bovard

IRVING DILLIARD [JULY 1949

O. K. Bovard, a legendary figure as managing editor of the *St. Louis Post-Dispatch,* is remembered here by one of his juniors, Irving Dilliard, later editorial page editor of that paper. Dilliard was one of the first group of Nieman Fellows, in 1938–39. He retired from the *Post-Dispatch* in 1960 but not from writing. His works include books about Judge Learned Hand, Mr. Justice Brandeis, and Mr. Justice Black. Since 1963 he has been Ferris Professor of Journalism at Princeton University. He is also an elected trustee of the University of Illinois. And he writes an editorial column for *Chicago's American.* The Bovard article first appeared in the printed program of the 1948 Page One Ball given by the St. Louis Newspaper Guild.

Not the least of the problems in writing about the complex man who was the great managing editor of the *St. Louis Post-Dispatch* for thirty years—from 1908 to 1938—is the question of what to call him.

His parents named him Oliver Kirby Bovard. Since he regularly threw the blanks from *Who's Who in America* in his vast, desk-high waste basket, it is doubtful whether his full name appeared in print more than a few times in the seventy-three years of his life.

When he was a young reporter, his intimate *Post-Dispatch* colleagues called him Jack. A St. Louis newspaper legend has it that he himself wrote "30" to that nickname. He was still Jack to fellow reporter Harry James one hearty night in 1900. The next morning James called the office, then on the east side of Broadway between Olive and Pine. James was unaware that his associate of the night before had been promoted to city editor, effective that day. The new city editor answered the telephone.

"Hello, Jack," said James.

A cold voice at the office end of the telephone said formally: "This is Mr. Bovard, the city editor. Please keep that in mind, James." There are those who say that this story is not fair to Mr. Bovard, but so runs the legend. He knew where authority rested on a newspaper and whose responsibility it was to exercise it, and on what terms.

He signed himself O.K.B., on office memos. Using the editor's blue pencil, he wrote his initials, not large, not small, usually on an upward slant, and all connected, with a quick, encircling loop of the blunt pencil for emphasis. When his devoted stenographer, Phil O'Connell, typed memos for him, they closed with the same three letters, O.K.B. Yet he did not call himself O.K.B. and it is unlikely that many persons, if indeed anyone at all, addressed him in conversation as O.K.B.

In all his dealings at the office as city editor and as managing editor, he was simply and plainly just "Mr. Bovard." That was the way he identified himself on the telephone. That was the way his editors and reporters spoke to him. Paul Y. Anderson, who was for years his favorite reporter, once said: "We never addressed our superior except as 'Mr. Bovard.' "

He was a fine figure of a man. He was tall and erect and carried his handsome head high. He kept himself in excellent physical form by daily exercises. His eyes were gray steel and just as sharp and at times equally hard and penetrating. His lips were firm and tight. There was a suggestion of a downward turn at the corners of his mouth, but it could and often did break into a smile, which now and then was the quick forerunner of a rich laugh. His nose was long and straight and seemed somehow to suggest its acuteness for news.

He spent much of his time away from the *Post-Dispatch* in the out of doors. A consequence was that his face was tanned almost around the calendar. In later years, hair that turned from gray to white was a striking complement to the bronzed skin. He would have made a magnificent Indian chief.

Mr. Bovard ran a one-man school of journalism throughout nearly forty years of news planning and editing on the *Post-Dispatch*. His course of instruction was particularly severe and intense when he was city editor, from 1900 to 1908. One of the cubs in that period was Charles G. Ross. Not long after Ross came to the staff, Mr. Bovard sent the freshman reporter to get the facts about the fall of a painter from a high smoke stack in the extreme southwestern part of St. Louis.

It was a hot summer day and a trip to the scene of the accident was a long one. Not only was transportation slow and involved, but it ended much too soon and when the youthful news gatherer alighted from the last street car, he had a lengthy walk. At last he found the factory, where he proceeded to collect information—name, address, and age of the painter, the place, how he happened to fall, the extent of his injuries and so on. The reporter then reversed the weary transportation process, returned to the office and wrote the short item which was indicated. Thinking he had done a good job, he turned the item in to the city editor.

Mr. Bovard glanced over the few lines and called his cub to the desk. "Ross," he asked, "how tall is this smoke stack?"

The new reporter could not say. He gave an "about so-and-so" estimate and repeated that it was quite "tall."

The one-man school of journalism said firmly: "Ross, 'tall' is a relative term. I want you to go back and find out the exact height of that smoke stack."

Young Ross retraced the long, hot trip to the factory. When he at last returned to the office, his weary day had passed into night. But he had the precise height of the smoke stack in feet and inches.

Forty-two years later, as he recalled this journalism lesson, Charles G. Ross sat in the office of the presidential press secretary at the White House. He was not sure whether the short item about the painter's fall found its way into print. But printed or not, it taught him a lesson he has never forgotten—"get the facts, including the color of eyes—and the exact height of all smoke stacks."

Richard L. Stokes was another cub in the days when Mr. Bovard rode the city desk. One of Stokes' first assignments was City Hospital, where the reporter noted that a particularly fat orderly was much in evidence. Stokes soon found occasion to write about the orderly and, describing him, quoted Hamlet: "Oh, that this too, too solid flesh would melt."

When this passed under the eye of Mr. Bovard, the city editor called the reporter before him and said: "Stokes, I want to realize on your sense of humor." He issued certain instructions, preparatory to giving the reporter assignments which would permit him to employ humorous and descriptive writing. Not long afterward Stokes was entrusted with writing the story of the Veiled Prophet's Ball. It was a big assignment for a young reporter and he threw every adjective in the dictionary into his story.

His masterpiece at length completed, the glowing young author delivered it to the city desk. In due course Mr. Bovard began to cross out a word here and a word there. He kept on crossing out words down through the first page. Stokes could tell that all his cherished adjectives were going out, one by one.

When the reporter could stand it no longer, he went to the city desk and said: "Mr. Bovard, if you cut that, it will bleed."

Mr. Bovard did not look up. He said, "We will staunch the flow," and went on cutting out adjectives.

In the early 1930's Marquis W. Childs was writing features for the *Post-Dispatch*'s Sunday magazine. Mr. Bovard watched Childs' work with much interest and satisfaction. When Harry Niemeyer retired to Hollywood, Childs applied to Mr. Bovard for the vacant post of movie critic.

"Childs," said Mr. Bovard, "you don't want to write about movies. I'll have to find something for you. Leave the matter with me."

Within two weeks, Childs was assigned to the *Post-Dispatch*'s Washington bureau.

The editor who sent Ross back to get the exact height of the smoke stack, who took the adjectives out of Stokes' magnum opus, and who assigned Childs to Washington rather than let him write movie reviews was one of the most paradoxical of men any newspaper ever saw.

He was cold and ruthless and even rude. He could end a telephone conversation with "I've heard enough of this" and hang up. He could close a conference at his desk without so much as formal dismissal. Times without number he merely picked up the latest edition on his flat-top desk and began to read.

The same Mr. Bovard was warm and considerate and generous. Raymond P. Brandt thinks of him, as do many others who came up under his editorship, as the reporter's friend. Behind the stern taskmaster was an editor who was after all only the master reporter. When a reporter had proved his trustworthiness, Mr. Bovard placed full confidence in him. Then Mr. Bovard trusted the reporter just as he trusted himself.

When a voice on his telephone complained about a news story written by Grattan Kerans, for years the *Post-Dispatch*'s highly competent city hall reporter, Mr. Bovard said:

"I have never had the pleasure of meeting you. I do know Mr. Kerans. Good bye."

He did more than stand behind the reporter. He put himself in the reporter's place. He knew that it took a long time to get some stories. When he allowed a reporter six weeks for an assignment, he meant the reporter had that much time in which to do everything necessary to bring in the completed work. Long before the coming of the Guild, he was quick to reward outstanding performance with bonuses and extra holidays.

As Paul Anderson said, if Mr. Bovard was the highest-salaried managing editor in the country, he more than anyone else probably was responsible for the relatively high reporters' salary scale in St. Louis. He was sparing in his praise, but when he sent a reporter congratulations it meant something and the reporter knew it.

Although Mr. Bovard was severely reticent about details of his life, he did finally prepare a short statement of "biographical facts." This was after "differences" with the publisher, which he described as "irreconcilable," led him to announce his retirement July 29, 1938.

The typed account said that he was born in 1872 in Jacksonville, Illinois, "the son of Charles W. and Hester (Bunn) Bovard, natives of Ohio and Illinois respectively." Editing it, he wrote in his birthday, May 27. The account then told that the family removed from Springfield, Illinois, to St. Louis in 1880, that the father was a printer, later an editorial worker, that for several years before his retirement in 1904, the father was telegraph editor of the *Post-Dispatch.*

Continuing in the third person, the sketch reported how its subject's "formal education ended with grammar school; he passed the entrance examination for high school at the age of 14, but was unable to go to high school. He worked at various clerical jobs for several years, and took his first job as a newspaper reporter on the *St. Louis Star,* in 1896. He joined the *Post-Dispatch* staff in 1898, and was made city editor two years later."

The next paragraph recounted how he made a decision not to go to New York.

"He was made managing editor in 1908, but in 1909 was sent to the *New York World* on an indefinite assignment for examination and training by direction of the elder Joseph Pulitzer, founder of the *Post-Dispatch,* and then still directing head of the *World* and the *Post-Dispatch.* Mr. Bovard spent a week with Mr. Pulitzer at Bar

Harbor, Me. At the end of 10 months in New York he was offered his choice between remaining on the *World* as assistant managing editor, or returning to the *Post-Dispatch* with 'increased authority and emoluments.' He chose St. Louis in preference to 'playing second fiddle' to the man who had been selected for first place on the *World*."

In this self-prepared sketch, Mr. Bovard took notice of only one thing in his forty years on the *Post-Dispatch*. He wrote:

"When the false report of the signing of the Armistice came Nov. 7, 1918, four days before the actual signing, Mr. Bovard gave it no credence, and the *Post-Dispatch* at no time published it. The report that the Armistice had been signed was available to the *Post-Dispatch*, and could have been played up in the paper. The Associated Press carried the fact that such a report, not officially verified, had been picked up in a cable message intercepted by the Navy Department's intelligence service."

Another paper had issued an extra, "out about noon of the 7th," which said that "the signing took place at 11 A.M., French time." Mr. Bovard did not fall into the error, this despite the fact that he was subjected to tremendous pressure, not only from outside, but within his office. *Post-Dispatch* newsboys were stoned on the streets and angry crowds gathered at the doors of the *Post-Dispatch*. But Mr. Bovard sat at his desk, immovable and seemingly calm. In explaining why he did not join in the common error, he continued:

"Analysis of the official news from France at the time showed that the German armistice commissioners had not entered the French lines up to that hour, and that Pershing's army was heavily engaged in front of Sedan as late as 1:45 P.M. It was further obvious that the signing in all probability could not take place for several hours after the meeting of the parties. Finally, the message bore no inherent mark of truth; no authority was given. It was mere assertion. While this was not a factor in reaching the decision, it was interesting to note."

Below that in the familiar blue pencil, the connected initials, "O.K.B.," the enclosing loop, and the date, "August 1938." Thus he ended his sketch of himself.

One by one his star reporters received Pulitzer prizes for distinguished work which he guided or in which he in effect collaborated. John T. Rogers was awarded the reporter's prize for 1927 for the news investigation which resulted in the resignation under fire of Federal Judge George W. English of Illinois. Two years later another reporter's award went to Paul Anderson for work in the oil-reserves-missing-bonds disclosures.

In 1932, Charles Ross received the Pulitzer prize for correspondence for a piece of work which Ross himself is the first to say was in considerable part the planning of Mr. Bovard. This was "The Country's Plight," an extended analysis of the economic troubles of the United States at that time, together with challenging suggestions as to "what can be done about it." In 1937, under Mr. Bovard's direction, the news resources of the newspaper were thrown into an investigation of election frauds in St. Louis. The findings were strikingly portrayed with photographs of empty houses and the number of ghost voters written across the pictures. This graphic campaign brought the *Post-Dispatch* the public service award in 1937.

Mr. Bovard's capacity as a directing editor was shown by two vastly different stories. One was the baby hoax of Nellie Muench and the ramified disclosures which went with that fabulous case. The other was the detailed, almost sociological analysis of Chicago as an American phenomenon which was one of Paul Anderson's most incisive pieces of work.

For years his special delight was his Washington bureau, which he often telephoned five or six times a day. So complete was his confidence in the men he put there that not once did he enter the bureau in the twenty years that he directed its operations. He did not attend a Washington Gridiron dinner until 1939, the year after his retirement, and it was then that he first saw the inside of the Washington office to which he gave so much thought and energy.

A scene, never to be forgotten, after that Gridiron dinner, was a forensic battle between Mr. Bovard and Mr. Justice Frankfurter. With a roomful of spectators ringed about for many minutes, the two strong men locked themselves in verbal combat. The judge told the editor how to run a newspaper and the editor countered by telling the judge how to conduct his business on the Supreme Court.

In his latter years, Mr. Bovard became intensely interested in political philosophies and systems. He printed articles by Mussolini on Fascism in Italy. He gave a great deal of attention to what went on in Russia and ran the text of the Soviet constitution. His columns were the only ones in the country to carry in full an epoch-making speech by Stalin, sent to St. Louis by Brandt who was then in Russia.

Mr. Bovard always knew what he wanted to accomplish and he planned accordingly. In 1931, Brandt collected a wealth of material on Russia and came home in the summer to write a series of articles. The managing editor held up the publication of the series until fall. He would not print the articles in August when many of the very people he wanted to inform were out of the area on vacations in the North and East.

Over the years he developed a department which became known in shop talk as the "dignity" page. Heading the editorial section Sunday and daily, it presented well-thought-out articles on serious subjects and notable personalities. In time it became an outstanding vehicle in American journalism for news interpretation and appraisal.

Mr. Bovard had blind spots and every reporter who worked with him could name one or more. Like as not they grew out of his lack of formal education. For although he was among the most intelligent of men, he often discovered late in life facts or ideas with which a university education would have equipped him in his early twenties. Had he met Marxism as a college student, he doubtless would have been less taken with the idea in his sixties.

In the Bovard book, Franklin D. Roosevelt was "the Kerensky of the American Revolution." He thought the New Deal President should have nationalized the banks at the outset of his administration and taken other steps to control capitalism. While some persons hated F.D.R. for going too far, Mr. Bovard criticized him for not going far enough.

But this intensely political editor was Mr. Bovard in his last years. Mr. Bovard who was the great editor was the man of an earlier time.

The earlier Mr. Bovard developed the memos that were models of clarity. He was the editor who laid out the grand strategy and left it for his reporters to execute the tactics. He was the editor who could celebrate brilliant achievement with one breath and condemn slovenliness with the next. He was the editor who looked askance at comics and the other entertainment features of newspapers, the editor who sought to make the newspaper he served into a daily "people's university." He was the editor who held himself aloof from the business office, who took satisfaction in demonstrating that an advertiser enjoyed no special privileges in the news columns.

To a degree that he himself probably never recognized, Mr. Bovard was successful because of conditions around him. The first of these was the fact that his publisher, Joseph Pulitzer, gave him the widest opportunity to exercise his remarkable talents. The second was his access to seemingly unlimited resources for expensive news investigation and coverage. The third was the corps of editors and reporters under him: he could have done little as chief of staff without officers to assist and advise him and carry out his mission.

Letter to a Young Journalist from His Father

BARRY BINGHAM [JANUARY 1961

Mr. Bingham is editor and publisher of the *Courier-Journal* and the *Louisville Times*. This piece was first published in the *Courier-Journal*.

Dear Worth: As a young man in the early years of a newspaper career, you ought to expose yourself to a book called *The Fading American Newspaper*. You have already been around news rooms long enough for some of the writer's points to make you good and angry. But such anger can be a healthy thing, so long as it is not blindly defensive.

The book is by Carl Lindstrom, a professor of journalism at the University of Michigan. His strictures on the American press cannot be dismissed as the mouthings of an egg-head theorist, however. Nor can they be brushed off as the work of an uninformed layman, as happened in the case of the *Report on Freedom of the Press* by the Hutchins Commission. Lindstrom is a newspaperman to the core. For years he was executive editor of the *Hartford Times*, an active and widely respected member of the profession.

His message is one that young journalists would do especially well to ponder. He tells us that the newspaper is not necessarily here to stay. "Electronic and film transmission of news, even new printing methods are leaving it behind, and it is entirely possible in the not so remote future that it will go the way of the street car."

That statement is guaranteed to make newspaper people hot under the collar. No doubt he aimed to produce that effect. He is like a psychiatrist administering shock treatment, in an effort to shake up the mental pattern of a patient whose thinking has fallen into a dangerous rut.

Lindstrom notes that "journalism, the recorder of change, has feared change as if it meant death." He argues that without deep-piercing change, the press may fade and die. He tells us that "indignation has an exceedingly low boiling point in editorial offices when the press critics start shooting." Then he begins to shoot.

He aims his shafts directly at some of the sacred cows of journalism. He deplores the familiar "pyramid lead" on a news story, the old demand to tell the what, where, when, and why in the first sentences. He is scathing about the traditional display headline: "It makes correct quotation almost an impossibility; it accounts for most of the misconstructions and distortions; it offends intelligence and rips the envelope of context; it is a constant libel risk."

You can judge from these samples the nature of the fire and brimstone Lindstrom heaps on our heads. But he is not merely being a fuss-budget. He is making a salient point that the American newspaper is dangerously resistant to change in a changing world. He submits that the press itself has not recognized the movement from violent street-sales competition to "home delivery journalism," which is the order of the day in Louisville and in most American cities. He finds no sense in competing press services that will "run the risk of hypothecating accuracy to get there first even if with the least. Rivalry of this kind is old fashioned and amusing."

He is interesting on such matters as run-of-paper color: "It is a mistake to embark upon competition in which you cannot possibly win, unless the issue is liberty, patriotism, or moral principles." He makes a valid criticism of education reporting: "The progressive movement crested and subsided, and all during this critical period newspapers in general never took it upon themselves to go into the classroom and find out what was going on."

I like his statement that "the press, along with other printed matter, is the last bulwark of the language." That's why I think we have to strive for a more exact and meticulous use of language than

99 per cent of our readers would ever attempt. I like his quoting Franklin P. Adams that "nothing is too good for the newspaper." This is no pat on our professional backs. It is a way of demolishing the excuse that serious criticism of the arts, a liberal use of foreign news, and adult writing are not feasible because they are over the heads of newspaper readers. I like his stressing the old saw: "Never underestimate the reader's intelligence, or overestimate his information."

Sometimes Lindstrom overstates his case, perhaps deliberately in order to stir up the sluggish animals of the profession. He is telling wholesome truth when he warns that newspaper circulation, while it is growing, is not gaining nearly as fast as the population of the country. He is being provocative without supporting evidence when he declares that "television is learning by its mistakes much faster than newspapers."

Some of his assertions make me long to sit down with him in one of those bull sessions dear to the hearts of newspapermen.

For instance, I find no justification in any poll of readership for his assertion that "women probably read editorial pages more than men do." I think he woefully oversimplifies the issue when he announces that "the crusading newspaper is not a money-maker, and this discovery profoundly changed journalism." Here he seems to be falling into the easy cynicism which is one of the journalistic traits he excoriates. I suspect him of an old news-room prejudice against editorial writers and their "Ivory Tower pallor."

You may disagree, as I do, with many other charges that flow from his typewriter. But Lindstrom is indisputably on the side of the angels. He is for better writing, higher standards of taste, more alert responsibility, a faster response to changing conditions which could save us from the fate of the mastodon (or the street car).

He makes me seethe and want to talk back, but he also makes me want to do a better job, if only to prove him wrong in some of his nettling charges. I am in wholehearted agreement with his conclusion that "the way to meet competition is not to cheapen the product. The way to meet it is to make the product better."

Your affectionate

FATHER

Tom Stokes: What He Was Like

RICHARD L. STROUT [JULY 1959

The first award of the Thomas L. Stokes Award Committee was made posthumously to Tom Stokes. His friend, Richard L. Strout of the *Christian Science Monitor,* made the address at the awards dinner at the National Press Club, May 5, 1959.

Every now and then some exceptional new reporter joins the Washington press corps, some crusader, some hell-raiser, and it's funny how after the years the experienced newspaperman can generally spot him. He may be aggressive, like the late Paul Y. Anderson, or Bob Allen, or he may start out relatively young and shy and mild as Tom Stokes did.

These men are a little different from their fellows. Journalism to them isn't just a business. They would shudder at the word but it's a kind of lifetime crusade. It's a way of tilting at the smug and mighty, and of somehow yanking out the truth against obstacles. That kind of reporter when he hits Washington is likely to stay, and die, in harness: You can't somehow imagine a Nate Robertson or an Ed Lahey or a Ray Clapper or a Clark Mollenhoff ending up in a fat-cat public relations job for General Motors or U.S. Steel They don't necessarily have to be radicals though a lot of them are; Joe Alsop is a good Republican but it's hard trying to imagine him toeing some chamber of commerce line or passing out handouts for some corporation.

These men have a purpose in life, a goal, a fire in their bellies; they are not using journalism as a step-ladder to something else; they are generally here to stay. That's what Tom Stokes was when he came to Washington way back in 1921.

He was 23 years old. Outwardly, I am told, he looked mild and shy and amiable. He was bright, he had got a Phi Beta Kappa key at the dreamy old Confederate university town of Athens, Georgia. I arrived in Washington three or four years later and ultimately came to know Tom. He liked to tell how he was in the SATC camp at college and one day was told to report to the 6-foot regular Army officer. Tom presented himself with a snappy salute. "What's your name?" demanded the officer crisply.

For the life of him Tom couldn't remember. It was part of Tom's personality both that this incident actually happened and that later he could look back on it without mortification. The officer dismissed Tom kindly and told him to come back some time when he could remember his name.

Once as a youngster Tom volunteered in church to go as a missionary to China and though he didn't go he remained a bit of a missionary all his life. His mother died when he was 13 and his world seemed to crash about his ears. He came to Washington from a newspaper in a small town in Georgia where a hideous lynching had occurred. He was a sensitive, imaginative person and I think the sickening affair haunted him. There was that element in Tom under his gaiety. I guess that most of us, whether we admit it or not, feel some degree of guilt over the state of the world and some go their quiet way, as well as they can, trying to expiate it.

I asked some of Tom's old friends what was the single characteristic that they thought differentiated him from anybody else?

He was a liberal, of course; not a namby-pamby liberal but rather a fierce liberal when he discovered what he considered to be injustice. But there are a lot of liberals. He was also cheerful, and intelligent, and good company. Granted all that, there are other people like that, too (not enough, but some).

It got to be funny, the way I constantly got the same answer to my question, expressed in different ways but meaning the same thing.

"It was the way he managed to hold his own strong views and yet managed to retain the affection of people whose views were harshly antagonistic to his." In my lifetime I have never seen anyone who had this attribute to a stronger degree than Tom Stokes. He liked people and he was gay and companionable.

I don't mean that Tom didn't have critics—or perhaps even enemies. But consider the fact that Tom never hesitated to lecture the South on civil rights and that he yet remained one of the few columnists the South would listen to on that subject. It was the same with most people of all shades of opinion. I have seen it many and many a time. When he sat down at the press table in the Senate restaurant, or at his favorite place in the National Press Club, others would always crowd in. They would sit down and not go away.

People who weren't on speaking terms with one another would drop down if Tom were there, chat amiably and then go off and perhaps not be on speaking terms again. It was really something to analyze. He was a warm, comfortable stove; he was a walking truce, and yet he would not yield his liberalism an inch in the festive atmosphere. I really can't explain it: I suppose part of it was that he had no malice at all, and no arrogance at all.

Tom richly deserved the Pulitzer prize which he won. But it is ironic that he got the award not for exposing reaction (as he did all his life), but for his equally fair and determined crusade against the political use of WPA relief funds in Kentucky in behalf of the New Deal Democrats, in the 1938 mid-term election. Tom was right in his exposé, and it represented a splendid bit of reporting though it made some of the "liberals" mad at the time. But it is a chance which the progressive reporter must take. Stay on your own side of the fence and things will tend to remain quiet and you probably won't get many prizes. But stray out briefly and attack fellow liberals and you run the risk of being tagged with a Pulitzer.

Like every old-time newsman I have a metal file cabinet of clippings by my desk. How often when I turn to it I still find some first-rate clipped item from the Stokes' column! These columns remind me that Tom was one of the few who kept his balance of objectivity in the otherwise all-but-universal paeans from the press after the 1953 inauguration.

I have always felt that the American press—or a good part of it—deprived the Eisenhower administration for several years of something to which it was legitimately entitled, a virile opposition. Every president needs this unending, critical press scrutiny. The administration and the country lose it at their peril.

Tom's normal style in his columns was simple, direct, and unpretentious. He had a grim concern with many matters which other columnists found too humdrum to explore. I think he was the one who first brought to my attention the role of the *regulatory agencies* in Washington—the great "fourth branch" of the American government. It was something that back in 1953–1955 hardly any other writer seemed interested in.

I think that more than any other man Tom was responsible for

Sherman Adams' departure. In a column as early as 1955 Tom charged flatly that Adams was "directing the fight against power development." In later columns he spoke out on the drearily complicated Dixon-Yates give-away. Sherman Adams, he charged, "meddles constantly in the business of these regulatory commissions, which is really none of his business."

In the last column I have of Tom's, November 20, 1957 (six weeks before he stopped writing for good) he came back to this same subject and Sherman Adams. "Anybody," he declared, "who is constantly around Congress during this Administration finds his tracks all over the place."

Well, that's where Tom signed off. But a man named Sam Rayburn took notice of these and similar columns and got the House to appropriate $300,000 for the first investigation of regulatory agencies in history. The inquiry followed. You know how it unexpectedly snagged Sherman Adams. I am interested in this because in a piece I wrote last summer for *The New Republic* entitled, "Tom Stokes and Sherman Adams," I argued that Tom had sparked the inquiry. I added sadly,

"I suppose a posthumous prize is out of the question."

Well, I seem to be wrong.

A Habit That Was Handed Down

Moberly Bell and His Fight to Save the London Times

LOUIS M. LYONS [APRIL 1948

This was a review of *History of the Times: The Twentieth Century Test (1884–1912)*, which was published by *The Times,* London, in 1947 and is volume III of the complete history of the paper.

When Northcliffe, by elaborately concealing his identity, obtained control of the London *Times* in 1908, his first complaint of the editor of that august paper was that he daily opened all the editorial mail with his thumb. Northcliffe added that the *Times* hadn't had a piece of news in fifty years and when it had any it handled it on the maxim that news like wine improves by keeping. That was not the way he had brought the *Daily Mail* to a million circulation and become himself the First Press Lord. Yet he had coveted the *Times* with its 37,000 more than the *Mail* with its million. The 37,000 were all the right people, always had been through the century and a half of *Times* history, entwined as it was with the history of British imperialism and its eager instrument. At times it was uncertain whether the *Times* was the voice of the Government or Government policy a mere echo of *Times* views. Yet Northcliffe was never really to reach the *Times* readers.

Northcliffe saved the *Times* from bankruptcy. But the *Times* editors by their stubborn jealous custody of its institutional character saved the *Times* from Northcliffe. The struggle of Moberly Bell, the manager at the turn of the century, to save the *Times* as it met the crisis of modern competition is one of the great stories of journalism, and here greatly told by historians who remain, in *Times* character, anonymous.

To newspapermen, the fight to save the *Times,* against all the internal and external factors that seemed to ensure its destruction, is the essence of this most fascinating of all journalistic histories. But beyond that it is a rich chunk of the inside history of British imperialism in its most Kiplingesque outcroppings. For the *Times* paced the policy of that imperialism. For a generation it was the key of German policy to send ambassadors to capitals of Europe who could cope with the *Times* correspondent, usually a more formidable foe than the British Foreign Office. *Times* editors often retired to the Foreign Office. Humorless and old-fashioned, but the best informed group of men on earth, the *Times* editors at the end of the century cared nothing for sensationalism, but everything for the last bit of exact information. "In the use of material, the foreign editor took into account first the diplomatic effect of a dispatch, second its value as news. He had in mind rather its effect upon statesmen, British and foreign, than on the world at large."

Moberly Bell himself was a co-conspirator in Jameson's Raid that set off the Boer War. His understanding with Cecil Rhodes was that he was not to start it on a Saturday, for the *Times* had no Sunday edition. The *Times* pushed Gladstone's anti-imperialist government into sending Gordon to Khartoum and then when he was hopelessly involved there, to send a relief force. Its own correspondent was one of the two Englishmen with Gordon, and died with him. His dispatches were not merely exclusive; they were all the information the British public or government had for many crucial months on a situation strategic to British policy.

"The paper's policy towards Gordon and the Sudan sprang from its belief in the general desirability of the expansion of the British Empire." It was Bell who engineered the Egyptian adventure, from Cairo.

The *Times* always knew more than it printed and rationed its disclosures to what it felt in the interest of sound public policy. It had also its innate restraints. When Queen Victoria was so indiscreet as to send an uncoded telegram to the Paris embassy expressing her horror at the verdict against Dreyfus, the *Times*'s colorful, incredible de Blowitz got hold of it and triumphantly sent it. But the *Times* suppressed it. It was bound to leak out and it did. But "what we felt we could not do was to take the initiative of giving publicity to a private communication of the Queen."

Everything about the *Times* of the period when Moberly Bell took charge, 1889, was incredible, including its very existence. In the eighteenth century the *Times* was started as a means of advertising a printing business of one Walter. Thereafter there was always a Walter as chief proprietor. But the Walter family by the third generation had become the languid but acquisitive collectors of profits from a paper that was a subsidiary and supporter of an obsolete print shop whose fat profits were gained by bleeding and starving the greatest journalistic enterprise in the world. The end result was that the feudal Walter family lost control of the whole works to an uppity yellow journalist whose papers they despised—Northcliffe.

The British ruling class had learned to take in the *Times* by the Battle of Waterloo which upped its circulation. By mid-century under the great Barnes and Delane it had attained its journalistic pinnacle and 70,000 circulation. It was after Delane that it ran to erudition, diplomacy, and ponderosity. The institutional character of the paper was firmly set by 1884 when this history opens. Its audience by then had defined itself: "Reading the *Times* was more than a habit; it was a habit that had been handed down." The editors asked themselves not so much what their own convictions were as "What should the *Times* say?"

John Walter III, in his last years as the story opens, had survived from the great days of Delane. "The passage of two score years had deepened his sense of trusteeship. The *Times* so long as he was alive would never depart from the old ways. Nor was it necessary for him to intervene directly. The staff were in full sympathy with his desire to maintain the old standards. Walter was happy to be ruled by the custom of the office and he was happy that the Editor should accept the same rule. Thus after 37 years service the chief proprietor relied confidently on the influence that work in the atmosphere of Printing House Square exercised over his own mind and over the servants of the paper. It was upon this influence that George Earle Buckle, the editor (1884–1912), relied for his inspiration during a period of 30 years that embraced the most profound of issues, domestic and foreign."

There is a kind of obsolete magnificence about this. And about the instructions that Foreign Editor Donald MacKenzie Wallace gave to his correspondent in Turkey: "If you do your duty you will not satisfy the authorities. Already I have received complaints about your dispatches and I have replied that I do not believe any man with the independence of judgment requisite in a *Times* correspondent can possibly satisfy the authorities."

Into this impenetrable atmosphere in 1889 came a new man with new vigor, to save the *Times*. Moberly Bell, Egyptian born, British educated, had been a *Times* correspondent first as a pleasant side line from his banking. He was weaned away from the banking house in Cairo to become *Times* manager and to stand between the academic editors and the dilettante proprietor—a massive man with the imperial reach of a Rhodes, an intellect capable of reorganizing and keeping in close touch with the far-flung foreign correspondent system on which the *Times* was based, a meticulous man who kept all the accounts of the *Times* in his own hand ledger and wrote all his voluminous correspondence by hand, disdaining typewriter and secretary, except for filing. The sanctum of his editors was inviolable and he left them alone. They resisted the use of the telephone, even to the Paris office, in the twentieth century. Wallace would have none of de Blowitz' beats by phone. He'd rather have them late and accurate, and you feel sure the two were synonymous with him. He was suspicious of scoops and tended to hold them until he could send a man over to investigate. The makeup was left to the printer who suited his convenience. None of this would Bell change, nor consider any tampering with the standard of the paper. But he re-energized its foreign staff, and recognizing that a subsidy must be found to maintain the paper, set out successfully to create one—by publishing books to make up the deficit.

Bell had his troubles with some of Wallace's erudite correspondents. A classic instance was an expense account from the Balkans correspondent in 1904 for two dispatches filed in 1893 and 1894. He had lost the keys to his desk drawers. Bell was sure that nobody was interested in the Balkans—his own imperial concepts stretched through the length of Africa and Asia. "As a rule the British public only care for one thing at once and two things in the Balkans would be more than they could stand" he said, refusing an assistant to the Balkans correspondent.

The *Times* reached a peak of prestige on the Sudan issue. Then in a few years it lost it. Lost in a piece of bad judgment. Fighting Parnellism and Home Rule for Ireland, they bought some letters that seemed to show Parnell involved in the political murder ring then operating in Ireland. The resulting legal action was costly, and the space it took dutifully to print all the evidence against it cost the *Times* the chance to print news just as the new penny press was becoming real competition. But that was not all. "The mid-Victorian legend about the inerrancy of the *Times* was exploded. Something of the awe of Holy Writ which had clung to its columns now faded away. The *Times* had been deceived and might be deceived again." This deepened the crisis for the twentieth-century test of the new competition the *Times* was organically, temperamentally and financially unequipped to meet.

The archaism of the paper was well illustrated by its first brush with American journalism. The occasion was the peace treaty of Portsmouth where Theodore Roosevelt refereed between Japan and Russia. It was attended on behalf of the *Times* by its great Far Eastern correspondent, Morrison, by Smalley from Washington, and by Wallace the foreign editor, who bore messages from King Edward for President Roosevelt and the Russian ambassador. But he might as well have stayed at home as he was soon complaining. Smalley, though British, had been a dozen years in America and had become Americanized in his news sense. He played it for the news and having control of the telegraph because it was in his territory, he disregarded the daily views of his senior colleagues to cable what his excellent pipelines were yielding. As the Russians proved the most communicative, he played their line. This mightily confused the ever-watchful Germans who detected a shift, as it appeared, in *Times* policy. Wallace protested but Smalley was scoring beats and Bell was selling the service in New York.

The *Times* survived that Americanism, and it is to be noted that Bell alone of the office appreciated its value. But his other American venture precipitated a crisis. Bell had found the *Times* losing money and was convinced it must continue to lose it if it was to keep its character. He was determined to find a subsidy that would not cost its independence. He brought out an atlas in 1896 with modest success. Two American publishers, Horace E. Hooper and W. M. Jackson, saw in this a chance for a larger enterprise. For a decade the profits of book ventures made dividends instead of deficits for the *Times*. Bell seemed to have solved his problem.

But it ended in a revolt of the small proprietors, descendants of collateral relatives of Walter. Minority shareholders, with no influence in the management, they had exercised their prerogative of bickering and badgering for many years. A real issue was the relation of the paper to the printing firm, but a final irritation was the venture into books, and its American connection. The printing company, parent of the *Times,* was the property solely of the Walter family. The small proprietors' shares were only in the *Times*. The Walters ran the printing company like a pre-Roosevelt holding company. It charged the *Times* peak rates regardless of the paper's earnings and it ran the print shop regardless of the paper's typographical needs until by absentee control the printing house became a junk shop of obsolete type faces and antiquated machines. But it was still taking $150,000 a year from the *Times* even though the paper was on the ragged edge of bankruptcy.

The stubbornness of the Walters went on until the most vindictive of their relatives got them into court with a formidable case. When this seemed approaching settlement the cousins and aunts rebelled anew over the book sideline with its American enterprise. This though the books were making $100,000 a year while the *Times* was losing $80,000.

This insanity impelled Bell and the Americans to propose to Walter to let Hooper and Jackson buy out the small proprietors.

But they were rejected by a faction that wanted to oust Walter and Bell too. Finally in desperation Walter made a deal with one of the most successful of the new newspaper publishers, Arthur Pearson, to take over the *Times*. To the *Times* editors this was the ultimate surrender. They despaired. All but Bell. He schemed and labored and negotiated with men of money all over England and by the most resourceful and even devious means, he defeated the Pearson deal. It meant defeating his own chief proprietor as well as all the litigious relatives. It meant, in a final recourse of desperation, bringing in Northcliffe. This was so far more shocking than the Pearson deal that Bell had to conceal it even from the court. It was as "Mr. X" that Northcliffe bid $1,700,000 and got the *Times*.

The rest of the story is a last-ditch struggle to the death—literally so for Moberly Bell—to keep Northcliffe from using the *Times* for his own shifting political feuds. Bell had deluded himself that he could control Northcliffe. He served as shock absorber for three years of increasing pressure by the outside proprietor. The issues are meaningless today but in 1911 they spelled to *Times* editors issues of independence and integrity. Bell carried the whole load and kept the editors, even Walter himself—still nominal director—from ever knowing the completeness of control Northcliffe had wrung from him in his desperate need. Northcliffe wore him down under an avalanche of daily directives and demands, a calculated pressure to exhaust the old man. Bell died at his desk at 61 as he finished a letter urging his colleagues to go along with one more compromise which he argued was not yet vital to principle. With Bell gone, Northcliffe moved fast to force out Buckle as editor and to introduce modernization that was to bring the *Times* to 200,000 circulation. But the young men who succeeded the old never yielded on the essential issue of the continuity and character of the *Times*. Geoffrey Dawson was to resign the editorship a decade later on the same issue. The final salvation came after Northcliffe's death in 1923 when another Walter with Major J. J. Astor steered the *Times* into the protection of a unique form of trusteeship against external control. But that is beyond the bounds of this history which closes in the crisis of 1912.

Moberly Bell died a defeated and deluded man. But there is a grandeur about his delusion and a nobility in his defeat that rises above the involved imperialism, the obsolete methods and the feudal exploitation of the *Times*. Here you had a great institution whose people grew old or old-fashioned and its arteries hardened just as new competition came in which it could not meet. Yet its standards, though not its techniques, were superior to the new. Its editors were born thirty years too late. Its ownership was feudal, and that defeated the change of new vigor in the person of Moberly Bell, who was resourceful and able, to meet the change. "It was an article of faith with Bell that the *Times* must not cease to be the *Times*." He was defeated first by the antediluvian ownership, then by his own gamble on Northcliffe, a dominating man who would not brook independence. The strain killed Bell. But the magnificent thing is that the fight went on. The institution had the traditions and the men of a stubborn integrity to hold to its character so tenaciously that it weathered the long crisis to survive finally on its own terms.

APPENDIX

I. LIST OF NIEMAN FELLOWS THROUGH 1964–65

II. LIST OF ASSOCIATE NIEMAN FELLOWS THROUGH 1964–65

INDEX

APPENDIX

I. LIST OF NIEMAN FELLOWS THROUGH 1964–65

(Each name is followed by academic year at Harvard, position at that time, and position as of April 1965; asterisk means Pulitzer prize)

Allen, C. Stanley, 1941–42, reporter, New Haven Register; now in public relats., Keats, Allen & Keats, Wash., D.C.

Allen, J. Edward, 1939–40, reporter, Boston Herald; now intl. repres., American Newsp. Guild, Weymouth, Mass.

Anderton, Piers B., 1954–55, teleg. ed., San Francisco Chronicle; now ABC, Wash., D.C.

Andrica, Theodore, 1943–44, nationalities ed., Cleveland Press; same now.

Armstrong, John A., 1957–58, Sun. ed., Portland Oregonian; now dir. inf., Reed College, Portland.

Ashmore, Harry S., 1941–42, polit. writer, Greenville (S.C.) News; now Center for the Study of Democratic Institutions, Santa Barbara.

Barschdorf, Arthur C., 1952–53, reporter, Hammond (Ind.) Times; now dir. public inf., Minn. Power & Light Co., Duluth.

Barth, Alan, 1948–49, edit. writer, Washington Post; same now.

Batal, James, 1945–46, ed. and pub., Cleghorn Courier, Fitchburg, Mass.; now lecturer on Arab affairs, Coral Gables, Fla.

Bauer, Malcolm C., 1950–51, city ed., Portland Oregonian; now assoc. ed., same.

*Beech, Keyes, 1952–53, foreign corr., Chicago Daily News; same now.

Bergenheim, Robert C., 1953–54, city hall reporter, Christian Science Monitor; now asst. to pub., same.

Berger, Daniel, 1962–63, edit. writer, Indianapolis Times; same now.

Binzen, Peter H., 1961–62, educ. reporter, Philadelphia Bulletin; same now.

Bonafede, Dominic D., 1959–60, reporter, Miami Herald; now Wash. corr., New York Herald Tribune.

Booker, Simeon S., 1950–51, city ed., Cleveland Call-Post; now chief, Wash. bureau, Jet-Ebony.

Bordner, Robert, 1944–45, reporter, Cleveland Press; now retired, Thanksgiving Hill, Peninsula, Ohio.

Botter, David E., Jr., 1944–45, reporter, Dallas News; deceased 1963 (prof. of journalism, Northwestern Univ.).

Braestrup, Peter, 1959–60, reporter, New York Herald Tribune; now foreign corr., New York Times.

Brandle, Lowell S., 1960–61, reporter, St. Petersburg Times; same now.

Brazier, Donald G., 1960–61, asst. city ed., Seattle Times; same now.

Brelis, Dean, 1957–58, free lance; now foreign corr., NBC.

Brown, Barry, 1953–54, edit. writer, Providence Journal; now USIA.

Brown, Robert W., 1951–52, ed., Columbus (Ga.) Ledger; now ed., Rock Hill (S.C.) Evening Herald.

Browne, Millard C., 1942–43, edit. writer, Sacramento Union; now edit. page ed., Buffalo News.

Brunn, Robert R., 1948–49, San Francisco corr., Christian Science Monitor; now Wash. corr., same.

Burby, John P., 1959–60, city hall reporter, San Francisco Chronicle; now press sec. to Gov. Brown of California.

Burke, Donald, 1941–42, staff writer, Time, Inc.; now Interplan Planning Organization, Rome.

Buttedahl, Oscar, 1939–40, ed. Bismarck Leader; now stockbroker Santa Rosa, Calif.

*Caldwell, Nathan, 1940–41, reporter, Nashville Tennessean; same now.

Campbell, Robert F., 1956–57, edit. writer, Winston-Salem Journal & Sentinel; now edit. page ed., same.

Carey, Francis E., 1946–47, science writer, AP, Wash.; same now.

Carter, Hodding, 1939–40, ed., Delta Democrat-Times, Greenville, Miss.; now publisher-editor, same.

Champion, Hale, 1956–57, reporter, San Francisco Chronicle; now dir. of finance, State of California.

Chaplin, George, 1940–41, city ed., Greenville (S.C.) Piedmont; now ed., Honolulu Advertiser.

Cherniss, Norman A., 1958–59, edit. page ed., Riverside (Cal.) Press-Enterprise; same now.

Clark, John McL., 1938–39, edit. writer, Washington Post; deceased 1950 (pub., Claremont, N.H., Eagle).

Clark, Robert P., 1960–61, science reporter, Louisville Courier-Journal; now managing ed., Louisville Times.

Clark, William H., 1944–45, feature writer, Boston Globe; deceased 1955 (retired 1951).

Clay, Grady E., 1948–49, reporter, Louisville Courier-Journal; now real estate ed., same.

Clinchy, Evans, 1958–59, educ. reporter, Hartford Times; now Educational Services, Inc., Watertown, Mass.

Colvin, James E., 1941–42, rewrite, Chicago Daily News; now public relats., Field Enterprises, Chicago.

Cooper, Sanford L., 1941–42, cable ed., Pittsburgh Press; now public relats., S. L. Cooper, Inc., Wash., D.C.

Corry, John J., 1964–65, copy ed., New York Times.

Crandall, Robert S., 1951–52, Sun. ed., New York Herald Tribune; now asst. news ed., New York Times.

*Crider, John H., 1940–41, Wash. corr., New York Times; now public relats., Morgan Guaranty Trust, New York City.

Daniel, James M., 1942–43, reporter, Washington Daily News; now roving corr., Reader's Digest.
Davies, John O., Jr., 1951–52, reporter, Newark News; now ed., Camden Courier-Post.
Davis, Alvin, 1953–54, reporter, New York Post; now managing ed., same.
Davis, Harry M., 1940–41, Sun. feature writer, New York Times; deceased 1950 (science ed., Newsweek).
Davis, Neil O., 1941–42, ed. and pub., Lee County Bulletin, Auburn, Alabama; same now.
Day, John F., Jr., 1942–43, reporter, AP, Huntington, W. Va.; now pub., Exmouth Journal, England.
Dearmore, Thomas L., 1959–60, co-editor and pub., Baxter Bulletin, Mountain Home, Ark.; same now.
de Roos, Robert, 1948–49, reporter, San Francisco Chronicle; now free lance.
Dickinson, William B., 1939–40, news manager, UP, Minneapolis; now managing ed., Philadelphia Bulletin.
Dickson, Robert, 1941–42, telegraph ed., New York World-Telegram; deceased 1947 (was in same position).
Dilliard, Irving, 1938–39, edit. writer, St. Louis Post-Dispatch; now Ferris Professor, Princeton Univ. (home, Collinsville, Ill.).
Donohoe, Edward J., 1942–43, reporter, Scranton Times; now managing ed., same.
Dougherty, John L., 1955–56, teleg. ed., Rochester Times-Union; now asst. managing ed., same.
Doyle, James S., 1964–65, state political reporter, Boston Globe.
Dreiman, David B., 1948–49, science writer, Minneapolis Star; now book pub., Platt & Munk, New York.
Drew, Robert L., 1954–55, corr., Life Magazine; now TV producer.
Dudman, Richard, 1953–54, reporter, St. Louis Post-Dispatch; now Wash. corr., same.
Durdin, Tillman, 1948–49, China corr., New York Times; now foreign corr., same.
Duscha, Julius, 1955–56, edit. writer, Lindsay-Schaub Newspapers, Decatur, Ill.; now natl. corr., Washington Post.

Eaton, William J., 1962–63, Wash. corr., UPI; same now.
Eberhardt, Charles, 1953–54, ed., New Mexico Newspapers, Inc.; now USIA.
Eddy, Bob, 1950–51, teleg. ed., St. Paul Pioneer Press; now asst. to pub., Hartford Courant.
Edmundson, Charles, 1940–41, edit. writer, St. Louis Post-Dispatch; now reporter, Memphis Commercial Appeal.
Edstrom, Edward, 1944–45, asst. Sun. ed., Louisville Courier-Journal; now Wash. corr., Hearst papers.
Eggleston, Arthur D., 1940–41, labor columnist, San Francisco Chronicle; deceased 1959.
Elliott, Robert C., 1942–43, war news ed., San Francisco News; now dir. public relats., Henry J. Kaiser Corp., Honolulu.

Emmerich, John O., Jr., 1961–62, managing ed., McComb (Miss.) Enterprise-Journal; now reporter, Baltimore Sun.
Etheridge, James P., Jr., 1942–43, edit. writer, Tampa Daily Times; now exec. sec., Florida Educational TV Commission, Tallahassee.
Evans, Paul L., 1946–47, exec. ed., Daily Republic, Mitchell, S.D.; now dir. inf., TVA.

Farrell, Robert E., 1953–54, reporter, Wall Street Journal; now Paris bureau chief, McGraw-Hill World News.
Fentress, J. Simmons, 1957–58, edit. writer, Charlotte Observer; now Wash. corr., Time, Inc.
Fernsworth, Lawrence A., 1943–44, copy ed., New York Daily News; now Wash. corr., various papers.
Fischer, Stephen M., 1946–47, reporter, San Francisco Chronicle; now public relats., Scientific American.
Fisher, Roy M., 1950–51, reporter, Chicago Daily News; now book ed., Field Enterprises, Chicago.
Fitzgerald, Stephen E., 1939–40, reporter, Baltimore Evening Sun; deceased 1964 (public relats.).
FitzHenry, Charlotte L. See Robling.
Fleming, Robert H., 1949–50, polit. writer, Milwaukee Journal; now Wash. bureau chief, ABC News & Special Events.
Foisie, Jack, 1946–47, reporter, San Francisco Chronicle; now foreign corr., Los Angeles Times.
Foss, Kendall, 1944–45, staff writer, Time, Inc.; deceased 1964 (managing ed., Business Week).
Foxhall, Mrs. Lewis (Lois Sager), 1947–48, reporter, Dallas News; now in Memphis, Texas.
Frazier, Robert B., 1952–53, reporter, Eugene (Ore.) Register-Guard; now edit. writer, same.
Freehoff, William F., 1951–52, ed., Kingsport (Tenn.) Times-News; now assoc. news dir., radio station WKPT, Kingsport.
Friedman, Saul, 1962–63, reporter, Houston Chronicle; same now.
Fuller, Wesley, 1938–39, reporter, Boston Herald; deceased 1958 (ed., Bell Tel. Labs.).

Galphin, Bruce, 1962–63, reporter, Atlanta Constitution; now edit. writer, same.
Geiselman, Arthur W., Jr., 1964–65, reporter, York (Pa.) Gazette & Daily.
German, William, 1949–50, copy ed., San Francisco Chronicle; now news editor, same.
Gilmore, Charles W., 1947–48, reporter, AP, Atlanta; now editor, Toledo Times.
Givando, Joseph, 1951–52, copy ed., Denver Post; deceased 1953 (managing ed., Fort Dodge Messenger).
Glasgow, Robert W., 1947–48, reporter, New York Herald Tribune; now regional ed., Arizona Republic, Phoenix.
Goldman, Peter L., 1960–61, reporter, St. Louis Globe-Democrat; now associate ed., Newsweek.
Gonzales, Donald J., 1949–50, diplomatic reporter, UP, Wash.; now vice-pres. Colonial Williamsburg.

Gordon, William, 1952–53, managing ed., Atlanta Daily World; now USIA, Nigeria.

Gorey, Hays, 1949–50, city ed., Salt Lake Tribune; now news ed., same.

*Graham, Gene, 1962–63, edit. writer, Nashville Tennessean; now lecturer in journalism, Univ. of Illinois.

Grant, Donald S., 1941–42, reporter, Des Moines Register & Tribune; now UN corr., St. Louis Post-Dispatch.

Grant, Lester H., 1947–48, reporter, New York Herald Tribune; now M.D., New York Univ. School of Medicine.

Griffith, Thomas H., 1942–43, asst. city ed., Seattle Times; now senior staff ed. of Time, Inc., publications.

Gross, Rebecca F., 1947–48, ed., Lock Haven (Pa.) Express; same now.

Guthman, Edwin O., 1950–51, reporter, Seattle Times; now national affairs ed., Los Angeles Times.

*Guthrie, A. B., 1944–45, city ed., Lexington (Ky.) Leader; now author.

Hale, Edward, 1955–56, asst. night city ed., Buffalo News; now exec. asst. to Lt. Gov. of New York.

Hall, Max, 1949–50, Wash. corr., AP; now social science ed., Harvard University Press.

Hamilton, John A., 1961–62, assoc. ed., Lynchburg News; now assoc. ed., Norfolk Ledger-Star.

Handy, Mary, 1957–58, educ. reporter, Christian Science Monitor; deceased 1958 (was in same position).

Hansen, Robert H., 1955–56, reporter, Denver Post; deceased 1960 (was in same position).

Harrison, John M., 1951–52, edit. writer, Toledo Blade; now prof. of journalism, Penn. State University.

Harrison, Selig S., 1954–55, foreign corr., AP, India; now India corr., Washington Post.

Harwood, Richard L., 1955–56, reporter, Louisville Times; now Wash. corr., same.

Hayes, Harold T. P., 1958–59, assoc. ed., Esquire; now ed., same.

Healy, Robert, 1955–56, reporter, Boston Globe; now polit. ed., same.

Heinecke, Burnell, 1956–57, reporter, Chicago Sun-Times; same now.

Heldt, Henning, 1941–42, reporter, Jacksonville (Fla.) Journal; deceased 1950 (Miami Herald).

Hempstone, Smith, Jr., 1964–65, foreign corr., Chicago Daily News.

Hepner, Arthur W., 1945–46, reporter, St. Louis Post-Dispatch; now John Wiley & Sons, publishers.

Herbers, John N., Jr., 1960–61, state manager, UPI, Jackson, Miss.; now in Wash. bur., New York Times.

Hewlett, Frank W., 1945–46, war corr., UPI; now Wash. corr., Salt Lake Tribune.

Hill, Ernest M., 1942–43, state polit. writer, UP, Oklahoma City; deceased 1959 (foreign corr., Chicago Daily News).

Holland, Elmer L., Jr., 1948–49, edit. writer, Birmingham News; now edit. page ed., same.

Holles, Everett R., 1941–42, night cables ed., UP, New York City; now dir. of communications, General Atomic, San Diego, Calif.

Holly, Hazel, 1953–54, reporter, San Francisco Examiner; now information officer, Dept. of Health, Education and Welfare, Washington.

Holstrom, Ben F., 1944–45, reporter, Minneapolis Star Journal; now advertising, Ojai, Calif.

Hopkins, Frank S., 1938–39, reporter, Baltimore Sun; now State Department, Wash., D.C.

Hornsby, Henry H., 1946–47, reporter, Lexington (Ky.) Herald-Leader; now exec. ed., same.

Hoyt, Robert E., 1953–54, asst. city ed., Akron Beacon Journal; now with Detroit Free Press.

Hughes, John, 1961–62, foreign corr., Christian Science Monitor; same now.

Hughes, Paul J., 1943–44, reporter, Louisville Courier-Journal; deceased 1955 (feature writer, same).

Hulteng, John L., 1949–50, edit. writer, Providence Journal; now dean, School of Journalism, Univ. of Oregon.

Ivey, Alfred G., 1951–52, assoc. ed., Winston-Salem Sentinel; now dir. of news bureau, Univ. of North Carolina.

James, Weldon B., 1939–40, reporter, UP, Washington; now edit. writer, Louisville Courier-Journal.

Janson, Donald D., 1952–53, copy ed., Milwaukee Journal; now midwest corr., New York Times, Kansas City, Mo.

Jenkins, C. Ray, 1964–65, managing ed., Alabama Journal, Montgomery.

Jennings, Charles S., 1943–44, copy ed., Chicago Daily News; deceased 1961 (Wash. bureau, U.S. News & World Report).

Johnson, Carlton M., 1954–55, city ed., Columbus (Ga.) Ledger; ed., same.

Johnson, Philip J., 1958–59, reporter, New Orleans Item; now edit. dir., WWL–TV, New Orleans.

Johnson, Vance, 1940–41, managing ed., Amarillo (Tex.) Daily News; now dir. promotion, Field Enterprises, Chicago.

Jones, Clarence H., Jr., 1963–64, reporter, Jacksonville Journal; now reporter, Miami Herald.

Jones, Victor O., 1941–42, sports ed., Boston Globe; now exec. ed., same.

Joyce, Thomas H., 1960–61, reporter, Detroit News; now Wash. corr., same.

Karnow, Stanley A., 1957–58, Paris corr., Time, Inc.; now Far East corr., Saturday Evening Post.

Karsell, Thomas G., 1954–55, managing ed., Delta Democrat-Times, Greenville, Miss.; now reporter, Louisville Courier-Journal.

Kelley, Wayne P., 1963–64, Atlanta bureau chief, Southeastern Newspapers; same now.

Kelly, Frank K., 1942–43, feature writer, AP, New York; now vice-pres., Center for the Study of Democratic Institutions, Santa Barbara.

Kelly, J. Patrick, 1958–59, teleg. ed., Atlanta Journal; now exec. news ed., Winston-Salem Journal & Sentinel.

Kendall, Donald M., 1964–65, farm-polit. ed., Hutchinson (Kans.) News.

Kendrick, Alexander, 1940–41, news review and book ed., Philadelphia Inquirer; now CBS news analyst.

Kieckhefer, Erwin D., 1942–43, farm ed., Minneapolis Star Journal; now reporter, Memphis Commercial Appeal.

Kilpatrick, Carroll, 1939–40, assoc. ed., Montgomery Advertiser; now natl. affairs reporter, Washington Post.

Kole, John, 1962–63, reporter, Milwaukee Journal; now Wash. corr., same.

Korengold, Robert J., 1963–64, Moscow corr., UPI; now Moscow corr., Newsweek.

Kraslow, David J., 1961–62, Wash. corr., Knight Papers; now Wash. corr., Los Angeles Times.

Kraus, Albert L., 1954–55, financial writer, Providence Journal; now asst. financial news ed., New York Times.

Kumpa, Peter J., 1957–58, Wash. corr., Baltimore Sun; same now.

Lahey, Edwin A., 1938–39, labor reporter, Chicago Daily News; now Wash. bureau chief, Knight Papers.

Lambert, William G., 1959–60, reporter, Portland Oregonian; now Los Angeles corr., Time, Inc.

Larsen, Carl W., 1947–48, rewrite, Chicago Sun-Times; now dir. public relats., Univ. of Chicago.

Lasch, Robert, 1941–42, foreign news ed., Omaha World-Herald; now ed., edit. page, St. Louis Post-Dispatch.

Lasseter, Robert C., Jr., 1943–44, ed., Rutherford Courier, Murfreesboro, Tenn.; now advertising, Murfreesboro, Tenn.

Lauterbach, Richard C., 1946–47, foreign corr., Time, Inc.; deceased 1950 (feature ed., New York Star).

Leary, Mary Ellen. See Sherry.

Lee, Robert E., 1952–53, Wash. corr., UPI; now Deputy Asst. Secretary of State.

Levitas, Mitchell R., 1958–59, reporter, New York Post; now staff writer, Time, Inc.

*Lewis, Anthony, 1956–57, Wash. corr., New York Times; now London bureau chief, same.

Limpus, Lowell M., 1940–41, polit. ed., New York Daily News; deceased 1957 (New York Daily News).

Lindsay, John J., 1957–58, reporter, Washington Post; now Wash. corr., Newsweek.

Linford, Ernest H., 1946–47, ed., Laramie (Wyo.) Republican-Boomerang; edit. page ed., Salt Lake Tribune.

Lisagor, Peter, 1948–49, reporter, Chicago Daily News; now Wash. bureau chief, same.

Liston, Harold V., 1956–57, city ed., Bloomington (Ill.) Pantagraph; now assoc. ed., same.

Locke, Francis P., 1946–47, edit. page ed., Miami Daily News; now edit. writer, Riverside (Calif.) Press-Enterprise.

Loftus, Joseph A., 1960–61, Wash. corr., New York Times; same now.

Lyons, Herbert, 1938–39, chief edit. writer, Mobile Press-Register; now advertising, Denhard & Stewart, New York.

Lyons, Louis M., 1938–39, reporter, Boston Globe; retired 1964 as Curator, Nieman Fellowships.

Maguire, Frederick W., 1943–44, ed., Lowell Sun-Telegram; now prof. of journalism, Ohio State Univ.

Maldonado, Alexander, 1964–65, edit. columnist, San Juan Star.

Manning, Robert J., 1945–46, State Dept. corr., UPI, Wash.; now exec. ed., Atlantic Monthly.

Marder, Murrey, 1949–50, reporter, Washington Post; now diplomatic corr., same.

Martin, Fletcher P., 1946–47, city ed., Louisville Defender; now USIA, Accra.

Martin, Robert P., 1951–52, war corr., CBS; now Far East corr., U.S. News & World Report.

Mathis, James V., 1961–62, Wash. bureau chief, Houston Post; now co-publisher and editor, The Daily Review, Edinburg, Tex.

Mayne, Calvin W., 1952–53, reporter, Rochester Times-Union; now edit. page ed., same.

Mazie, David M., 1963–64, reporter, Minneapolis Tribune; same now.

McCarthy, Justin G., 1947–48, labor reporter, Chicago Sun-Times; ed., United Mine Workers Journal, Washington.

McCartney, James H., 1963–64, Wash. corr., Chicago Daily News; same now.

McCary, Robert L., 1960–61, teleg. ed., San Francisco Chronicle; deceased October 1960.

*McCormally, John P., 1949–50, reporter, Emporia (Kans.) Gazette; exec. ed. Hutchinson (Kans.) News-Herald.

McCormick, Kenneth F., 1942–43, reporter, Detroit Free Press; now public relats., Michigan Gas Utilities Co., Monroe, Mich.

McDougall, William H., 1946–47, foreign corr., UPI; now a Monsignor in Salt Lake City.

McElheny, Victor K., 1962–63, science writer, Charlotte Observer; now European corr., Science.

McIlwain, William H., 1957–58, copy ed., Newsday; now managing ed., same.

McNeil, Neil V., 1959–60, Wash. corr., Scripps-Howard; now instructor of journalism, Northwestern University.

Mencher, Melvin, 1952–53, state house reporter, Albuquerque Journal; now asst. professor of journalism, Columbia University.

Menzies, Ian, 1961–62, science reporter, Boston Globe; now financial ed., same.

Meyer, Sylvan, 1950–51, ed., Gainesville (Ga.) Times; same now.

Miller, Edward M., 1941–42, Sun. ed., Portland Oregonian; now asst. managing ed., same.

Miller, Robert C., 1946–47, foreign corr., UPI; same now.

Miller, William J., 1940–41, rewrite, Cleveland Press; now vice-pres. for public relats., Federated Department Stores, Cincinnati.

Mintz, Morton A., 1963–64, reporter, Washington Post; same now.

*Mollenhoff, Clark R., 1949–50, reporter, Des Moines Register & Tribune; now Wash. corr., Cowles Newspapers.

Molony, Charles, 1951–52, Wash. corr., AP; now asst. to Board of Governors, Federal Reserve Bank, Wash., D.C.

Montgomery, Harry T., 1940–41, cable ed., AP, New York; now deputy gen. mgr., AP.

Mooney, Richard E., 1955–56, Wash. corr., UPI; now foreign corr., New York Times.

Morgan, Perry, 1958–59, assoc. ed., Charlotte News; now managing ed., same.

Morris, Hugh, 1950–51, state polit. corr., Louisville Courier-Journal; now chief state polit. corr., same.

Munger, Guy E., 1954–55, asst. ed., Greensboro Daily News; now business ed., same.

Murphy, John R., 1959–60, state polit. corr., Macon Telegraph & News; now polit. ed., Atlanta Constitution.

Musgrave, Arthur B., 1942–43, copy ed., Houston Post; now prof. of journalistic studies, Univ. of Mass., Amherst.

Nakatsuka, Lawrence K., 1951–52, labor reporter, Honolulu Star-Bulletin; now admin. asst. to Senator Hiram Fong.

Neal, Fred W., 1942–43, Wash. corr., Wall Street Journal; now prof. of international relations, Claremont (Calif.) Graduate School.

*Nelson, John, 1961–62, reporter, Atlanta Constitution; now Atlanta corr., Los Angeles Times.

Nixon, Glenn C., 1939–40, reporter, U.S. News; now reporter, U.S. News & World Report.

Norris, Hoke M., 1950–51, reporter, Winston-Salem Journal; now book ed., Chicago Sun-Times.

Nossiter, Bernard D., 1962–63, natl. affairs reporter, Washington Post; now foreign corr., same.

Obert, John, 1956–57, city ed., Park Region Echo, Alexandria, Minn.; now ed., same.

Odell, Jay C., Jr., 1946–47, copy ed., Philadelphia Inquirer; now in business, Venice, Fla.

Okin, Robert, 1942–43, reporter, AP, New York City; now dir. of publishing, American Heart Assoc., New York.

Ostrow, Ronald J., 1964–65, financial writer, Los Angeles Times.

Otwell, Ralph, 1959–60, asst. city ed., Chicago Sun-Times; now asst. managing ed., same.

Owens, Patrick J., 1962–63, edit. page ed., Pine Bluff (Ark.) Commercial; now edit. writer, Arkansas Gazette.

Parsons, Arch, 1954–55, UN corr., New York Herald Tribune; now with Los Angeles Times.

Paxton, Edwin J., 1938–39, assoc. ed., Paducah Sun-Democrat; now pres., same.

Pearce, John Ed, 1957–58, edit. writer, Louisville Courier-Journal; same now.

Pillsbury, Fred, 1956–57, edit. writer, Boston Herald; now feature writer, same.

Pinkerton, William M., 1940–41, Wash. corr., AP; now News Officer, Harvard.

Plumb, Robert, 1959–60, science reporter, New York Times; same now.

Pomfret, John, 1960–61, labor reporter, Milwaukee Journal; now Wash. corr., New York Times.

Porteous, Clark, 1946–47, reporter, Memphis Press-Scimitar; same now.

Press, Harry, 1955–56, reporter, San Francisco News; now city ed., same.

Pugh, Thomas, 1960–61, asst. city ed., Peoria Journal-Star; now assoc. ed., same.

Qualey, Jacob S., 1943–44, northwest ed., Minneapolis Star Journal; now literary agent, New York.

Rand, Christopher, 1948–49, China corr., New York Herald Tribune; now corr., New Yorker.

Raymont, Henry, 1961–62, Latin American corr., UPI; now Latin American corr., New York Times.

Reed, Roy E., 1963–64, reporter, Arkansas Gazette; now southern corr., New York Times, Atlanta.

Revell, Aldric R., 1948–49, polit. reporter, Madison Capital Times; same now.
Roberts, Gene L., 1961–62, polit. reporter, Raleigh News & Observer; now in Atlanta bur., New York Times.
Robertson, Cary, 1945–46, Sun. ed., Louisville Courier-Journal; same now.
Robertson, Nathan W., 1944–45, Wash. corr., PM; deceased 1950 (was in same position).
Robling, Mrs. John S. (Charlotte L. FitzHenry), 1945–46, wire ed., AP, Chicago; now public relats., Winnetka, Ill.
Rodgers, Wilfrid C., 1958–59, reporter, Boston Globe; same now.
Roevekamp, Fred, 1956–57, reporter, Christian Science Monitor; now public relats., New York City.
Rooney, Edmund J., Jr., 1959–60, reporter, Chicago Daily News; same now.
Ross, Thomas B., 1963–64, Wash. corr., Chicago Sun-Times; same now.
Rundle, Walter G., 1947–48, China manager, UPI; now assoc. ed., Newsweek.

Sager, Lois. See Foxhall.
Samson, John G., 1959–60, reporter, AP, Albuquerque; now radio news ed., KGGM, Albuquerque.
Sancton, Thomas, 1941–42, reporter, AP, New York; now vice-pres. for public relats., Walker Saussy Adv. Agency, New Orleans.
Sargent, Dwight E., 1950–51, chief edit. writer, Portland (Me.) Press Herald; now Curator, Nieman Fellowships.
Scates, Shelby T., 1962–63, reporter, AP, Oklahoma City; now reporter, AP, New York.
Schecter, Jerrold L., 1963–64, Far East corr., Time-Life; now Tokyo bureau chief, same.
Schmeck, Harold M., Jr., 1953–54, reporter, Rochester Times-Union; now science reporter, New York Times.
Schmidt, Dana A., 1950–51, foreign corr., New York Times; same now.
Seagle, Don, 1955–56, reporter, Charleston (W. Va.) Gazette; same now.
Secrest, Andrew M., 1960–61, ed. and pub., Cheraw (S.C.) Chronicle; same now.
Seeger, Murray A., 1961–62, state polit. reporter, Cleveland Plain Dealer; now reporter, New York Times.
Seigenthaler, John L., 1958–59, reporter, Nashville Tennessean; now ed., same.
Seney, Edgar F., Jr., 1955–56, pub., Florida Keys Keynoter; now managing ed., Miami Beach Daily Sun.
Shapiro, Henry, 1954–55, Moscow bureau chief, UPI; same now.
Shaplen, Robert M., 1947–48, Shanghai bureau chief, Newsweek; now corr., New Yorker.
Sherry, Mrs. Arthur H. (Mary Ellen Leary), 1945–46, polit. reporter, San Francisco News; now West Coast corr., Economist and London Observer.
Shively, John W., 1943–44, real estate ed., Kansas City Star; now Urban Renewal Administration, Wash., D.C.
Simmons, Boyd T., 1940–41, reporter, Detroit News; same now.
Simons, Howard, 1958–59, news ed., Science Service; now science reporter, Washington Post.
Sims, Watson S., 1952–53, reporter, AP, Chattanooga; now ed., world services, AP, New York.
Smith, Robert C., 1960–61, assoc. ed., Norfolk Virginian-Pilot; now edit. page ed., Charlotte News.
Sochurek, Howard J., 1959–60, photographer, Life Magazine; same now.

Spencer, Steven M., 1939–40, science ed., Philadelphia Bulletin; now assoc. ed., Saturday Evening Post.
Steele, John L., 1951–52, Wash. corr., UPI; now Wash. bureau chief, Time, Inc.
Steif, William, 1952–53, reporter, San Francisco News; now Wash. corr., Scripps-Howard.
Stephens, Oren M., 1942–43, Sun. ed., Arkansas Democrat; now dir. of research and analysis, USIA.
Sterling, Donald J., 1955–56, reporter, Oregon Journal; now edit. writer, same.
Stern, Mort, 1954–55, night city ed., Denver Post; now asst. to the pub., same.
Stewart, Gilbert W., Jr., 1946–47, Wash. corr., Newsweek; now asst. dir. of information, TVA.
Stewart, Kenneth N., 1941–42, national news ed., PM; now prof. of journalism, Univ. of Calif., Berkeley.
Stockwell, Richard E., 1945–46, news ed., WCCO–CBS, Minneapolis; now public relats., G. E. Aircraft, Cincinnati.
Strohmeyer, John, 1952–53, reporter, Providence Journal; now ed., Bethlehem Globe-Times.
Stucky, William M., 1949–50, city ed., Lexington Leader; deceased 1961 (assoc. dir., American Press Institute).
Sullivan, J. Wesley, 1957–58, news ed., Oregon Statesman, Salem; same now.
Svirsky, Leon, 1945–46, science writer, Time, Inc.; now edit. consultant, Basic Books, Scientific American, New York.

Tanner, Henry, 1954–55, foreign news analyst, Houston Post; now Moscow corr., New York Times.
Terry, John B., 1943–44, Wash. corr., Honolulu Star-Bulletin; deceased 1944 (war corr., Chiacgo Daily News).
Thuermer, Angus M., 1950–51, wire ed., AP, Chicago; now foreign service officer, State Department, Munich.
Torrey, Volta W., 1939–40, news review ed., AP, New York City; now ed., Technology Review, M.I.T., Cambridge, Mass.
Toth, Robert C., 1960–61, science reporter, New York Herald Tribune; now Wash. corr., Los Angeles Times.
Townes, William A., 1942–43, asst. city ed., Cleveland Press; now asst. managing ed., Baltimore Evening Sun.
Trewhitt, Henry L., 1953–54, reporter, Chattanooga Times; now foreign corr., Baltimore Sun.
*Turner, Wallace L., 1958–59, reporter, Portland Oregonian; now San Francisco corr., New York Times.

Vogel, William P., 1939–40, reporter, New York Herald Tribune; address now unknown.

Waggoner, Walter H., 1947–48, Wash. corr., New York Times; now reporter, same.
Wagner, Charles A., 1944–45, Sun. ed., New York Mirror; now exec. sec., Poetry Society of America, New York City.
Wakefield, Dan, 1963–64, free lance; same now, Hudson, N.H.
Wales, Wellington, 1950–51, edit. writer, Auburn (N.Y.) Citizen-Advertiser; now chief edit. writer, Knickerbocker News, Albany.
Wall, Marvin, 1956–57, reporter, Columbus (Ga.) Ledger; now edit. writer, Atlanta Constitution.

Wallace, Kevin, 1951–52, reporter, San Francisco Chronicle; now staff writer, New Yorker.

Wallace, Richard J., Jr., 1949–50, polit. reporter, Memphis Press-Scimitar; now secretary and ed., Atlantic Council, Wash., D.C.

Waring, Houstoun, 1944–45, ed., Littleton (Colo.) Independent; same now.

Wax, Melvin S., 1949–50, asst. news ed., Rutland (Vt.) Herald; now reporter, San Francisco Chronicle.

Weiss, Lawrence G., 1948–49, reporter, Boston Herald; now edit. writer, Denver Post.

*Weller, George, 1947–48, foreign corr., Chicago Daily News; same now.

Werner, Ralph J., 1940–41, financial writer, Milwaukee Journal; now public relats., Milwaukee.

White, Leigh, 1943–44, CBS, Wash., D.C.; now free lance, 20 Third St., S.E., Wash.

Whitt, Wayne, 1953–54, reporter, Nashville Tennessean; same now.

Wicker, Thomas G., 1957–58, Wash. corr., Winston-Salem Journal & Sentinel; now Wash. bureau chief, New York Times.

Willis, C. Delbert, 1948–49, reporter, Fort Worth Press; now city ed., same.

Wilson, Kenneth E., 1952–53, managing ed., Santa Rosa Press-Democrat; now asst. news ed., San Francisco Chronicle.

Woestendiek, William J., 1954–55, Sun. ed., Winston-Salem Journal & Sentinel; now asst. exec. ed., Houston Post.

Worthy, William, Jr., 1956–57, corr., Afro-American, Baltimore; same now.

Wright, Lawson M., Jr., 1956–57, reporter, Richmond Times-Dispatch; now city ed. Charlotte Observer.

Wyatt, Edward A., 1939–40, assoc. ed., Petersburg (Va.) Progress-Index; now ed., same.

Yablonky, Ben, 1945–46, rewrite, PM; now prof. of journalism, Univ. of Mich.

Yahraes, Herbert C., 1943–44, feature ed., PM; now free-lance science writer, Stanfordville, New York.

Zagoria, Samuel D., 1954–55, reporter, Washington Post; now admin. asst. to Senator Clifford Case (N.J.).

Zuber, J. Osborn, 1938–39, edit. writer, Birmingham News; now ed., The Constructor, Wash., D.C.

Zylstra, Donald L., 1953–54, managing ed., Redwood Journal, Ukiah, Cal.; now Wash. corr., American Aviation Publications.

II. LIST OF ASSOCIATE NIEMAN FELLOWS THROUGH 1964–65

Baumfield, David L., 1964–65, parliamentary corr., New Zealand Herald, Auckland.

Chiang, Te-cheng, 1961–62, managing ed., Ta Hua Evening News, Taipei; now govt. inf. officer, Taipei.

Cornwell, John, 1956–57, agric. corr., New Zealand Herald; now ed., New Zealand Farmer, Auckland.

Cowan, Mrs. C. D. (Daphne Whittam), 1958–59, assoc. ed., The Nation, Rangoon; now at School of Oriental and African Studies, University of London.
Creery, Timothy W., 1964–65, Ottawa corr., Southam Newspapers.
Cross, Ian, 1954–55, chief reporter, Wellington (N.Z.) Dominion; now executive, Felt & Textiles of New Zealand, Ltd.
Eswaran, V. V., 1959–60, parliamentary corr., Hindustan Times; now Calcutta corr., same.
Flower, John H., 1952–53, asst. chief of staff, Sydney Herald; now gen. manager, Newcastle Sun, Australia.
Flowers, Fred C., 1954–55, special corr., Melbourne Herald; now broadcasting mgr., same.
French, William H., 1954–55, reporter, Toronto Globe & Mail; now book ed., same.
Goodman, Martin W., 1961–62, reporter, Toronto Star; now London corr., same.
Grant, Bruce, 1958–59, chief leader writer, Melbourne Age; now Wash. corr., same.
Hudson, Lionel, 1953–54, foreign corr., Australian Associated Press; now news dir., Australian Broadcasting Commission.
Ichinose, Yukio, 1961–62, science reporter, Kyodo News Service, Tokyo; same now.
Ishihara, Hiroshi, 1957–58, foreign news writer, Yomiuri Shimbun; now Wash. corr., same.
Jones, Maurice, 1958–59, deputy chief reporter, Southland Daily News, Invercargill, N.Z.; same now.
Kane, Herbert J. E., 1951–52, chief reporter, Christchurch (N.Z.) Press; deceased 1953.
Kidd, Paul, 1962–63, feature writer, Hamilton (Ont.) Spectator; same now.
Kim, Yong-koo, 1962–63, staff writer, Hankook Ilbo, Seoul; now ed., same.
Kleu, S. J., 1961–62, financial ed., Die Burger, Cape Town; now on leave for advanced study.
Krishnaswami, P. N., 1963–64, city ed., Economic Times, Bombay; same now.
Kuroda, Kazuo, 1956–57, staff writer, Nippon Times; same now.
Lamarche, Guy, 1963–64, polit. ed., La Presse, Montreal; same now.
Lawson, David, 1957–58, edit. writer, Auckland (N.Z.) Star; now with Whitcombe & Tombes, book publishers, Christchurch.
Leiterman, Douglas S., 1953–54, reporter, Vancouver Province; now public affairs producer, CBC, Toronto.
Mackay, Shane, 1951–52, chief, legislative bureau, Winnipeg Free Press; now exec. ed., same.
Maeda, Hisashi, 1955–56, foreign news writer, Asahi Shimbun, Tokyo; same now.
Malkani, K. R., 1961–62, ed., The Organiser, Delhi; same now.
Marshall, John L., 1957–58, senior reporter, Perth Daily News; same now.
Mead Garth L., 1953–54, deputy chief reporter, Nelson Evening Mail; now gen. manager, Rotorua Post, N.Z.
Morinaga, Kyoichi, 1964–65, staff writer, Mainichi Shimbun, Tokyo.
Nakasa, Nathaniel, 1964–65, asst. ed., Drum, Johannesburg.
Nielsen, Robert, 1952–53, reporter, Toronto Star; now edit. page ed., same.
Nkosi Lewis P., 1960–61, staff writer, Drum, Johannesburg; now documentary producer, Transcription Center, London.

Onruang, Chirabha, 1963–64, educ. ed., Siam Sikorn Daily, Bangkok; same now.
Otani, Satoshi, 1959–60, foreign affairs reporter, Sankei Shimbun; now Moscow corr., same.
Pang, Woon-yiu, 1963–64, reporter, Overseas Chinese News, Hong Kong; same now.
Parasuram, T. V., 1958–59, parliamentary corr., Press Trust of India; now Wash. corr., Indian Express, Bombay.
Park, Kwon-sang, 1964–65, edit. writer, Dong-a Ilbo, Seoul.
Plater, Ronald, 1955–56, senior sub-ed., Brisbane Courier-Mail; same now.
Prasad, Sharada, 1955–56, news ed., Indian Express, Bombay; now ed., Indian Planning Commission, New Delhi.
Pun, Chiu-yin, 1962–63, city ed., Sing Tao Evening News, Hong Kong; same now.
Reddy, G. K., 1956–57, foreign affairs writer, Times of India; same now.
Saez, Juan V., 1957–58, reporter, Manila Times; now press officer, Philippine Embassy, London.
Sarda, Shankar, 1964–65, magazine ed., Maharashtra Times, Bombay.
Sarkar, Chanchal, 1960–61, asst. ed., The Statesman, New Delhi; now dir., Press Institute of India, New Delhi.
Sayres, Ross, 1952–53, chief reporter, Auckland (N.Z.) Star; now ed., same.
Shen, Shan, 1959–60, city ed., China News, Taipei; now public relats., Hong Kong.
Shirakawa, Michinobu, 1960–61, science ed., Kyodo News Service; same now.
Siddiqui, Manzur, 1956–57, contributing ed., Dawn, Lahore, Pakistan; address now unknown.
Sparks, Allister, 1962–63, polit. reporter, Rand Daily Mail, Johannesburg; same now.
Steyn, Robert C., 1963–64, polit. corr., Cape Argus, Cape Town; same now.
Stone, Desmond, 1955–56, edit. writer, Southland Times, Invercargill, N.Z.; now reporter, Rochester Times-Union.
Sussens, Aubrey, 1960–61, asst. ed., Rand Daily Mail, Johannesburg; now public relats., Johannesburg.
Thai, Nguyen, 1962–63, former dir., Vietnam Press Bureau (exiled); now returned, Saigon.
Tipping, E. W., 1951–52, chief of staff, Melbourne Herald; now columnist, same.
Warner, Denis A., 1956–57, S.E. Asia corr., Australian newspapers; same now.
Whealan, J. P., 1955–56, reporter, Windsor Daily Star; now edit. writer, same.
Whittam, Daphne E. See Cowan.
Wickramasinghe, Piyal, 1957–58, reporter, Times of Ceylon; now program adviser, Asia Foundation, Ceylon.
Wong, Francis, 1960–61, ed., Singapore Sunday Mail; now edit. writer, Straits Times, Kuala Lumpur.

INDEX

(SEE ALSO ALPHABETICAL LISTS OF NIEMAN FELLOWS AND ASSOCIATE NIEMAN FELLOWS STARTING ON PAGE 421)